LUTHER'S WORKS

LUTHER'S WORKS

VOLUME 20

LECTURES ON THE MINOR PROPHETS III ZECHARIAH

HILTON C. OSWALD
Editor

CONCORDIA PUBLISHING HOUSE · SAINT LOUIS

CONCORDIA PUBLISHING HOUSE
Saint Louis, Missouri

Library of Congress Catalog Card No. 55-9893
ISBN 0-570-06420-1

MANUFACTURED IN THE UNITED STATES OF AMERICA

Contents

General Introduction

THE first editions of Luther's collected works appeared in the sixteenth century, and so did the first efforts to make him "speak English." In America serious attempts in these directions were made for the first time in the nineteenth century. The Saint Louis edition of Luther was the first endeavor on American soil to publish a collected edition of his works, and the Henkel Press in Newmarket, Virginia, was the first to publish some of Luther's writings in an English translation. During the first decade of the twentieth century, J. N. Lenker produced translations of Luther's sermons and commentaries in thirteen volumes. A few years later the first of the six volumes in the Philadelphia (or Holman) edition of the *Works of Martin Luther* appeared. Miscellaneous other works were published at one time or another. But a growing recognition of the need for more of Luther's works in English has resulted in this American edition of Luther's works.

The edition is intended primarily for the reader whose knowledge of late medieval Latin and sixteenth-century German is too small to permit him to work with Luther in the original languages. Those who can, will continue to read Luther in his original words as these have been assembled in the monumental Weimar edition (*D. Martin Luthers Werke.* Kritische Gesamtausgabe; Weimar, 1883 ff.). Its texts and helps have formed a basis for this edition, though in certain places we have felt constrained to depart from its readings and findings. We have tried throughout to translate Luther as he thought translating should be done. That is, we have striven for faithfulness on the basis of the best lexicographical materials available. But where literal accuracy and clarity have conflicted, it is clarity that we have preferred, so that sometimes paraphrase seemed more faithful than literal fidelity. We have proceeded in a similar way in the matter of Bible versions, translating Luther's translations. Where this could be done by the use of an existing English version – King James, Douay, or Revised Standard – we have done so. Where it could not, we have supplied our own. To indicate this in each specific instance would have been pedantic; to adopt a uniform procedure would have been artificial – especially in view of Luther's own inconsistency in this regard. In each volume the translator will be responsible primarily for matters of text and language, while the responsibility of the editor will extend principally to the historical and theological matters reflected in the introductions and notes.

Although the edition as planned will include fifty-five volumes, Luther's writings are not being translated in their entirety. Nor should they be. As he was the first to insist, much of what he wrote and said was not that important. Thus the edition is a selection of works that have proved their importance for the faith, life, and history of the Christian church. The first thirty volumes contain Luther's expositions of various Biblical books, while the remaining volumes include what are usually called his "Reformation writings" and other occasional pieces. The final volume of the set will be an index volume; in addition to an index of quotations, proper names, and topics, and a list of corrections and changes, it will contain a glossary of many of the technical terms that recur in Luther's works and that cannot be defined each time they appear. Obviously Luther cannot be forced into any neat set of rubrics. He can provide his reader with bits of autobiography or with political observations as he expounds a psalm, and he can speak tenderly about the meaning of the faith in the midst of polemics against his opponents. It is the hope of publishers, editors, and translators that through this edition the message of Luther's faith will speak more clearly to the modern church.

JAROSLAV PELIKAN
HELMUT LEHMANN

Introduction to Volume 20

THIS volume contains Luther's *Lectures on Zechariah* according to the Altenburg text and according to the German text. The complicated history of the transmission of Latin texts in the case of Luther's lectures on the minor prophets will be outlined in the introduction to Volume 18 of *Luther's Works.* It is dealt with in great detail in Volume XIII of the Weimar edition of Luther's works, pages vii–xxxvi.

Luther began these lectures on the minor prophets with Hosea in March 1524 and continued, with brief interruptions, until probably March 1526. Taking the books in their Biblical order, Luther arrived at the prophet Zechariah in the last weeks of 1525 and completed the book in early 1526. We have chosen to translate the Altenburg manuscript of the Latin lectures. This manuscript has the disadvantage that it suddenly, without explanation, brings Zechariah to a close at the end of chapter 13, as if Luther had not treated chapter 14 at all. But this is also the end of the whole manuscript, for neither the closing lectures on Malachi nor the opening lectures on Hosea are given. The reason for stopping abruptly at chapter 13 of Zechariah is obviously that of the compiler. In other respects the Altenburg manuscript is complete. It is, however, not a direct product of the lecture hall but the result of considerable editorial work on the basis of perhaps more than one notebook no longer identifiable.

The Altenburg manuscript of the lectures on Zechariah was first published by Johannes Linke in the Erlangen edition of Luther's works, *Exegetica opera,* XXVIII, 5–200, and later, with many corrections, in the Weimar edition, XIII, 646–669, from which we have translated. A German translation of the Weimar text is given in the St. Louis edition, XIV, 1976–2159.

The second half of this volume contains the German commentary on Zechariah, published by Luther himself in December 1527. As even a cursory comparison of the two texts will show, this is not a translation by Luther of the Latin manuscript from which the lectures were originally delivered, although it may safely be assumed that Luther's lecture hall notes and manuscripts were the basis of the manuscript he now prepared for publication. On January 1, 1527, Luther wrote to Michael Stifel, "I am struggling to let my Zechariah see the light of day," and to Nikolaus Hausmann on January 10, "My Zechariah is in the press and taking shape toward publication, and the book is still growing day by day under my hand." But the printing was not completed until almost a year later. Luther was at the same time occupied with the treatise *That These Words of Christ, "This Is My Body," Still Stand Firm* (*Luther's Works,* 37, pp. 13–150) and determined to finish it first. Also, the first half of the year 1527 was a time of serious illness both for Luther himself and for those near and dear to him. For several months Luther was not able to work at all. On November 22, however, Luther wrote to Wenzeslaus Link, "I have almost finished Zechariah." On December 28 he could write to Spalatin, "I am also sending you my Zechariah." The printer's date at the end of the book is 1528, perhaps because the new year was thought of as beginning on Christmas Day.

This edition apparently won instant popularity, for it was almost immediately translated to Latin by Laurentius Span and in that form later printed in the Wittenberg edition of Luther's works (1566). This Latin retranslation was somehow consistently preferred to all other versions of the lectures, even though shorter authentic manuscripts written down by students at the lectures were available.

That Luther issued his German commentary on Zechariah as a kind of definitive version of the content of the lectures to supersede the various Latin copybook versions is to be doubted. The opening remarks in his three German commentaries on the minor prophets point to other reasons. In the preface to his German commentary on Jonah, for instance, Luther tells us that he has undertaken this commentary to counteract the devil's strategy "to tear him away from the Scriptures and inveigle him into his quarrels and ultimately catch him outside the Scriptures and ruin him." In the preface to "Zechariah," on the other hand, Luther expresses particular concern for the layman. Recalling that it seems to be the fashion of the day to write commentaries on the more difficult books of the Bible in order to impress people with scholarship and enterprising allegory, Luther points out that he has chosen to treat Zechariah to show that even in the more obscure prophets the most important point is the "simple faith in Christ."

H. O.

LECTURES ON ZECHARIAH

The Latin Text

1526

Translated by
RICHARD J. DINDA

ON THE PROPHET ZECHARIAH [1]

From the earlier prophets and from Haggai we can understand the intent of Zechariah and, in fact, of all the prophets who prophesied to the Israelites after the Babylonian captivity. This purpose obviously involved especially one matter — to comfort the remnant of a dispersed people wretchedly afflicted by captivity and to encourage them not to despair. They should not lose confidence that the divine promises made to them about their coming King would be fulfilled: that Christ their King would finally come in spite of their totally desperate situation, in spite of their devastated land, in spite of a dispersed people facing a miserable death. For this to happen, the people had to be renewed according to the flesh, and for this renewal Christ continued to be promised as their King-to-come. To convince his people of this, the prophet develops their confidence with many visions and discourses. All of this he intends as comfort for shaken hearts, that they not lose confidence at so critical a point in their history but rather put their hands to work to begin to till the land and to finish the temple they have begun. He says that the Lord will be present as He has promised.

To be sure, all this points to the fact that we should know that God wants His people to undertake nothing, and that He approves of nothing, unless He has first sent out His Word, from which we are completely informed concerning His will. But He does not approve of what we decide to do by our own reason or strength, from however pious a mind this may appear to us to come. This happens so that He may give us the greatest assurance in our consciences that what we do at His command in every way pleases Him; and, contrariwise, that what we ourselves invent for ourselves without the Word of God displeases Him greatly. Furthermore, those who want to decide anything in the area of righteousness without God's Word cannot be sure in their consciences that what they have decided pleases God. Con-

[1] The Altenburg manuscript originally read "Jeremiah."

sciences must constantly be in doubt and admit that they do not know whether or not a work is God-pleasing. Therefore with many and varied consolations the prophet through the Word of God strengthens those wretched people, who were so long oppressed in wretched captivity and scarcely dared draw a breath. This he does so that their consciences may be completely assured that God will be with them and will bless what they have begun, since He bore witness concerning His own will with such rich testimony. This purpose of the prophet we can gather from the very circumstances of the situation. You see, at that time the condition of the Israelites had degenerated so much that in the whole sphere of the Judaic world there existed not a single nation which did not bitterly persecute and scoff at Israel, not a single nation which did not rejoice over the adverse straits of the Israelites; that is, over their property reduced to nothing now that Israel itself had been carried off into captivity. Indeed, there was [2] nothing to raise even the hope of the restoration of Israel. In the judgment of the flesh it appeared absolutely impossible for the kingdom to be restored with the acquisition of a king and, in fact, to be glorified as it had never been before. There simply was no room for hope. With many words and visions the prophet consequently strengthens a people so weak and uncertain of mind and nourishes their faith.

But all this has been written also for our instruction, that we may learn that God really has this purpose — to declare things that are totally impossible to our mind and reason — and that there is nothing less in agreement than His Word and our judgment. In fact, His Word and our judgment are involved in constant warfare with each other so that afterwards, when He has done and accomplished what He promised, our glory may perish and He may be glorified who creates all things out of nothing and the possible out of the altogether impossible. Indeed, for Him nothing is impossible, as Christ says, so that our own judgment and reason are brought to naught and we trace to Him all things as items received. So far is it from being true that we owe anything to our own powers that they are even something that militates completely against the Word of God. They do not believe the Word; they consider it impossible. Thus the prophet here beautifully points out this weakness of the mind in a people terrified by the difficulty of their situation, by the baseness of the priest, etc., as he records in chapter 3. In fact, the prophet removes all things from be-

[2] The manuscript has *nihil non erat,* but the *non* seems spurious.

fore their eyes and sends the people back to God's Word, saying that God will fulfill His Word, even though all creatures resist. For it is He who makes life out of death, righteousness out of sin, the greatest wealth out of abject poverty. Briefly, it is He who makes all things out of nothing and calls the things which are not as if they were, etc. (Rom. 4:17). This is something vitally necessary for us to note in every temptation – that we may have faith in God and learn to commit ourselves to Him, that He will free us beyond every judgment of our reason as we would not have dared to hope. Obviously, this is a reason for and function of the prophecy which can be useful also for us, lest we appear merely to read history as we read what happened to Israel.

CHAPTER ONE

1. *In the eighth month, in the second year of King Darius.* Earlier, at the beginning of the commentary on Haggai, I mentioned that these two, Haggai and Zechariah, were contemporaries. Haggai preceded Zechariah by two months, as the initial sentence in each case indicates: Haggai prophesied in the sixth month of the second year, but Zechariah in the eighth. Also, under the direction of Haggai the foundations of the temple were laid. On the other hand, at the very beginning of his work, Zechariah came and urged the people to push to completion what they had begun, lest their minds begin to waver, and to go on strenuously, not at all frightened by the nations surrounding them. All these wanted to keep the Israelites from making progress, for they often bitterly opposed the Israelites. Against all these, I say, he urged them to be secure. He reminded them that the Lord would protect them against all their foes, etc. In my commentary on Haggai I have also said who I think Darius was, namely, Darius Longimanus, who succeeded Cambyses and the sons of Cambyses on the throne. Now, this Darius was kindly disposed to the Jews, a fact we learn from Esdras, where he writes (1 Esdras 6:27-34) that Darius sent letters ordering that the people not be hindered from being able to finish the building they had begun. The Septuagint translators number the kings of the Persians differently from the way I have numbered them on that list I published.[1] I do not believe, however, that I am in error. You see, historians differ concerning this matter. Perhaps the jury is still deliberating this point of dispute as to who of us has the more correct idea.

2. *The Lord was very angry.* No Latin writer would have added the words "with wrath." [2] The phrase rather was added in the Hebrew

[1] The reference is not, as was earlier supposed, to Luther's general chronology entitled *Supputatio annorum mundi* (W, LIII, 21—184) — prepared for Luther's "own use" originally but published in 1541 and again in 1545 at the urging of his friends — but to a shorter chronological table of the Medo-Persian kings, prepared especially for the students who attended the lectures on the minor prophets. Cf. W, XIII, xxxi f.

[2] The Latin text of the Vulgate reflects the Hebrew redundance: *iratus est . . . iracundia.* The English translation uses the adverb "very" instead.

fashion. For the Hebrew says, "I rejoice with joy, I desire with desire, I am angry with anger." The Latin simply says, "I rejoice, I desire, I am angry." He begins his prophecy by repeating their past disaster. He admonishes and frightens them not to disbelieve the Word of God as their fathers had done. He says, as it were: "You have the clear Word of God. Also God has sent you two witnesses, Haggai and me. Therefore you must listen to this Word ahead of all your sacrifices. The difficulty of being obedient, the impossibility of the situation, the fierceness of your foes, the imminent destruction of all your property – all these terrify you. Do not be disturbed by these, but be careful that they do not become reasons which keep you from obeying God, even as your fathers did not obey."

The flesh always has the power to be able to dispute or oppose the eager pursuit of God's Word. Recall what they say in the Gospel (Matt. 22), "I have married a wife, I have purchased [five] yoke of oxen. I cannot come." [3] Today, too, many people are concerned about wives, children, goods, friends, position, reputation. Were they not concerned, they would fully confess the Gospel. Yet there ought to be no reasons to draw us away from following God. Obviously that is a weakness and blindness of the flesh, as if God, who has given you even those things about which you are anxious, could not give you more. The Germans have a way of saying, and it is well said and Christian too: "God has even more than He has ever given away." [4] So, if you must give up your wife on God's account, let her go. Let the children, the house, friends, reputation – let them all go. God has more than enough good things to give back to you, should it redound to His glory. Indeed, He has made us the very clear promise that we would receive a hundredfold (Mark 10:30), even in this life, if we should suffer loss of property for His glory, and that, finally, we would receive eternal life. Moreover, the rich will go hungry and poor. However, "those who seek the Lord lack no good thing," as we read in Ps. 34:10. After all, which do you think is preferable: to lose goods, wife, children, and, finally, even life; or to lose the Lord who can give life, justify, and sanctify, and who finally can shape new heavens and a new earth? Surely it will be better to have lost temporal goods than to be deprived of eternal ones and of God Himself. However, because

[3] Luther freely quotes the excuses from Luke 14:19-20. They are not given specifically in Matt. 22.

[4] *Gott hat noch mehr, denn er je vergeben hat.*

the flesh has a concern only for the things of the present and the loss thereof, the story is told to her who is deaf, as we say in the proverb.[5]

3. *Thus says the Lord of hosts.* The prophets and the Scriptures everywhere call God "the Lord of hosts," for צָבָא means the military or the army. He is, then, the Lord of soldiers or of the military. This certainly is a wonderful name for God. It is given to us not only to teach but also to comfort us. For teaching, you apply it this way: all those who confess the name of this King or Lord must be soldiers. They must always be armed and in the field, just as Job says (Job 7:1): "Man's life on earth is military service." We have very dangerous and very powerful enemies both against our good character and even against the Word, and that is the greatest evil. The world threatens death. It even threatens to take away life along with our property. Likewise the closest army is our own flesh, that foe in one's own house. The flesh harasses us with a concern for the nourishment of our body and of those people who are close to us. It seduces us into shameful activities. Then too, Satan never ceases assaulting us with spiritual hosts of wickedness (Eph. 6:12), with despair against faith, and with the uncovering of sin. All the while the devil erodes our conscience in every way, misleads us to a lack of hope, and never ceases prowling around, seeking someone to devour, as Peter says (1 Peter 5:8). So we must lead the life of active soldiers as we are assailed by very powerful foes and as we do battle under the Lord our God. Then He is called the Lord of hosts to comfort us, that we may know that He who is in us is greater than he who is in the world (1 John 4:4). For He has overcome the world, according to John 16:33. Indeed, not even the prince of this world has any power against Him (John 14:30). Instead, He has overcome both the world and the prince of the world, but He has overcome them on our behalf. Therefore it is our consolation that this good Lord of ours faithfully comes to our aid and battles for us in the field. He fights for us at our side, lest we lose faith, regardless of what great evils assail us. So this is why the prophet Zechariah here repeats the expression "the Lord of hosts" three times, as if to say: "Whatever you fear, whatever it is that you are concerned about, be confident. The Lord does battle for you. He goes ahead of you as general of the war as He fights in the field, etc.

[5] Cf. Terence, *Heautontimorumenos,* II, 1, 10: *quam mihi nunc surdo narret fabulam,* and Horace, *Epistulae,* II, 1, 199—200: *narrare asello fabulam surdo.*

Return to Me, says the Lord of hosts. Because all the sophists have taken this passage as a declaration in favor of free will, we must not leave this unnoticed. However, they are drawing a very incorrect conclusion. Anyone with a bit of judgment who is not devoid of common sense can judge it as incorrect. This is the way they draw this conclusion: " 'Return to Me, says the Lord, and I will return to you.' Therefore we have free will." I deny the consequence which is drawn from the imperative verb to the indicative. After all, what is this consequence? "The Law says: 'You shall love the Lord with all your mind and all your strength'; therefore I have the power to love." Certainly, so terrible and total is our blindness if, when we lack the grace of God, we pursue the light of nature and of our reason in matters of godliness. Today we see men laboring in this blindness whom our age considers most learned, most outstanding – men whom both kings and princes look up to. I am not told here what I can do but what I should do. You see, "Return to Me, etc.," is the word of the Law. Consequently this text does not speak in favor of our will but against free will. Lawyers speak this way – and correctly – that bad habits produce good laws. After all, laws are publicized because what is required by law is not happening. You see, whenever I demand something of someone, I immediately convince him that it is not being done by him. Otherwise I would be making a foolish demand. Thus any child who knows his ABCs can laugh at this lack of logic. But if we had had to concede this to those who favor free will, they would have all the laws of Scripture on their side, and with all of them they would be able to establish the power of the will. Indeed, this turning is twofold. One is our turning to God; the other is His to us. After all, it is one thing when God turns toward us, and another when we turn to God. The Lord demands that we turn, not because this is something we can accomplish by our own power, but rather that we may acknowledge our own weakness and implore the help of the Spirit, whose prompting can turn us. This, then, is the conversion caused by the Gospel. There is, you see, a twofold conversion – that of the Gospel and that of the Law. The Law merely gives the command, but nothing is accomplished; something is accomplished, however, through the Gospel, when the Spirit is added. He renews hearts, and then God turns toward us. This is the conversion of peace, that is, that we are not merely righteous but also filled with joy and find delight in God's goodness. This is what Paul always wished the Christians: "Grace and peace."

4. *Be not like your fathers.* As I mentioned above, he sets before their eyes their earlier disaster. He exerts himself particularly to persuade [6] them that they should not lose confidence in God's Word and that they should not neglect that Word. These are points which all the prophets urged strongly.

Return from your evil ways. The prophet is speaking spiritually and passes a spiritual judgment on their behavior. The prophets condemn and label as wickedness, idolatry, and evil ways whatever seems good to carnal sense and whatever the judgment of reason cannot but approve. In this way the Jews were drawn by their own imagination and by the appearance of good to establish new rituals and ways of worshiping God. However, because they had themselves discovered all these, because they had themselves fabricated them, they did not please God, as I already mentioned at the beginning. Therefore the prophets always condemned all those inventions and testified that they were idolatry and not worship of God. Today, too, that thinking of the flesh greatly hinders the Gospel from its efficacy in many people inasmuch as it still imposes on them the appearance of right. The hypocrisy of human traditions is like this. This is what the prophet here calls "evil ways." He does this to terrify them with the example of their fathers, to get them to abandon their pursuits and to learn to cling solely to the Word of God. This is what all Scripture always and everywhere requires. Since, however, the flesh cannot but be consistent with itself, it holds the Word in contempt and approves of that which it has contrived itself. The prophet adds:

And they did not heed Me. All power lies in listening and giving heed, as it is always to the end of time. The prophets everywhere speak this way. God is not giving a command about burnt offerings. Instead, this is the Word "which I commanded them, that they hear My Word which I speak to them, etc." [7] But because God's Word has the habit of making demands that are impossible in the judgment of the flesh, we abandon the Word, hold it in contempt, and follow both our own sense as well as things we see placed before our eyes. This I have mentioned earlier in considerable detail.

5. *Your fathers, where are they and the prophets?* He says, as it were: "You see that both your fathers and the false prophets who were holding sure sway before the captivity and considered My Word a joke

[6] We have preferred the reading *permoveat* to *permoneat.*

[7] Cf. 1 Sam. 15:22; Jer. 7:22-23.

have already paid the penalty, while I have spoken in vain to them through genuine prophets. Look – none of them now exist. Their kingdom has been destroyed. They themselves have been led off into captivity and have died wretchedly. This is obviously the way I avenge My Word; and that terrifies you. Taught by this example of your fathers, you become terrified by that wrath when you see that because of their contempt for the Word fathers as well as prophets have perished, disciples as well as teachers, men who would not cease opposing My Word and who wanted it destroyed by every means. But it is they who have perished; My Word is still safe." This is a neat threat, which rightly should terrify us that we, too, may take the Word to heart and that we may not be listless and negligent, as if it had nothing to say to us and as if we were scorning it as something cold and dead. Otherwise we will pay the same penalty as they did for neglecting the Word and holding it in contempt.

Do they live forever? To the Hebrews "forever" means indeterminate time. This is revealed very clearly in Ex. 21:6, "And his master shall bore his ear through with an awl; and he shall be his slave forever." Here "forever" cannot refer to "eternity" but a kind of continuous state, that is, "always and continuously he will be his slave." Therefore the meaning here is as if he were saying: "See how false are your fathers and the prophets who kept saying things to please your fathers, for they surely are now long dead. Therefore, are they alive as men who are still unharmed?" For so, according to the sense, we must read in the indicative what the Hebrew language in its own idiom renders in the future. Indeed, the false prophets kept promising their hearers peace, righteousness, the favor of God, the safety of all their possessions, a calm kingdom, and a tranquil life. They kept saying, "Peace, peace," and there was no peace,[8] as also Micah 3:11 repeats: "Is not the Lord in the midst of us? No evil will come upon us." To statements of this sort on their part the Lord alludes here in the prophet, as if to say: "Had their promises been true, they certainly would be alive and in power now."

6. *But My words and My statutes.* Rather, this happened to them: They wanted to be saved themselves, and they wanted My Word to perish; therefore the evil fell back upon their own heads, because the laws and ceremonies which I prescribed kept accusing them and destroyed them as they neglected such prescriptions. So also today, what

[8] Cf. Jer. 6:14; 8:11.

is written in the Law and the Prophets bears witness against the Jews and judges them guilty of punishment because of their transgression. By the way, where we read [9] "statutes," we can just as accurately translate with the word "ceremonies."

So they repented and said: As the Lord of hosts purposed. I believe the meaning of this passage is simply this: The Law has now caught them; their experience has taught them. So now they are feeling the Lord's vengeance and already recognize their error for which they are being afflicted. And finally they have now been put to shame – which in the days when they refused to let go of their own nature they absolutely believed would never occur. That is how secure and confident they were of their cause. Therefore the prophet here takes a look at the shamelessness and impious obstinacy in which they felt secure and because of which they believed no evil would befall them. It is as if he were saying: "Now they no longer strut proud and puffed up but are already feeling the punishment of the Law." Thus it is "sheer terror to understand the message" (Is. 28:19). So also today, because we are flesh and wicked, we do not believe the Word. We hold faith in contempt and we want to learn by experience. Moreover, we shall doubtless learn from experience, as did they, to our great loss. And then, when we shall have thus been caught up by our disaster and will want to recover our senses, it will all be over. Because we neglect the Word and hold it in contempt, it is impossible for great disaster and wretchedness not to await us. Please God that this may not engulf us too while we are still alive, but may God give us His grace that we die in grace. You see, just as the best and holiest prophets among the Jews could accomplish nothing to call the people back from wickedness, even though such prophets were inspired by the Holy Spirit, so also we are totally without confidence that we shall accomplish anything to keep the flesh from being true to itself, that is, wicked and without belief for every Word of God. No, the flesh does not believe until it has already been caught up and engulfed by evil and sees that its case is already lost. Therefore, we must commit the matter to God.

Until now we have been commenting on the prophet's first discourse, which he delivered in the manner of the Law. It performs the duty of the Law, as it causes consciences to tremble in order to humiliate them and bring them to an understanding of themselves. Indeed, this is the way the Holy Spirit operates. First, He humbles. Then He

[9] In the Vulgate.

lifts up and brings back saved those He has humbled and condemned or hurled down into hell. The spirit of Satan operates differently. With swelling words he promises salvation to deceive poor unwary consciences. And when in hypocritical guise he has thrown these into the error of wickedness, he cannot bring them back, etc. But for those who are thrown down, for hearts that are humiliated and frightened, there follows a great and clearly evangelical comfort. And so the prophet has followed the correct order of the Spirit.

7. *On the twenty-fourth day of the eleventh month, which is the month of Shebat, in the second year of Darius.* This is the prophet's second discourse, which he delivered much later. The books of the prophets are thus to be divided into many discourses, as I have mentioned several times in regard to other prophets. As I have said, he richly comforts an afflicted people terrified by his rebuke. Here and there throughout his entire prophecy he intersperses quite a lot of material regarding Christ. Therefore both Christ and the apostles also cite many testimonies from this prophet. What I have said about the discourses of the prophets is true: that they delivered some at one time, others at another, and that they did not deliver them all in a single address. This passage most clearly convinces me of this, because we see that the prophet hid for almost three months after his first discourse. While he began his earlier discourse in the eighth month, he began this one in the eleventh month. Thus we see that the prophets did not always preach at a single urging and prompting of the Spirit but rather preached this at one time and that at another time, according to the revelation of the Spirit. For the Holy Spirit functions the way Christ says in John 3:8 about the wind of the Spirit: "It blows where it wills, and you hear the sound of it, but you do not know whence it comes or whither it goes." Moreover, for the Hebrews March was the beginning of the year. If you count the months in their correct order from that point, the eleventh from March will be January, which they call Shebat (with a short first syllable [10]). So he began this discourse in January.

8. *I saw in the night, and behold, a man riding, etc.* There is no difficulty if we only remain consistent in the plan and purpose of the matter, lest anyone vainly imagine certain difficulties for himself. In sum, this is what he discusses here: a comforting vision is here re-

[10] Thus Luther distinguishes this proper name שְׁבָט from the common noun שֵׁבֶט, "rod, staff."

vealed to the prophet, which he is to explain to an afflicted and numbed people. This is what all the circumstances indicate. Consequently, because the prophet had a clear vision, the people should have no doubt that they had a favoring God and a kindly Father. You see, God generally connects words closely with signs so that He may positively strengthen total human weakness, to which all the words and works of God cannot but seem absolutely impossible. Therefore it becomes quite obvious that He strikes down that fear and makes the heart courageous, lest it doubt that God does care and that it has a kindly God. After all, what is greater than that God, all-good and all-mighty, be kindly disposed to insignificant man, full of sin, that God have regard for him and take care of him, etc.? Certainly such operations are incomprehensible. Only those who have experienced them understand them. For when a man's heart has adopted such confidence that he believes God cares for him, that God is kindly disposed to him, that God will be a very faithful Guardian and Companion in every need, then he no longer is a man who believes this but already a divine creature, since he now has a divine zeal and power in his heart. This fires his heart and makes it grow against every fear, against all the foes he faces, in short, against all creatures. Therefore, because this is a situation of such great dimensions, we need an abundant and rich supply of the Word so that we may finally be strengthened by it, etc. Now we shall examine all the details of the vision.

In the night. Night undoubtedly points to the state of the people. The vision fits the sort of people they were in their hearts (that is, the sort of thing they thought about). You see, in this people there was no light; that is, no joy, no happiness. Instead, there were the terror of consciences, sadness, dismayed minds. The word "night" stands for all of these. Thus for a people completely destitute of every help, for a people already standing in the midst of death, there comes a light and the greatest comfort. This they still did not think would happen, as we shall see. For at first sight everything in the vision was terrible. Everything kept threatening the appearance of a greater evil, like red horses among the myrtle trees in the glen. Seeing all these, the prophet is terrified. For the weakness of the human heart is such, and its fear and terror are so great, that the heart flees even those things which are going to be good and comforting. It even flees salvation and in its distress loses faith. It believes that all these portend its destruction. So here, in the person of his people, the prophet is afraid of the vision which kept promising nothing but the greatest comfort and peace. So we, too, run away from God if He ever plunges one of us into poverty or illness. Yet these are very clear evidences of divine favor. But immediately, I say, we despair of God's goodness and favor toward us, and we look for salvation among creatures. Therefore we cannot but think the worst at any sign or word from God. This is clearly the intent of the prophet's word when he asks, "What are these, my lord?"

9. *The angel of the Lord who talked with me said to me.* I believe that the angel who is riding the horse (in its idiom the Hebrew says he is a man mounting a horse, but the Latins say it differently) and the angel who speaks with the prophet are the same person. But I consider it insignificant if anyone believes they are two different people. At any rate, all these riders agree that "all the earth remains at rest" (v. 11), that is, that the Lord is favorably inclined, that they need fear no warfare, that no kingdoms will rise up against Judea, etc. After all the circumstances of the vision have been searched out and examined, they will testify that this is the true and genuine meaning of it. First, *the myrtle* is a joyful happy tree. The heathen, too, believe that it was dedicated to Venus on this account. They would use the myrtle to celebrate and dance beneath it. Why, even we Germans indicate a very pleasant place by saying *unter einer grünen Linde,* as many of our songs reveal. The equestrian angel rides among the myrtles, that is, among the happy trees. He portends very great joy. So the two signs, the horse and the myrtle, contest with each other. It is as if he were saying: "You fear horses as portents of a coming war, but be confident! I have settled all wars, and I have settled them in the midst of peace." Next,

In the glen. This, too, is a safe and pleasant place. For there are more pleasant and more delightful places in the valleys than in the hills, where the wild beasts' runways are, just as we Germans also say *in der hübschen, grünen Aue* ("in a pleasant green meadow").

Red, sorrel, and white horses. These point to the very powerful nations – the Medes, Persians, and others. In this way also he points out that the authority of all these nations, however powerful and warlike they may be, will nevertheless not rage against Israel but will have become inclined toward peace. He says in substance: "Those kingdoms and their power are safe. They have not been destroyed or crushed. They are still 'horses,' but they are peaceful, for I have caused all things to be at peace."

The riders are undoubtedly angels through whom God manages this visible world. This the Epistle to the Hebrews 2:5 reveals, "For it was not to angels that God subjected the world to come, of which we are speaking," as if to say: "He subjected this visible world to them as He made them His ministering spirits" (cf. Heb. 1:14). Also: "He will give His angels charge of you to guard you in all your ways" (Ps. 91:11). And Christ says: "Their angels always behold the face of your Father, etc." (cf. Matt. 18:10). In this vision there are four orders of riders, or angels. This prophet, more than others, delights in the number four. The number four will follow often as we delve deeper into this book. With these four orders he means the peoples of the four corners of the earth, that is, that peace will come to Israel from all peoples of the earth so that there will be absolutely nothing to drive a contrite Israel to despair, but that everything will be peaceful and Israel will be comforted and helped.

Now, however, we are not completely in harmony about the colors of the horses. Most certainly we know what sort of horses are red, for the color *red (rufus)* is what we call *rotfarb*. *Sorrel* – more recent writers say that horses colored in this way are what the Latins call *spadices* ("chestnut").[11] To be sure, I am not certain what that color is.[12] I believe it is pinkish, an off-red, as crimson is an off-red. We call horses of this sort *die braunen Schimmel*. The *white (glaucus)* has a bluish cast like the color of the sea. These we will call *die apfelgrauen Hengste* ("dapple-gray stallions"). Our interpreters say that these four orders point to four kingdoms: Persians, Chaldeans, etc. However, it does not seem right to me to make such an interpretation. I believe that they mean all the kingdoms in the four quarters of earth or sky. As a result, that number four has to do more with the division of the parts of the earth: East, West, North, and South. This also the

[11] Cf. Vergil, *Georgics*, III, 82, where *spadices* and *glauci* are given as the "good" colors for horses, *albi* ("off-white") and *gilvi* ("yellowish") as "the worst" colors.

[12] Luther's own uncertainty about these colors is further reflected in some of the manuscripts of this passage. One has the marginal remark, "The writer is not sure whether he understood the doctor correctly," another crosses out the line concerning "the color of the sea" as applied to the white color, apparently hoping that a fellow student might help him correct later what he did not seem to understand at the moment. Cf. W, XIII, 558, n. 18.

colors can indicate. One by one they approximately fit each quarter of the earth.

What still remains of this chapter is easy, for the very allusion or vision reveals it. Indeed, he discusses nothing else throughout this chapter except to reveal and amplify the vision.

10. *These are they whom the Lord has sent to patrol the earth.* This is the explanation of the vision. It is as if he were saying: "You are very fearful. You are fainthearted, terrified by the ferocity of the nations who oppose you. You are not pushing forward the building of the house of the Lord that you have begun. You are afraid of the power and the weapons of neighboring nations. But have faith! Every occasion for every evil has been removed. The Lord cares for you. He has sent His angels to visit the earth to help you. Their ministry the Lord uses to manage all nations, for they are ministering spirits." Clearly then, we are not so forsaken that He sends His guardian and world-managing angels to search us out. This is the force in the word "The Lord has sent them," that it reveals their office, namely, that they will see to it that no misfortune happens to Israel and Judah at the hands of those nations of all the earth which they had before considered the most hated of all.

11. *And they answered the angel of the Lord who was standing among the myrtle trees.* In Dan. 12:1 Michael is proclaimed as the great prince who would rise and stand up before the people of the Lord, etc. They feel that he is the angel among the myrtles.

All the earth remains at rest. The books of Joshua and Judges often use the word for "being at rest" which we find here. For instance, "And the land had rest from war" (Joshua 11:23), that is, everything was peaceful. The wrath and cruelty of empires no longer existed. There were no more tumults and wars. So here the meaning is this: All the earth is untroubled and at rest. Each man enjoys his substance in peace.

12. *How long wilt Thou have no mercy on Jerusalem?* Up to this point the prophet has set forth the vision in this way, that all happy and prosperous events are being announced, and the vision completely fits this declaration, for just as the angels speak, so things appear.

Now follows an amplification and enlargement of the exposition.[13] This passage is genuinely delightful and wonderfully comforting. Now

[13] The Zwickau manuscript of these lectures has *consolationis* instead of *expositionis*.

Prince Michael himself intercedes for the people that the Lord might have compassion on Jerusalem. All this serves the purpose, as I have said, fully to strengthen an afflicted people. Therefore the meaning is as if he were saying: "Lord, Your people alone are wretched and fearful. They alone have suffered calamities beyond every other nation of the world; and although it would be proper for them to be supremely confident and filled with glory, nowhere is the land being tilled less than in Your land, nowhere is there peace less than in Your people of peace. Meanwhile, all other nations are safe and flourishing." So powerful is prayer with contention when it relies on the divine promise, as if to say: "If You deal kindly with the Gentiles, why do You not rather deal kindly with Your people, to whom You gave the promise that You would be with them, people whom You said You wanted to save against the insults of all the nations of the earth, etc?"

This is already the seventieth year. The angel responds with an objection, as if he were hearing the Lord say in reply that it is not yet time to help Jerusalem. So the angel says that it is now time, that the people must be glorified again, according to the promise made about the seventieth year. That prophecy is in Jer. 29:10: "After seventy years are completed for Babylon, I will visit you and I will fulfill to you My promise, etc." With that promise as many as survived the captivity were saved. Otherwise none would have been saved, because the captivity kept militating against the promises about David's eternal kingdom. After all, what seemed less true than that David's throne would continue forever when both king and people had been carried away? Consequently the Lord was adding another promise so that His people had no doubt that, even though they were captives, they would still return to their own land and be glorified.

13. *Gracious words and comforting words.* It is not for the prophet's but for the people's sake that all things happen. They are revealed to the prophet, however, that he may tell them to the people, that he may strengthen and confirm their contrite hearts, as if to say: "Fear not, but rather have faith and rejoice. The Lord is uttering comforting and gentle words."

14. *Cry out.* The angel commands the prophet to tell the people these very comforting words. "To cry out the Word," as it is here used, ought properly to be expressed with "to preach the Word," to indicate the office. We frequently find this expression in Moses. Now the angel directs the prophet what to preach.

I am exceedingly jealous for Jerusalem and for Zion, etc. As I have mentioned, this is a very beautiful passage – one of greater comfort than we have had so far here. All the words are perfectly suited. He grants jealousy to His people, wrath to the Gentiles. Jealousy properly is an anger which by nature involves love, as a man feels jealous about his wife. Briefly, it is a hatred of evil in the object of one's love, a friendly, loving hatred, or anger. It is like the anger of parents toward wayward children. Therefore the Lord takes away every suspicion of wrath with this single statement, as if He were saying: "My jealousy was great against Jerusalem, but now that that is finished, love overcomes wrath, for it was not so much wrath as jealousy." Our good and great God loved that people because of His Christ, who was destined to be born of the flesh of that people. Therefore He becomes indignant over the faults of His people, much like a husband who cannot bear the love of other men for his wife, or conversely, in the case of a wife, the love of other women for her husband.

15. *But I am very angry with the nations.* That is, "I was jealous over Jerusalem. For her I turned everything into good, because I loved her. But I am angry with the heathen with a great wrath. I shall destroy all their foundations because they are at ease." What God hates in the heathen is this: They are many, they are powerful, they are at ease, that is, they trust in their own might and power. And because they relied on these, they were contemptuous of both God and His people. So God hates the pride, the scorn, the self-confidence of the heathen.

For while I was angry but a little. Here He explains what He means by "jealousy." He says in effect: "I did not want My people to be ruined and abandoned; I merely reproved them in the direction of the good. I wanted to cure them, not kill them." In this way He offers complete comfort to their afflicted minds, and He does this with very sweet words. After all, what is sweeter and more pleasant than to know that God punishes just like a father? When the heart knows this, there is surely more sweetness in this understanding of the Father's will than there is pain because of His punishment. In fact, when the heart understands the Father, this mitigates all the pain we indeed feel as we are being punished. Hence this statement can be a source of comfort in finally any adversity at all. When God throws us into poverty or disgrace, when He nails us to a cross, when He allows our property to be taken from us, let us always say: "Let it go.

God intends nothing bad."[14] He does everything out of a fatherly love. His jealousy is that of a father. He cannot be angry always. But when this happens, more than half of the bad that can happen has already happened.[15]

They furthered the disaster. This, too, is a marvelous statement, no less comforting than the preceding. It means this: "The heathen have proposed mutual efforts and conspire together against My people to destroy them completely, leaving not even their name." Ps. 137:7 repeats these words of the heathen: "Raze it, raze it! Down to its foundations!" That conspiracy of the heathen He calls "furthering the disaster." As I have said, this is a very sweet statement. The Lord is showing that He not only is not angry with us as He whips us but also that He hates the whipping He uses against us. This passage is worth observing, for it can console us too when by the will of God our adversaries scourge us for some good and godly purpose. We know then that it is a paternal scourging, that no evil threatens us, and finally, that the Lord hates our foes. When we know this, a joyful spirit fills us so that we gladly endure the Lord's hand and turn our defense over to the Lord. We can regard our foes with contempt, however much they howl and rage against us.

16. *I have returned to Jerusalem with compassion.* "Because I am now compassionate, I promise mercy. I shall no longer scourge, because My anger has ceased." This is a very generous promise. When it comes to the heart of man and bears fruit, he becomes the master of death, sin, and hell. Thus there is nothing that can frighten such a person. What man who relies on very generous divine comfort of this kind would not dare build a temple reaching to the clouds?

And the measuring line shall be stretched out. He uses a circumlocution with which He shows that not only the temple but even the city are destined to be rebuilt. That is, so great will be the peace and security that the workers will go out safely and almost leisurely to build the city. They will not hurry because of fear or be forced to break off the work they have begun, as happened before.

17. *My cities shall again overflow with prosperity.* That is, not only Jerusalem but also the land of Judah and all other cities of my land will abound in good things. In Hebrew "overflow" is an elegant word. We cannot render it very well with a single Latin word. We

14 Luther uses the German expression *Lass gehen, Gott meint's nicht böse.*

15 Luther uses a German phrase: *so ist es mehr denn halb geschehen.*

can translate it literally from the Hebrew this way: "My cities still will be sprinkled with blessings," that is, there will be various cities dispersed here and there, and yet none of them will lack its own prosperity. He addresses Himself not to the abundance of the blessings but to their distribution.

For these bountiful promises the prophet certainly used up many sermons (even with many sermons he was hardly able to set forth the power and magnitude of these promises). And for us, too, these promises could surely provide full and rich material for many sermons, because all of these matters are so sweet and full of comfort. If the prophet examined them according to all their details, if he related them to each of the cities in proportion to the calamity each had suffered, he needed many sermons. And of course they are worthy of a very detailed treatment. After all, what could have been more comforting to wretched and tormented consciences than to hear that Jerusalem would be rebuilt, the cities restored to their pristine grandeur, the people glorified by the Lord? For all the heathen thought that this people had been wiped out and their case settled. And now, after Jerusalem had been so utterly destroyed, what could be more comforting than to hear at long last that the Lord again had chosen Jerusalem, that He favored her and wished her well?

18. *And behold, four horns!* Here is another vision which adds to the comfort of the previous one. What I mentioned earlier about the number four must again be noted here. Everywhere in Scripture "horns" mean thrones – even in the historical sense.[16] The prophet Daniel especially reveals this. Therefore the four horns mean the thrones spread throughout the four corners of the earth.

21. *These are the horns which have scattered.* He does not mean the carpenters here, as could seem to be the case from our poor translation.[17] He is using a Hebrew construction. For Hebrew generally places the relative first and the demonstrative in the second place, as Ps. 1:4 shows: "Like chaff which the wind drives it from the face of the earth." Another psalm (68:16) shows the same thing: "The mount which God desired it for His abode." Because our translator has not noticed this, he has thus confused the order of the construction. Ac-

[16] The contrast is between the *sensus historicus,* the Biblical report of an event in history, and the *sensus propheticus principalis,* the even more important meaning of the historical event for the future. Cf. W, IV, 476, 8—21.

[17] The Vulgate.

cording to the Hebrew, the correct reading is this (v. 21): "He spoke, saying, 'These horns, which have scattered Judah, one man after another, none of whom has lifted up his head, these have come to frighten them away, etc.'" But the Latin would construe it this way: "They have come to frighten away all these horns which have scattered Judah, etc." The meaning is: "They have come to put to flight, to terrify, and to drive away from My people the threatening power and tyranny of all the kingdoms of the earth." The word which our translator renders with "frighten away" *(deterrere)* is an elegant one. Moses used the same word in Gen. 35:5: "A terror from God fell upon all the cities which were round about them."

When He has compassion on us, the Lord sends His Word in such great supply and with such fullness that there is no way to measure it. His kindness and gentleness pour forth boundlessly. They have no limit. On the other hand, when He is angry, there is no way to measure His wrath. When He takes away His Word, then one rage always follows another. That is a great misfortune, a dreadful blindness. But when He promises to be our Father, He reveals Himself fully. There is no bitterness, no terror; and all things are safe and peaceful. Here we see what great and varied comfort and what great eagerness our very wonderful and gentle Father has used to revive and strengthen fearful and contrite hearts that they no longer fear anything but believe that they will have a gentle Father. So determined is God to comfort and strengthen a terrified, trembling conscience and to have man finally return to Him. You see, this kind of terror of consciences is monstrous and horrible beyond measure. The conscience is so delicate. weak, and helpless a thing that, once it has been terrified, the great concern and greater comfort of the holy Word can barely renew it to keep it from becoming more and more desperate every day. The people who in our time write much about developing man's character do not know this. If these people had learned just once how great the anguish and terror of the afflicted conscience is, how great its fear, they would soon stop urging character so much. Almighty God knows His handiwork; He knows our weakness. Therefore He also sees what manifold and sweet promises and comfort we need. O God, it is a much greater thing that this kind of conscience be lifted up than as they think, etc.

This, then, is the historical sense of chapter 1: that trembling hearts be revived and strengthened, that no power frighten them from going on with building the house of the Lord which they had begun; that there is nothing so difficult or so cruel that they should be afraid of it; that the Lord will be at their side; that He will not allow the heathen to rage wantonly against His people anymore and to destroy them utterly (He speaks of it here as "scattering them man for man"); that the Lord will not allow the heathen to lift up their horns anymore, that is, to charge through them like an angry bull.[18]

18 Luther uses the German expression *mit dem Kopf hindurchgehen.*

CHAPTER TWO

In chapter 2 the prophet himself, in the manner of a preacher, turns history into an allegorical prophecy. For as he spoke earlier of the current state of Jerusalem, so here he will speak about her future – that all things signify in spirit that grace will be revealed through Christ throughout the world. Here he will also explain why he takes such pleasure in the number four.

Therefore with all those ideas above about great peace and external calm, about rebuilding Jerusalem, etc., he is showing this: all things are happening because of the coming grace to be revealed through Christ. Here in this chapter he adds the spiritual realm of Christ. He himself explains the horses and the horns that scatter. He shows that everything has a spiritual meaning. Now comes, as I have said, the reason for using the number four. The Gospel had to be noised abroad and propagated to the ends of the earth, to all nations, as Ps. 72:8 reveals: "May He have dominion from sea to sea, etc." Also, Christ says in Matt. 24:31: "They will gather His elect from the four winds, etc." Then, too, we read in Is. 60:4: "Your sons shall come from far, and your daughters shall be carried in the arms." Here and in all similar passages hides the mystery in the words "comforting" and "having dominion," just as here, too, we must understand the enlarging of Jerusalem as a spiritual enlargement. After all, these matters cannot fit a physical Jerusalem, as we shall see as we go through the chapter. Here is the mystery of the second and first chapters:

The angels with horses are the kingdoms of the entire world. They stand among the myrtles, that is, they are peaceful and at rest. The people of Judah had to have physical peace so that Jerusalem and other cities could be rebuilt. This was the significance of history. The mystery is as follows: That external peace signifies the spiritual joy and security of the church, that is, of the righteous who believe in Christ. Their consciences are calm and peaceful, so that there is nothing which can separate them from the love of God, even though warfare and hatred surround them. For as Christ says, "In the world you will have tribulation, but in Me you will have peace" (cf. John 16:33).

The world does not stop raging against and persecuting the members of Christ, and "the rulers take counsel together against the Lord," as we read also in Ps. 2:2. Yet in all this Christians do not succumb. So great is the peace of Christ, "which passes all understanding," as Paul says (Phil. 4:7); that is, so great is the peace in our hearts that in every tribulation we are so far from being overcome by fear that we even rejoice, as Paul says in Rom. 5:3. Thus by not turning away evils or enemies but by turning them loose, the Lord causes us to feel safe, to rejoice always, not to be overcome by any evil, even though the whole world may bare its fangs against us. Let the pope rage. Let the emperor and his princes threaten us with evil. We shall sit in the beauty of peace, even though they throw us into prison. If they are allowed to give themselves over to their wrath, if finally they even slay us, we will rejoice no less than if we had been invited to a wedding. This is the response St. Agnes gave to the tyrant who was about to kill her, etc.[1] The carpenters are the preachers of the Gospel, as are also the angels riding horses. Because these are ministers of the Word, they fight not with their own strength but with the Word. Their fighting capability appears insignificant, their weapons very weak. Yet with that very Word, which the world sees as some ridiculous fiction, they cause the greatest and most powerful kingdoms to flee from us. They cause us to pity them rather than to fear them and to grieve because they are so vainly wasting their wrath and indignation. At the expense of property, body, and soul they set themselves against us, but all in vain. For we always have our horses among the myrtles. Thus our foes are forced to submit to us, while they can overcome in us nothing less than our spirit, which, like a bronze wall, stands firm and unafraid and holds their threats as well as their might in contempt. This is one thing which causes the devil great grief. When he invades our body, he intends to overcome our soul. Otherwise he considers hurting our body worthless. All of this the prophet gives us in this second chapter, which I call an allegory of the preceding chapter. After all, that cannot be the physical Jerusalem which the prophet sees here, as the context itself proves.

1. *And behold a man with a measuring line in his hand.* That man is Christ, who has received the gift of the Holy Spirit from the Father and who most surely measures the church, that is, makes small or great by means of very specific gifts of the Spirit, for He gives to each man

[1] Cf. *Luther's Works,* 12, p. 177; 17, p. 258.

as He wills, just as the apostle says in Eph. 4:7, "according to the measure of Christ's gift." So the church does not extend beyond the Spirit of Christ. See 1 Cor. 12. Surely this is the meaning of the measuring line – the Holy Spirit with His gifts.

3. *And he came forward to meet him and said.* Here I omit what Jerome dreams up – that the angels did not know of the mystery of the incarnation.[2] I also omit the hallucinations of Dionysius about the celestial hierarchy – that some angels teach others, that some are of very low rank, some of very high rank, and I don't know what all he writes so shamelessly as if he himself had seen it.[3] Christ says, "Their angels . . . behold the face of My Father" (Matt. 18:11). Therefore it is God who illumines the angels and who uses their efforts. It is not true that some angels illumine others. However, because all of this takes place to comfort an afflicted and terrified people, we had to give some attention to this nonsense.

4. *To the young man.* The young man is Zechariah.

Jerusalem will be inhabited without a wall. In Nehemiah and in Ezra the command had been given about rebuilding Jerusalem and the walls around the city. Consequently, it is clear that we cannot take this passage to refer to the physical Jerusalem but to the Jerusalem whose borders are the entire world. It is as if he were saying: "There will be no city so broad and vast as to be able to hold the Christians, so many of them will there be, seeing that they will be living throughout the entire world." I am not displeased by the idea of those who translate "men" as "those robust in the faith" and "cattle" as "weaker people." After all, Christ's body has flesh and bones, that is, the strong and the weak. Because His is a kingdom of love, however, the one patiently bears the weakness of the other, as Paul writes (cf. Rom. 15:1).

5. *I will be to her a wall of fire.* That spiritual Jerusalem will have no physical wall. Nevertheless, it is going to have a fiery wall instead of a stone wall. This fiery wall the Lord Himself promises He will be. This is a very rich comfort, but though it is a richer comfort than anything before, no one believes it unless his heart is illuminated by the Spirit. Here we must have the sort of eyes Elisha had when he saw fiery chariots and horsemen all around and told his servant, "Those

[2] Jerome, *Commentaria in Zachariam prophetam, Patrologia, Series Latina,* XXV, 1433.

[3] Cf. *Luther's Works,* 1, p. 235; 13, p. 110, n. 55.

who are with us are more than those who are with them" (2 Kings 6:16). This is also very clear in Ps. 125:2: "As the mountains are round about Jerusalem, so the Lord is round about His people." If only we believed this! God cannot lie. For those who are faithful to Him He is a wall of fire, that is, He is a terrible God who absolutely annihilates all who oppose Him. For what might and power would be so great as to be able to stand against this wall which eats away and consumes everything it comes into contact with. Here Satan and all the foes of the Word must give ground. After all, who will overcome the Lord, the Divine Majesty, who scatters all of His enemies for the church and reduces them to nothing just like dust? These things, however, are said in spiritual terms. We must understand them spiritually as well. For this, we must have faith, for to the flesh this appears like the very opposite, while our enemies beset us, take us captive, rage against us as they like, and finally even kill us. But the Lord says that He is a wall of fire, as if to say: "Be confident. Though they may beset you, they will not overcome Me. They will not escape My vengeance. For in a short time it will come to pass that they are nothing, that their name will scarcely survive after I have torn down and destroyed their foundations." This is something He stated very well in the case of that terrible rejection of the Jews. When they had been scattered throughout the world, scarcely a bare remnant of them survived – and then in a most pitiable condition. He declared the same point, too, in overthrowing the Roman Empire. That was certainly the most flourishing world power. At that time it was making vicious attacks upon the holy martyrs of Christ. But finally that wall of fire so scattered and destroyed it that its capital city no longer has even the appearance of a city. So deep are the dregs of impurity, so great the confusion there, that one finds it impossible to see there the reflection of a once so splendid empire. I want our princes to take warning today; they who threaten us with evil, who rage against us as if they wished to swallow us alive. But let them rage, let them indulge the impotent madness of their mind. They will soon become nothing, and men will scarcely recall their name anymore, whether it be the Margrave or Duke George.[5] From the beginning God has not spared those who have held His Word in contempt. So also He will not be sparing now.

[4] We have read *videri* for *videre*.

[5] Margrave Joachim I of Brandenburg (1485—1535) and Duke George of Albertine Saxony (1471—1539), both bitter enemies of Luther and the Reformation.

He will be a wall of fire. If anyone strikes against this wall, He will be turned into ashes and become nothing, etc.

And I will be the glory within her. He removes the entire glory of the flesh so that whoever glories may glory in the Lord and we may glory only in our Lord Christ. The glory of physical Jerusalem lay in her people, her armies, her bravery, her blessedness, her justice, her law. She could boast about all these. The unique glory of the Christians, however, lies in Christ alone, in whom they believe and whom they trust.

6. *Ho! ho! Flee from the land of the north.* After he has set forth the promise and the comfort, the prophet adds the exhortations that the Jews should not despise the great grace and unspeakable mercy of God. This the prophet saw was going to happen: that almost all Israel would regard both Christ and the promised grace in Christ with contempt; and that they would have to be cast down in order that a mere remnant of them might be saved. This is the one particular thing, too, which causes all the good Gospel preachers to grieve. They see the world not only despising the Gospel of the glory of God Almighty but even persecuting it. This can be an argument that the world is not merely stupid and ignorant of God but also full of devils and is driven along by this fact. This passage bothers Lyra. In fact, he upsets himself as he asks why the Lord calls His people back only from the land of the north, even though He had scattered them to the four winds throughout the world. Skipping mystical allegories, I think the simple meaning here is this, that they had recently been brought back from Babylon. We grant that under both this and the Assyrian captivity the Children of Israel were scattered everywhere throughout the world, as I have also mentioned earlier. The kings of the Chaldeans and Assyrians had also thus scattered them, whereupon some kept seeking safety for themselves in flight. Therefore the greater part of the captivity was in Babylon. So it happens that He calls them back only from Babylon, because there was a greater number, a greater transporting, there. It is as if he were saying: "Great things are at hand. Christ, your King and Savior, soon will come. Don't tarry among the Babylonians. If you don't come to the physical Jerusalem, at least come to the spiritual one." Yet He had promised that out of Zion would go forth the Law, and the Word of the Lord from Jerusalem (Micah 4:2).

8. *After His glory He sent Me.* This is a confirmation and ampli-

fication of the promise about that new Jerusalem of amazing size to be built throughout the world. Indeed, He is describing the builder and leader, or head, of this new Jerusalem. Surely we cannot take these words to mean an earthly Jerusalem, since it is a fact that Jerusalem never subjected the Assyrians, Chaldeans, and Egyptians to itself. Therefore we must understand this as a reference to spiritual subjection. Also, the Lord God of hosts is speaking here, and not Zechariah, who had been sent as a prophet only to the Jews to strengthen them, and not to the Chaldeans and Assyrians. And so also the grammatical sense here proves that Christ is true God and true man. For the true Lord of hosts sends the true Lord of hosts; but He is sent to the heathen, not in His own person but in His Gospel and in His Spirit, as Paul writes to the Ephesians (Eph. 2:17). He comes "after the glory," just as He says here. Our interpreters trouble themselves surprisingly much with this text. I think we ought to understand it simply to mean that Christ is saying that He would come "after the glory," that is, after the synagog and the throne have again been brought back from Babylon and restored. He says in substance: "I have promised to restore both the priesthood and the throne of this people, to rebuild the cities of Judah, to give My people the pleasure of My peace, etc. When all this will have happened and they will gradually begin to totter again, then I will immediately appear, not in the glory but after the glory, in humility and contempt. In vain will you wait for Me to come in royal processions and splendor. Do not be disappointed if you stand gaping at armor and power and want Me to be surrounded with royal paraphernalia."

Isaiah also agrees with this meaning when he says: "There shall come forth a Shoot from the stump (or trunk) of Jesse, and a Branch shall grow out of his roots" (Is. 11:1). For Christ came into the flesh at the time when the tribe of David was lying completely neglected and had almost ceased to exist. No longer was there a king born of the seed of David sitting on David's throne. The priests and high priests had already risen up and were struggling against the tribe of Judah for control of the state. This is clear from the history of the Maccabees and from Philo.[6] Furthermore, the priests won out, so that the tribe of Judah had no hope of recovering its royal position, for heathen nations were ruling. So, with the situation of the tribe of Judah damaged

[6] Luther may be referring to Pseudo-Philo, *Breviarium de temporibus,* edited by Annius of Viterbo, which he used in the preparation of his chronology, the *Supputatio annorum mundi* (Cf. W, LIII, 19—21).

and in difficult straits, Christ came to take the throne again, just as had been promised. This is what Isaiah calls a Shoot and a Branch coming from a dead trunk. Jacob's prophecy also pertained to this – that the scepter would not depart from Judah nor the ruler from his loins until that Shiloh come, etc. (cf. Gen. 49:10), that is, Christ would come at the time when the tribe of Judah had lost its controlling authority and royal dignity. When He says that He would come "after the glory," that is, after His people and especially the ruling tribe of Judah had been humiliated, He relates this to the disgrace and debasement of the tribe of Judah.

For he who touches you. He says: "I shall be sent to the heathen as if to avenge you, for they have despoiled you and made you subject to them. I shall subject them in turn, but that will be a miraculous subjection. Indeed, it will happen while they are harassing and attacking you. But still, as they touch and hurt you, they will touch and hurt Me." That is what He means with the word "touch," as we also read in the psalm (Ps. 105:15): "Touch not My anointed ones." Here, then, we must take this passage to have a completely spiritual sense. It is as if He were saying: "Put aside all pomp, all gaudy, royal paraphernalia, for you will be kings, but marvelous ones. For you will be touched, that is, you will be afflicted; you will be forced to carry a cross; the heathen will threaten you with opposition, etc. Nevertheless, you will be superior to all this; you will be equal to such great disasters. The heathen, on the other hand, who are confident that they are the victors, will succumb." This is a marvelous contradiction – one which is completely foreign to every judgment of reason. The person who becomes subject conquers; the one who is superior is conquered. For while Christians have been oppressed by the judgment of the world and are overcome by adversities, they are conquering by the power of the Spirit of God. Here again we see a very generous promise. Were we to have our hearts strengthened by it, what calamity, what violence either of the world or of the devil, could be so great as to conquer us? We would not just be equal but far superior to it. Indeed, the Lord gives us such worth, takes such great care of us and loves us so much, that He says that the pupil of His eye is touched when we are touched, this is, when we are afflicted and oppressed. Since there is nothing more sensitive than the pupil of the eye, the Lord says that whoever touches Christians touches the pupil of His eye. Therefore, the meaning, in sum, is this: "I love you and take care of you no less than I do

My own eyes." But such matters demand faith. They don't want to be grasped by reason, neither can they, for the opposite is what appears to reason, that while He says He exercises as great a care for us as He does for the pupil of His eye, He meanwhile puts us into prisons, causes us to lose our property and children, forces us to flee, and finally permits us to be killed.[7] Thus He allowed His very dear friend, John the Baptist, to die so disgracefully and undeservedly that the head of a very saintly man was given in payment for the lewd dancing of a shameless whore. Says the judgment of reason: "A great concern of God, indeed, for His saints! This is obviously to love them as the pupil of His eye!" However, as I have said, faith feels and believes this when a person is being afflicted and learns that new kind of warfare and that new kind of victory – through the cross. Were we to believe this, we would never cease weeping over the wretched blindness and wickedness of our foes when they persecute us. For we know that they are touching the pupil of the Lord's eye – a terrible sin, which God certainly won't forgive them.

9. *For behold, I will shake My hand over them.* This means: "I am strong. I shall exercise My power against those who have despoiled you. In fact, I shall conquer them with your weakness." For through the weaknesses of the world, He thus overcomes everything strong. He sets the wretched worm, the weak midget, the earthen vessel, against the bronze mountains, against the strong and powerful spirit of Satan, who devotes all his might to accomplish one thing – to break that weak vessel into pieces and reduce it to nothing. And Satan would certainly accomplish without difficulty whatever he wished if God were not to wrap Himself into our weakness and thus overcome Satan through us. Otherwise we are nothing else than dust and the lightest ashes before his might. This is what happened at the beginning of the newborn church. The number of the faithful grew because of their many deaths and wounds. No force or tyranny could be so great as to frighten the Christians away. In fact, they always became more and more courageous. Their number increased just as fresh heads, born from the blood, kept growing on the Lernean Hydra for Hercules.[8]

And you will know that the Lord. He says in effect: "When you

[7] The text has *occidere,* but *occidi* was probably intended.

[8] The reference is to the second of the 12 labors of Hercules. For every head Hercules cut off the Lernean Hydra, two new ones would immediately appear.

are in tribulation, when your foes will attack you, then your experience will have taught you, and you will know and understand that I have accomplished all this."

10. *Sing and rejoice, O daughter of Zion.* This is the congratulation for recognizing and possessing great glory under the disgraceful cross. This genuine joy is incredible when we realize that with our weakness we are overcoming the tremendous power of Satan. Here there is no tribulation, no adversity, which that joy cannot remove from our hearts.

And I will dwell in the midst of you. God dwells in us, that is, in our hearts through faith, as it is written in Eph. 3:17. Also John says: "He who is in us [9] is greater than the one who is in the world" (1 John 4:4). Therefore, to have God living in us is to have a heart filled with faith in Christ, who wants to be merciful. To have God dwelling in us means that the Father is a kind Father, who protects us in every adversity.

11. *And many nations shall join themselves to the Lord.* This is the same point which he mentioned earlier about extending Jerusalem throughout the earth; namely, that by the Word and through faith all nations would be converted to believe in Christ and would be implanted in and become inhabitants of this Jerusalem. This is an outstanding passage about the conversion of the heathen to the Gospel.

12. *And the Lord will inherit Judah as His portion in the holy land.* Clearly he distinguishes land from land, as if to say: "No longer will the Lord abandon Judah. Instead, He will inherit it and take it up again as His property and portion. This will happen in a land of holiness, a land which is not polluted, a land which can be neither befouled nor profaned; just as Isaiah says [10]: "For never again shall the wicked come against you." We certainly cannot take this to mean the land of Judah, where many wicked people lived. Rather, he is speaking about the true church which Christ's Spirit sanctifies, "for all who are led by the Spirit of God are sons of God," as the apostle says (Rom. 8:14).

13. *Be silent, all flesh.* This is an apostrophe to all the nations. It is as if he were saying: "Because such a kingdom and such holiness are going to exist in the world; therefore, be silent, ye nations. The kingdom of Christ is coming." You see, the kingdom depends on a

[9] Luther changes the pronoun from "you" to "us."

[10] The ascription is incorrect. The passage quoted is from Nahum 1:15.

coming and running as the Word is sent and preached among all nations. *Be silent,* that is, "Believe, give place, rest from your own pursuits and presumptions; let the Lord Himself reign."

For He has roused Himself, that is, He has set the Gospel in motion. Already He has begun to govern with His Gospel.

CHAPTER THREE

IN the preceding chapters we have seen that the prophet's purpose has been to encourage and strengthen the people to continue pressing forward in the work of building the house of the Lord which they had begun. Here in these next chapters he comforts their leaders – men who were responsible for both the spiritual and civil concerns of their people. Joshua was the priest in charge of spiritual matters; Zerubbabel was the leader in matters political. Both of these the prophet encourages with the greatest and sweetest comforts and promises. Indeed, it is very important that people have a courageous ruler who leads the rest of the multitude by his example. Then, frightened by no difficulty, they follow their leader, as we generally and commonly say, "A good leader deserves every honor." [1]

Here we should note especially that moral problem, how very difficult it is to submit to God's call and what great effort and comfort are necessary finally to put aside our own thoughts and affections and to listen to the divine call. See how fearful the people were before! See how the prophet accomplished almost nothing with his generous and sweet comfort! Notice here in the case of the priest, and later in the case of the king, how there is nothing but trembling and pure desperation. They could scarcely be compelled to finish the work of the Lord they had begun, even though the prophet had encouraged them with great comfort. The nature of the divine call is such that first one approaches the situation with great fear, trembling, and desperation. Here nothing happens precipitously. There is no need for rashness, for audacity or arrogance, but rather for great comfort. Therefore we must particularly mark this section that we, too, may approach the work of our calling with fear and trembling. Otherwise whatever venture we attempt more arrogantly than we ought, relying on our own plans and boldness, will turn out badly. The genuine Spirit cannot be in those people who, so to say, boast and triumph at the very beginning of their call and are willing to try everything. Surely, they finish everything quickly, as if they have already overcome Satan, although

1 Luther quotes a German proverb: *Ein guter Anheber ist aller Ehren wert.*

they have not yet seen him. If these people, when adversity assails them, are ever forced to give a reason for what they have begun, it is strange how they lose confidence in their cause and cannot pursue it farther. This is something we have seen in the case of our own prophets. The prophet Isaiah clearly opposed the Lord, who was sending him. As an excuse, he pleads the impurity of his lips in Is. 6:5. Moses and Jeremiah both kept pretending a lack of eloquence to prevent their being sent out. But God in His every work surpasses all the thoughts, powers, and understanding of reason. He requires and wants far more sublime and difficult things done than human intellect can achieve. In fact, all these human efforts appear very weak. Therefore we need another Master that we may break out of this, that is, that we may close our eyes and ears and cling solely to His Word; that we may give God the glory for being truthful; and that we may have no doubt that He will complete whatever He wished to accomplish in us. This is what Paul says: "God is able to do far more abundantly than we think" (cf. Eph. 3:20).

Here we see exactly the same thing. What an impossible situation this seemed to the priest; how many things there were to terrify him! First, because of his burdened and poorly bolstered conscience, he was frustrated by that common question: Who knows if I, a sinful man, am pleasing God? The guilty conscience cannot do any good thing. Always uncertain about the will of God, it approaches anything with fear and, in fact, with the greatest uncertainty. Therefore God cannot approve its efforts, because the mind fluctuates so much. In fact, we must do a good work with a conscience completely good, so that we believe it is not our work, not a work of our strength or planning, but a work of God. With a sure and mature conscience we must trust that the Lord will accomplish what He has planned through us and with our ministry so that we recognize that we are God's "tools" (ὄργανον). Otherwise, if the heart does not become that strong, it is impossible for us to begin over again. You see, the size of the task, the great difficulty of doing it, our reason, and Satan frighten us immediately. Satan so exaggerates the task that he calls us away from it. He reviews the difficulty, threatens us with many evils, and then has us go back to our work. Also, he reveals and exaggerates our sin and weak flesh by pointing out that God does not approve of sinners but rather casts them out and punishes them, and that this is work for saints who are in charge of divine tasks of this sort, etc. This surely places us in a very violent wrestling match. For when we stand strong and are equal to this temptation, we are overcoming sin, death, and Satan at one time. The heart no longer fears anything. It has no doubt about the will of God. It is sure that God approves of it, although weakness and sin is still present. It is sure that God wants to use its ministry, even though to the flesh the opposite appears to be the case. Surely, to overcome those three is not within the capability of human powers. Therefore the Holy Spirit must be present within us as the Paraclete, who encourages the heart so that we overcome joyfully, allow God to use our ministry, and are not at all frightened by the fear of death or sin; or if we are not completely joyful and bold, that we still overcome in the midst of our weakness and uncertainty, always keeping our eyes fixed not on our weakness but on the will of God, for He has thrown us into such a calling with His own will, etc. This same idea appears beautifully in this chapter where the prophet treats this point in general to strengthen an uncertain priest who is terrified by the magnitude of his task, by the evils which threaten him, and finally by his own sin and to encourage his priest against all those insults, etc.

1. *The Lord showed me Joshua the high priest.* The prophet did not see the actual figure of Joshua the high priest but some likeness by which the high priest Joshua was represented as if present.

And Satan was standing at his right hand. "Satan" generally and quite properly signifies any opponent. I think it here signifies especially the devil. Again we must understand here that he saw some likeness of the person who was always opposing the priest and frightening him away from whatever he had begun.

This is a wonderfully choice vision, for it very vividly reveals to us the heart and innermost emotions of the priest. He had heard the clear command of God to rebuild the temple. Then, after hearing that Word, he thought that he should listen to God, but he still kept wrestling with himself over the problem thus: "Who knows whether God intends to approve? Perhaps God will reject us sinners." This is exactly the way the human heart battles against sin in the presence of God. For Satan so inflates and exaggerates sins that the heart becomes convinced that God will reject it. It can conceive of no other God but one who now threatens it with a beating or a flogging. So here the high priest Joshua, crushed and terrified by his sins, does not dare go on with his task. Therefore he is strengthened and encouraged to believe that the Lord is not angry, that He has turned away the accusation of Joshua's conscience and is accusing Satan himself, who so discourages the heart with the heinousness of its sin that it cannot go on to serve its calling.

2. *The Lord rebuke you.* This is a very wonderful and sweet comfort. Everything is contained in the fullness of this comfort, so neatly has he arranged all his words, as if to say: "From now on, Satan, stop opposing the priest. The Lord orders all things cursed which you inspire the timid priest to think about and which frighten him from his task. You are causing him to be downcast before God and to dare nothing before men. You are acting as if the Lord had completely rejected Jerusalem. But the Lord has not done this. On the contrary, He has chosen it and loves it as His own possession."

Is not this a brand plucked from the fire? "You are doing this that the foundations may be destroyed and Israel perish, so that not even the remnant will survive and be saved. However, the Lord will preserve the remnant for Himself. He will glorify and save them. For that priest along with the few who survive will be exactly like a brand plucked out that terrible captivity." We have the same simile in Isaiah, where he calls the two kings "Two smoldering stumps of firebrands" (Is. 7:4), and above, in Amos 3:12, we read: "As the shepherd rescues from the mouth of the lion two legs, etc." These are the wonderful, mighty works of God. He treats His people as if He were completely incapable of protecting them. He permits them to be swallowed up [2] almost totally. Yet He preserves a very few and protects them in such a way that absolutely no power either of the world or of the devil is so great as to be superior to those few.

3. *Joshua was clothed with filthy garments.* An angel is always added to signify accurately the wrestling of the conscience in God's presence. The priest, although silent, has always reflected to himself just as he is pictured here in the vision. What the filthy garments are the prophet himself explains: the corrupt priesthood and sins of the priest. Frightened by these, he was becoming anxious and was losing confidence that his priesthood would please the Lord. It was the priestly function to pray for the sins of the people and to offer up sacrifices for those sins. But Joshua the high priest with his disturbed conscience always thought that God was the avenger of sin, that he was a sinner, and that his intercession before God for the sins of the people would be useless. Terrified by the terrible and wretched re-

[2] We have read *degluti* (with the Zwickau text) for *deglubi*, "to be skinned."

jection of the kingdom and people, he could not set the mercy of God before his eyes. Therefore he still thought that God was angry and that whatever he – just one man – would try would be in vain, because his circumstances were so constricted, afflicted, and in fact hopeless. So he takes off the dirty clothes and puts on fresh. This is a comfort against his sins, just as earlier he kept on being strengthened against the temptations of Satan. And let me give you this additional warning: what Lyra and Jerome dream up here about the filthiness of the garments is purely worthless imagination.[3]

4. *Behold, I have taken your iniquity away from you.* Everything in this vision is revealed in such a way that the vision declares and reveals God's will to the priest. It strengthens the priest so that he no longer doubts that God will approve of his ministry, that his filthy garments have been changed, and that his sin has been taken away. Now he wears new clothes, that is, a happy and joyful conscience which no longer flees from God, which thinks nothing evil about God but hopes for every good thing. Thus the fresh clothes do not mean works but grace and faith. The conscience is equipped not with works but with faith in order to find peace in God's presence. And so the heart which has been strengthened in faith rejoices and is afraid of nothing. It has no further anxieties about the insults and violence of all the heathen, about Satan, nor about sin. Instead, it joyfully despises them and performs the Lord's work with gladness.

5. *A clean turban on his head.* The turban was the priestly turban. See Lev. 8:9. Now that the person is approved and made worthy, the priestly office is also approved. Therefore the turban is here set on his head so that he may go on to be a priest, to signify that the Lord will approve of all he does. Clearly, the purity of a person's character always should come before the purity of his duty, for if his character is pure, all the rest is pure too. How would an impure person perform pure works? "A bad tree cannot bear good fruit, etc." (Matt. 7:18).

6. *And the angel of the Lord stood and enjoined.* Now that Satan has been driven back, the priest strengthened, and his sins taken away, the angel adds an encouragement. He neatly connects Christ's priesthood to that external and legal priesthood. For everything was happening for only one purpose and had been established merely to be

3 Cf. Jerome, *Commentaria in Zachariam prophetam, Patrologia, Series Latina*, XXV, 1436: "This is understood in a threefold way: in regard to an illicit marriage, the sins of the people, or the squalor of the captivity."

a sort of minimal preparation for that coming priesthood of the great High Priest, Christ. All this was taking place solely on His account. Because the promise had been given that He would come from that people, both the people and the priesthood had to survive and be preserved until He should come. Therefore the passage means: "Now you have been established in your priestly office. Your works please God. Go then and carry out that priestly ministry of yours. If you shall have done this,

7. *You shall rule My house.* That is, "you will be a judge in My house. You will be in charge of the people and their rulers in those matters related to the worship of God." This, however, is law. He is speaking legally, for this discourse is in the subjunctive, as the language of the Law usually is. The Gospel says: "I do. I do, etc."

And I shall give you the right of access among those who are standing here. Some interpreters take this to mean angels. My idea very simply is that it does not mean angels but rather that the Lord plans to give also a people and listeners, who are going to listen to the priestly teacher, who are not going to despise him. Consequently, this will be a blessed priesthood.

8. *Hear now, O Joshua the high priest.* Beautifully he connects, as I mentioned a bit earlier, those two priesthoods – the legal one and that true one of the great High Priest, Christ. In substance he is saying: "High Priest Joshua, listen to what I intend with that external priesthood of yours. I am renewing the promises about the coming Christ. For the manifold promises of the Law have this point, that Christ will be a priest. So go ahead! Take charge of that external priesthood until He comes. For it is on His account that both the people and the priesthood had to be restored, that the promises might come true."

For they are men of good omen. We must take it in a good sense rather than in a bad sense when He calls them "men of omens" *(portentosos).* The same meaning and wording we find in Is. 8:18: "Behold, I and the children whom the Lord has given me are signs and portents in Israel, etc."[4] So the meaning is this: "You and those who are standing next to you are men of good omen and sources of wonder to the world," that is, as Paul interprets it, "You are a spectacle to God, the world, and the angels" (cf. 1 Cor. 4:9). You see, Christians try and undertake absolutely impossible situations, matters

[4] Cf. *Luther's Works,* 16, p. 93.

which are foreign to every judgment of reason. All this is beyond human understanding, as I mentioned at the beginning of this chapter in sufficient detail about the victory over Satan, death, and the conscience.

Behold I will bring My Servant as He buds.[5] This correctly refers to Christ alone. Also, what we read as "as He rises" *(orientem)* we should read more accurately as "as He buds" *(germinantem),* just as grasses or fruits bud and sprout. So Christ is described in Is. 4:2: "In that day the Branch *(germen)* of the Lord shall be beautiful." We read in Jer. 23:5: "I will raise up for David a righteous Branch *(germen).*" In this text, too, I would prefer using the word "Branch," so that the passage would read "I shall bring forth My Servant as a Branch." He calls Christ a Branch, just as Isaiah calls Him a "Shoot" (Is. 11:1) and says that He sprouts forth like an outstanding and excellent young plant (Is. 53:2). With this expression Isaiah indicates that Christ's kingdom is always growing. You see, the Spirit and Christ's Word are always in a state of growing. They move forward constantly, and as a consequence they bear greater fruit. The world sets itself against it with might and main to cause this branch to wither and dry. It attacks the branch with death, disgrace, poverty, and every evil. God, however, always causes it to grow. He supplies it with enough moisture so that it still grows and flourishes even in the burning summer sun.

9. *For behold, upon the Stone which I have set.* He is also called a stone in Ps. 118:22: "The Stone which the builders rejected"; and in Is. 8:14: "a Stone of Offense and a Rock of Stumbling to both houses of Israel"; and again in Is. 28:16: "Behold, I am laying in Zion for a foundation . . . a Cornerstone, etc." Christ is called Stone because all of us who are Christians lean upon Him. He alone is our firm foundation on whom we can rely. Paul also interprets Christ this way (cf. 1 Cor. 3:11).

There are seven facets. This is what Isaiah says: "The Spirit of the Lord is upon Me because the Lord has anointed Me" (Is. 61:1). The seven facets, then, are the seven spirits or gifts of the Holy Spirit which Christ has distributed in the church. These gifts cause that Branch to blossom forth, even though the world, Satan, and all creatures always stand against it.

And behold, I will engrave its inscription. Exegetes upset them-

[5] Cf. p. 69, n. 7, below.

selves in different ways as they interpret this passage. One takes it to mean the development in the Virgin's womb; another, the bestowing of the various gifts of the Holy Spirit, even though the seven facets have already spoken of them. As for me, I think that we must interpret this inscription as Christ's sufferings, as if God were saying: "I shall carve My own inscription, that is, I shall finally chip Him away and get Him ready through suffering that He may be the Cornerstone on which the building is erected." For Christ has been carved and shaped by His suffering and resurrection. This is the way He first began His true kingdom.

And I will remove the guilt of this land. On the day of His suffering He bore all our sins, as Isaiah writes (cf. Is. 53:4): "He Himself carried our sins." You see, through and in the crucified Christ, God took away the sin of the whole world. In this way the prophet indicates that that true Priest finally will come to take away the sin of His people and to free them from their sins. This finally will be the true sacrifice, of which the priesthood of Joshua, the high priest of the Law, was incapable. He further declares that this will happen *in a single day.* With this one phrase he annuls the entire Old Testament, as if to say: "He will need one other day, and that alone will be enough. With this one day He will take away the sins of the whole world. With one sacrifice He will make all things perfect." Thus later there will be further need for no other day, no other priesthood, no other sacrifice. See Heb. 7.

10. *On that day everyone of you will invite his neighbor, etc.* This is a proverbial statement. He says, as it were: "Frequently you have been stuffed full of many promises about the great peace and complete security yet to come. This, however, is not yet fulfilled. It will be fulfilled at the time when He will come. His will be a kingdom of peace and security. This peace is the peace of consciences and of the abundance of every spiritual blessing." In this way He takes a common proverb and gives it spiritual force. No one should think that the promise offers bodily and external peace and security. After all, the Christian life is not a life of pleasure. It does not consist of good days. "All who desire to live a godly life in Christ Jesus will be persecuted" (2 Tim. 3:12). This is how they become "conformed to the image of the Son of God, etc." (cf. Rom. 8:29).

CHAPTER FOUR

In the preceding chapter we have seen the very great comfort with which the Lord through His prophet consoled the high priest. The priest was one of the two leaders of a people who had been brought back out of captivity and was rebuilding the temple and city. We have also seen how the prophet himself and on his own initiative has dealt with the allegory of his visions. The fact that the high priest Joshua, dressed in dirty mourning clothes, took off the dirty garb and put on clean decorated robes indicated that at some time a Priest would come to suffer and die to take away the sin of all men; that He would rise again to glorify us and to make us His co-heirs to all the blessings of His Father. This Priest was Christ Jesus, etc.

Now that the prophet has given that comfort to the first leader, he follows with this comfort for the other leader, Zerubbabel. I have mentioned earlier several times that it is a tremendous matter, completely incomprehensible to human reason, that the human heart can lay hold of divine favor, especially at a time when it is crushed by sin and aware of its adversaries, that is, that it does not doubt that it has a favoring and kindly God. In that way we, too, must be strengthened with such a rich Word, with many visions, and promises. In this chapter we see this very thing happening. The prophet is again stirred up to encourage and strengthen a leader at a time when the situation is so chaotic that we may clearly see that not everybody is so easily moved by the Spirit as certain men in our day boast, men who are filled and inflated with their own way of thinking. The Divine Majesty places a greater value on His Spirit than that one should hold it so cheap. Consequently, those wicked men are not to be trusted – men who with such pride and bombast vaunt their own spirit. But I have mentioned this several times earlier.

1. *And the angel came again.* Here again the prophet begins another discourse which he delivered at another time and on another day after he had finished the prior one.

Like a man that is wakened out of his sleep. The prophet does not refer merely to his own state of mind when he is awakened from sleep but to that of the ruler and of all the people. He is saying in effect: "You are lazy, sluggish idlers when you thus stop the work of the Lord as if you were sleeping and snoring." So this means: "I am wakened like a man who has been sleeping." In the person of the prophet, then, we must see a reflection of his entire people and how they had been affected.

2. *I see, and behold, a lampstand all of gold.* Moses in Ex. 25 also uses the same device when he describes the tabernacle. But the holy writers have argued in different ways about the lamp above the head of the lampstand. We answer briefly that the prophet meant that hollow, or the plates, of the lampstand where the lamp sits – *die Schalen,* in German. "Above the head" is a Hebraism for "atop," so that the meaning is "seven lamps on it."

3. *And there are two olive trees by it.* We translate badly when we put the olive trees "above" it,[1] because there immediately follows, "One on the right side of the lamp, and one on the left."

This second part does belong to the vision. But even now it all appears absurd to those who still do not understand the interpretation, which we shall shortly supply. Then they will see that it is all very sweet and pleasing.

Now we have frequent questions, both of the prophet for the angel and of the angel for the prophet. This occurs that we may see that the prophet has not just wasted words. On the contrary, we see that all things have to do with his straightening out that sleepy state of mind of the people. Thus while he has lingered with these questions, he has created more attentive listeners and has held their minds in suspense so that they carefully pay wide-mouthed attention to whatever it is the Lord intends with the vision.

6. *Not by might, nor by power, but by My Spirit.* This is the interpretation of the vision. It nevertheless does not seem to fit quite what the prophet saw. After all, what commonality or what harmony does the Spirit have with lights or lampstands? Yet actually it all fits together very harmoniously. The meaning, then, is as if he were saying: "Your mind, Zerubbabel, is still so busy with carnal ideas that you are almost asleep, so does it give you an undecided mind. On the one hand, you know that you must, according to the Lord's word, rebuild the temple. On the other hand, you fear the kings and peoples who

[1] The Vulgate text had *super* ("above"), for which Luther now quotes *iuxta* ("next to").

oppose you, and consequently you do not get to work. You do not see that you can be equal to the great might and power of your foes. The Lord says that there is no need for weapons, might, or power; that you require none of these; that you need only the light of the Spirit to receive some confidence of mind."

With these words he needles the ideas of Zerubbabel about the power, weapons, and might of his foes. He commands him to feel secure against all these. All that is necessary, he says, is faith so that he does not lose confidence in the Lord. Wherever this faith is present, the Lord without question promises that He will repel and crush all weapons, power, and might – however great these may be – even of all the world. Here, then, we have a rich text about the confidence of the heart that comes by faith. With that confidence, alert and righteous people are secure against every power of their temporal and spiritual foes. This parallels the external victory over the wicked, where every power and the victorious outcome also lie in resoluteness of mind. Consequently, whoever said, "Hearts are more powerful than hands, for hearts have all power," seems to have described this precisely. I have heard the same thing also from people who have at times fought on the battlefield. They maintain that they can guess and predict, on the basis of obvious signs and intelligent guessing before the battle begins, which side is going to lose. For they say that all the signs on the one side show destruction because everything is very confused, and even the horses with lowered heads have some ominous presentiment. On the other side, the one which is destined to be victorious, everything promises victory; the minds of all the soldiers are alert and the horses whinny eagerly. In short, there is nothing which does not promise an absolutely sure victory. Therefore only that courage conquers which the Lord gives those whom He wants as victors. We Germans, too, have a common saying which is very true: *Gott behüt mich vor einem, der mich meint,* etc.[2] Therefore, since this happens among the wicked, how much more do the righteous who are encouraged by faith and the Spirit overcome and conquer.

Next, everything which the prophet saw in his vision is made of gold. Nothing is of iron, which befits weapons, but all is of gold. You see, in warfare there is no use for gold, but gold indicates peace. Furthermore, the lamp is lighted, as if he were saying that there is

2 "May God protect me from him who has it in for me." A parallel use of the German verb *meinen* is found in Luther's couplet *Der alt böse Feind, mit Ernst er's jetzt meint.*

need for light and fire. For the Holy Spirit burns, that is, He kindles and illumines the heart that it may be secure, feel courageous, and fear nothing.

Therefore everything fits together beautifully in the vision. Those people who intend to interpret Moses have here an opportunity to reflect, from which they should learn that in the entire building and construction of the Mosaic tabernacle the Lord meant nothing else than what happens in the world through the ministry of the Word. The table signifies the Word of God. This the Psalm (23:5) reveals very clearly: "Thou preparest a table before me, etc." Also: "Let their own table . . . become a snare" (Ps. 69:22). You see, the Word is food. It feeds us to protect us against the north wind (according to the text of Moses, the table had been set up in that way in the tabernacle), that is, against the temptations of Satan. The lampstand indicates peace, because it is made of gold. Wherever the Word is preached, there nothing happens by force, armor, or warfare. Rather, people rest quietly and at peace. Therefore the lampstand is the ministry of the Word, which teaches and feeds the church. The altar of incense is true prayer, spoken in faith and in the Spirit. True prayer is something which only those can utter who have the Spirit of Christ. Others thus may speculate more widely about this matter, for it's a long, wide field. The lampstand, however, which the prophet saw in this vision was located between two olive trees. Those trees are Zerubbabel and the high priest Joshua. It is as if He were saying: "There is nothing for you to fear. The Holy Spirit is in your midst. He shines among you. So you need neither weapons nor power. You have Me, your kind and gracious God."

The various objects around the lampstand indicate the ministers of the Word. Equipped with various gifts of the Holy Spirit, they promote the ministry of the Word, for each minister does not have all those gifts. The apostle Paul goes into great detail about just this in 1 Cor. 12 and in Eph. 4. The lamp reservoirs are the prophets; the actual lamps are the preachers. These latter teach others what they have received from the prophets.[3] Again, not every minister has the gift to plumb all the depths of Scripture. Those whom the preachers teach are the various decorations on the lamps. Yet they, too, are all of gold, etc.

7. *What are you, O great mountain? Before Zerubbabel.* This,

[3] We have read *prophetis* for *propheticis.*

too, still refers to the vision. The teaching has been finished, that is, the vision has been explained. Now the Lord adds encouragement. The Lord turns from Zerubbabel and speaks to his enemies to comfort Zerubbabel. The Lord did the same thing earlier, in chapter 3:2, when by apostrophe He turned the conversation to Satan: "The Lord rebuke you, etc." Also, just as the earlier verses of this chapter address themselves very carefully to the thoughts of Zerubbabel, so this verse pertains especially to this point. The prophet imagines that Zerubbabel was thinking: "What will I – one lone man – be able to accomplish against mighty kings and savage enemies?" For Scripture calls princes and the nobility "mountains" and "hills." [4] He develops the idea that that great heap of enemies – the rulers of the Persians as well as very powerful peoples – is a lofty mountain. He directs Zerubbabel's attention to that host of enemies, to the might of their weapons, and to the power of their armies. Terrified by all these, Zerubbabel interrupted the work he had begun. Now the prophet calls him back to faith and to the Spirit. Then, he says, that mountain will easily be leveled, no matter how huge it may appear. Let me also tell you this. Other people divide this passage in different ways. I divide it simply and read it this way: "What are you, O great mountain? Before Zerubbabel you will sink into level ground." This is to be a rebuke for the enemy, the great mountain, as if he were saying: "May the Lord rebuke you, a great mountain standing in the way of the prince Zerubbabel, keeping him from continuing the work he had begun according to the will of God." *To level ground* [5] is elliptic speech, as if to say: "May the Lord reduce you to level ground to keep you from frustrating the prince further, to keep you from filling him with fear."

And he shall bring forward the top stone, that is, "Even against your will – in fact, after you have been reduced to level ground and your powers have been crushed – Zerubbabel 'will bring forward the top stone.' He will push forward and complete the work which he had started, since he had already laid the foundation under King Cyrus. He will completely finish the temple of the Lord and will hurry to erect it just as he laid the foundation."

And he will equate grace with its grace. This is a difficult passage. I cannot come to a definite decision about it, because there is not just one Hebraism in it. Holy writers have troubled themselves variously

[4] Cf. *Luther's Works,* 16, pp. 37, 115, 191, but also p. 139; 17, pp. 9, 75.

[5] The Vulgate text has only the adverbial phrase *in planum.*

in making many graces, but those are trifling attempts. I shall tell you what it seems to me to say. First, from the Hebrew I translate this way: "And with shouting or cheering, 'Grace! Grace for it!'" Thus the meaning is: "That great mountain which up to now has stood in the way of Zerubbabel will be reduced to level ground. Then Zerubbabel will bring forward the top stone and will raise up the temple he had already earlier begun, so that not just one man but all the people will shout and cheer (the repetition indicates this). Thus all will shout, 'Grace! grace!'" We have exactly the same meaning as in Haggai about the splendor of the new temple: "The latter splendor of this house shall be greater, etc." (Hag. 2:9). Furthermore, he has used repetition in the Hebrew fashion, as if to say that the nations from all parts of the earth will eagerly run together and offer their joyful cheering about the erection of the temple, even though it lies there now as an object of contempt. In Scripture the word "grace" signifies favor, as in Prov. 1:9 "That grace be added to your head," and elsewhere: "Grace is deceitful, and beauty is vain" (Prov. 31:30). Here it does not so much mean "favor" as that which is very proper and which causes one to be highly regarded. In substance, then, he is saying that "many additional decorations will still be added to this temple. There will be still more beautiful treasures added to it." For with uproar and shouting the people will vie to decorate this temple – which later did happen. So we must always take repetitions of this sort in a distributive sense. We see it this way in Ezekiel (14:4): "Man after man of the house of Israel," that is, "any man of the house of Israel"; and in Moses: "Staff upon staff, etc." [6]

9. *The hands of Zerubbabel have laid the foundation of this house.* He explains with clearer words what he seemed to have said more obscurely above about bringing forward the top stone, erecting the temple, and the great glory of the new temple, so that many nations will gather there eagerly and congratulate Zerubbabel. Paul says the same thing about Christians: that they should be pursuers of good works, or zealots; that is, that they should vie with one another in good works so that one is eager to outstrip another in good works (cf. Titus 2:14). The same sort of rivalry, he says, will occur among those who

[6] The expression *virgam et virgam* does not seem to occur in the Pentateuch. Perhaps Luther has in mind the directive for the Passover *tenentes baculos in manibus*, "with staffs in your hands" (Ex. 12:11). To emphasize its distributive meaning ("each with his own staff in hand"), Luther uses the Hebrew idiom of repetition.

are going to congratulate Zerubbabel on the building of the temple. Therefore the meaning of this passage is this: "The temple is going to be finished while Zerubbabel himself is still alive, even though the situation is so chaotic now that no hope seems less capable of fulfillment. But when the work will have been finished, you will know, finally, that the Lord of hosts has sent me to you and that I have prophesied these things at the Lord's command. Then for the first time the will of the Lord will become clear, however completely it is now being neglected because of the many things which keep you from listening to the Word and will of the Lord."

It is an absolutely wonderful thing and completely beyond human understanding to know for a fact that some work pleases God. Otherwise the temple was an unimportant matter. To the world, it appeared as something cheap and contemptible. The world was of the opinion that nothing pleased God less than some building of this sort. So, with all his power, Satan kept getting in the way so that they might not listen to the will of God and that the Lord's will might not be done, for Satan cannot but be opposed to those matters which relate to righteousness and the worship of God. So evil is that spirit, for he can bear anything at all rather than that which pertains to God. No doubt the foundations of many great buildings were constructed throughout the world at the time when the temple was built, but that evil spirit had nothing to say against all of them. He kept attacking only this one, because it belonged to God, because it aimed at the glory of God. This is the way the devil always works, for we know his thoughts. It makes him unhappy that man has this gift of sight. He does not only always set a trap for our soul but for our sanity as well. We have already seen a terrible enough example of this strategy in the case of the seditious and rioting peasants, among whom one can always see the wickedness and power of Satan, etc.[7] The will of God stands firm, however, and what the Lord wills is finally carried out, even though Satan and all the gates of hell resist it.

10. *For whoever has despised the insignificant days.* Again He takes away their timidity by carrying them away from their view of the situation or of the difficulty of finishing their task and by bringing them to His Word. As a result, they should place before their eyes not the

[7] Luther had issued his tract *Against the Robbing and Murdering Hordes of Peasants* (*Luther's Works*, 46, pp. 49—55) in the spring of 1525. The lectures on Zechariah were begun late in 1525 and carried over into 1526.

magnitude of the task, the imminent perils, the power of the neighboring nations, but the will of God. He says, as it were: "The mountain which stands in your way is a huge one. You are suffering severe attacks from all sides. All this spawns in your minds a realization of the difficulty you face and a certain lack of confidence. Everything appears hopeless. There can be no comparison between your powers and those of your foes. So the days appear insignificant, that is, in these days the people, their situation, and their works all appear to be insignificant when everything they do produces too little fruit. But why are you delaying your work? Why do you not believe Me when I speak? Why do you not keep your eyes focused on My Word rather than on your own timidity? I can moderate all great difficulties and turn them into very simple matters." So divine goodness has a way of making all things out of nothing, the greatest happiness out of a total despair over everything, glory out of disgrace, gold out of ashes – however impossible this may seem. In this way does He show His concern over their deepest emotions.

They will be gladdened and will see the plummet in the hand of Zerubbabel. Because the Hebrews lack impersonal verbs, they cannot conveniently express impersonal phrases. Christ, for instance, says in the Gospel (Luke 6:38): "They will put into your lap" instead of "it will be put"; also (John 15:6): "They will gather it and throw it" instead of "It will be gathered." Thus here we have "They will be gladdened, etc.," that is, "there will be rejoicing." Furthermore, this whole passage is ambiguous because of the two meanings it can have. The first of these is that the prophet is speaking about the Kingdom of Judah and says that it is going to rejoice over the erection of the temple. In this way the plummet becomes the temple – decorated, finished, and beautifully completed under the direction of Zerubbabel, etc. In my opinion, however, all of this seems to be something that should be applied to Christ, because of whom the temple was rebuilt and the people led back again from captivity. Because Christ had been promised to the Jews and was going to be born of their flesh, therefore the kingdom and priesthood had to be preserved. In short, that entire time following the Babylonian captivity was waiting for Christ. Everything was happening on His account. But one can see the marvelous plan of God Most High – how He works in His own way that He always calls into existence those things which do not exist as if they did exist (cf. Rom. 4:17) and brings down to Sheol before He leads to heaven, etc. (cf. 1 Sam. 2:6). As He is about to bring forth Christ the King, as He promised, He allows the Persians to come to power after the Jews have been carried off into a wretched captivity. Now nothing would appear less possible for a kingdom and priesthood which, along with all the people, had been carried away than that the people would be led back home, the temple rebuilt, the people restored to their original position of honor, and finally, that their kingdom would last forever, as had been promised. That is why the prophets always connect with that time the kingdom of Christ and the new glory which was to come through Christ the King. We have also seen above in chapter 3 how he treated the passage about the stone which was going to take away the sin of the world, etc. That we can understand in no other way except that he is speaking of Christ. Haggai, too, adds to his second chapter (vv. 9, 8): "And in this place I will give prosperity, says the Lord," and "the Desire of all nations shall come," as if to say: "As soon as the temple is finished, Christ will come and enter upon His throne." This is the first reason which prompts me to think that we must take this verse to mean Christ. Another reason is that He makes a clear distinction between stones. At first, he was speaking about the cornerstone of the new temple. He said that it was going to be brought forward not without great glory, applause, and congratulation of many people, as we have said. But here he names another stone and refers to that earlier discourse which he had with Joshua the high priest about the precious Stone. A third reason is that he repeats the seven eyes. We have already noted how he signifies the Holy Spirit and all the gifts of the Spirit with the number seven.

Accordingly, the summary of the meaning of the verse is as if he were saying: "The days appear insignificant to you, but you do not know what I am doing or what I am attempting. You see, I am going to do more wonderful and glorious things in these insignificant days than I have ever done before. I will raise up a joy. The joy is going to be great." The occasion for this joy will be

The plummet, or the leaden mass. He calls this leaden to distinguish it from the first Stone – the Cornerstone. Thus the meaning is: He will be made of lead – shining, polished, and smooth, like lead. This Stone is the resurrected Christ, placed in the foundation of the church through the preaching of the apostles. This preaching offered the occasion for great joy when it announced all joyful and blessed news – grace and eternal life. And this Stone, he says, will be seen

In the hand of Zerubbabel. This will happen, even though Zerubbabel will no longer be alive at the birth of Christ. But it is the way of the prophets to speak in this manner. For instance, it is said of Christ that He would sit on the throne of David (cf. Is. 9:7). Also, earlier, in chapter 3, the Lord says that He will bring forth that great Stone in the presence of Joshua the high priest. The meaning is this: That administration of Joshua the high priest now has been restored, and the people who are now under Joshua will see that Stone. This is the way we must also understand what he is saying here about Zerubbabel, that they are going to see a plummet in the hand of Zerubbabel,

Along with the seven eyes of the Lord, for so I read and construe, that is, "with the Holy Spirit." The Gospel brings both Christ and, at the same time, the gifts of the Holy Spirit, which traverse the whole world wherever the Gospel is preached. He calls the Holy Spirit an eye, because Christ's kingdom is the kingdom of faith. It is situated only in knowledge, as Isaiah says (cf. Is. 53:11): "By His knowledge shall My Servant make many righteous." That knowledge he calls an eye. In this way the prophet himself wanted to relate his allegory to a vision of physical things. That is the way he interprets the genuine temple and the real lampstand. This is the custom of the prophets.

11. *What are these two olive trees?* Although he now understands the lampstand, it still bothers him that in the tabernacle of Moses he had not seen the lampstand between two olive trees. This then produces his question.

People have troubled themselves in various ways as they interpret this passage. One takes it to mean grace, another something else. I merely follow my meaning which I mentioned earlier. The two olives are that twofold administration: of the Mosaic law by Joshua, and of the external polity by Zerubbabel. Therefore I simply take these two olive branches to mean the single Judaic people who had that double administration. Thus the meaning is: Those people are in divine favor. In their midst they have the lampstand; that is, the Holy Spirit is prepared to advance both of those administrations until Christ comes. In the meantime nothing will be fruitless while the olive branches are there, that is, everything in this kingdom will flourish peacefully, so that the kingdom will bear fruit for God and His Word.

12. *Which are beside the two golden spouts.* "Spouts" *(rostra)* he calls the little holes of the lamps, *die Schneuzen.*[8] Moses, too, wanted the spouts of the lamps to be exactly opposite each other.[9] Thus here also the prophet saw the spouts arranged in a straight line, and the one olive set up on the right, with the other on the left.

14. *These are the two sons of the oil,* of splendor.[10] This is the second part of the vision explained, that is, Joshua with his spiritual administration and Zerubbabel with his political administration. They are the "sons of olives," that is, the sons of good fortune and prosperity. You see, this is the way the Hebrew language generally speaks, as, for instance, in the psalm: "Upon the son [11] of your right hand" (Ps. 80:17). The Latin [12] renders this absurdly, but it is the same thing [13] as we mean when we say in Latin: "This is a matter of your right hand." After all, what would sound less proper to Latin ears than for a vineyard to be called a "son of the right hand"? So we also read in Is. 5:1: "On a fruitful hill." [14] Many psalms are filled with Hebraisms of this sort. So the prophet again has exhorted and encouraged the prince with many words to go on cheerfully and quickly with the completion of the temple he had begun according to the will of God and to fear nothing, regardless of how difficult a matter this undertaking may appear to be. You see, this is how all the works of God appear. They militate against every judgment and idea of human reason. They appear absolutely impossible. That is why the righteous do not immediately rush headlong to complete such works. Instead, fearful and weak-hearted, they can scarcely be attracted and stirred by many generous words of comfort to undertake their duty to do what the Lord has commanded. This I have spoken of earlier in great detail. Hence it becomes clear how we must place no confidence in those inflexible braggarts who say they understand nothing but the Spirit but who attempt everything very easily.

8 Luther uses *Schneuzen* ("snuffers") in his German Bible both here and in Ex. 25:38 and 37:23. In Is. 6:6 he translates the Hebrew word with *Zange* ("tongs").

9 Cf. Ex. 25:37.

10 The Weimar text prints *splendoris* as if it were a part of the Biblical quotation, but it is explanatory to *olei.*

11 The Vulgate has *virum,* but Luther quotes *filium.*

12 The Vulgate.

13 For *item* we have read *idem.*

14 Cf. *Luther's Works,* 16, p. 58.

CHAPTER FIVE

Saintly writers have treated this chapter in various ways. Let us, however, omit nonsense of this sort and the ideas of men, and let us rather pursue the real message as best we can.

In the earlier chapters the prophet has encouraged and strengthened the prince, the high priest, and the people. This we have explained already in sufficient detail. Then he applied everything to the coming and present kingdom of Christ which, as he had described, would be a kingdom of joy and great calm. Now in this chapter he will speak in the manner of all the prophets. They all have the custom that they not only describe in fullest and sweetest detail the kingdom of Christ but also add the horrible treachery and ruin of Israel, which refused to receive and recognize this King and Savior. So it is with visions, lamentations, and a multitude of prophecies that the prophets declare the eternal fall of that wretched people.

The apostles, too, followed this pattern. Paul and Peter very clearly declare that after the preaching of the Gospel false teachers will come like wolves who will go about at will against the flock of the Lord and will tread underfoot whatever they wish. So also the prophet Daniel says (Dan. 12:10): "All the wicked shall do wickedly." As I have said, Zechariah does exactly the same thing here. When he has made his prophecy about that plummet, he at the same time immediately adds what must happen to these people who are not going to receive this kingdom of Christ. This is the summary of this chapter. It deals directly with Pharisees, Sadducees, and other scribes whom Christ found among His people when He declared that He was King and Savior but whom He also left behind.

1. *And I turned and lifted up my eyes.* Before his eyes he had the Spirit, who was consoling Prince Zerubbabel and the people in turn as we have seen. He saw that after the kingdom and the priesthood had been restored the temple was going to be rebuilt. But now he looks behind the scenes at the terrible and tragic things which are going to happen as soon as those very blessed things have come to pass. This is the prophet's purpose when he says that he turned and

saw a flying scroll. This reminds us of Abraham turning around as he was about to sacrifice Isaac and seeing a ram caught in the briars by its horns (Gen. 22:13).

2. *A flying scroll.* The imagery is appropriate and elegant. The scroll can mean nothing other than teaching or law, because there is nothing here of the apparatus of war – no swords, no horses, no weapons. So the prophet sees that after him another kind of wicked teaching is going to come, for the sects have been developing – the Sadducees, Pharisees, and Essenes.

Its length is twenty cubits. Here some people bring up the question of numbers. I simply think that if there is any hidden meaning in the numbers, these merely refer by number to the length and width of Solomon's portico and allude to that [1] structure, as if he were indicating with that scroll that what is being taught is not true things but only externals, as the portico was outside the temple. Otherwise I would simply want to relate the number to the account of the vision, namely, that heresies and wicked teachings are creeping about and spreading widely. As Peter says, "They have more imitators of their own destruction" (cf. 2 Peter 2:2). Thus the dimensions of the scroll indicate the power and efficacy of the wicked teaching. The prophet himself interprets the scroll.

3. *He said: This is the curse that goes out over the face of the whole land.* The scroll is an excellent herald calling attention to wicked doctrine, because it calls such teaching a curse. You see, it takes away the benediction and grace which the Gospel shows to all men. Because the Gospel is the Word of salvation, it is called the Word of benediction, as: "By your descendants shall all the nations of the earth be blessed" (Gen. 22:18). That is, through the Gospel a benediction will be made known to them, for the Gospel takes away wrath and vengeance and confers the benediction and favor of God.

The land, that is, that of the Jews.

Also the apostle seems to have looked back into this section not just once. He frequently uses such vehement verbal attacks against impure doctrine as, for instance, in his Epistle to the Galatians (3:10): "All who rely on works of the Law are under a curse."

Every thief, just as it is written there, will be judged. The Hebrew text seems to suggest an entirely different meaning, for the Hebrew

[1] We have read *hanc* for *hunc.*

translates this way: "For from it every thief will in such wise be judged innocent." This is the proper sense of the Hebrew word. I do not recall ever reading otherwise in Scripture, for there is exactly the same word in Ps. 18:23: "Then I will be guiltless and absolved (or innocent) of a very great sin." Therefore also what follows must be rendered: "From it everyone who swears falsely will similarly be judged innocent." It is as if he were saying: "This is the sort of book which gives freedom from sinning and promises the hope of safety from punishment. It sets rascals free to do arbitrarily whatever they wish. So the papist laws have allowed usuries for the priests and for the entire so-called clergy so that they might enrich themselves. Why, the pope even allows robbery and theft, provided that a certain fraction of the gain comes to him, so that in this way he may, under the guise of religion, turn a profit, legally or illegally. So also those who swear falsely are absolved. This properly pertains to doctrine, because every doctrine comes under the name of the Lord. The heralds also confirm their doctrine in the name of the Lord when they say that they come in the name of the Lord. This is evident from all the prophets. So, too, Christ confirmed His discourses with an oath. Therefore, in sum, this passage means: The doctrine which is going to come is the sort which will teach unrighteousness. Thus the thievery signifies all the corrupt laws that encourage robbery and usury. The false swearing signifies all the wicked laws that encourage impiety. These things become very clear once we have placed the papacy before our gaze. One part of the papacy is that it teaches confidence in works as opposed to Christ and the grace shown the world in Christ. The other part is that the decrees of the pope, as I have said, smell of nothing but greed – which the teachers of the decrees themselves admit. So they first rob the souls with their wicked doctrine; then they rob the bodies, too, when they suck people dry of their goods and skills with their trickery and deceit. This is the way we can understand this section. You see, the Pharisees, too, did exactly the same thing. The Gospel account reveals how they served their belly and their greed. Christ also rebuked them with very bitter reproaches in Matt. 23: "You devour widows' houses," and the part about swearing by the gold which is in the temple. Christ also rebuked their false doctrine, when they taught confidence in works. All the Gospel writers tell us this in detail – how the Pharisees always resisted Christ when He taught. For it cannot be otherwise when we have lost Christ and His pure doctrine but that we become blind, serve our lusts, and consider our belly our god, as the apostle says (cf. Phil. 3:19). This, you see, is the way all the wicked ideas of the monks and their sacrifices developed.

4. *I will send it forth, says the Lord of hosts.* He is saying, "I shall bring forth this scroll," that is, "when they will have sinned enough with that wicked doctrine of theirs, when they have reached the highest point, then I shall declare how all their teachings are wicked thefts and perjuries; I shall declare the wickedness of their doctrine – that, under the pretext of My holy name, they have only destroyed souls by taking My name in vain"; just as He here says that it shall come "into the house of him who swears falsely by My name." The Gospel has accomplished that revelation of wrong, because it came to the house of thieves and of those who swear falsely. That is, it takes revenge on them because of the wrong they have done openly; and just as they have devoured both souls and bodies, so also are they and all theirs going to be devoured. Therefore He says: "I shall not permit it to go unavenged." That this is clearer than the light of noon no one can deny. So wretchedly have the Jews been scattered throughout the world that they do not even have one tiny place where they can live in safety. Blinded by God, they live everywhere as miserable, abject exiles. This is the first vision. The second follows.

5. *Lift up your eyes and see.* This imagery, too, pertains to the same point, for this prophet has the practice of almost always using two visions for the same purpose. We have seen this in his earlier chapters. So he saw an ephah going out. (The ephah is a common measure among the Jews, just as a peck is among us. A gomer was a tenth of an ephah. We could translate ephah as a cask.) Second, he saw [2] a weight of lead and a woman sitting within the cask, but in such a way that she sticks out above the cask on an elevated chair. But he saw the weight of lead fly up. It was so large that it completely filled the mouth of the cask from above. Then he immediately adds that the weight of lead was thrown back over its mouth, namely the cask's, while the woman was terribly frightened. The prophet himself interprets the woman but not the weight of lead. He has very neatly described the wicked life; so we must seek out the reason or cause why he has used such imagery.

6. *This is the eye of those in all the land.* "Eye" here means the appearance and form of the things which are on earth. This is the

[2] We have read *vidit* for *videt.*

way Hebrew generally uses the word "eye." We read, for instance, in Ps. 6:7: "My eye wastes away because of grief." Also in Ex. 10:15: "Locusts covered the eye of the earth," that is, the face or surface[3] of the earth. The meaning, then, is what Paul says (2 Tim. 3:5): "holding the form of religion but denying the power of it." Thus the prophet indicates that the cask is the very shape or form which follows that doctrine of theirs. Thus the shapes of papal decretals are their caps, tonsures, the cinctures with which they are girded, ceremonies, stated days, definite forms for prayers, etc. All of these are very carefully measured as if with a cask. They are all reduced into definite forms limited by certain places, times, and persons. The form of the cask, then, refers to wickedness. The function of the cask is related to greed, because the papists were born only to consume the fruits of the earth. Gluttons they are, creatures of the belly, since their belly is their god. In that cask sits a woman, not a man. She is human reason, the wicked heart, and its impure ideas. All these are not controlled by the Holy Spirit so long as they believe they are pleasing God. Furthermore, she is seated, that is, she presides, rules, teaches, just as Christ says about the Pharisees who "sit on Moses' seat" (Matt. 23:2). The fact that he also says *in all the land* shows that that wicked doctrine spreads widely "like gangrene," as Paul says (2 Tim. 2:17).

Furthermore, the weight of lead[4] is carried up into the air, that is, their hypocrisy is not yet suppressed. The woman still sits secure, but she sees that a blocking up of wickedness is going to come, as he now adds.

8. *And he thrust her back,* that is, he took away her seat. Thrusting her down from her lofty seat into the cask, he threw her into confusion. Earlier that seat was carrying her above the cask, but now the weight of lead is sent back down onto the mouth of the cask, and she is closed up inside. This means that wickedness indeed is embarrassed by the Gospel and is put to shame. However, the Gospel does not correct it. The hypocrisy always remains and cannot be corrected. In fact, those who have thus given themselves over to hypocrisy become more and more hardened and sink more deeply into their wickedness, even though the Gospel overcomes and confounds them. We see the same thing happening in our time as happened with the Jews. Christ has

[3] This translates *superficiem,* the Latin word used in the Vulgate in the passage quoted.

[4] The Weimar text has *auri* ("of gold") instead of *plumbi* ("of lead").

rebuked them, but they still lie immersed, as it were, in their wrong. They have no hope of coming to the surface. In fact, day by day they are still guilty of further blasphemy. Therefore they become more blinded, because God has cast them down into a very wretched situation. They have no temple, no kingdom, no priesthood, no public schools. If they teach anything, they teach their own topics. If they teach anyone, they teach their own children. This teaching they do in private whispers and in nooks and crannies as they have been pushed down into that cask and closed up therein so that they cannot come forth. The same thing will happen to us who hold the Gospel in contempt. The Gospel will again be taken away, even if human affairs are going to continue to exist still longer.

The leaden weight certainly is what the prophets call "the burden," as when they say, "The burden of the Word of the Lord." Briefly, it is the weight of the judgment of the Lord, which presses down the heart and conscience of those who are so immersed in hypocrisy that they cannot come out of it. As I have said, the Jews have been crushed by the Gospel and have been cut off completely from faith. Still, they persist in their works; they protect them tooth and nail. Yet their consciences are so confused and terrified that, although they wear themselves out because of their many works, they never dare to lift their heads in freedom. Their hearts are that burdened, their minds that downcast. Not even once do they glory and rejoice in God. They never reach the point of tasting divine goodness and mercy. That lead is a terrible weight pressing them down. This must happen in the case of every hypocrisy, which at first puts up a pretty front but, as I said before, it comes to this end, etc. This is what the psalm says in this vein: "The wicked [5] . . . came trembling out of their fastnesses." It is the nature of hypocrisy to bind, close up, and press down the conscience. On the other hand, the Holy Spirit draws the conscience out into a broad place, that is, into freedom. It lifts up the heart. It makes the conscience rejoice and be at peace. Scripture uses the same expression in Ps. 18:19: "And He brought me forth into a broad place"; also: "Thou enlargest my understanding" (Ps. 119:32); and: "There is no peace for the wicked" (Is. 57:21).

[5] In his "Song of Deliverance" (2 Sam. 22; Ps. 18) David used the Hebrew phrase בְּנֵי נֵכָר ("foreigners") in the verse here quoted (46). Luther changed the Vulgate's literal translation *filii alieni* to *impii* ("wicked," "godless"), which indicates what "foreigners" really meant — "alienated from the commonwealth of Israel and strangers to the covenants of promise, having no hope and without God in the world" (Eph. 2:12).

9. *Behold, two women coming forward,* that is, two women were being brought or led forward, or they were coming forward.

The wind was in their wings, that is, the wind was moving their wings. They had movable wings, as Isaiah saw the Seraphim also flying with two wings (cf. Is. 6).

Like the wings of a stork. I have mentioned several times already that the linguists of the Hebrews differ much in their choice of words for different objects. Here there is doubt about the word which our translator [6] renders *milvus.*[7] I translated it "stork," following the verse from the psalm: "The stork has her home in the fir trees" (Ps. 104:17).

And they lifted up the ephah, that is, as they flew, they were lifting up that ephah which the weight of lead had closed, and they were holding it up between heaven and earth.

11. *In the land of Shinar.* Where the location of Shinar is is revealed in Gen. 11. There the sons of Noah are said to have set out to the east, where they found the plain of Shinar. Later the tower of Babel was built there. The plain there is said to have been very broad and pleasant. Then, what we read as *when this is prepared* is more correctly read "when this is let down." Now we shall treat the meaning of this suggested translation of mine. After the ephah was closed up by the lead, the prophet saw it being carried away from his sight upward into the sky. This means that wickedness is not going to remain among this people. Rather, those two flying women will carry it away to a different place. The carrying away is a complete inversion: the Jews were carried away from Babylon to Jerusalem, but the ephah is being transferred from Jerusalem to Babylon. In sum, this means that those whose place the Lord has given to us will be completely uprooted and thrown out of the church – as Paul argues in detail in Romans (Rom. 11). Furthermore, women are carrying it. This signifies the office of teaching. You see, there is no doubt that the two cherubim before Moses [8] and Isaiah [9] indicate the ministry of the

[6] The Vulgate.

[7] *Milvus* is used in the Vulgate to translate the Hebrew words for "falcon" (Lev. 11:14; Deut. 14:13), "kite" (Is. 34:15), and "stork" (Jer. 8:17). Luther's choice of "stork," as supported by his reference to Ps. 104:17, embarrasses him at least to the extent that he admits, according to the Zwickau manuscript of this passage, "Some say 'stork,' but the stork nests on top of houses. Let's make it: 'like the wings of the heron.'" Cf. W, XIII, 600, n. 7.

[8] Cf. Num. 7:89.

[9] Cf. Is. 6:2. This passage does not specify *two* seraphim, but compare in Luther's *Jesaia, dem Propheten* the line *Es stunden zween Seraph bei ihm daran.*

Word. At the same time, there is in the middle of them the means of propitiation, that is, Christ, to whom all Scriptures look and whom alone the ministry of the Word treats. The seraphim are winged because the Word flies; it runs swiftly. This is what the poets, too, wanted to picture with their Mercury, the winged messenger of the gods, and that is how his name was chosen, why he should be called "Hermes." So also Vergil described rumor as winged, because there is no other evil which spreads with greater speed.[10] So, just as the righteous ministry of the pure Word, "with wings" means this, so also here in unrighteousness, a wicked ministry of a wicked word is meant. Hence these two winged women signify everything which the Jews or their wicked word teach. These are women who are flying, not married men. That is, all their teaching, all their preaching, all their words, are carnal. There are two women, just as there were two cherubim, because the Word is between speaker and hearer. Similarly Christ also sent out men two by two to preach. The summary, then, of all this is that the suffering and disaster of the Jews is so great that not only are they being held closed up in the ephah so that they are unable to escape but also they are never going to hear the pure Word, that wicked teachers have to be brought together to keep the people from ever hearing the pure Word, locked up as they are in the worst wickedness. So the Lord also threatens in Isaiah (Is. 5:6): "I will also command My clouds that they rain no rain upon it." In such grim terms he describes the hopeless destruction of that people – so hopeless that not even a small remnant of them remains to be restored. They are going to be rejected forever. They will not be converted lest they be saved. Then we must also remember that the flying women are carrying the ephah on high between heaven and earth. This means that their doctrine touches neither heaven nor earth, that is, they do not teach the kingdom of God nor do they compass the kingdom of this world. They no longer have either a spiritual or a physical kingdom. Both administrations have perished – that spiritual one of Joshua the high priest as well as the physical, or political, one of Zerubbabel the prince. In sum, they have lost both their kingdom and their priesthood. Even if the Jews see and know this, they are still so wretched and blind that they cannot recognize their error. So they allow themselves to be carried on high – between heaven and earth. Their stubbornness makes them irreconcilable.

[10] Cf. Vergil, *Aeneid,* V, 174—177.

To build a house for it in Shinar. He does not deign to give it its recent name but its original one. He does not say "in Babylon" but "in Shinar." There, he says, a house will be built and prepared for it. There is a question about the place, for it is a matter of comparing the two places, so that there is no need to imagine some definite physical location. Briefly the meaning is this: The people who are now in a double administration, spiritual and political, have been called back from Babylon. They will also be transferred finally into the true Jerusalem. Moreover, the remnant who are destroyed will not remain in Jerusalem but will even be transferred to Babylon, and to a mystical Babylon; that is, to a confused place, to total blindness, to a place where the wrath, judgment, and vengeance of God are present. There there is no peace, no grace, no mercy, no Jerusalem. All this pursues them wherever they may be.

And they will set it down there. The most wretched and terrible thing of all is that this is an irrevocable error; that that rejection lasts forever. And so do the warnings of the Lord everywhere in Scripture sound frightful indeed: "I shall have no more mercy on them" (Hos. 1:6); also: "I shall forget with an eternal forgetfulness" (Hos. 1:6); as one can see everywhere in the prophets. So then, when they have been set down "on their base," that is, on their hardness, obstinacy, and wicked stubbornness so that there is no hope of being called back, they have been broken and cut off from the tree, as the apostle says in Rom. 11:22-24, etc.

CHAPTER SIX

THIS chapter is quite obscure by itself, and a variety of interpretations makes it even more obscure. So it happens that I, too, have in one way or another some doubt about its real meaning. Yet I think that I am not going to interpret it badly. It would be too long to list and refute each opinion of every interpreter. However, there is the general consensus that they want the four chariots to stand for the four empires — the Babylonian, the Persian, the Greek, and the Roman — about which Daniel gives much detail; however, this single refutation of mine will point out how these do not fit: The prophet has only this practice here: in all his visions he discusses events which are still to come — not events which have happened, or past history. This we see from all his earlier visions and from those which follow. This, of course, will not fit the interpretation of those who use the four-empire explanation. For with the first chariot they must go back to the Babylonian empire, and this does not fit the prophet's practice. I do not approve of their allegory for another reason. They are being absolutely ridiculous and nonsensical when they interpret the four red horses of the first chariot as martyrs, the white horses as virgins, the black horses as confessors, and the spotted horses to represent the diversity of all the saints — and all sorts of other, more ridiculous things. After all, in every allegory one must show that it conforms to faith; that is, that it is related to faith or to the ministry of the Word. Those allegories which are related to works are worth nothing at all, since there is no consideration for works; all of them are external things: virginity, hand, and foot. This is worth noting, lest we be misled by the example of those who, because of their delight with works, become very trifling and imagine all sorts of improper and absurd interpretations.

In this chapter we shall present what the Lord has given. You be the judge. If there is anyone whom we do not satisfy and who has a better interpretation, he should communicate with us. Yet I believe that I am going to hit the mark.

In sum, the prophet discusses in this chapter the same thing as he has in all the previous chapters. He comforts and encourages his people, who have been terrified and dejected because of their fear of the nations of the north. You see, I have mentioned several times earlier how the neighboring peoples had kept the Jews from going on with the temple which they had begun and which they had been ordered by divine command to erect. The Jews did fear the might and armies of the nations of the north. Earlier those nations had taken them captive and had treated them wretchedly. The Jews still remembered this calamity and were always afraid because they knew what they had suffered before. So that recollection of a bygone disaster always terrified them with the fear that something similar – or even worse – might happen. Therefore they always continued to hold the north in suspicion, because it was from that direction that Jeremiah had prophesied every evil would come. Against that fear or terror of the north the prophet here comforts his people that they pull themselves together and remember the words of the Lord, who said that everything would be safe, and that the north – the area to be feared – not only would not oppose them but would even be in harmony with them, be faithful, and believe the Word. Consequently, it is the prophet's intent to remove every cause of their fear. This is my feeling about and my review of this chapter. You see, everything in it will refer to the idea that it be related to the ministry of the Word. In this way this chapter will also be very closely connected with the previous chapter. In that chapter we saw the vision about the flying scroll, the cask, the leaden cover, the flying women, etc. That vision exposed the wicked Pharisaical doctrine which was going to be in control at the time when Christ's coming would be near. In this chapter he reveals what is going to happen when Christ has already come and rules; that a new light – the teaching of the Gospel – will be kindled. That light not only will drive out wicked doctrine; it will also be spread throughout the world and will bear fruit among all nations. So, as I have said, this chapter closely follows in direct order that preceding one which we have just completed. We shall now get at the text.

1. *And I turned and lifted up my eyes and saw.* When he says that he turned, he reveals that the matter is going to be after his time and that it has not yet happened. So he also says in the previous chapter that he turned when he saw the flying scroll. This is what I mentioned in my introduction, that what they interpret about the

four empires does not fit, since the prophet indicates that he is speaking about a future matter which has not yet occurred.

And the mountains were mountains of bronze. This is a Hebraism which the Latin merely renders: "Between two mountains of bronze."

Four chariots. The vision of a previous chapter, chapter 1, also had horses; but here not only horses but also chariots are presented, to indicate that this is a completely different vision from that earlier one, where the horses are scattered into the four corners of the world and cause the Spirit of the Lord to rest throughout the world. Thus we can understand that vision in no other way than that it refers to the ministry of the Word.

2. *Red horses.* These are sorrels. The spotted ones are dappled, speckled, pied. They are horses of the sort we call *die grauen Schimmel,* which have many spots. We have the same word [1] in Genesis too. Jacob placed twigs with their bark removed at the place where the sheep would drink. There the sheep bred and conceived spotted sheep.

5. *These are the four winds of heaven.* This is the interpretation of the vision, but it is quite obscure. We must depend on our interpretation which we set forth earlier, that everything may be harmonious. The chariots are called רוּחוֹת, that is, spirits. You see, in this place we don't want that to be translated with the word "wind," even though the Hebrew word signifies both wind and spirit.

Who are going out to stand before, etc. In the earlier vision, the riders were returning with the horses. Here they are not returning. Instead, they are being sent out away from standing in the presence of the ruler of the land (that is how it reads in the Hebrew). For the Word of God always runs; it is never at rest. You see, Scripture makes the angels the ministers of God who assist God, as we read, for instance, in Daniel (Dan. 7:10): "A thousand thousands served Him," that is, were assisting Him. There the prophet speaks about the ministry and assistance of the angels. The sophists go through bitter torture to explain this vision, and especially Dionysius has developed some quite laughable theories about the heavenly hierarchy.[2] But when Zechariah here speaks of a ruler of the earth, he has in mind Christ, who is properly called "Ruler of the earth" in the Psalms, as for instance, in Ps. 8:1: "O Lord, our Lord, etc." And earlier we saw

1 The word is probably *maculosus* ("spotted"). Cf. Gen. 30:39.

2 Cf. *Luther's Works,* 36, p. 109.

the same thing in this prophet. We must carefully observe everything in this vision. The red horses which draw the first chariot are passed over in complete silence. The black horses and the white ones on the second and third chariots are sent to the north. Consequently what I have mentioned earlier is now clear: we cannot take these chariots to refer to four empires. After all, they do not come from the north but from Jerusalem. They move from the sight of the prophet to the north. The fourth chariot with the spotted horses goes off to the south. In Hebrew the words are joined together thus: "the spotted and the strong horses." [3] These are the same horses, and yet he speaks as if he were speaking about different ones.

8. *And he cried to me and said.* In Hebrew this is an expression of great emphasis: "He shouted to me." Here is the sum and substance of the entire chapter. This is as far as the first part of this chapter goes – a part which we shall clarify to the best of our ability.

Earlier I have several times mentioned that the number four signifies the four quadrants of a circle, that is, the earth. Therefore he means the sending of the horses with the chariots into the four quadrants of the world. He says nothing about the red horses of the first chariot. We, too, shall say nothing about them. The horses of the second chariot are sent to the north, as are also those of the third. This relates to the comforting of the people. It is as if he were saying: "You fear the northern quadrant, but be confident. Summon back your courage and dismiss sadness and fear. The Lord is going to stir up a war against that quadrant. He will fight for you against the north, now that He has sent the two chariots." When the prophet spoke this, the Jews probably did not understand to what it applied. Yet he is offering comfort that they may be lifted up and encouraged to quit their fear and terror; to consider a Lord who has every concern for them, so that those whom they fear so much are being restrained by two chariots sent against them. So we see that what I said really proves to be true, that his point in this chapter is that his people may be encouraged and strengthened against their fear of the enemies to the north.

Allegory: if we accept the color of the horses as allegorical, then everything will square with the ministry of the Gospel, to which we must relate all things, and not to the foolish ideas and ridiculous fictions of good works.

[3] In v. 3 above. The Vulgate renders this with *varii et fortes.*

First, there are *two mountains.* They signify the twofold church – of the Jews and of the Gentiles – which He has made one, as Paul says (Eph. 2:14): "Who has made us both one." They are called mountains, for everywhere in Scripture a mountain signifies a multitude or gathering of peoples and the power of their kingdoms. This he mentioned earlier when he said (Zech. 4:7): "What are you, O great mountain, before Zerubbabel?" Isaiah also calls the church a mountain in Is. 2:2: "And it shall come to pass in the latter days that the mountain of the house of the Lord shall be established, etc.," that is, "the power of the Word will exalt and glorify Christ's church." He is, of course, speaking of spiritual exaltation and glorification. Furthermore, the mountains are *of bronze* because the church is invincible against every violent attack of Satan and of the gates of hell and the world. The church is not a bloodthirsty warrior. No one should think that bronze relates to that here. Rather, the bronze signifies the unconquerable resolution and perseverance of the church, as it is written in Micah (4:13): "I will make your hoofs of bronze." We must still interpret the colors of the horses. The red horses of the first chariot he passes over in silence. Briefly, we shall take the colors of the horses for the effect which they caused among those people to whom they were sent. Here then, the color red signifies the effect of the Gospel among the unbelieving, carnal Jews. That is, the Gospel brought about only carnal wickedness in them, it stirred up in them only bitter jealousy against the Gospel of Christ and its heralds, while only few – barely a remnant – were saved. So then, the ministry of the Gospel accomplished nothing in Jewry at first. It only made the Jews more carnal, so that they became more bloodthirsty and savage against the saints. The black and the white horses are those of the second and third chariots. The philosophers say that black and white are the extreme colors. Red is halfway between them, for it is made naturally from black and white if you mix the two.[4] We see this in coal, glass,[5] and the like if we put them in a fire. Briefly, black is the color of darkness and death; white is the color of light and life. These two colors signify the Word. First, it declares people guilty; it condemns and de-

[4] The basic theory here referred to is one of the theories advanced by Aristotle in *On Sense and the Sensible,* 3, 439b and 4, 442a, to explain the sensation of color.

[5] For *vitro* ("glass") we might read *nitro* ("native soda," or "saltpeter"). Then coal would be the black substance, saltpeter the white substance, and fire the resultant red. This is suggested in *Dr. Martin Luthers Sämmtliche Schriften,* XIV (St. Louis, 1898), 2053, n. 1.

stroys them. Then it justifies and saves those whom it has destroyed. The spotted horses are the apostle Paul and other ministers who have preached the Gospel among the different and remote nations. These are the bravest, too, for the apostle Paul labored more than all the other apostles in his ministry of the Word. He himself testifies about himself in this respect (1 Cor. 15:10). He put on many colors as he adjusted himself to various peoples. These horses are ready to run in any direction; that is, Paul with his men came into the midst of fierce and strong nations – even to the Romans. Therefore very powerful heralds had to be sent there to teach the Word of the Gospel with great confidence of mind and with great energy.

Behold, those who go to the north country. He applies the vision in proportion to what they understood and how they had been affected at that time. If indeed they could not then understand that obscureness, which we have now explained, then the prophet is doing this merely to strengthen their trembling hearts, lest they still be concerned about the north.

My Spirit. This is obviously the Holy Spirit, not "wrath," or "vengeance," as others interpret it. The same wording occurs in Is. 11:2: "And the Spirit of the Lord shall rest upon Him." So here we have: "They have set My Spirit at rest in the north country," that is, "He will reign there through the Word and the Holy Spirit." Furthermore, he applies the vision only to the north, as I have said, because the prophet is accommodating himself to the comprehension of his hearers, for at that time they did not fear all the other nations of the earth as much as they feared the people of the north. So he speaks about the north alone, even though the same thing is true for the whole world, but it is necessary to apply it there because of the fear in his people's consciences. Heralds of the Word must thus assume the responsibility of directing the Word to that place where they see consciences suffering the most, where they seem the most frightened.

10. *Take from the exiles, from Heldai, etc.* We have now finished the visions of this prophet in which there has been great difficulty and on account of which the prophet has been considered most obscure. Here at the end he adds a sign as a confirmation of all his earlier visions and discourses up to this point. This, you see, is a custom of all the prophets and everywhere in Scripture – to add some sign which confirms the Word. For instance, Isaiah, in chapter 20, is commanded to loose the sackcloth from his loins, take the sandals off his feet, and

go about naked and barefoot. With this sign he was confirming his preaching of the devastation and stripping of Egypt (which he had prophesied) by the king of the Assyrians. There are many signs of this type in Jeremiah as well – in chapter 13, for instance, where he speaks about the loincloth that rotted when Jeremiah had hidden it. With this sign the Lord wanted to confirm His humbling of the Jews, who had gone away from true worship and the correct Word in their wickedness. Jeremiah also has this kind of sign when the cup of the Lord's fury is given to him so that he may give to the heathen to drink (Jer. 25:15); and again, when he wore a wooden yoke about his neck to signify thereby that all nations were going to be subject to the power of the king of the Chaldeans, that they all would come under the power of that king (Jer. 27:2). Thus through all time signs are added to the Word. Noah had the rainbow,[6] and we have Baptism and the Eucharist. The same thing occurs also in this prophet.

"Take from the exiles," that is, from those captives who have returned from the Babylonian captivity. Here he names Heldai, Tobijah, and Jedaiah. With these men he is ordered to enter the house of Josiah, who will be their fourth companion. All four of those, you see, had been prisoners in Babylon and had been led back. We must not argue about the persons. Two are named in Ezra, and there is no doubt that Jedaiah was of the household of Joshua and Tobijah of the tribe of Zerubbabel. Ezra does not call the other two by the names you have here, but this is not unusual. After all, many of those people often had two and even three names. It is very probable that those four belonged to the two tribes of Judah and of Levi, because in sum he makes this point with that sign, that Christ is both Priest and King, as the words are very clear. It is significant that he added "from the exiles," that is, from those who have come from Babylon, that those who had returned from captivity might be the more strengthened and might believe and that the others also might not doubt once they saw the sign.

11. *Take gold and silver,* that is, the sacred gold and silver which had been offered for use in the temple and in its sacred services.

And make crowns. One would not sin here were he to add "two," so as to read: "Make two crowns."

Set it on the head of Joshua. He does not want the crown placed

[6] The German version of these lectures shows that we should read *arcum* ("rainbow") for *arcam* ("ark"). Cf. p. 253 below.

on the head of Josiah or of Heldai, but on the head of Joshua the high priest. It is in this that the force and purpose of the sign consist – that the chief priest wears that double crown. To this sign are added the words:

12. *Behold the Man whose name is Growing, for a growing will occur under Him.* This is the way I translate from the Hebrew, just as I have also done earlier. In chapter 3, where the same word occurs, I have treated the text in sufficient detail. The evangelist Luke seems to have had this passage in mind when he says (Luke 1:78): "The Dayspring has visited us from on high." He used the word ἀνατολή ("rising"). It is more expressive, however, when we translate it with the word *crescere* [7] ("to grow"). The meaning of this passage is: "Up to now I have comforted you with many discourses and visions that you may be absolutely certain that the temple is going to be erected, that you have been saved, and that in your midst the coming kingdom of Christ is developing. Therefore do not be afraid. No one will be able to overcome or hinder you from your building. For because Christ is going to come, all things must be done. When He will have come, He will take up both the kingdom and the priesthood at the same time. He will grow exceedingly, and there will be much growing under Him, that is, the Gospel will prosper against the gates of hell, against the powerful attacks of Satan and of the whole world." Christ will be effective against all the wisdom, righteousness, prudence, and bravery of the world, as we have explained above in greater detail in chapter 3. Therefore it becomes clear that we must not apply this text to Joshua the high priest, who is merely a sign and figure of that coming Man about whom he speaks, namely, the growing Christ. Just so, too, the things which follow will clearly state this when He is described as the One who is going to sit on His own throne, which was not the prerogative of the high priest. For the kingdom and royal power belonged only to the tribe of Judah, not to the tribe of Levi. So when he says here that both come to one person, we must take this to mean Christ, who became both our King and Priest to eternity, as Scripture has it.

13. *And He Himself shall bear the honor.* In Hebrew these are

[7] For the Greek word in Luke 1:78 the Vulgate has *oriens* ("rising"). Luther proposes that a more expressive translation is *crescens* ("growing"), from the verb *crescere*. In his comment on Zech. 3:8 above, Luther preferred *germinantem* ("budding") to *orientem* ("rising"). The Hebrew word involved is צֶמַח, "sprout, growth, bud."

outstanding words. Because we do not have a complete comprehension of this language, we cannot translate them with words that are appropriate or expressive enough. "Honor" here signifies praise and celebration, as is revealed from that passage which is used frequently in many psalms (cf. Ps. 104:1): "Thou art clothed with honor and majesty," that is, praise and comeliness, *ein köstlicher, hübscher Schmuck.*[8] This is the sort of elegance and beauty with which girls are adorned when they wear gold and silver bracelets, pendants, and necklaces and all sorts of jewelry. This we call "adornment," or "elegance," in Latin, but "praise" in Hebrew. There is a clear passage in Exodus (Ex. 28:2): "garments for glory and for beauty." Here, therefore, we must see that elegance and adornment, or the great spreading abroad of Christ's kingdom. As His kingdom is not physical, so it cannot be decorated with physical adornments. In addition, it has no other elegance than the preaching of the Word of the Gospel. That is the great adornment and praise of Christ. Kings of this world are purple-clad, clothed and bedecked with gold and jewelry. But Christ wears the light. Through the Gospel are preached His gentleness, sweetness, righteousness, holiness, and kindness. When He is preached "full of grace and truth" (John 1:14), then He is adorned with His finest jewelry and most splendid glory. In this priesthood and kingdom there is nothing external, such as there was in the Mosaic priesthood. Here all things are spiritual. We see the same thing in that very beautiful little verse of the psalm (Ps. 145:5): "Of the glorious splendor of Thy majesty and of Thy wondrous works they will tell and speak." There the prophet explains what he means with the splendor of majesty. We also find the same phrase in Deuteronomy:[9] "Place something of your praise on Joshua," that is, adorn him, commend and praise him in the presence of the people. So also God is adorned when we preach Him in Word and faith. In this way the earth becomes filled with the glory of the majesty of the Lord.

And He shall sit, that is, like a teacher. This is the second badge of honor of Christ.

[8] Luther's German translation of Ps. 104:1 has *du bist schön und prächtig geschmückt.*

[9] Recalling the Lord's order that Moses commission Joshua as the new leader of Israel for the entry into Canaan, Luther probably had the Vulgate version of Num. 27:20 in mind: *Dabis ei . . . partem gloriae tuae,* which he here paraphrases as *pone de laude tua super Josue.* The same incident is reported in Deut. 3:28, but there in words somewhat removed from the Hebrew idiom here being illustrated: *Praecipe Josue et corrobora eum.*

And He shall rule, that is, like a king. This is the third badge of honor. Also,

There shall be a priest upon His throne. He is going to be at the same time both Priest and King, so that the functions of the two tribes will be placed in that one person. This is something which had never happened before. In fact, it was not even permitted. This, you see, is what the prophecy stated – that the scepter would not be taken away from Judah until He whom all nations desired would come (cf. Gen. 49:10; Hag. 2:7). Obviously, then, Christ is at the same time both our King and our Priest. He is our King as He rules over us and guards and protects us against every might and power of physical as well as spiritual foes, so that no creature can harm us without His permission. He is our Priest – and this is by far the sweetest and greatest comfort for consciences – as He intercedes for us before His Father and bears the iniquities of us all as if they were His own to make us coheirs with Him of all the good things of His Father and to reconcile us to His Father. Thus the Father can be angry with us or reject us as little as He could do so in the case of His own Son, Christ, for it was His will that He be our Chief Priest.

And peaceful understanding shall be between them both. Some interpret this as applying to a unity between Jews and Gentiles, as Paul says in Ephesians that both have become one because the wall of hostility has been taken away (cf. Eph. 2:14), that is, the Law, which separated Jews from Gentiles. The Jews wanted to appear more worthy and better than the Gentiles because of their divine reception of the Law. The Jews believed that by this reception of the Law they were going to be justified and that the Gentiles would be damned because they did not have the Law. That wall of hostility, the apostle says, Christ took away and nailed to the cross so that both Jews and Gentiles might know that they would be saved by faith alone without any works. This meaning is not bad *per se.* Nevertheless, if I were not too daring, I would approve another which has greater appeal to me, namely, that the prophet is speaking about the union and harmony of the two offices of royal authority and priesthood; that both were in Christ at the same time. In this sense, it becomes completely clear that we can by no means take this to refer to the priesthood of Joshua, as some think, since royal authority pertained solely to the tribe of Judah and not to the tribe of Levi, which had the responsibility for the priesthood. The twin crowns indicate, too, this double administration – physical and spiritual. Both of these a priest of the Law could not hold. Those crowns likewise signify the sort of kingdom it is: One is golden; the other, silver. The golden one signifies faith; the silver one, the ministry of the Word – a truth that is clear from many passages in Scripture. Solomon says in Proverbs (Prov. 10:20): "The tongue of the righteous is choice silver." Also, we read in the psalm (Ps. 12:6): "The promises of the Lord are pure like silver seven times refined." Faith alone is the price which God Almighty requires of us.

14. *And the crowns shall be as a reminder to Heldai, Tobijah, Jedaiah, and Josiah.* It is a very common occurrence in Hebrew that there are some double and even triple names. Sometimes this produces an obscurity for readers when such names are switched at other places. Here the names of two – the first and fourth – were changed. But the Lord orders those crowns to be hung as a reminder of that matter. We, too, have the same custom of hanging weapons and battle flags of certain persons in our churches or public buildings as reminders for our posterity. The Lord wants the same thing done here. He wants the names of those four to be written down there so that the people would not doubt that what had been promised and signified by that sign was going to be fulfilled. Thus those crowns endured as seals of God's promise until Christ came.

15. *And those who are far off shall come and build in the temple of the Lord.* This some people interpret as the kings and realms of the wealthiest nations. All of these, impressed by the renown of the undertaking, sent gold, silver, and other precious gifts to Jerusalem for use in the temple. The equipment of the temple was most splendid and magnificent, so that Christ's apostles, too, were amazed at that structure, as is recorded in the gospel (Mark 13:1). However, I adhere strictly to the sequence and order of the text. After all, the prophet is speaking about that "growing" Christ, who is going to establish at the same time a new kingdom and a new priesthood. He says that many people who are far off are going to come to this from distant lands, that is, that all nations from all parts of the earth are going to come together to Him, as Scripture reveals everywhere, to finish that true temple where He will be glorified and preached by the faithful – Jews as well as Gentiles.

If you will have listened to the voice of the Lord your God. Clearly he adds this to terrify the Jews greatly. After all, this signifies the falling away and miserable destruction of that people, which he also prophesied in dire vein earlier in chapter 5. Then too, Isaiah, throughout his book, presses this point especially. It is as if Zechariah were saying: "These things which I have foretold will happen. You, however, see to it that you do not regard the Word of God with contempt. The voice of the Lord will build that structure. He will use that voice only for so glorious and magnificent an undertaking. With the ministry of the Word He will accomplish all things. Consequently, if you wish to be in that temple too, you must believe His Word; you must receive that Word without stopping to gaze at its external beauty or equipment."

Thus we have completed the most difficult passages of this prophet. Certainly, it is only with great effort that we can barely call the mind back away from the senseless interpretations of the "scholars," which hold us back on every side much more than does the very genuine understanding of the prophet. Those interpretations vary widely and confuse everything. Jerome is especially guilty of this. Why, he can barely write a single meaningful line about the whole prophet. Therefore it is particularly fitting that we free the meaning from the interpretations of all these people as if from some inescapable labyrinth.

CHAPTER SEVEN

These next two chapters are quite clear and simple *per se,* now that we have taken care of the difficulties of the visions. The prophet took almost two years to reveal the first six chapters. This the inscriptions at the beginning of the book as well as of this seventh chapter indicate. He had begun in the second year of King Darius, and here he says that Darius had begun his fourth year. So he preached to the people for two years before he began this sermon. Let me summarize these two chapters. After the people had been established in and recalled to the good and true way to walk in the Law and Word of the Lord, Satan or wicked human reason began to find the path of human traditions and inventions which are outside of and beyond the Word of God. You see, Satan generally and everywhere pushes himself into those matters which relate to God and the holy worship of God. This is something the Germans express beautifully in the proverb: "Wherever God has built a church, the devil will have a chapel close by." [1] As a result, what the entire fifth chapter earlier described in quite terrible terms about the flying scroll had to happen among these people. So the Lord allows this to happen while the prophet is still alive that the people may be warned by this example not to depart from the Word but remain in its truth and purity. In the entire Old Testament there is scarcely a place so clear – as we shall see here in this chapter – against the traditions of men and that religion of the angels [2] which, because of its hypocrisy, appears so saintly to the judgment of reason. Yet the blindness of the papists is such that they bring this text forward in favor of their traditions, for they are blind men and strangers to all common sense. Indeed, this is the famous text they use to support fasting in the church of the pope. It has even stimulated them to establish fasts for each of the four seasons of the year.[3] Such is the

1 *Unser Herr Gott hat nirgend eine Kirche, der Teufel will auch eine Kapelle daneben haben.*

2 Cf. Col. 2:18.

3 The reference is to the ember days in the four quarters of the Roman Catholic church year. Their name *Quatember* is derived from *ieiunia quattuor temporum* ("fasts of the four seasons"), and they may be Jewish in origin.

blindness of human reason which so shamelessly abuses the Word of God according to its own whims. It hears only a few syllables and ignores the logic and context of the whole discourse. Thus because there is mention of fasts here, they immediately set their teeth firmly into that word and believe that it establishes what they themselves are dreaming up. Yet those fasts have no Scriptural authority. They were the self-chosen [4] works and voluntary religious acts of that people, as Paul says,[5] and the Lord here completely condemns them.

The text, however, offers no reason for that fasting. And it did not matter that a reason be added for something worthless. For who could give sound reasons for all their foolish teachings? Satan thinks up a thousand tricks with which to persuade the unwary to consider religion what they establish under his authorship. Finally, if it is absolutely necessary that we add reasons, we shall be content with those which the Jews propose. On these Jerome has commented in great detail.[6] We shall not spend time, however, to determine which are genuine and which are not.

For *the fast of the fourth month* [7] they give this reason: it was in the fourth month that the king of the Babylonians first laid siege to Jerusalem, tore down the walls, swept into the city, and captured it. This was the month when the king had fled and Jerusalem came into the power of the enemy. As a memorial for this loss, that they might bear witness that they were mourning the disaster of the holy city, it seemed right to them to consecrate a fast of mourning which they observed precisely as if they had received an holy precept of God. In our day we have people who are exactly like those Jews. They are those superstitious people who in their foolish religious rites bury that wooden image of Christ and abstain from all food on the day of preparation until that wooden image again is raised. They do this to honor the passion of Christ, but in the meantime they have neglected the genuine significance of that passion. The Jews, too, had a superstition like that. They fasted during the fourth month every year because Jerusalem was captured during it. In addition, I should also note this: their fourth month is June, because they begin counting their months from March.

[4] We have read *electicia* for *delecticia.*

[5] The reference is probably to Col. 2:23.

[6] *Commentaria in Zachariam prophetam,* on Zech. 8:19, *Patrologia, Series Latina,* XXV, 1474—1475.

[7] The four fasts here discussed are taken from Zech. 8:19.

The fast of the fifth month indicates that the Jews also fasted in the fifth month. For this fast they offer the following reason: in this month, after the city had been taken, the temple of the Lord and the palace were burned. Sacred history vouches for this. They were deeply moved by the great tragedy that the king of the Babylonians was not content with plundering and laying the city waste but also destroyed the temple of the Lord and with fire vented his wrath on some of the finest royal palaces. As a result, they established a fast also for this.

The fast of the seventh month. This is the month of September.[8] To establish this fast they used the pretext that it was in this month that Gedaliah was killed.[9] The king of the Babylonians [10] had established him as the governor of the land of Canaan to be in charge there. There is something about this in Jeremiah,[11] when he rebukes them for fearing evil against themselves at the hands of the king of the Babylonians [12] and for fleeing to Egypt. This murder of Gedaliah later was the occasion of a great disaster.

The fast of the tenth month, that is, of December. To establish this fast, they say that they were influenced by the fact that in that month the report of the burning of the temple and the flight into Egypt first reached the ears of those who had been led into captivity in Babylon.

These, then, are the matters which, in sum, these next two chapters treat. The Lord condemns those self-chosen works of righteousness and says that such works displease Him, because He has neither instituted nor commanded them. This is certainly a very clear passage – as I mentioned at the beginning of this section – against the traditions of men and self-chosen works, regardless of how good they may appear. After all, who can deny that fasting is a good work? And yet here the Lord rejects it. He demands instead that they be godly, kind-hearted, and devoted to the Word of God, that they be involved in those works which God has commanded. He says that there is no need to invent self-chosen works and will worship,[13] as Paul calls it.

1. *In the fourth year of King Darius,* that is, "was the Word given

8 The Weimar text has "November" but corrects this reading in a footnote.

9 Cf. Jer. 41:1-3.

10 The Weimar editor has so corrected the text's "Assyrians."

11 The original text has "Isaiah," but reference is to the same context as in the previous lines. The Weimar editor suggests the correction to Jeremiah 39—44, but he does so in the form of a question.

12 The original text has "Assyrians."

13 ἐθελοθρησκεία, Col. 2:23.

to me to preach and publish." This happened in the month of November – the month they call "Chislev." Actually, the Jews reckon their months according to the lunar cycles, beginning with the new moon's appearance, but we do not, for we have fixed months and fixed days of the month. Because of our system, we must use intercalary days, which they do not need.

2. *And they sent to Bethel.* Here Jerome has dared too much, for he translates this word "Bethel" which the Hebrew has as "the house of God." This is the proper name of the place, so it did not have to be translated as a common noun. For wherever Scripture mentions the temple of the Lord, it uses other words – like הֵיכַל אֲדֹנָי. I have no knowledge of any place in Scripture where we must translate "Bethel" as a common noun. Therefore read it this way: "And they sent to Bethel." In substance he says: "Let those be ashamed of their wickedness who are still attached to that condemned place, because of which they had suffered grievous affliction." Now, Sharezer and Regem-melech were the ones sent to implore the favor of the Lord. This they were to do with the gifts and offerings, which people generally sent as a pledge. Finally, when they had sacrificed and made their offerings at Bethel – this was a great wickedness, for the Lord had rejected and outlawed that place – they went to the priests of the house of the Lord in Jerusalem and to the prophets to question them.

3. *Should I mourn?* According to the Hebrew, one should read: "Shall I still weep in the fifth month for my sanctification as I have done for many years?" Look at the Book of Numbers for information about the Nazarites: how abstemious they were, how they never cut their hair, and how they observed who knows what else.[14] The apostle Paul also did this because of the weakness of the Jews, as one reads in the Acts of the Apostles (21:23-26). To such observances the prophet alludes here in that question proposed to the priests and prophets of the Lord, as if to say: "Must I still mourn, abstain from wine, fast, and have superstitious regard, as it were, for the rites of the Nazarites in memory of that disaster which followed the overthrow of the city and the burning of the temple?" He is asking, then, whether he ought to proceed with that self-chosen religion, now that the temple has been rebuilt. This is the same thing which some weak people do today when they stir up questions about their ridiculous vows.

5. *When you fasted and mourned.* The Lord rebukes that stupid

[14] Num. 6:1-21.

superstition and says, as it were: "Your eating and drinking give Me no pleasure. What is this to Me, since I have given you no such commands? It had nothing to do with Me that you were walking about sad, weeping, and hungry because of your captured city and burned temple. And while all this went on, you did not change your way of life. You did not cease your idolatry. You kept on despising the Word of God. You had no faith in Me and not even an enthusiasm for love." He will add a similar rebuke about their unjust judging and their perversion of justice against widows and fatherless children. There is a very similar passage in Malachi (Mal. 3:14): "It is vain to serve God. What is the good of our walking as in mourning, etc." To sum up, the Lord is saying here that fasting is not done for Him, that all these things are worthless because He has not commanded them, but that He approves of those things which stem from a good source – from a faithful heart. You see, once the heart is sanctified and pure, whatever comes afterwards is also pure and holy, whether one fasts or eats, whether one keeps watch or falls asleep.

6. *And when you eat and when you drink.* There is a similar passage in Jeremiah (Jer. 7:21): "Take your sacrificial victims and eat their flesh," that is, "Don't bother Me with your eating and drinking and with your fasts." We read also (Ps. 50:13): "Do I eat the flesh of bulls and drink the blood of goats?" Again, Ps. 50:12: "If I were hungry, I would not tell you, etc.," that is, "Neither your fasting nor your eating pleases Me." Paul, too, says the same thing (1 Cor. 8:8): "We are no worse off if we do not eat. Food will not commend us to God." Whatever happens, nothing hinders Him; He approves of everything. But these are only externals. Whether you eat or fast, whether you drink or fall asleep – what is this to God? He wants the heart to be godly and pure. So Paul did well when he cut his hair along with the other Jews, as he records in the Acts of the Apostles (21:26).

7. *Are not these the words, etc.?* This is the way I read this verse: "Are these not the words which the Lord preached through the mouths of the earlier prophets when Jerusalem was still standing?" And these are the words: "You fasted, you went about mourning, you established self-chosen religious acts, etc. But I don't want all these. I do not approve of them. With them you have only provoked Me to wrath. And although taught by your previous experience, and this to your great harm, you did not cease before I rejected and hated those practices and self-chosen works of yours. How long will you abuse My long-

suffering? How long will you continue in your wickedness?" For hypocrites commit a double sin: first, they desert God and invent something that is contrary to the Word of God; second, they blaspheme the name of God. When they add their concept of righteousness to their works and practices, they think this is worship of God and that God approves. In this way they "call evil good and good evil," as Isaiah (Is. 5:20) has it. This is something even public sinners and the openly dissolute do not do.

9. *Thus the Lord of hosts had spoken.* This is the way I would want to render this verse to make it fit the preceding section. You see, He is explaining Himself as to what those words are which they had heard from the prophets, when He adds:

Render true judgment. He is saying in substance: "My prophets did not speak this way: 'You must fast, mourn, lament!' They said absolutely nothing like this, but rather: 'Render true judgment.' So isn't this now enough madness? Do you want to go on with it still longer? Hear what the Lord says. Listen to what He requires of you: that you have just magistrates, princes, and judges to administer the government fairly; that you have people with a concern for the Law to pronounce judgment 'without respect for persons' [15] – people who remain uncorrupted by bribes and who do not pervert the Law and oppress the poor." This is their first sin – that they have "gift-hungry rulers." [16] Then the Lord requires kindness of everyone, and mercy toward his neighbor. These, you see, are the functions of love which pertain equally to all men, as Christ Himself also said, "I desire mercy and not sacrifice" (Matt. 9:13). Mercy, moreover, is the blessing by which we are obliging to others. It is as if He were saying: "Each of you, treat each other well. Be of mutual help to each other with love. Then also show mercy to each other, that is, each person should be kind to his brother and have compassion on his neighbor in every need. Let each of you forgive the offense of another. Lift each other up, if you should ever slip. Then do not falsely accuse the stranger, the widow, the orphan, and the pauper, who are otherwise destitute of every avenue of aid. They are wretched *per se.* Therefore, do not add evil to evil. Otherwise, 'the poor will be lying helpless everywhere.' " [17]

[15] Luther quotes the Greek word προσωπολημψία of Rom. 2:11; Col. 3:25; James 2:1.

[16] Luther quotes the Greek expression βασιλῆας δωροφάγους from Hesiod, *Opera et dies,* 264.

[17] Luther quotes *pauper ubique iacet* from Ovid, *Fasti,* I, 218.

11. *But they refused to hearken.* Intent on their own pursuits and lusts, they turned their ears away from the truth and hardened their hearts like steel. I do not know if the Hebrew word really means "steel," for I have often said that the Hebrew linguists are unsure about words for objects. In Exodus we translated it with the word "diamond," but there a different word is used.[18] The word does mean the wicked stubbornness of the Pharisees which ruled in their hearts and kept them from listening to the Word of God.

12. *By His Holy Spirit through the hand of the prophets.* He says in substance: "I have hewn them by the prophets," as Hosea [19] (Hos. 6:5) has it. "I have spared no effort, no hardship, to call them back from their wickedness over against the Word of God. But they have continued obstinately on their way. They have turned their backs to Me." From this text was taken that statement which we read in the Nicene Creed: "Who spoke by the prophets," and what Peter says in his epistle: "Men moved by the Holy Spirit spoke from God" (2 Peter 1:21).

13. *And just as they did not hear.* "Just as the prophets preached and they did not hear, so also, when they would cry out, I would not listen." So this should have been translated with the subjunctive,[20] for the Hebrews do not have a subjunctive. The Lord Himself bears witness that they did invoke the name of the Lord. This certainly was an excellent practice. If one ever concedes anything to the power of what people call free will, here much is conceded to it, namely, the invocation of the name of God. But still, because they refused to listen to the Word of God, it was impossible that God should listen to their cries. We learn from this, then, that if we want Him to listen to our prayers, we must first listen to the Word of the Lord. Otherwise He will not listen, even though you weep and cry out – even if you burst.

14. *And I scattered them among all the nations.* The word which our text [21] translates as "scatter" is an elegant and powerful word in Hebrew. The Hebrew reading is: "I have thrown them out among all nations with a whirlwind," as if to say: "I have scattered and driven

[18] In Ex. 28:18 the Hebrew word is יַהֲלֹם ("jasper," "onyx"); in the present passage the word is שָׁמִיר ("flint," "adamant").

[19] The Weimar text has "Isaiah."

[20] Instead of *clamabunt* the Vulgate should have had *clamarent,* Luther means to say.

[21] The Vulgate.

them in all directions with the onslaught of a storm. No one could resist, so the terrible storm snatched them up. That they were grief-stricken hindered Me not at all."

The land they left behind them was desolate, because there remained behind no farmer, no resident. Everything was reduced to desert.

And the desirable land was made desolate. We have the same word here for "desirable" as we have in Haggai [22] (Hag. 2:7): "The desire of all nations shall come in." The Jews were particularly delighted with the city of Jerusalem and with their land. They took it hard that they were being pulled out of that land. Yet, regardless of how much their land pleased them, the whirlwind turned them out and scattered them.

[22] The Weimar text has "Genesis." The Hebrew word in question is חֶמְדָּה.

CHAPTER EIGHT

THIS chapter is easy and clear because of its relation to what precedes. I said[1] that one had to do this: that one had to see how the prophet was setting forth two eras. The first was when the people were brought back from captivity and when the temple and city were rebuilt, that the Lord might kindle a fire from a tiny remnant – as from a glimmering spark – which would sweep the whole world. For this purpose some were saved for the sake of the promises. The second era is the one in which He describes Christ as already present and ruling. The prophet uses this chapter as a summary to repeat everything which he earlier discussed with his abundant imagery and many visions. Here he repeats all the same points with very clear language. Thus we can easily call this chapter an explanation and interpretation of everything which has come earlier.

2. *I am jealous for Zion with great jealousy.* Earlier I have explained in detail what jealous means. In sum, the Lord says this: "Until now I have been very angry with Zion. Through the Chaldeans I destroyed it and afflicted it severely. However, I still did not reject it completely. Instead, as a husband rebukes his wife because of his love for her when he sees her remiss in anything, so I, too, etc. You see, I shall no longer be angry, for I have already returned to Jerusalem. Mercy and peace now follow, not vengeance or hatred."

3. *The city of truth and the mountain of the Lord.* He calls Mount Moriah, which lies in the middle of the city of Jerusalem, "the mountain of the Lord." These are lofty titles, very honorable heralds – for both the city and the hill. However, He does not ascribe that holiness and truth to the inhabitants of the city because they themselves are holy or true, but because He Himself is going to live in Jerusalem, and He is holy. In fact, He is holiness itself and absolute truth. If you look at the people, they are profane and wicked people who killed the prophets and even Christ Himself. But on account of the Word which the Lord speaks here, the city becomes holy and the mountain

1 See Luther's introductory paragraphs in chapter 1.

truthful, and then the people who have the Word of God also become holy. For we may say that God lives in a given place when He dwells there through His holy Word and through His Holy Spirit. These were present in Jerusalem, so that the people could have no doubts about the will of God, because He had promised that He most certainly would be present in that place and would hear them when they called upon Him. Briefly, what we have in Christ they had in their temple. Thus God Almighty always wants to lead consciences with some external sign and to reassure them that they should have no doubts about His will, should not wander about uncertain as to what God approves of, and should not, like the blind, aim at some uncertain target. Therefore we have the greatest assurance in Christ that God does listen to us, that we do understand His will for us. In the same way, they had the greatest assurance, when they revered the temple, that God was present and was listening to them. In sum, then, the prophet is saying this: "They will be faithful people. I will again lift up the true worship of God. They will have the pure Word of God, through which I shall always be present."

4. *Old men and old women again shall dwell.* These words we must relate to the emotions of the people to whom the prophet speaks them. At that time they had been greatly disturbed by their current situation. Nothing was secure. Nothing they tried was successful. Their crops were turning out poorly. All their prayers were receiving bad answers. Then, too, they had been hemmed in by foes who kept abusing them and who were keeping them from pursuing the building of the temple. Cambyses, the king of the Persians, and his wicked lieutenants kept them from being able to finish the building they had begun under Cyrus. In short, almost only plotting, warfare, trickery, and deceit were the rule of the day, so that they could see nothing else but the deplorable condition of their entire situation. They kept thinking that it was all over for them and their kingdom. To these and similar emotions of theirs the Lord here adapts Himself. He comforts them lest they lose their faith that the kingdom would be safe, renowned, and densely populated. You see, Haggai and Zechariah first set forth consolation of this sort, as if to say: "All things will be peaceful, disturbances or uprisings will no longer be heard in the land, the city of Jerusalem will be crowded with people, children will play safely in the streets, etc. This indeed seems impossible to you, but be confident, I shall bring it to pass very easily."

7. *Behold, I will save My people.* This verse, along with others which follow, some people apply to Christ. This is not altogether bad. If anyone should want to keep close to the emphasis, he could maintain this. I, however, prefer to treat and to apply to Christ only those statements which properly pertain to Christ and which effectively consider His kingdom; and I pass over those which can be disallowed in one way or another. He says that the city will be populous, that the streets will be filled with old people, girls, and boys; even though now there are very few people, even though everything seems to be falling apart and lost. We have our evidence of this in Nehemiah: scarcely 10 percent of the city had been rebuilt at that time. The other 90 percent had been destroyed and burned. So nothing seemed less likely to happen than that the city, deserted and devastated, was going to turn back into a renowned, densely populated, pleasant place. But God has this power to create all things out of nothing, lest we do any boasting about our own powers. So He immediately adds: "I shall save My people from the east country and from the west country," that is, "I shall call Judeans as well as Israelites back from Babylon and from other parts of the world, wherever they may be, and Jerusalem will have inhabitants."

8. *In truth and in righteousness,* that is, "Your worship of Me will be lawful, genuine, and sincere because of My Word and the godly individuals who are among the people." Otherwise idolatry would never have ceased among those people. Because of the Word and the Holy Spirit, who has been present in some men, He says that He wants to spare them from fear of another destruction.

10. *Indeed, before those days there was no wage for man.* He is describing the wretched conditions of the state existing before this prophecy – that no undertaking was successful, fields did not return due seed with interest, abject poverty and fear of plots were rampant. This we can see from Haggai, chapter 1. Therefore savagery, cruelty, and total disaster to all their possessions were then controlling the people. They had no peace, no truth, no righteousness. It is an idiom of Scripture to say, "There was no wage for man"; we translate negatively in this way: "What the people worked for was a lost cause, it brought no results." People were throwing everything into a sack with a gaping hole in the bottom. So we see how Scripture speaks about the merits of men, namely, about the results of man's efforts, not about the merits.

12. *There shall be a sowing of peace.* Again we have a Hebraism.

In substance He is saying: "From that tiny remnant I shall raise up for Myself a numberless people. From an insignificant spark I shall kindle a great fire. They will be My sowing of peace, that is, they will be well and prosperous. They will multiply like seed." He now adds much detail.

13. *O house of Judah and house of Israel.* He includes Israel, too, in the promise, even though the prophecy had stated that Israel would never be brought back. I have said, however, that we must understand that in this way, that there is no doubt that many of the Israelites were brought back, but their throne and name was never restored. To Judah the name, throne, political administration, and priesthood were restored. Israel was carried off to the Medes and never afterward recovered its prince, divine worship, or any political organization. Accordingly, if any people of Israel were brought back, they were counted as people of Judah. But that they were to be a curse for the heathen or a blessing means that they were to be an example, as the Latins say. They were an example of a curse when some would call down on others as miserable a rejection and captivity as had happened to them because of the wrath of God.

14. *As I purposed to do evil to you.* He constantly has regard for their afflicted consciences, which had been so wretchedly oppressed earlier. There still always remained some sense of the past calamity. He keeps calling their consciences back from those evil and frightful awarenesses of past ill-fortune, and He strengthens them again with very broad, rich, comforting promises. But a strong faith to apprehend those promises was required for this. After all, as far as reason was concerned, everything seemed lost.

16. *Speak the truth to one another.* He does not urge ceremonies or sacrifices, which they considered very valuable. Instead, He demands the finest works of love, as we have mentioned in sufficient detail in the previous chapter. It is as if He were saying: "Just as I am righteous and truthful, so you should be too."

Render judgments that are true and make for peace. This is a wonderful arrangement of words. They mean: "May each of you be sincere and candid with his neighbor. Let each of you do what he says he will do, and say what he does. Let him not pretend to be a friend and prove to be an enemy. Let him not hold out bread in his one hand while he carries a stone in the other. Then rightly render fair judgments, for from unfair judgments rise hatreds; from hatreds, plots;

from plots, sedition and warfare." This is the way I interpret the judgment that makes for peace.

17. *Do not devise evil.* Thus Scripture everywhere requires mercy and not sacrifice: that we do good to each other; that one help the other, either with action or with advice. But the Lord especially wants to commend to our care those who have been oppressed and afflicted. For such people He says He has regard, as Scripture everywhere tells us. The eyes of the Lord have regard for the poor.

Love no false oath. This we can take to refer to false worship and religion, when we misuse the name of God for the purposes of our own traditions and fraudulent worship, as I interpreted in chapter 5 earlier. But each must pursue what he wants.

19. *The fast of the fourth month and the fast of the fifth month.* Here the question about the fast is answered. We proposed it earlier and explained it in detail.[2] He completely abrogates all those human traditions, saying in substance: "I do not want you to be afflicted. I do not want you to go hungry. After all, what is your fasting to Me? But I shall change that grief of yours into joy so that, just as you were sad during those earlier days, now you will eat more freely and be joyful." But this is translated badly in our Bible[3] as *in solemnitates praeclaras* ("noble feasts"). We should rather translate it *in solemnitates iucundas et bonas* ("pleasant or good feasts"). The poorer translation perhaps has given wicked priests an opportunity to misapply this passage to confirm their own wicked traditions, to conclude that their fasts are noble and worth being spread abroad and proposed to the people for imitation of the custom. Yet the prophet clearly says that they must no longer follow such practices. But the prophet fosters works of love so diligently because it is the nature of hypocrisy and of human traditions to turn away from the truth and from a concern toward the neighbor. This is something which all those wicked orders of monks, and especially the orders of those who are considered the most holy, like the Carthusians,[4] still very clearly teach today.

20. *Peoples will still come and live, etc.* Even this verse people apply to Christ. Although this may not disagree with the meaning, yet

[2] Cf. p. 75 above.

[3] The Vulgate.

[4] For Luther the Carthusian monks seem to exemplify monastic life at its worst, particularly in the matter of fasting. Cf. *Luther's Works,* 2, pp. 338 f.; 7, p. 344; 17, p. 111; 22, p. 461; 23, p. 263.

the whole verse cannot be applied to Him. Therefore we shall continue to use that first meaning. He is saying: "The inhabitants of many cities will gather here, not only you but the residents of many cities (we must read it this way),[5] and the residents of one city will say to those of another: *Let us go to entreat the favor of the Lord.*" Then, a little farther down, He adds "to seek the Lord of hosts in Jerusalem." Now, if that last section had not been added, I would apply this verse to Christ, too. Therefore we are applying this to literal and legal worship. Thus the meaning will be that which Luke explains in Acts 2:5: [6] "There were dwelling in Jerusalem . . . devout men from every nation under heaven." The temple finally was so highly regarded that even princes and queens from distant lands honored it with their gifts, as Josephus relates.[7]

21. *I am going also.* Jerome feels that this part was not spoken in the person of God as others want it, but in the person of the people.[8] This is ambiguous. Which meaning is the better I leave unresolved. If it was said in the person of God, this will be the meaning: "I shall be in the midst of them, and I shall be their God," as He says elsewhere.[9] Thus we should understand this as referring not only to the Jews but to all the righteous of all the nations of all the earth that gathered there to worship God.

23. *In those days ten men will take hold.* He connects the time of the return from captivity with the time of the kingdom of Christ. He says that ten men of every tongue of the nations of all the earth are going to take hold of the fringe of the robe of a single Jew to go along with Him. The Jews bear down hard on this passage in wondrous ways and say that it has never been fulfilled. There is, however, a great incongruity in their interpretation so that it cannot be understood in the way they are dreaming. Consequently we cannot apply this to the external and physical edging of a robe, but to the preaching of the Gospel. It is as if He were saying: "The Gospel will be preached throughout the earth. It will bear such great fruit that one apostle (or, as others wish, Christ) will with his preaching convert many

[5] Luther proposes to read *habitatores civitatum multarum* for the Vulgate's *habitent in civitatibus multis.*

[6] The Weimar text has "Acts 1."

[7] Flavius Josephus, *Antiquities of the Jews,* XI, ch. 5.

[8] Jerome, *Commentaria in Zachariam prophetam* on Zech. 8:21, *Patrologia, Series Latina,* XXV, 1476.

[9] E. g., Zech. 2:10.

thousands of people to righteousness. They will follow spontaneously, not because the Law compels them but because the Holy Spirit leads them." Because the number ten is the cycle of all numbers, it indicates the universality of those who are going to be converted to the faith in any language. Then the prophet also quietly indicates that they will not come into this kingdom unless they have been selected and limited to a certain number. This definite number is God's business. He calls, and He selects, according to His own will, whom He wishes. Nothing of this lies within the province of our powers and exertions, but in His mercy.

CHAPTER NINE

We have about completed the first section of this prophet. In the chapters which follow, he will prophesy about the future, namely, about the succession of time up to and after Christ. The first part of this chapter is strangely obscure. All the exegetes have treated it in different ways, yet all that variety still does not leave me satisfied. Some interpret this to be about Babylon; others, about the Maccabees. Jerome relates it all to Christ.[1] Yet all of them do not aim straight. What the prophet says about the burden is completely clear and manifest. After all, the heading of the chapter has this. Therefore, where there is a burden of the Word of the Lord, there must be some evil; or else a coming oppression is being declared and signified. This is normal in all the prophets. And yet here he immediately mixes grace with the prophecy of devastation, as he adds within the chapter: "I shall take away its blood from its mouth, and its abomination from between its teeth" (v. 7). Briefly, this is what I believe is the meaning of the first part of the chapter: the prophet wants to prophesy and foretell that it will come to pass that the neighboring peoples around Jerusalem – Tyre, Sidon, and all Palestine – are going to be converted to Christ by the Gospel revealed throughout the world. Yet a great disaster, a destruction and affliction, will precede that grace, that is, it is indeed going to happen that our neighbors also will go with us, that both we and they will have the same faith. However, they are not going to reach that grace unless they have been well chastised. First, they are going to pay the penalties for their godlessness and because they have so often caused us wretched, savage affliction. That seems to me to be the real meaning. If it does not agree, I see no other by which to explain for myself that remarkable obscurity. After all, the prophet says everything somewhat obscurely, so that the prophecy, now obscured, was not understood until the Jews saw it happen. About Tyre and Sidon, these very rich cities (for they were coastal cities overflowing with every kind of fine merchandise), we

[1] Jerome, *Commentaria in Zachariam prophetam,* on Zech. 9:1, *Patrologia, Series Latina,* XXV, 1479.

must consult the history books. These cities were destroyed twice, once by Nebuchadnezzar, king of Babylon. Ezekiel recalls in great detail the destruction he caused: "Nebuchadnezzar, king of Babylon, made his army labor hard against Tyre, etc." (cf. Ezek. 29:18). The second destruction occurred at the hands of King Alexander, who was called Alexander the Great. This account the historians of the Gentiles write. Mention of this overthrow we find also in the accounts of the gospels, when Christ says: "Woe to you, Chorazin! Woe to you, Bethsaida! for if such mighty works done in you had been done in Tyre and Sidon, etc." (Matt. 11:21). In this passage Christ Himself bears witness that those cities had been overthrown and completely destroyed. That happened in the more recent destruction at the hand of Alexander the Great. Then, after Alexander had died, there was perpetual discord, very bitter hatred, and armed conflict between the kings of Egypt and Syria. They were often involved in bitter warfare with each other – not without great disaster and destruction for those cities which were lying between them. For whoever would win, to him they would become subject, and by him they would be plundered. See the histories of the Maccabees and Josephus.

1. *In the land of Hadrach.* Jerome thinks that this word is composed of two separate elements.[2] Perhaps this is not bad. It is a new word which the prophet invented to obscure the prophecy. It means *ein Schenck* – a cupbearer. The prophet has misused the etymology of the word to describe the mores of those cities as luxurious, pampered, and very wealthy. He is saying as it were: "We are now poor and destitute. Our entire situation is in a deplorable state. We are suffering great hardship in rebuilding the temple and in repairing the wretched ruins of our city. On the other hand, you Syrians are cupbearers. All your produce shows a happy increase. You are flooded with an abundance of all things. In leisure and security you indulge your appetites. You have no worries about anything bad. But in a short time it will come to pass that your cities, too, will be destroyed and your luxurious living checked in order that, now that you have been thus repressed, you may rejoice with us over the grace revealed through the Gospel."

And will rest upon Damascus. He is speaking of Syria, of which

[2] Jerome, *Commentaria in Zachariam prophetam* on Zech. 9:1, *Patrologia, Series Latina,* XXV, 1479.

Damascus is the security or capital. The Syrians are especially confident of it and rest secure in it.

For to the Lord belongs the eye of man. This is the Scriptural idiom which the prophet also uses in Ps. 3:8: "Deliverance belongs to the Lord," that is, *Bei dir steht die Hilfe.* Thus here the fact that men and all the tribes of Israel see does not belong to them themselves but to the Lord. It is He who furnishes the seeing. The meaning of the passage is this: "Soon another change will approach and threaten. The burden is before their hands. There will soon be another kingdom. The Lord will give His eye to all men, that is, light will rise up from the Lord." You see, this passage demands that we understand this in terms of spiritual eyes.

And of all the tribes of Israel. He says in substance: "You Syrians and Palestinians appear to yourselves to be intelligent people. You believe that everything has been set out into the light for you and that we are lying wrapped in darkness. But there is another light, another sight, different from the one you have in mind. That light belongs to the Lord, who will give His eye to all of us and to all the tribes of Israel that we may not only see what we should see but also rejoice about what we have seen." This is the way Scripture often uses the word "to see." Furthermore, that new light is the Gospel, which illumines hearts and the deepest darknesses.

2. *Hamath also, which borders thereon, Tyre and Sidon, though they are very wise.* That is, this burden will weigh down not only those heavy drinkers and pleasure lovers but Hamath as well (this is the city that they call Antioch today), which borders on Damascus. These people, he says, all seem to themselves to be wise. Indeed, they are wise in the eyes of the world. However, there is need for another wisdom. But he explains that wisdom of the world and of reason, for which that entire area was distinguished. He notes Tyre in particular as he adds, "Tyre has built her rampart, etc.," as if to say: "Because strong walls gird her, because her wealth abounds everywhere, Tyre believes that she will be safe against every onslaught of her foes. She has many leaders for her government, she has a great supply of silver and gold. But none of these will help her. She cannot be saved." Now, that city was very wealthy and very prosperous. So it was not without great difficulty for his armies that Alexander the Great could conquer her. But finally Tyre was conquered. The prophet immediately adds:

4. *Behold, the Lord will take possession of her, for her might will*

be cast into the sea. This is the way I connect the continuity of his discourse here. Otherwise it has no unity. Also, I take the fact that he says that the Lord is going to take possession of Tyre as something good. Thus the meaning is: "Through His Word the Lord will dwell even in Tyre. A great disaster, however, will precede His taking possession. First the might of Tyre will be cast into the sea, and first she will be devoured by fire.

5. *Ashkelon shall see it and be afraid.* He next explains the burden as applying also to the rest of the neighboring cities. He names the capital and principal cities of the kingdom of the Philistines which were especially flourishing. Although this was a small kingdom, it still dared go against very powerful and very large kingdoms. It caused much trouble for the Jews, for it often conquered them, too. But here the prophet says the Philistines will lose their self-confidence, for we read: "because its hopes are confounded" (the word "its" is superfluous). That is, they will lose their assurance. The men who can give good advice to preserve their state will be taken away from them, and when they are lacking in a state, strength, resources, or armor cannot suffice.

6. *And a mongrel people shall dwell in Ashdod.* Jerome applies this to Christ,[3] but that simply does not fit. In the Hebrew we have מַמְזֵר, "a bastard," will dwell in Ashdod. That is, the natives, and genuine citizens will be driven away and annihilated, foreigners and strangers, to whom Ashdod did not belong, will dwell in it. Therefore, he says, they will perish completely; just as they now say that scarcely a remnant of those very wealthy cities survives. Yet at one time they were so powerful and well known that I am often amazed at their power, however small they may have been.

7. *And I will take away its blood from its mouth.* This passage promises grace — as I mentioned at the beginning of this chapter. The meaning, then, is this: "They are murderers and robbers, idolaters and great sinners. All these sins I shall take away from them (for this is what he calls 'blood' — the sins of the flesh). I shall take them away through the Gospel." This did happen through the preaching of the apostles, who traveled through these cities.

It, too, will be a remnant for our God, that is, it, too, will be part

3 Jerome, *Commentaria in Zachariam prophetam,* on Zech. 9:6, *Patrologia, Series Latina,* XXV, 1482 f.

of the remnant of the people of God, who will be saved through the Gospel.

And it shall be as a governor (or teacher) in Judah, that is, it will be converted so thoroughly, and the Gospel will produce so much fruit, that it will even have leaders in the Word to be similar to and to be able to vie with the teachers and leaders of Judah. Thus the prophecy with which the prophet wanted merely to indicate that the kingdom of Christ would be present in spiritual hearts has been made obscure. The Gospel did teach and cleanse these hearts, even among the heathen. And that was something the Jews never believed would come to pass.

And Ekron shall be like the Jebusites, that is, Ekron will be a proselyte of the faith, just as the Jebusites were proselytes and associates-in-the-faith of the Jews in Jerusalem. They will believe the Gospel of Christ just as the Jews believed it.

8. *Then I will encamp around my house some of those who march under arms.* In Hebrew it reads: "I shall pitch a camp." We have the same word in Ps. 34:7: "He will send His angels [4] to camp around those who fear Him," that is, in the manner of an army He surrounds godly men with the protection of the angels, and He makes the angels their guards, lest they be harmed in any way. We have the same expression here, too, as if to say: "I shall strongly fortify that church which I have gathered to Myself from the Gentiles and the Jews," *so that no oppressor shall again overrun them,* "so that the godly may no longer be harassed by the oppressor, that is, by the lawgiver, but may be ruled and led by the Spirit. Therefore I shall give zealous and watchful apostles [5] and heralds of the Word, who will perform their duty well and save the flock entrusted to them, lest wolves attack that flock, lest false teachers beset it and scatter and destroy its souls." Thus those who are in charge of the ministry of the Word are the soldiers of Christ. They go out, spread the Word, and do bitter battle against Satan as much for their hearers as for the Word, for Satan never ceases going around, seeking whom he may devour, as Peter says (cf. 1 Peter 5:8), and whom he may call away from Christ through his oppressors, that is, through the teachers of works and of human righteousness.

For now I have seen. Now that the Law has been repealed and

[4] Luther quotes Ps. 34:7 as *immittet angelos suos,* but the Vulgate has *immittet angelus Domini.*

[5] The Weimar text has *epistolos.*

destroyed, I see a spiritual people coming together into one fold – both Gentiles and Jews.

9. *Rejoice greatly, O daughters of Zion!* This is, as I have said, the second part of this chapter, in which he describes the very rich comfort and broad propagation of the kingdom of Christ throughout the world among all nations. This passage is quite familiar. The evangelists have cited it (Matt. 21:5; John 12:15), and we have treated it in detail in the Postil.[6]

He comes to you a just Savior. This is quite a wonderful description of this King. Just as He is very different from all the kings of the world, so also His area of responsibility and His royal apparatus are clearly different from those which fit a king of this world. Here there is no violence, no armor, no power, no anger, no wrath. All these, you see, are proper for kings of this world. Here there are only kindness, justice, salvation, mercy, and every good thing. In short, He dispenses the sweetness and the mercy of God. He is just, because He justifies. He is Savior, because He saves. These are qualities which no king could ever bring to his throne. They are qualities far greater than those which befit a man. Moreover, all of these properties are spiritual and depict a spiritual kingdom, which the coming and accession of this just King reveal. For He comes in humility, riding on an ass. Then, too, He is not surrounded by the powers of His subjects. The powers of the people lie in their King rather than the reverse, which is true in the case of worldly kings. Here the entire passage agrees with the antithesis. For if that King of ours is just and does come to save, then we are clearly wicked and condemned sinners. Otherwise He would come with a vain intent to make us righteous and to save us.

Poor. The Hebrew word does not exactly mean "poor." One would translate it more correctly with the word "lowly," or, in German, *elend.* Luke wanted to translate it that way in the song of Mary (Luke 1:48): "For He has regarded the low estate of His handmaiden." The meaning, then, is this: "Your King is coming to you. He will bring justice and salvation. But He lacks all pomp, all royal equipment; He appears with no glory or magnificence but comes like a humble person, a common man, like one of the *hoi polloi,* like anyone of the common herd, not distinguished from others by any royal insignia. Then, too, no horses follow Him, no chariots. The lowliest animal, a jackass, carries Him."

[6] Cf. p. 287, n. 7, below.

10. *And I will cut off the chariot from Ephraim.* We have a singular (chariot) instead of the plural here. He again includes both tribes – Israel as well as Judah. The Kingdom of Israel was in Ephraim; that of Judah, in Jerusalem. Therefore this passage is filled with quite rich consolation. It is as if He were saying: "Although Israel was moved out into Media and was never brought back, yet I shall take them up along with Judah and make them one kingdom, that Israel as well as Judah may have the same faith and same Spirit. Moreover, this will be a spiritual kingdom. Therefore I shall cut off all external weapons, chariots, horses, and whatever pertains to an external kingdom. None of this weaponry has to do with My kingdom. I use none of it. There is nothing less I carry before Me than some external sign – either weapons or some symbol of an external kingdom. I am a just King and the Savior. So that kingdom of Mine is also going to be poor and humble on the surface. In it nothing regal will be apparent. But I shall clothe with spiritual power those who will be My soldiers in this kingdom of Mine. They will have dominion not over men but over death, sin, hell, and Satan, so that no creature can prevail against them. They will be My princes of salvation." This is what He calls cutting off the chariots of Ephraim. This is what Isaiah (Is. 2:4) also says: "They shall beat their swords into plowshares, etc." That is the same thing, too, which the prophet adds here: "I will cut off the war horse from Jerusalem, and the battle bow shall be cut off," that is, there will be no further concern for weaponry. Animals will not be equipped for warfare.

Because He will speak peace with the nations. Here He gives the reason [7] why He said what He did in the previous verses. That is, He will preach the forgiveness of sins to reconcile God and men. Wherever there is forgiveness and reconciliation, mutual love and peace must also follow among us. It becomes easy to reject and lay down weapons. Certainly this holds true, for Christians do not fight among themselves. After all, they are people of peace. They are like their King. They bless those who speak evil, they do good to their enemies, and they give up the cloak also to one who takes away their coat.[8] But he says *among the nations.*[9] You see, Ephraim was scattered among the na-

[7] Luther gives the technical name for this rhetorical device: αἰτιολογία.

[8] Cf. Matt. 5:38-45.

[9] Here Luther quotes *inter gentes.* At the beginning of the paragraph he had quoted *cum gentibus.* In both places he is obviously trying to paraphrase the Vulgate's *gentibus.*

tions. Therefore even Ephraim will find that predicted peace among the nations.

And His dominion shall be from sea to sea. He takes this statement from Ps. 72:8: "He will have dominion from sea to sea, etc." This is a very clear passage about the spiritual kingdom of Christ, who will close the mouths of the Jews who fancy a carnal kingdom for themselves. Here Christ the King is clearly said to be going to have dominion through the entire world – but without violence, without weapons. This cannot happen in a physical kingdom.

11. *As for You also, in the blood of Your covenant, You have set free your captives.* The emphasis is on the pronoun "You." He has already described the King and the kingdom of peace. Now he describes the way in which this kingdom was prepared and how much the preparation of the kingdom cost the King. And this entire passage is a kind of contrast, for he clearly distinguishes the blood of the old covenant from the blood of this King. "Indeed, Moses had blood, but it was the blood of goats and calves, but You have Your own blood with which You establish Your covenant." The author of the Epistle to the Hebrews explains this passage beautifully (Heb. 9:12): "He entered once for all into the Holy Place, taking not the blood of goats and calves but His own blood, thus securing an eternal redemption, etc."

This point about ransoming captives Jerome and Lyra interpret as applying to the fathers saved from the edge *(limbo)* of hell.[10] This they do with a word which they themselves have invented. It is strange that such great men have so often and so stupidly erred because of their laziness, and this in passages of the greatest comfort, where the sum of our salvation is dealt with. They have done just that here, when they speak of their dreams about the fathers, although this is spoken about the salvation of all believers, which the shedding of Christ's blood is to prepare. But if the fathers had not been saved and made righteous before they arrived in hell, they would never have been brought back. There would be no salvation for them. After all, forgiveness of sins must precede salvation; and we must receive that forgiveness while we are alive. This is exactly what happened to the fathers. While still alive they were freed and saved by that faith by which we are to be saved. For "all ate the same spiritual food, and

[10] Jerome, *Commentaria in Zachariam prophetam,* on Zech. 9:11, *Patrologia, Series Latina,* XXV, 1485.

all drank the same spiritual drink, etc." (1 Cor. 10:3-4), except that that blood had not yet been revealed. They did believe, however, that it was to be revealed. Against very clear passages of this sort, the holy fathers have some terrible hallucinations, so that their laziness in matters of Scripture disgusts me. Besides, I do not believe that the limbo exists of which these people boast so much, but without cogent testimony of Scripture. Scripture says that our dead fathers sleep in the Lord, that they are being kept in the hand of the Lord.[11] It does not say that they are relegated to limbo. Here the prophet is speaking about the covenant of Christ. That clearly is not related to the dead, because they cannot hear. It pertains to the living. Therefore to us while we are alive are declared the Gospel and the forgiveness of sins in Christ's blood shed for us. Thus by comparison he contrasts this blood of the King to the blood of goats and calves which Moses used in his covenant. Indeed, the King's own blood has confirmed this covenant – the remission of sins and eternal salvation, just as the writer said in the Epistle to the Hebrews (cf. Heb. 9:15). This is the way we must take what he says about the freed captives. He says, as it were: "In the earlier covenant the captives were freed from Egypt and were transferred to the land of Canaan. You, on the other hand, transfer captives from *the pits in which there is no water,*[12] that is, from death, sin, and hell. You see, those who have the feeling of sin also truly have the feeling of death and hell. They have neither peace nor consolation, but eternal thirst. We suddenly find ourselves in that pit when we are at the point of death, unless Christ brings us out of it.

12. *Return to your stronghold.* This is both exhortation and consolation. He is saying in substance: "Now that Christ, the King and Savior, has been revealed, and after you have heard the Gospel, return to your stronghold!" He designates no special place for this stronghold, but he still goes on with his continuing contrast. The earlier covenant had a destination where they were going – the land of Canaan. Yet, many of them murmured in the desert, and some murmured elsewhere. As a consequence, they perished and did not reach what they were wishing for. The Epistle to the Hebrews also goes into this matter in detail. Consequently, lest the same sort of thing happen to you also, lay hold of the Gospel and believe, since you have been brought back from the pit, lest you be deprived of your consolation in the end, as

[11] Luther may have in mind such passages as Acts 7:60 and 1 Thess. 4:14.
[12] The picture is the same as in Jer. 38:6.

they were deprived of the land of Canaan, which had been appointed very definitely beforehand and toward which they were struggling. To this definite location he here contrasts the "stronghold." Nevertheless, he does not name a definite place. He says, as it were: "This is that stronghold. When you will have reached it, you will be safe against every onslaught of sin, death, and hell."

Prisoners of hope. With this phrase he answers the objection of the flesh, which cannot see in Christians that dominion over every creature. In fact, the opposite seems more true. After all, Christians have been exposed to many evils. They are wretched objects of contempt before the world. They suffer persecution. They have a consciousness of their sin, the fear of death, etc. Against such thinking, he responds in sum: "You do not see the stronghold. You are still captives. Nothing is more evident than how you are still under death and sin. But be of good cheer! You are prisoners of hope. That is, you were saved in hope, as the apostle says (cf. Rom. 8:24). That liberation from the pit through the blood of Christ is based on hope. Salvation and righteousness are not visible; they lie hidden. But calling them "prisoners of hope" is a Hebraism, just as Paul also calls himself a prisoner of Christ.[13] He calls his chains the bonds of Christ and of the Gospel,[14] for those bonds are what he suffers for Christ and for the Gospel.

Today I also declare that I will restore to you double. This "today" has already been explained very well in the Epistle to the Hebrews.[15] One could take this doubling to mean the people or the Spirit multiplied because of hearing the Gospel. It is as if He were saying: "You used to be My only flock, an insignificant flock in Judea. However, by declaring the Gospel, I shall bring it to pass that you will be doubled for me and that Israel and all the nations of the earth will believe along with you." However, I am much more pleased with another statement which we find in Isaiah (Is. 40:2): "She has received from the Lord's hand double for all her sins." And here we have, "Today I declare that I will restore to you double." There the word "restore" brings no merit into the picture, lest some wicked person assign anything to his own merits or worth. Rather, this is pure grace when He restores double grace in the place of sins which have been taken away, that is, He removes from us both the Law and

13 E. g., Eph. 3:1; Philemon 1.

14 E. g., Phil. 1:13; Philemon 13.

15 Cf. *Luther's Works,* 29, pp. 147 f., on Heb. 3:7.

sin. These are the two greatest evils. Death regularly accompanies the Law and sin. After all, "the sting of death is sin, and the power of sin is the Law" (1 Cor. 15:56). It was not enough that we be freed from sin unless the author of sin also be taken away. That, of course, is the Law, which causes sin to abound, and [16] it makes demands on us and accuses us so that no conscience can ever be joyful. But that redemption is brought about by the blood of the King. In sum, the prophet is doing the following: he describes the way in which that King has arrived at this kingdom of salvation and righteousness. Through the Word we are justified and freed. We are moved from the kingdom of darkness into the kingdom of light by the power of Christ's blood. Then we live in hope.

13. *I have bent Judah as My bow. I have made Ephraim its arrow.* There follows a compounding and spreading of this function. You see, from Judah and Ephraim, He says, that grace is to be spread also among all nations. But He accords this honor to Judah and Ephraim, to name them first, for Christ was properly their own because He had been promised to them. John says (John 4:22): "Salvation is from the Jews." Paul, too, always places the Jews first when he speaks about the justified Jews and Gentiles. He says (Rom. 1:16): "To the Jew first and also to the Greek." But what follows now seems to disagree with His previous words, where He said that He would take away the bows and chariots from Ephraim and the horses from Jerusalem, and where He established the entire kingdom on the Word and the Spirit (cf. v. 10). But here He mentions armor, bows, and swords again. I respond this way: The previous statement is the very sum of truth when the lowly King is described as walking without any royal equipment. Thus He did walk. He even described in the same way His kingdom and those who belong to it. These points He made in clear words, without any metaphor, so that they could not be understood any other way. Therefore to that earlier simplicity we must apply the present words as figurative. We must understand the sword, bow, and other things metaphorically that they may not appear to disagree with His earlier clear statement. The meaning, therefore, is this: "I shall take up both of these kingdoms – Judah as well as Ephraim. I shall use their conversion not only to convert the Jews but also to convert all nations throughout the world when I spread the Gospel throughout the world through them. I shall use their works that these

[16] We have followed the Erlangen edition in reading *et* for *ut*.

works may declare also to the Gentiles that salvation has been offered to them through My blood. I shall stretch Judah as My bow. That is, with Judah I shall shoot My arrow of the preaching of the Gospel in order that many nations may be wounded by that bow of Mine and become subject to Me." We also have this in Ps. 45:5: "Your arrows are sharp. The peoples will fall beneath You."

And Ephraim. That is, I shall fill the apostles and other disciples with the Holy Spirit that they may fire arrows among the nations with the Word of grace. This is an interpretation of that which he said earlier: "He will speak peace to the nations, and His dominion shall be from sea to sea" (v. 10).

Like a warrior's sword. The Word of the Gospel will be effective. It will burst forth among the nations and will produce rich fruit.

14. *And the Lord God will appear over them.* The disciples, apostles, and heralds of the Gospel will declare and bear witness of the power of the Word with miracles and with steadfastness. No one who has seen these signs and the strength of character in the apostles would be able to deny that the power of God was in them and that the Lord was using their efforts as tools of a sort for His purpose.

Like lightning. No one will be able to hinder the Word. It will run and burst forth rapidly from east to west like lightning. No one will slow it down as it runs and flashes. So also, no one will be able to slow either the effectiveness or the course of the Word.

With a trumpet, that is, with the Gospel. *And He will march forth in the whirlwinds of the south.* A storm from the south is the most powerful of all. With this expression He indicates the power of the Gospel as it is preached. He says, as it were: "The Word will go forth with great power. Like a whirlwind and a storm, it will snatch up nations and peoples. It will humiliate and scatter them in such a way that it will first mortify and condemn them and then bring them back to life and save them." This is the way the Holy Spirit operates in converting the wicked.

15. *He will protect them, and they shall devour, etc.* He takes delight in a sort of pleasant affectation for metaphors and in figurative language. With all of these, he describes the power of the Gospel as it is preached, and commends its magnificence and glory. But He indicates that ministers of the Word have been, in times of persecution, exposed to many perils and have been destined for death, as we read

in Ps. 44:22. They are prisoners of hope. Therefore they need the Lord to defend them, and He does defend them, just as He says (Matt. 10:30): "Even the hairs of your head are all numbered." Also (Zech. 2:8): "For he who touches you touches the apple of My [17] eye." Moreover, He does not merely defend the body. Even after the body has been killed, He sees to it that the Word is effective and stands firm against Satan and every foe. This redounds to His glory.

They will devour, that is, they will lay hold of and will censure sinners, just as Christ says (cf. John 16:8): "The Holy Spirit convinces the world of sin." Once they have mortified them, they will eat them, that is, they will incorporate them to themselves through the faith of the Gospel. This is the same thing which He says about the cornerstone. He says, as it were: "They will hurl and thrust My Gospel out among the nations, and their preaching will be effective."

They shall drink and be full of talk, that is, they will cause a disturbance. With all these expressions He signifies the blessed success of the Gospel among the heathen. That is, they will rejoice over the conversion of the heathen as the drinker rejoices over his wine when he drinks his pleasant fill.

They will be filled like bowls. This is another metaphor, drawn here from bowls – the bowl is *eine Schale* ("a shallow vessel"). They were used in sacrifices to hold wine and the blood of sacrificed animals. He says in substance: "They will toy with the heathen as the priests toyed with the bowls and other vessels of the sacrifices. They will sacrifice and offer the heathen with their preaching." This, too, is what Paul says (Rom. 15:16): "I am in the priestly service of the Gospel . . . so that the offering of the Gentiles may be acceptable," that is, "through the Gospel I make the Gentiles a sacrifice and bring it to pass that Gentiles thus sanctified become an acceptable offering to the Lord." In this way, all the heralds of the Word offer sinners and the unrighteous to the Lord when those heralds kill and drive them to despair with the Word in order to turn them to righteousness. Thus the apostle Paul was filled with the blood of many Gentiles. And so with this one word the prophet here has explained the entire rationale for the sacrifices of the Old Testament as concerns what they relate and pertain to, namely, the ministry of the Word.

16. *And the Lord their God will save them.* That is, He alone is

[17] Luther changes the pronoun to suit his construction.

the means to salvation. We must anticipate no salvation other than that which happens by the Word of the Gospel, about which we are now speaking. But its revelation lies in the future. All of this now is only the prelude until salvation becomes known. Thus the prophet uses many different metaphors. In our language these are quite difficult; in Hebrew, however, they are most appropriate. Indeed, because the Jewish people regularly used sacrifices, they could easily accept metaphors therefrom – something we cannot do. Yet, the metaphors related to eating and drinking which he mentioned here are frequent even among other nations. We have this in Job (Job 5:5) also: "The strong will drink of his wealth," and in Ps. 79:7: "They have devoured Jacob." Also (Ps. 14:4): "They have eaten up My people, etc.," that is, they have exhausted them. They have flayed them. Even the Latin uses this terminology. They all have become drained.

The flock of His people. Christ and the apostles had studied this prophet quite closely. For they use many words from this prophet in their prayers. They even bring out some passages here and there. In this way Christ always has on the tip of His tongue the word "flock" when He calls Christians His sheep.

Because they will be lifted up as holy jewels above His land. We noted the rite of the Nazarites from Num. 6: how the Nazarites were sanctified for the Lord, how they never shaved and went about bareheaded, etc. The Hebrews call that rite נֵזֶר which we translate as *Zucht* ("discipline") in German. But they had a certain voluntary abstemiousness with which they would serve God, lest they backslide into idolatry. Indeed, they were very pleased to be religious people. And here, it is to this rite of the Nazarites and, in fact, to all sacrifices, eatings, festivals – briefly, to all ceremonies – that the prophet alludes. And through allegory he relates all this to Christ. This is what the apostles and the true heralds of the Word do. For this is what the apostle Paul calls building gold, silver, and precious stones on the foundation (cf. 1 Cor. 3:12). The apostle Paul presents the same thing in Gal. 4 when he allegorically interprets the account of the two brothers Ishmael and Isaac. Here, then, the prophet speaks about Christ with many obscure metaphors and figures of speech because he has discussed the same matter earlier with clear and direct language. Therefore the Nazarite jewels are the apostles and heralds of the Gospel, who, he says, are to be lifted up above His earth. But the Hebrew word does not exactly mean "to lift up" but "to be raised" as an ensign or banner is raised in war. This is apparent in Ex. 17:15 in connection with the altar which had been built. There Moses adds: "And called the name of it 'The Lord is my נִסִּי ("banner"),'" that is, the banner or military ensign which attracts the eyes of onlookers to it. In this way, then, he calls apostles and ministers Nazarite jewels, who are to be lifted up like a banner. The apostles and the heralds of the Word are the foundation of the church, but they must be as dedicated and consecrated to the Lord as the Nazarites were, that is, they must teach the Gospel and faith in the purest way. They must not pollute these with human teachings or mix them with the leaven of hypocrites. The apostles were men like this, as Zechariah here prophecies about them.

They shall be lifted up, namely, through the Holy Spirit in the land, like leaders or like banners at which the hearers of the Gospel would look. Indeed, where the Gospel is preached, there a battle begins, because the world and Christ cannot be in harmony. So then they do battle. The godly apostles, trusting in Scripture, oppose the enemies of godliness and close their foes' mouths. This is the way the Holy Spirit exalts them when He supplies faithful heralds of the Gospel who do not seek their own greatness, who do not curry the favor of others, who do not hunger after wealth and honor, but who seek only to enrich Christ, to return both the talent they received and rich interest, and thus they are dedicated and consecrated to Christ alone. Then they are true Nazarites, when they teach the pure Gospel of Christ without mixing in their own hallucinations and human doctrines, as does follow. But this is an opportunity to see the wonderful result and reason for what has come earlier. He says (v. 15): "On that day the Lord their God will save them, etc. For they shall be lifted up like the jewels of נֵזֶר, etc." But the prophet is discussing this to indicate by what plan or in what way He wants to save, namely, through the Word, by sending apostles to declare Christ, to draw to Him by their preaching those in whom the Gospel is effective. Of course, these apostles must be "jewels of נֵזֶר," that is, they must be dedicated to the Lord. They must teach the unspoiled Gospel sincerely. Otherwise they are not "jewels of נֵזֶר."

17. *Yea, how great is His goodness.* This passage has been twisted very badly in favor of the Sacrament of the Eucharist. That happens because it mentions grain and wine. So great obviously was the intolerable negligence of the holy writers, especially when it would have been proper to be extremely sober and vigilant. Jerome, along with

the Jews, charges the Septuagint with ignorance because they translated "grain of young men and new wine that brings forth maidens." But I feel that Jerome is the one who has translated this badly. I subscribe to the Septuagint version, and that is the way I read *frumentum electorum et vinum* [18] *germinans virgines.*[19] And so the meaning of the passage is this: Not with might, not with physical armament, not with a warlike attack will Christ save His people. He will do this with beauty and delight. He will save not with the savagery of weapons but with majesty and beauty, as we have it in Ps. 45:4. This is what he here calls grain and wine: the Gospel, which is Christ's greatest honor and beauty. With this Gospel He attracts hearts which taste that sweetness of the Gospel. You see, the Gospel is the light and ray in which Christ is glorified, because He now has praises, celebration, magnificence, majesty, beauty, and the thousand things the Psalms call by other names when they describe the beauty of Christ. This Gospel, he says, will be something pleasant. In fact, with the Gospel He will produce strong young men and women, not helpless infants such as are born from the weak begetting of the flesh. No, these will immediately be healthy young men and beautiful maidens, as such young ladies generally are when they are about to be married, and such as young men in the flower of youth are wont to be. As a result, there is a miracle connected with their birth. In sum, He indicates that the people of the Gospel will be robust, energetic, and cheerful, both in spirit and in faith. After all, in Christ there is no old age but an everlasting bloom of youth. In Christ, there is no sad senility which begins to trouble one with various ills – the sort of problem which happens to those who have left adolescence far behind and have reached a ripe old age. Youth has none of those ills. It makes the hearts of young men energetic and immune to all grief and worry. Just so, too, are the girls who are still in the bloom of youth, etc.

18 We have subsituted *vinum* for *mustum* to give the Vulgate reading Luther has in mind: "the grain of the elect and the wine springing forth virgins."

19 Luther means to say that the Septuagint version is the way he understands what he quotes in the Vulgate version. The Septuagint version is σῖτος νεανίσκοις καὶ οἶνος εὐωδιάζων εἰς παρθένους ("grain for young men and flavorous wine for virgins").

CHAPTER TEN

The prophet continues to play with allegories, metaphors, and figures of speech, just as he had begun. But this section is cited almost word for word in Matt. 4, where the evangelist describes Christ's preaching in Galilee. This entire section consists of contrast, too; for he separates genuine preachers and the genuine Word of God from hypocrites and false teachers who are not "the jewels of נֵזֶר" but speak of the vision of their own heart. Here, then, is the meaning.

1. *Ask rain from the Lord in the season of the spring rain.* The emphasis here is on *the Lord.* He says, as it were: "Stick with God and 'beware of the leaven of the Pharisees' (Matt. 16:6), lest they impose it on you in the guise of right and lest they cause you to wander off into the desert just as sheep become lost when the shepherd goes away." All this has happened. After all, when Christ came, everything had become mixed with human traditions and Pharisaical leaven.

Scripture in many places mentions a twofold rain. I have discussed it elsewhere in detail. The first is the one which enriches the earth so that it may receive what has been sowed. The other one wards off dryness after sowing has been received to water the growth, lest it wither. The first rain was the teaching of the Law. He says in substance: "You have the prophets with you. They rebuke and restrain you with the Law alone as with a sort of overseer. It is a difficult thing for you to endure those prophets. Therefore I give you another bit of advice. Leave the Law. Ask for the second rain. Stick to the grain of young men and the fresh wine of maidens. Then your consciences will be lifted up when the tyranny of the Law has been removed. So long as you fear that tyranny, you must be afraid; you must carry a very heavy burden." Thus he speaks in contrasts, as I have said.

The Lord will make the storm clouds and showers of rain. What our translator [1] calls *showers of rain* is a single word in Hebrew.[2]

[1] The Vulgate.

[2] *Pluviam imbris* in the Vulgate translated the Hebrew מְטַר־גֶּשֶׁם ("rain-shower"), a single word but in compound form. The problem word, however,

Grammarians are not yet agreed as to exactly what it[3] means. In all of Scripture it is used three times: twice in Job (Job 28:26 and 38:25) and here in Zechariah. The Septuagint translators render it φαντασίας ("bright signs"). However, to me it seems to mean that storm which generally occurs in spring after winter has passed, when a little louder thunder shakes the earth. They do say, after all, that thunder benefits both earth and growth; that because of that thunderclap the earth is opened and fertilized. This, then, is the meaning I give: It is as if he were saying: "When you will have asked the Lord for the spring rain, He will grant you a rich increase. He will give more than you will have asked, for He will give the abundant, great, and heavy rain with the spring storm, which customarily enriches the ground. *That each may have vegetation in his field,* that is, wherever people will have asked for the Gospel, there it will be preached with the greatest increase. It will produce the richest fruit.

2. *For the teraphim have spoken.* He uses different figurative language to describe false teachers, just as he has earlier described Christ's genuine preachers. He calls false teachers idols, diviners, liars, dreamers, etc.

The dreamers.[4] He means those who are preoccupied with dreams and foolish hallucinations. Jude in his Epistle (Jude 8) also calls them dreamers. They connect their dreams to everything they say when they prescribe works with which they deceive the unwary and with which they want wretched consciences to comfort themselves. And they add that God approves of works of this sort. For this they promise God's favor. In this way they destroy souls with a false promise about which not even they are sure. This is a situation which ruins souls. So he adds:

Therefore, the people have been scattered like sheep; they are afflicted for want of a shepherd. He indicates that the scattering is not a common or simple one but the sort of one in which each sheep seeks forage for itself when in some way the shepherd has been removed. Then it happens that the sheep wander here and there, become weak,

with which Luther deals in the following sentences is the Hebrew word חֲזִיז ("thunderbolt," "lightning flash"), which the Vulgate translates with *nives* ("bright clouds," or "storm clouds").

[3] To make this and the following references true, we must think of חֲזִיז as the antecedent.

[4] From this point on and up to v. 7 the verse numbers in the Weimar text are incorrect. We have corrected these numbers.

and perish. We have absolutely the same statement with clear language and without any figures of speech in Isaiah (cf. Is. 53:6): "Each has turned to his own way. All we like sheep have gone astray." Here the prophet has to write these things in obscure terms and with figurative language. Otherwise, had he said this in direct language so that they had understood, he who was connecting and preaching the rejection and blinding of the people at the same time with their acceptance and restoration would doubtless have imperiled his own life. Then, too, the prophet had come for this; he had been sent for this: to comfort and cheer up an afflicted people who were very wretched and oppressed; to encourage them to go on with building the temple; to declare that the Lord would come and bless what they had begun; and finally, to remind them that the Lord would send the King He had promised to their fathers. Therefore, had he connected to those comforting promises clear threats which they understood, he would have frightened them away from their undertaking and from proceeding with building the temple. So he treated the threats and wrath of God with obscure terminology that, finally, only those might understand who should understand. In the number of those were the apostles, all the Jews who were converted to Christ, and we Gentiles who believe the Gospel, which promises the remission of sins in Christ, etc.

3. *My anger is hot against the shepherds.* This is not a complicated statement, but the grammatical arrangement slows us a bit. The meaning is this: "The shepherds are only scattering the flock. They are not taking them to pasture. They cause the destruction of souls. They are troublesome teraphim and diviners. They still are spreading their dreams. They are not the *Nezer*[5] of the Lord. Therefore I am angry with them. I shall bring punishment upon them."

And against the he-goats. This passage is also in Matthew (Matt. 25:32), when he says, "He will separate the sheep from the goats." So here he calls "he-goats" those foul teachers who only flay the flock. There is a similar passage in Ezek. 34:11: "I Myself will search for My sheep and will seek them out." So here he is saying that the Lord Himself is going to visit His flock – the house of Judah; that the Lord finally will come to feed and call His flock back from its wandering, etc.

And He made them like His proud steed. Here he repeats the earlier vision about the horses sent out before Jerusalem. This he has already described in chapter 6. But he is speaking in pictures. Above,

[5] Cf. Nazarites, p. 102.

in chapter 9, he said that the Lord would wipe out the horse and chariot from Judah. There he also described the spiritual kingdom of Christ. Here the prophet says that the Lord is going to take up Judah like His proud steed. These two ideas seem to disagree with each other. But here again we must warn you as we have warned you earlier. We must observe this principle especially in Scripture that earlier words to which those words which come later refer always take priority. Also, those statements which have been uttered very simply without any figurative language and obscure words interpret those which are uttered with figurative and metaphorical language. An open statement of words in which there is no figurative language carries by far the greater weight. This is something which the prophets of our time should know. They cry out, mix heaven with earth, and think that they have won the palm of victory over us when they can produce some obscure passage against us but meantime ignore many passages which say the same thing or the opposite very simply and clearly without any obscure figurative language. So it happens that, as far as they are concerned, Scripture is never in harmony with itself. Therefore we must also do the same thing here. Those statements which are spoken obscurely and with figures we must apply and interpret in connection with those which are spoken simply and without figures and cannot be understood in any other way. Here there is a metaphor. "I shall make them – My apostles and elect, who believe the Gospel – like My proud steed, like a beautiful, well-equipped horse, like a triumphant steed, decorated with caparison, bosses, and every kind of beautiful trapping." You see, this is what the word "praise" means, as I have mentioned before. Thus He is speaking of a spiritual horse and a spiritual battle, in which He treads underfoot the heathen through the preaching of the Gospel, through the preaching of the apostles and other heralds of the Word. They are, after all, proud steeds; that is, they are filled with the Holy Spirit. They break through with their preaching so that it becomes effective even when all creation battles against it. To this also that which follows pertains; and that cannot be taken just as the words sound.

4. *Out of it shall come the cornerstone; out of it, the tent peg.* He signifies that the people of the Jews will not be completely rejected, that a certain remnant will be saved. The same statement is made in clear language in Isaiah: "A remnant of Israel will return to the Lord their God" (cf. Is. 10:21). This clear statement the prophet here brings

out obscurely and figuratively as he speaks about a cornerstone and tent peg. This is the Hebrew expression which Ezra also used in a prayer of his: "Preserve for us, O Lord, the wall of Jerusalem and a peg from the house of the Lord" (cf. Ezra 9:8-9). Here the prophet says the same thing. He says in substance: "Even if the others have clung to their dreamers and wolves who are eager only to destroy souls, I shall nevertheless still take for Myself the cornerstone, although almost the entire house – that is, Israel and Judah – may have been rejected. From that cornerstone which I saved, I shall build Myself a new house, the church. I shall allow the people to be scattered and to wander, to be overwhelmed and to drown in their errors. I shall redeem for Myself a certain few who will be My tent peg. On them I shall hang the many beautiful vessels and ornaments of My house, as we read in Isaiah (Is. 22:23-24), that is, many faithful people will cling to those priests and heralds of Mine whom I have chosen. Those men will see to it that many are converted to the Gospel, that My house may have greater splendor, equipment, and decoration." In this way Paul is an outstanding peg in Christ's church. From him many great vessels were suspended: Timothy, Titus, Apollos, and others. Peter was another such peg.

The battle bow. That is, "I shall subdue many peoples with the preachment of the Gospel. For such preaching I shall use them as an archer uses his bow."

Every ruler. This refers to every teacher of the Law who only weighs down and oppresses consciences with the revelation of the Law. After all, Isaiah (Is. 9:4) does call the Law "the rod of the oppressor."

5. *They will be like mighty men.* The Hebrew word [6] is elegant. It means a hero or a giant, as is evident from Ps. 19:5: "Like a strong man runs with joy," and Ps. 45:3: "Gird your sword upon your thigh, O mighty one." For "giant" there we read "O most mighty one." Here we have the same meaning as we had earlier in chapter 9 regarding the grain of young men and the new wine of maidens. He says, as it were: "These will not be infants or weaklings but heroes and mighty giants, outstanding warriors, so that they can tread down anything easily." So he says that there will be wonderful heroes who are going to conquer not with weapons, not with arms and sword, but by treading upon. They have strength in their feet and in their step. By this

[6] גִּבּוֹר.

treading-upon the prophet here signifies nothing else but the ministry of the Word. This ministry Scripture everywhere compares with feet and running. For the Word of God runs, etc. In sum: They will dominate and make subject the necks of the proud, the self-righteous, the saints, and teachers of this world, for these are what he calls "mud." After all, through the Gospel we are told that our wisdom, righteousness, holiness, might, and power – briefly, whatever is in us – have been condemned. They have no use other than to be trampled on. We are further told that righteousness, wisdom, and salvation have been set forth and exhibited in Christ alone; that God has made Him alone our sanctification and redemption. Consequently, when the human heart hears and grasps this preaching, it immediately considers all its own righteousness as dung, as Paul also says that whatever does not come from faith is sin (cf. Rom. 14:23). But in our translation the reading is bad.[7] Read it this way: "They will crush them like clods of mud in the streets."

And they will fight because the Lord is with them. This is the interpretation of that sharp battle and successful trampling. In substance he says: "They will wage that great war not by force of arms but with a new kind of strategy, namely, through the presence of the Lord. This is what Paul says in 1 Cor. 3:7: "Neither he who plants nor he who waters is anything, but only God who gives the growth." Thus with their preaching the apostles only planted. The Lord, however, placed their word into the hearts of their hearers, and thus, by the power of the Spirit, which the Lord added to the Word, they trampled down all the boldest and wisest things of the world.

The riders of the horses will be confounded. The Lord will need no horses, no uproar of weaponry. Instead, merely with the Spirit, the Lord will carry on that wonderful battle of His with His new giants.

6. *And I will comfort the house of Judah and save the house of Joseph.* Earlier we heard several times about the eternal rejection of the kingdom of Israel; that the kingdom of Israel had not been restored, was not to be restored. But the kingdom of Judah has been restored. However, small remnants were the beginning of that restoration, and this happened because of the coming of Christ's kingdom. But here He says that He will comfort and save Israel as well as Judah (for the kingdom of Israel comes under the name "the House

[7] The Vulgate's *conculcantes lutum viarum.*

of Joseph"). These two clearly seem to disagree with each other, unless we apply to a spiritual taking up and bringing back what he says here about the Gospel preached in all the world, the Gospel which reconciled to God many from Israel who believed. That eternal rejection, however, applies to the external rejection of the kingdom and the priesthood; that Israel was not led back and the kingdom was not restored; that it did not have its earlier status. Therefore what follows proves that this passage is to be understood about a spiritual conversion. "Because I have pity on them, I justify them and forgive their sins. Thus it comes to pass that they please Me, that I take them up, etc." However, what we here read, "I will comfort the house of Judah," reads more meaningfully in Hebrew, "I shall see to it that Judah prevails," or "that Judah conquers." We have the very same statement in Gen. 7:18: "The waters of the Flood prevailed," that is, they overwhelmed everything.

And they will be just as they were. This does not indicate the way of life of the restored people. Instead He intends this, as if to say: "As they were in grace, as they had a kind and peaceful God before they were rejected; so also they will then have a God who is a gentle, protecting, pleasant Father, who wants to preserve and protect them."

I shall answer them. That is, "The mercy and their conversion will be so great because I am their God, who answers them." This statement embraces in totality the function of Christ's entire kingdom and the sum of Christianity. He says, as it were: "They will pray to Me, and I shall answer as they pray." This, after all, is the sum and substance of Christ's kingdom: to pray and to be heard. Under the word for "prayer" we include also the preaching and praise of God, that is, that we preach the Word of the Gospel and that this embellishes and praises the goodness and grace of God in Christ. Then, too, that we pray. You see, Satan, sin, the world, and our flesh attack us constantly. Many evils beset us daily. Therefore there never is a time when we do not need to pray that God's name be hallowed, that the Word of God bear fruit, and that Christ's kingdom be extended. This is the whole life of the Christian in the presence of God, as Paul also teaches throughout his letters.

7. *And Ephraim shall become like a mighty warrior.* Here we must take a very careful look at the prophet's plan. What is his goal? Where is he going? At what point is he in describing Christ's kingdom? Now, he clearly is using a comparison to show that he is speaking

metaphorically, lest the Jews imagine that they are being promised some sort of carnal kingdom and power. He says, "He will be like a mighty warrior," as if to say that they will not be physical giants or heroes (He does use the same word as he did earlier), but that they will be spiritual giants and heroes – by the power of the Spirit through the Word of the Gospel. In fact, they will be so mighty that no one will be able to overcome them and that they themselves will overcome, even though they now are scattered and thrown about among the Medes and Syrians.

And their hearts shall be glad as with wine. That is, they will have secure and happy consciences in the presence of God. No longer will the Law and sin be able to terrify and condemn them. Rather, they will believe that their sins have been forgiven and that they have received grace and redemption in Christ, as he adds here:

Their hearts shall exult in the Lord, as if to say: "That joy will lie not in their own wisdom and righteousness."

8. *I will signal for them.* This is a lovely phrase or idiom of Hebrew. It means to whistle or breathe upon, to stimulate someone's mind or emotions. It appears also in Isaiah:[8] "He will whistle for the fly which is in the land of Egypt" (Is. 7:18). That is, He will move it with His breath. He will cause a breeze, as He says elsewhere. The meaning, then, of this point is this: "I shall whistle for them. I shall encourage them. I shall cause them to approach their task with joy. I shall not give them many laws to coerce and drive them. They will not be hypocrites. On the contrary, willingly and joyfully they will take charge of their ministry of the Word, Christians are a voluntary people. In sum, through the Word I shall send My Spirit into them. He will stimulate them and make them active and enthusiastic. Thus I shall gather them together in the unity of faith."

For I have redeemed them. This is the sweetest signal which makes our hearts rejoice. When our hearts hear that Christ has died for our sins and that what He has done is sufficient, we have been moved from the kingdom of darkness into the kingdom of the brightness of the Son of God. We have become coheirs with Christ, etc.

And I shall multiply them. He explains this multiplication as he adds:

9. *I will scatter them among the peoples.* Everywhere he runs into

[8] The text has "Jeremiah," but Isaiah is quoted.

the carnal thinking of the Jews, for the Jews were thinking that all were to be gathered together in the land of Canaan, from which they had been driven by the judgment of God. But the prophet describes the strange gathering together and multiplying by saying that they would be scattered among all peoples, into the farthest parts of the world. We cannot take this to mean carnal multiplication, for it is so very clear so that the prophet may rescue us completely from the tangled errors of the Jews. The scattering, however, we must take as a blessing. In this way Peter, Paul, and the other apostles are those seeds and kernels of grain which are scattered among the heathen to preach the Word and to win them for the Lord through the Gospel.

And from afar they shall remember Me. This is a bad reading,[9] and this text has been badly mangled by punctuation as well. Read it this way: "Among distant peoples they will remember Me." As I have said, this is a strange gathering which simply does not fit that idea which the Jews had falsely imagined. The meaning is this: "They will remember Me among distant peoples. That is, they will preach Me. They will equip Me with heralds and will make Me known among all nations through the Gospel." For so Scripture uses the word "remember," as Christ also says: "Do this in remembrance of Me" (Luke 22:19). Therefore we must understand this passage to refer to the preaching of the Gospel which the apostles did in all the earth and to the gathering into the church of Christ through faith. Ps. 87:4 also has the same thing: "Behold, strangers and Tyre and the people of Ethiopia, 'These were born there.'" Also, we have it in Is. 60:4: "Your sons shall come from far."

And they shall live, and their children too. That is, they will be well taken care of. They will not mourn, as they did in their previous captivity. Evils will not oppress them, but they will rejoice and return with their children. "To live" here means to be well taken care of. That is, in the midst of death, sin, and hell, they will live by faith. No creature will separate them from the love of God. They will triumph over Satan and the gates of hell.

10. *And I will bring them home from the land of Egypt.* From the preceding verses and from those which follow, one is completely convinced that the prophet is speaking about a spiritual return, for he adds: "And I will bring them to the land of Gilead and Lebanon"; not

[9] Luther apparently objects to the Vulgate's *de longe,* for which he suggests the emendation *inter longinquos.*

to Jerusalem or Mount Zion, as they perhaps are thinking, but to Gilead. Gilead was the closest section of the Holy Land toward the north; Lebanon, the farthest. With this incongruity, He shows that He is speaking of a spiritual return. Surely the Jews were aware of this, that their captivity would be returned to Jerusalem, not to Lebanon or to Gilead. Therefore the meaning is this: There will be many Christians everywhere throughout the earth. We have absolutely the same meaning and same point at the end of Obadiah (Obad. 19): "Those of the Negeb will possess Mount Esau, etc." Jerome [10] relates that there were many outstanding Christians within the borders of Arabia at the time the church was founded there.

And no room will be found for them. He says, as it were: "There will be so many that one place will not be able to hold them all. Instead, they will have been scattered among distant peoples throughout the earth." This is the same thing Christ says: "The hour is coming when neither on this mountain nor in Jerusalem will you worship the Father" (John 4:21).

11. *And it shall cross at the channel of the sea.* "Channel" they call the narrows, or inlet, of the sea, where the sea is held in tightly and is constricted, and where it is narrow like a neck on a body. Beyond that channel it again opens up and spreads out far and wide again into its vast, broad expanse. The Hellespont is like this. He means that the Gospel is to be preached even among the Greeks.

And he shall strike the waves in the sea. He imitates the psalm (Ps. 65:7): "You who disturb the depths of the sea and the roaring of its waves, etc." He says, in substance: "He will strike those who live along the Hellespont and in the coastal cities and even the waves of the sea," that is, "He will strike the tyrants who hold sway in the coastal cities, who are in complete control and who persecute the Gospel. He will convert them so that those who a little earlier had hated the Gospel and its heralds with bitter hatred now have changed hearts and are friends of the Gospel.

The depths of the Nile. These are the chiefs, the tyrants, the wise, the righteous, and the powerful in whose hands is all control.

Thus the pride of Assyria shall be laid low. The prophet is taking a trip throughout the world. First he mentions Egypt, then Greece.

[10] Jerome, *Commentaria in Zachariam prophetam, Patrologia, Series Latina,* XXV, 1494.

Here he comes into Assyria to indicate the course and passage of the Gospel throughout the world among all nations.

And the scepter of Egypt shall depart. That is, no taskmaster, no tyrant of the Law, will afflict Christians anymore. No one will rule over them, because there is only one Lord who takes possession of the hearts of Christians. Everything else is left behind. There is nothing of the Law for any Christian.

13. *I will make them strong.* Again he adds this, of necessity, as if to say: "They will be strong, not in their own might but in Christ. In His name they will walk." That is, they will believe and live in the faith which has Christ as its object.

CHAPTER ELEVEN

Up to this point the prophet has foretold Christ's coming kingdom and what fruit the Word, to be published through the apostles throughout the world would produce; namely, that the heathen would be converted to the faith. All the prophets were aware of and knew well that that external kingdom of the Jews would end when Christ came; that that kingdom had to yield to Christ, the new King, that He might establish that new throne of His from which He intended to rule from sea to sea and over the lands of the earth. However, because the Jews had an insuperable stubbornness and were unwilling to yield to their new King, they were compelled to yield. Their kingdom as well as their priesthood were destroyed, and they themselves, miserable wretches, were thrown out and cut off from Christ's kingdom, while barely a tiny remnant was saved.

The prophet will discuss the same matter in this chapter. Here, however, he will do this with strangely obscure and involved language. You see, not only is the prophet himself quite obscure in this chapter, but the variety of interpretations also increases the obscurity. If we shall have disentangled ourselves from this chapter, I believe we shall have overcome whatever is obtuse and difficult to explain in this prophet.

1. *Open, O Lebanon.* Here he calls the temple at Jerusalem "Lebanon." As far as external matters were concerned, those people had nothing more lofty and sacred than that temple. He calls it "Lebanon," because they had built it with the cedars of Lebanon, as Ezra shows (Ezra 3:7). He also calls it "Lebanon" by metonymy to obscure the prophecy of the destruction of the temple by the Romans. That figure of speech, or metaphor, pleases even Latin writers. He calls the temple "Lebanon" because much timber from Lebanon was in the temple, and because the greater part of the temple consisted of logs from Lebanon. So we could say the same thing about the Hercynian Forest. Furthermore, he uses the imperative mood and indicates, nevertheless, that this still is going to happen. He says, as it were: "The temple which you are now building, preserving, and guarding will ultimately

lie open, deserted, and ruined when Christ comes. It will lie exposed to the entry of enemies from Rome. No might will be sufficient to keep the foes from breaking in."

Your cedars, that is, fire will destroy your buildings.

2. *Wail, O cypress.* He addresses himself to inanimate objects for the sake of the people. You see, he is referring to the sorrow of the people because of their ruined temple.

Your glories have been destroyed, that is, all the fine and wonderful decorations of the temple. For the ornamentation of the temple was outstanding, as I have already mentioned, and its sacrificial vessels were very beautiful, so much so that also the disciples of Christ admired the structure of the temple. The passage in the Gospel account (Mark 13:1) is well known.

Wail, oaks of Bashan. Bashan, beyond the Jordan, is the region of King Og. Later it was called Gilead and Manasseh. It is a well-known place in the land of Canaan. Oaks abound there – a fact which Isaiah reveals (Is. 2:13): "The Lord will be exalted above all the oaks of Bashan." Here, too, the prophet speaks to those oaks which had been carried away from there for use in building the temple.

The thick forest has been felled. Again he describes the destruction of the temple. But he calls the temple "the thick forest," as above he called it "Lebanon." Earlier he was considering the various architectural devices and the splendor of the timbers and columns of the temple.

3. *There is the sound of the wailing of the shepherds.* This is a Hebraism whose meaning is as follows: When the temple will be destroyed and the city also leveled, then one will hear the wailing of the shepherds, that is, of the princes and scribes, whose hands hold everything in their control. The kingdom, the priesthood – yes, every glory of the temple and of the city – will perish in the fire.

And the sound of the roaring of lions. Among the Hebrew-speaking, the rich and powerful are called "the young lions." Ps. 34:10 reveals this too, where we read: "The wealthy are in want and hunger," the Hebrew is, "The young lions are in want, etc."

The pride of Jordan. The Hebrew word properly means preeminence. In Moses' song, we read: "The Lord has triumphed gloriously" (Ex. 15:1). That is, in going up, He has become preeminent. He is conspicuous above all things. He rides high. So also here the prophet indicates greatness or preeminence. Moreover, he calls the people "Jordan." Certainly the Jordan is the principal river – the king of rivers – greater than others in that land. The Hebrew language has this custom, that the people or the land in which a great river flows or a lofty mountain stands bears the name of that river or mountain. This we see in Ps. 42:6: "I shall remember you from the land of Jordan and of Hermon, from Mount Mizar." Metaphors of this type please the Jews and are as clear to them as they are obscure to us. To summarize this passage then: The preeminence of that kingdom which is near the Jordan will be diminished and torn down.

4. *Thus says the Lord: Become shepherd to the flock doomed to slaughter.* He has described the destruction of the kingdom. In a new discourse he now goes on to describe their fault which earned them their destruction. This is a difficult and quite obscure chapter, as I mentioned at the beginning of our treatment of it. I have perspired much over it to arrive at the genuine meaning. Lyra applies this to their continuing history, but I disapprove of this. After all, in explaining the prophets we must take utmost care that we do not make them historians except when reason and necessity clearly compel us to do so. Consequently, this is the meaning I draw. He throws all the blame for the destruction on the wicked teachers and scribes, who shamefully abused the ministry of the Word in order to look after their own lusts and greed. Greed controlled the Pharisees when Christ came as the true Shepherd and King. So they used to laugh at Christ when He taught. They held Him in contempt. They remained servants to their own profits. Therefore this entire chapter exactly fits this time of Christ and His apostles. We should not twist it to mean anything else, for if one will take it to mean something different, everything in the chapter will not fit together.

Thus we have here the command of the Father in which He orders Christ to perform His office energetically, to preach the Word. The Father says as it were: "Christ, preach among those wretched people over whom nothing but slaughter holds sway." The "slaughter" is the error and destruction of their souls. After all, He is speaking of spiritual slaughter, which occurs as a result of the impious teaching of the wicked teachers. This is quite clear and obvious from the verses following. The evangelist Matthew also reveals this when he writes that Christ goes into Galilee and laments over the people because they were wandering without a shepherd (cf. Matt. 9:36).

5. *Those who had possessed them.* He calls them "possessors" to indicate the tyranny of the priests and scribes. Arbitrarily, they treat their subjects savagely. They destroy souls as well as bodies and property as if the kingdom had been entrusted to them rather than as if they were its ministers.

And they go unpunished. They destroy souls with impunity and fear nothing for themselves. There is a passage very similar to this in Ezek. 34:2 ff.

Those who were selling them. This is what Ezekiel says (Ezek. 13:18-19): "When they hunted down the souls of My people, they kept alive the souls of others. They profaned Me among My people for a handful of barley and a piece of bread, so that they killed souls, etc." That is, for the sake of their belly they hand souls over into the pit of hell.

They would say: "Blessed be the Lord, because I have become rich." Here the prophet shows the common utterance which the wicked teachers would use as their boast when they thought that they were pleasing to God and that wealth and honors were coming to them because of their own goodness. Thus they support their own wickedness with the name of the Lord. Isaiah also reproves the greed of the false teachers: "Woe to those who join house to house, who add field to field until there is no more room" (Is. 5:8).

They had no pity. Touched by no feeling of compassion, they just kept on fleecing the people. They destroy the souls as well as the property of their subjects. Such an insatiable desire for gain has overwhelmed them that there is no limit to their plundering. So their belly is always in want, as Solomon says (cf. Prov. 13:25). We see this also among our own pontiffs and bishops: how they have scraped things together.

6. *Therefore, I will not have pity.* Here he finally begins the warning with which he accompanies what he has said above, where he prophesied their destruction. He is saying, as it were: "The wickedness of their teaching causes Me to punish the people. Finally, I shall even destroy them, because they have cast Me aside and have preferred to listen to the seducers."

And behold, I will deliver men. From Josephus all these things are clear. This considered interpretation of ours is confirmed in the accounts of Josephus. He writes that when the Pharisees and Sadducees were in control, everything was very upset.[1] There was no safety, no tranquility. Murder and constant civil discord predominated among the Jews. You see, in addition to the internal ills so seriously afflicting that land, the power of the Romans was also besetting it. That power often sorely mistreated the Jews. All of this was the prelude to the final destruction. No other could be more calamitous or more terrible than that. And to that civil discord the prophet here alludes as he says *of his own king*, whom they serve, whether it be the king of the Syrians or of the Romans.

And thus the earth shall be crushed, that is, by those internal troubles and the onslaught of the enemy.

7. *And thus I tended the flock doomed to slaughter.* I believe that this is Christ's response to the aforementioned command which He had received in regard to feeding the flock. If this is so, these words tie in with what was said earlier. "Thus says the Lord, 'Feed the flock doomed to slaughter.'" "I have become the shepherd, etc.," that is, "just as the Father has commanded Me, so have I preached. I have done this for the sake of the poor of the flock, the downtrodden and oppressed among the people. For I shall save for Myself the weak, the humble, and the downcast, but I shall kill the rich and the proud of Israel." That which follows later is also proof that this is the unifying idea of the text (v. 13): "Cast it to the potter. And I cast them in the house of the Lord to the potter."[2]

And I took two wands. He describes how He has performed His teaching office which His Father had demanded of Him. The Hebrew word which our translation renders "wand" properly means a staff of the sort that shepherds use in taking care of their flocks. For here He is speaking of the way a shepherd feeds his flock. I would prefer to have kept the Hebrew words with which He names the two staffs and not to have translated them. The first staff He calls נֹעַם; the other, חֹבְלִים. There is no doubt that נֹעַם means "delight" – in German, *Lust.* But what חֹבְלִים is I do not understand as yet. I am uncertain as to its proper meaning. Some translate it as "a thin cord," others as "a chief," still others as "a sailor." Everyone may follow the translation he wants. Were I allowed to follow my own thoughts, I believe it means those who mourn, as that He intended different staffs to be understood; the

1 Cf. Flavius Josephus, *The Wars of the Jews,* I, ch. 5.

2 Both the Weimar and the Erlangen text print this quotation as if it were text commented on in the next paragraph.

first a delightful staff which does no harm to the sheep, which does not scatter but only gathers and brings them together to their feed, the other a threatening one with which he can protect the sheep and drive off the wolves, as if He wished to signify a club. But because we can come to no certain conclusion here, we shall not depart from the interpretation of the Septuagint and of Jerome. These translate it as a slender cord. Therefore, we take the first staff to mean *ein fein Rütlein* – a pleasant, soft wand; and the second, a staff to be used instead of a whip or as a whip itself. This is the grammatical rationale. Below we shall add the meaning.

8. *And in one month I destroyed three shepherds.* Zechariah now describes the Lord as He performs the duty of teaching. He says, as it were: "I have begun My ministry under rather blessed auspices. In fact, in one month – that is, in a very short time – I have destroyed three shepherds." Here all the exegetes worry themselves strangely over what He intends to signify with the three shepherds. I keep it in its completely simple context. A threefold order of chiefs was ruling the Jews: elders, priests, and prophets. The elders are the kings, princes, and judges, who are in charge of all things, who head the administration of the sword. The priests would rule with the Word. They performed the teaching office. The prophets would have inspirations. Later the prophets were succeeded by the scribes, who are called teachers of the Law (νομοδιδάσκαλοι). The Pharisees and Sadducees performed no legal administrative function, but they were sects. I believe that here the prophet is alluding to these three orders, as if the Lord were saying: "With My preaching I have ended the kingdom of the Jews. I have destroyed it spiritually, namely, with the Word." This was done from the baptism of John onward, when Christ took up His teaching office after the revelation from heaven occurred, etc.

And My soul was shortened. This is a Hebraism. It means to bear something impatiently, to be peevish. In German we have almost the same phrase: *er ist kurz angebunden,* that is, he is impatient. He easily takes things up wrong. Therefore, the meaning is "I hate that people. I can do nothing but reject and scatter them. Yet I shall save a few. On the other hand, their souls also became nauseated with Me. They had their fill of Me, and they were possessed by a hatred of Me. I don't want them; so they don't want Me in return.

9. *Therefore I said: I shall not be your shepherd. Whatever is to*

die, let it die; whatever is to be destroyed, let it be destroyed. The prophet here has used feminine words [3] for this reason, I believe, to point out that calamity which the people are suffering under those wicked presiding magistrates because they lack a head, a genuine, masculine shepherd, and that is Christ. The meaning, then, is as follows: "Because you refuse to accept Me, I in turn hold you in contempt. I am not concerned whether you die or are saved. Whoever dies, let him die. Whoever is destroyed, let him be destroyed. I shall not protect you. I shall not call you back. I shall not save you. I shall let you lie submerged in Epha (ch. 5:8 above), so that you cannot come out." This judgment of God, and more besides, the Jews still feel today. Entangled as they are in their errors, they cannot loose themselves so that they may come to their senses and be saved. They cannot come to an understanding of the truth. After all, he is speaking here about spiritual destruction and death, by which they are cut off from the congregation of the righteous and are erring about as if there were no God to care about these worldly affairs. Thus, with His judgment, God Almighty has allowed the whole world, too, to wander about before He returned His Gospel to us, through which we have been snatched away from Satan and are placed in the kingdom of the Son of God, etc.

10. *And I took My staff* נֹעַם. There is disagreement among the interpreters as to what these two staffs mean. I have thought of various ideas, but I see no better meaning than that which the text suggests. For it says clearly that "to break it," or to translate more correctly, "to break a piece off it" is the same as annulling an agreement. This is something we must note very carefully. Those two staffs mean the two preachments, the Gospel and the Law. The first staff is the Gospel — that sweet and very delightful Word which feeds, controls, and gathers the sheep that they may not wander but be fed with sweetness and delight. The other staff is the Law, which is preached to the hard and inflexible self-righteous people so that they may be terrified as it threatens death and hell. In this way Christ, too, used both staffs, but He did consider the first, the Gospel, of greater import. After all, He had come to preach the Gospel to the poor, to soothe contrite and disturbed consciences which the burden of the Law was oppressing. Against those who remained inflexible its harsh strength was needed. Now, He says that He has broken a piece off that first staff, that is,

3 That is, in the Hebrew text.

He has taken the sweetness and light of the Gospel away from the Jews. Therefore that breaking off applies rather to the people than to the staff, as if He were saying: "I have driven off the larger part of the people to wander in total blindness from which they are destined never to be led back. Yet I have saved a small remnant for Myself." This is exactly what Paul also says in Rom. 9:28: "The Lord will cause His Word to be cut short on the earth." That is, because the Word bears fruit in a few, He will cut many short who become unbelieving and are cast out of the congregation of the godly.[4] He adds:

11. *My covenant was annulled,* that is, the promise of the Gospel was annulled among that people. In the same way the Gospel has been taken away from them down to the present day.

And thus the poor of the flock knew. These are that very small piece of the broken-off staff – that piece which still remains in My hands. That tiny remnant which has been saved knows the sweetness and limitless treasure of the Gospel. Therefore they accept it and believe it. To everyone else the Gospel seems to be the word of Satan. This is clear: everywhere in the account of the Gospel, where the wicked Jews are described as most bitterly opposed to Christ, as people who did not want to know that Light and Salvation of the world. In sum, this entire passage holds out this idea: When the Gospel is preached, it offends whatever is outstanding, important, and wise in the world. Scarcely a handful accept it – the wretched and contemptible people in the eyes of the world. But among the rest, those who hold it in contempt, the Gospel is diminished. It is not that there is less of the Holy Gospel, which is always the power of God. Rather there is less of the effect which the Gospel has in the hearts of those who regard it with contempt, in the same way as Paul has the Antichrist seated above God (2 Thess. 2:4).

12. *If it is good in your eyes, give me my wages,* that is, if it pleases you. This is a common Hebraism in Scripture. For instance, in Gen. 1:31 we have: "God saw everything that He had made, and it was very good," that is, it pleased Him. Here the prophet adds an outstanding point in which he deals with the reason why the staff which he had already discussed was broken off. He also describes the wicked Jews who held Christ in contempt and treated Him so shabbily. After all, they held Him in such low regard that they even preferred the criminal Barabbas to Him. Then, too, they bought Him for

[4] We have read *piorum* (Erlangen) instead of *priorum* (Weimar).

30 pieces of silver – a point that is clear according to the Gospel account. So the prophet here charges them with this contempt and reproaches them as if to say: "By right you should have accorded high esteem to Christ, your true King and Savior. But you have scorned Him, paid money for Him, made Him worthless. Therefore He has rightly rejected you."

If it pleases. That is: "Do you or do you not wish to buy Me?" Therefore, since all of this does square very well with the Gospel account of the selling of Christ, we shall seek no other, remote interpretation. He gives them the option: "Do you want to buy Me or not?" He says that this is their decision – not because God so orders them to buy. Rather, he is noting the levity of the Jews' minds, that have placed so low a price on Christ that they were deliberating whether or not to pay a price of 30 pieces of silver for Him. Thus he is here imitating their deliberation, in which they argued over the price of the sale.

13. "Cast it to the potter." The evangelist Matthew (Matt. 27:10) translates this as "potter," and that is indeed correct. After all, the Hebrew word does mean "potter." This is quite clear from many passages of Scripture. Ps. 2:9 says: "And you shall dash them in pieces like a potter's vessel." Again, in Ps. 103:14 [5] we read: "He knows our frame." [6] Also we have in Jer. 18:6: "Like the clay in the potter's hand." Because the Jews are unable to remove so clear and obvious a point against themselves, they translate it differently. Others even render it "treasury."

A lordly (or magnificent) *price.* This is irony. He is saying, as it were: "My people are wonderful. I esteemed them so highly. I brought them out of Egypt with such great signs and with such great power. I selected them before all peoples of the earth. Now see how they regard Me with contempt. See what gratitude they return for My bountiful blessings, for My miracles, for My favors and My preaching. Is this not a wonderful price they pay for Me? Judas, who sells Me, is their ringleader and chief. But what shall I do? They regard Me with contempt. They buy Me; they sell Me. They destine Me for death, although I bear no guilt. Obviously, I have deserved this. Indeed, I shall allow Myself to be bought and sold. I shall allow Myself to be led like a sheep to the slaughter. I shall not resist."

5 The Weimar text has "Isaiah."

6 In the Vulgate *figmentum,* the product of a *figulus* ("potter").

And I took the thirty pieces of silver. The passage in Matt. 27:3-7 squares beautifully with this. Matthew writes that after Judas repented of his betrayal and after his conscience was touched because of the sin he had committed, he ran back to the scribes and Pharisees, threw their sale's price at their feet in the temple, and found the remedy for his grief in a noose; that later the price went to the "potter" when it purchased the field. Here the sacred writers trouble themselves. Jerome brings up the question why the evangelist Matthew cited this testimony as being from Jeremiah when it never appears in Jeremiah but in this prophet, Zechariah.[7] Briefly, I have this to answer: the evangelists do not generally cite testimonies from the prophets word for word. They merely bring out the sense. This is what Matthew also does in the passage we mentioned above in chapter 9:9, where the prophet said: "Rejoice greatly, O daughter of Zion. Shout aloud, O daughter of Jerusalem." Matthew cites this as follows (Matt. 21:5): "As it is written, tell the daughter of Zion, Behold, your King is coming to you, etc." Here, clearly, the words are different. Yet nothing of the sense has been changed. Then, too, Matthew added (Matt. 27:9) "by the children of Israel," which does not occur in the prophet. This Matthew obviously did to explain that buying and selling and to warn that the children of Isarel were responsible for it. As to the fact that He cites the testimony as coming from Jeremiah, I have nothing else to respond than this common answer, that the prophet perhaps had two names or that in the custom of other evangelists, too, Matthew was quoting generally, without any concern for the name of the prophet. Augustine (q. v.) discusses this passage carefully.[8] I would not readily believe that the names of the books of the prophets were exchanged because of changed titles. Then, too, there undoubtedly were with Matthew saintly and learned men, filled with the Spirit, who advised him that the Scripture which he cited was in Zechariah, not in Jeremiah. Admonished by their advice, he could have corrected that slight error, had he wished or had he thought it important. But there is no reason for us to bother ourselves with these and similar difficulties. After all, the life and sum of our faith do not lie in them. Those people who labor over nonessential matters of this sort are more than mad. Yet this is one thing which

[7] Jerome, *Commentaria in Evangelium Matthaei, IV,* on Matt. 27:9-10, *Patrologia, Series Latina,* XXVI, 213.

[8] Augustine, *De consensu evangelistarum,* III, ch. 7, pars. 28—31, *Patrologia, Series Latina,* XXXIV, 1174—1176.

the prophets of our day try to do when they read Scriptures for the purpose of searching out texts like this which they can use as the handle and material of debate and controversy. In the meantime, they neglect the lifeblood of religion, when they ought to be performing this one duty especially – teaching a ruling Christ. This is something all the apostles do with unanimous agreement. They teach everywhere the mystery of the suffering and resurrection of Christ as if they have forgotten all the rest of His miracles and activities.

14. *And I broke a piece off my other staff.* That staff is the administration of the Law, as I have interpreted it earlier. Now, he says that that last staff has been shortened. That is, not only has the Gospel, that gentle and very sweet preaching, been taken away from them, but the Law as well has been removed from them. Therefore they no longer have the Law from which they could establish priesthood, kingdom, ceremonies, and sacrifices. Instead, now that the Law has been taken from them, all those things cease to exist. That is, they can no longer preserve the Law. They lack polity, temple, priesthood. Therefore, they can perform no sacrifices. Today they merely carry their bare Bibles around with them along with their more than ridiculous dreams. We must not take this to refer to a spiritual annulling of the Law, as it has been abrogated for all the righteous, so that it no longer has the right to accuse and condemn them. Rather, it means that the Law has been abrogated for them neither in the letter nor in the spirit. That is, they have no use for the Law.

That I might annul the brotherhood between Judah and Israel. This refers to the brotherhood between the genuine Jews and the Jews according to the letter. Those who believed the promise about the children of Abraham are called Judah. Those who did not believe are called Israel. You see, in this prophet we must take those words in a spiritual sense, as the apostle Paul also interprets them,[9] so that those who believe come with the name Judah. For today Jerusalem exists throughout the world wherever there are believers. This is also clear from Ps. 87:4: "Behold, Philistia and Tyre and the people of Ethiopia – 'This one was born there.'" That fighting between the genuine Jews and the literal Jews never ceases. They are still fighting bitterly today about the Law. We see exactly the same thing in the Epistle to the Romans. However, because the Jews protect their own righteousness tenaciously, they never reach righteousness.

[9] Rom. 2:28 f.

15. *Take the implements of a worthless shepherd.* The sacred writers with perfect agreement apply this whole passage to the Antichrist. Lyra especially does this. I am convinced that a good third of his books are about the Antichrist. I do not understand this other than that here he is giving a sign of the preceding prophecy in order to confirm it. For it generally happens this way in all the prophets that signs are added to the discourses. This I have mentioned in detail earlier. Thus Jeremiah wore a wooden yoke (Jer. 29:2), and Isaiah walked about nude, etc. (Is. 20:2). Here, then, he adds a sign to the earlier discourse regarding the rejection and destruction of the people. The prophet is ordered to take the implements of a shepherd, that is, the shepherd's equipment: the cup, knapsack, cloak, staff. Also add a shepherd's pipe. But this is the equipment of a *worthless* shepherd, that is, of the sort of shepherd who in everything represents the "shepherd" in outward appearance but in actual fact really shows nothing so little as what is proper for a shepherd.

16. *I shall raise a shepherd in the land.* The prophet explains the sign. This is a singular instead of a plural, as if He were saying: "They have bought and sold Me, who was the true Shepherd and Savior. For 30 pieces of silver they sold Me. I came in the name of My Father, and they did not receive Me. Another will come in his own name. Him they will receive" (cf. John 5:43) – and this with great harm, for he will incline toward their destruction both of souls and property. For they will not gather what is scattered; they will not heal what is bruised, etc. What this is I have treated in detail in a sermon on a similar passage in Ezekiel.[10] In sum, this means: The true shepherd must keep watch. He must be zealous in the Word. He must give consideration to consciences, to comfort the sad, strengthen the afflicted, lest they despair, call back those who wander away, in short, he must win many for Christ. The worthless shepherds, he says, will do none of these things, because they no longer have the Word. That has been taken away from them. Both staffs have been broken. But when the Word is absent, all preaching is in vain. In fact, such preaching is most harmful and (like a terrible poison) destructive to souls. He immediately adds:

He tears off their hoofs. This is an elegant statement and one worth noting. That is, "He will make them useless." In Holy Scripture the

[10] The sermon for Misericordias Domini, 1523, on John 10:12-16, in which Luther discourses also on Ezek. 34:2 ff. W, XII, 531—535.

false teachers constantly hear that they destroy bodies as well as souls. To hoofs, however, the power of preaching is assigned, as Micah 4:13 reveals: "I will make your hoofs bronze." Now, when the prophet says here that those foolish shepherds are going to tear the hoofs off everyone, he indicates the calamity which results from wicked doctrine: the sheep are injured, afflicted, prevented from being able to go to pasture; consciences are incapable of coming to a knowledge of the truth. So even to this day the wicked teachers of the Jews hinder their wretched people from being able to escape from their errors. In fact, day by day those teachers involve and submerge them in greater errors.

17. *Woe unto this ghost of a shepherd.* That is, indeed, you resemble a shepherd in appearance, but without any function, just like a painted ghost that resembles someone.

Who deserts the flock. In the Hebrew we clearly read this in the plural. That is, like blockheads and ghosts, you all wear shepherd's garb, but actually you are totally foreign to shepherds. After all, you do not feed the sheep, you merely stuff yourselves with the milk and meat of the sheep.

The sword is above his arm. That is, he has no power (which is indicated by the right arm), no wisdom, no light of truth (which he understands with "right eye"). You see, the sword is above him. This is the wrath and judgment of God, which punishes, weakens, and blinds him, lest he have any power. That means that they lack the light of truth. Darkness and errors of every sort overwhelm them. They lie as if buried in them. They are covered up by them so that not even once can they aspire to the truth. Therefore they can offer no right hand, nothing good. They indeed have an arm, but it is the left arm. They perform and have a deep concern for the righteousness of the works of the flesh, but they are not works of the right hand. They lack light and truth. They are outside the faith. Therefore all that they do is sin. Then too, they have a left eye. That is, they are equipped with the eye of the wisdom of the flesh and of this world so that, even in this respect, they surpass the children of light, as Christ says (cf. Luke 16:8). But everything they do is lefthanded. Any knowledge they have is carnal. Whatever intelligence they have is death and "enmity against God," as the apostle says in Romans (Rom. 8:7). A sword of this kind is above all who have been cut off from grace, so that they can accomplish nothing, they know nothing, they understand nothing. Others take this passage simply to refer to the destruction of the false teachers. However, the former sense fits better and it appeals to me that the wicked man becomes a punishment for himself, as St. Augustine says. You see, as soon as a wicked man has departed from godliness, he has his own punishment. He lacks nothing except that that punishment has not yet been revealed. Certainly this entire passage can very well be applied to the Roman pontiff and bishops of our times. Beside the garb and badges of bishops they show nothing that befits bishops. They are posts and ghosts who were born only to destroy souls. They even lack a right eye and a right arm that they teach nothing good but only the destruction of souls.

CHAPTER TWELVE

THE interpreters work amazingly hard to explain this chapter. One troubles himself one way; another, another way. Lyra interprets it as relating to the persecution of the primitive church. Then he goes to the Antichrist, because he is going to sit in the temple at Jerusalem. He also mentions all sorts of other useless trifles. I do not censure – and in fact, I would rather follow – those who interpret this as referring to the time immediately after Christ and as explaining what fruit was produced by the Word of the apostles who were sent first into Judea and then among all nations throughout the earth.

1. *Concerning Israel.* In accord with our customary use of the name we are here compelled to take Israel for Christ's church. Indeed, the Gospel first began among this people. The apostle Paul even clearly distinguishes between the true and the carnal Israel, saying that not all of Israel is Israel (Rom. 9:6), but only those who are of the faithful seed. Cf. Gal. 3:7. The Israel of the flesh has never been restored nor is it ever to be restored. Therefore, when he speaks here about some burden which is going to be over Israel, we must understand that he is speaking about the faithful Israel, since Zechariah was making these prophecies when the kingdom of Israel had already been scattered and destroyed. Moreover, he says that a burden of this sort would come because Israel would suffer persecutions at the hands of neighboring peoples and of all the wicked, who would exercise their tyranny against the faithful who accept and believe the Gospel. Then he also says that not only would an exterior violence come but also a peril from false brothers who assail the truth with craft and deceit. This is a neverending battle against Christ's church, that some attack with violence, others with trickery, and plot [1] the destruction of the faithful. All these points he will discuss in great detail in this chapter.

Thus said the Lord who stretched out the heavens and founded the earth and formed the spirit of man within him. The prophet necessarily places this title first. After all, in it lies the sum of comfort against that very heavy burden of the enemies of the Gospel. He says, as it were:

[1] We have read *cogitent* for *cogantur*.

"Certainly, evil, misery, and tyranny at the hands of your adversaries will come, as well as the deceit of the false teachers. However, all of these will not hold you back. The Lord stands by you. This is the Lord who founds heaven and earth. This is the Lord who forms the spirit of man so that man can think nothing without the Lord allowing it. The word "spirit" means the mind, the movement or emotions of minds. This, he says, is instead of clay for the Lord; just as "clay is in the hand of the potter," so also plans, the reasons for plans, briefly, all the thoughts of man, come under the will of the Lord. He Himself is the Potter who changes, applies, and directs our plans according to His will where He wishes, as does any potter. You see, this is the same word which in an earlier chapter we translated "potter." Therefore the prophet is not speaking about the creation of men's spirits. Rather he is explaining how God Almighty directs hearts and thoughts already created and guides them as and where He wishes, so that we are incapable of thinking anything if God does not will it, much less accomplish anything we have thought of. This, I have said, is the very great comfort of all the righteous when they are under the cross, when they are held prisoner, when they suffer persecution, when they are under sentence of death. Therefore, they should not fear the violence and tyranny of the foes of the Gospel, as those foes plot evil against them and threaten them with death. Then, when the false teachers attack and assail the doctrine of faith, when, I say, they suffer all this, they should not despair. They should know that the tyrants are going to advise nothing other than what the Lord wills, for He forms their spirits. Thus we are absolutely certain that we are not in the power of our enemies, that they do not move a hair of our head without the Lord's permission, however much they rage against us, however many deaths they plot for us.

2. *Behold I am about to make Jerusalem a lintel of drunkenness.* It is strangely true that here most of the words have been translated ineptly in our Bible.[2] Jerome follows the Septuagint and translates "lintel," but I do not like this. First, therefore, let us solve the grammatical problem. After all, this is a very obscure passage. I translate and connect this passage as follows: "Behold, I am about to make Jerusalem a cup of commotion for all the peoples round about, who also are against Judah in the siege against Jerusalem," that is, in besieging Jerusalem they also want to lay siege to Judah. The fact that

[2] The Vulgate.

I translate "cup," or "goblet," and not "lintel" is based on the passage in Ex. 12:22, even though in that very passage Jerome translates – but badly – as "lintel" the same word which we have here. You see, we must read it thus: "Dip a small bundle of hyssop in the blood which is in the cup and sprinkle the lintel with it." Furthermore, what we have translated "commotion" is a word filled with significance. It properly means "staggering" or "reeling," as a drunken person generally does when neither his foot nor his mind performs its function satisfactorily. Hab. 2:5: "As wine deceives the drinker, so will the proud man be, and he will not be honored, etc."; and v. 16: "Drink, yourself, and stagger!" So, too, we read in Is. 51:17:[3] "You have drunk the cup of sleep to the last drop." There we have the same word, which you will read more correctly as "cup of commotion." Then, too, we have in Ps. 60:3: "Wine . . . that made us reel, etc." So the meaning is as if he were saying: "All the people, especially the wicked Jews who are round about the faithful, will move about as if intoxicated. Indeed, they will devour Jerusalem, but to their own great harm, for because of that devouring, it will come to pass that they will be upset. The food will not agree with them. They will move against Jerusalem and Judah whom they think they are going to devour completely. But with that devouring – or rather, with that drinking – they themselves will be devoured and drained. Thus again, pious hearts, oppressed beneath the cross, have here a very great comfort. They know that they are going to conquer even under the evil, for even when Christians are being killed, they still hold sway over their slayers. Through the cross, they are in control against persecution. Through death they attain life, etc.

Now we shall treat the mood of the chapter. That can be a two-sided victory – either in gentleness or in severity. That is, some of the enemies are devoured in wrath, some in mercy. As the church has her prayers answered that many of her foes and persecutors of the faith be converted to the faith, some indeed are devoured and perish because of the terrible judgment of God. So it happened with the Romans. Many of them, stirred by the blood of the martyrs, were converted to the faith and thus were saved, although they had persecuted the Christians most severely before. On the other hand, those who continued in their wickedness and did not stop swallowing up the Christians, finally paid the full penalties for their devouring. This

3 The Weimar text has "Is. 29."

happened because of Jerusalem, that is, because of the Christians, whose blood is so precious in the sight of the Lord that it would have been better not even to have touched the Christians. The same thing happened to the Jews. And the same will also happen to our pontiffs and princes who never cease their frenzy and fury against the Gospel of Almighty God as they lay up for themselves fire against their own houses. It is not that they hope that the Lord will not avenge their wickedness. You see, He hears the cry of His servants and the cry of innocent blood, as He says in Gen. 4:10: "The blood of Abel is crying to Me, etc." Next, He adds:

It will be against Judah also. This indicates the very bitter hatred and tyranny of the enemies of the Gospel. They are not content to have subjected Christians to themselves, as generally happens by right of war. They also want to wipe them out totally so that not even their name survives. They want to overthrow and destroy Christ's church just as completely, but Christ has said: "The gates of hell shall not prevail against it" (Matt. 16:18).

3. *I will make Jerusalem a heavy stone.* This is another comparison. The heaviness means properly a burden which one imposes upon himself. We have this in Gen. 42 and 44, when Joseph orders his brothers' sacks to be filled and loaded on the asses. You see, the German expression does agree: *Du wirst ihn auf dich laden* ("You will place the load on yourself"). The meaning, then, is this: The enemies of the righteous load themselves down with a heavy weight. They want to carry that stone up on high and throw it down that it may break into tiny pieces. They want to throw it completely out of the world. However, without their planning for this, it falls on their heads and crushes them like dust. Thus they themselves are broken into bits, and the Lord saves His own people whom He considers of no less value than the pupil of His own eye. This, too, can happen in two ways: for some, to their salvation; for others, to their damnation. We mentioned the same point earlier: that some are converted and made whole; others are severely condemned.

They will come together against her. He says in substance: "There are many very powerful enemies, all of whom stand against Jerusalem. They flex all their muscles to destroy her, to completely overthrow her. But, rage as they will, their efforts will not succeed. You see, I am going to turn back their iniquities upon their own heads."

4. *On that day, says the Lord, I will strike every horse with panic*

and its rider with madness. This is an explanation of the angered part of the battle. That is, He is describing the punishment of those foes who are neither changed nor moved to cease their vain opposition to God. Their horses will be struck with panic; they themselves, with madness. And this is the explanation of the "commotion" about which He spoke a little earlier. That is, the Lord strikes terror in the hearts of His enemies so that they cannot continue. They lose confidence in their side, as He says to the king of Babylon in Hab. 2:16, "And may you, too, stagger." That is, as you have raged and have overturned many kingdoms, as you have destroyed many nations, so now the same thing is going to happen to you. Now it will be your turn to be booty for your foes, etc.

Upon the house of Judah I will open My eyes. Thus everything will turn out contrary to what the wicked hope for. While they think that they alone are in control and are safely exercising their tyranny against the godly, they are perishing. This is what Ps. 37:35 says: "I have seen a wicked man overbearing, and towering like a cedar of Lebanon. Again I passed by, and lo, he was no more." But God saves and cares for the godly, while the world believes that they are done for. The Lord looks on them with mercy and with favor. He does not allow a hair of their head to fall. In the midst of death and troubles, He is close to them. Therefore He molds the spirit of the wicked so they cannot harm the righteous, however much they harass, attack, and threaten evil.

5. *Then the leaders of Judah shall say to themselves.* Although Judah will be thus oppressed, although it will experience the violence of tyrants, yet there will be comfort remaining in the hearts of the leaders. They will sustain the weary and weak, lest they lose their hope. That is, ministers of the Word will be concerned for their brothers. With the Word they will encourage and strengthen them to be steadfast. Moreover, they will be comforted not in their own strength, not in horses and weapons, as their adversaries are, but in their God, the Lord of hosts. Thus the tyrant's cross, bloodshed, tyrants, violence, prisons, death, evils, persecution – all these they see ahead of them. They are quite evident. And yet, with a marvelous victory which we do not see and which is not apparent (in fact, the very opposite appears) in all those, we triumph. We escape as more than conquerors because of Him who turns His face toward us and in whom is the sum of victory.

6. *I will make the leaders of Judah like a fiery furnace.* What our text [4] translates as "furnace" is "lip" in Hebrew. He takes this as a molten mass such as molten iron. He alludes to the bronze lip of a wash basin, which gleams like fire. Now He is describing the victory of the godly with other similes. He says, as it were: "My people are far from perishing, far from being oppressed and devoured, for they themselves are devouring the people who were threatening and even attacking them with death and every evil." This is the way the leaders of Judah will be against their enemies – like a molten lump stuck into wood, like a torch in straw, where nothing else remains save fire and burning. So they will prevail against every tyranny of the world, just as fire prevails over wood and a flaming torch over straw. Again He offers the most boundless comfort in which we see Almighty God compare all our foes and all the might of the world to wood and straw. But we who are weak in the presence of the world, we who are thrown into prison and are even killed – yes, we – He says, are torches to burn that dry straw and wood. We should be reminded of that that we may fill our hearts with rich comforts of this sort and may use them whenever we need to. You see, faith alone grasps them. They all appear different and seem impossible to the flesh, which is far from being able to believe, etc.

And thus Jerusalem shall still be inhabited. This, too, is related to our consolation, as if He were saying: "Although the tyrants want to destroy the church completely, it will nevertheless stand firm. Both the world and even the gates of hell will cry out against it. Yet the church will remain safe; and, on the contrary, the tyrants will perish. After all, we must not take this passage as referring to the physical Jerusalem, although the words appear to sound that way. You see, in Hebrew the words "beneath it" are clearly added. So the passage indicates that wherever Jerusalem is, there it will be preserved. It will not perish.

7. *And thus the Lord will give victory to the tents of Judah.* This is what I mentioned earlier – that partly the violence and partly the deceit of the false teachers assail the church continually. Here it is not that we hope for something better, for we, too, experience both of these today. And this can be proof that we have truly and sincerely received the Word of God from God. After all, we do not lack people to assail us with violence, to rather want us all destroyed in a single

[4] The Vulgate.

moment. Also, we have no dearth of false brothers and false teachers. In fact, our cup runs over with them. Against all these, however, the Lord gives victory to the tents of Judah, that is, He protects and preserves them in the same spirit in which He has always saved them. The house of David was the royal house. Therefore the royal family came with the name "House of David."

Inhabitants. So He calls those who dwell in the physical Jerusalem. He takes the glory away from all these, lest either the royal family or other citizens do any glorying in the flesh. After all, false prophets have a deep concern especially for one thing – seeking their own glory. Glory, as St. Augustine says, is the mother of all heresy. And yet people want nothing less than to seem so inclined, while they always have only this one thing on their lips, that they do all things for the glory of God. To summarize this passage, then: "I shall humiliate them with the cross and with tyrants that they may learn and know from experience that it rests with Me alone that they are saved, and so they should glory only in Me and not in their own wisdom, not in their own might, not in their own strength. As Paul says, 'Let him who boasts boast of the Lord'" (2 Cor. 10:17). Otherwise, the house of David immediately sets itself against Judah. One holds the other in contempt in comparison with itself. The false teachers want to appear to be the best. For this evil there is no quicker remedy than to come to a knowledge of God. This knowledge comes from the training of the cross, when people are sorely pressed by adversity to be forced to despair over their own strength and abilities and to give honor to God alone. Otherwise, as Paul says, they cannot keep from boasting in the flesh of the hearers (cf. 2 Cor. 10:16). Paul speaks of this everywhere so that he may take the glory away from the false teachers and not yield to them even a fingernail's breadth. We are well acquainted with many such texts in the Pauline epistles. For instance: "Are they descendants of Abraham? So am I. Are they Israelites. So am I. Are they servants of Christ? So am I, etc." (2 Cor. 11:22, 23).

8. *On that day the Lord will put a shield about the inhabitants of Jerusalem.* The prophet continues with his description of the metaphorical, or rather, spiritual, Jerusalem. On that day, namely, the day of the new covenant when the kingdom of grace comes, the Lord will protect. The prophet is speaking by contrast, as if to say: "Up to this time He has also defended Jerusalem to some extent – but scarcely, in small part. When the Gospel begins to rule and the grace revealed

through Christ will never end, His protection will also be constant and of the type which consists of the Spirit." This, you see, does not seem to the flesh to be protection but persecution. After all, enemies are constantly attacking, persecuting, and terribly mistreating the faithful. This we have described earlier in sufficient detail. Therefore that protection is a spiritual protection which is conceived by a faith which believes that there is victory in death, righteousness in sin, freedom in bonds – briefly, which believes that the Lord is on the cross.

And the feeblest among them on that day shall be like David. I believe that the meaning of this passage is very simple, for in Christ's kingdom the merit of the faithful will no longer be looked at, but only the mercy, grace, and goodness of God, because of which Christ's kingdom is also called the kingdom of grace. In sum, the meaning is: All things work together for good for those who believe, because they are the children of grace. All things are forgiven them. They can't go wrong. Even if they have been foolish and weak at times, divine goodness shuts its eyes to that. It holds them faultless. After all, all the sins of the faithful – however mortal – are nevertheless venial. But on the other hand, however much those who are outside of grace may weary themselves with many very good and very fine works, the Lord does not approve of them. They displease God no less than did Saul. Because God had cut him off from grace. He approved nothing that he did. Contrariwise, He forgave David the worst disgraces – adultery, murder, and the fact that he had given the heathen an opportunity for blaspheming the Lord. All this is in the sacred accounts. Although, as I say, all these were mortal sins, yet they were made venial. For David was one of His dear little children who just cannot go wrong. And here the prophet says that this happens with all the righteous, that David is a type and image of all the faithful; that just as David's sins – even the worst – were forgiven, so also the faithful in Christ are forgiven everything, provided that they do not fall away from the faith. Therefore he here presents an outstanding description of the kingdom of Christ. That is, it is nothing other than a kingdom of the pardoning, forgiving, and remitting of sins. But the job and task here is that we remain in the kingdom, that we do not fall away from it. You see, we must have this concern here, that that false idea which deceived many may not deceive us – the idea that while people think that they are in Christ's kingdom, they really are not. These major premises are very certain: Every child of the church is a child of remission and grace; and: No child of the church can sin mortally. But if you should add the minor premise: I am a child of grace, you are a child of grace, he is a child of grace; you could easily be deceived. Because of this, it happens afterward that the filthy pigs run into the sanctuary, where they befoul everything and become an occasion for others to blaspheme against the grace of Christ. David came to grace by no merit of his own, if indeed you consider merit. He had deserved judgment and wrath. However, because he acknowledged his guilt when he kept saying, "I have sinned," he received pardon. The prophet [5] immediately adds: "The Lord also has put away your sin" (cf. 2 Sam. 12:13). After all, if this confession is genuine in the heart, the Lord cannot but make them children of grace.

And the house of David shall be like the house of God. In the house of God, everything is happy, pleasant, and peaceful. Joy, dancing, security, peace, and mercy rule in it. He says that the church of Christ is also like this, for in it – as in the house of God – we lack no good thing. If any remnant of evil still remains while we live in our sinful flesh, Christ does not impute it to us.

Like the angel of the Lord before them. He adds this to describe the shape or dimension of the church, to tell how this kingdom of Christ is established in us while we yet live, lest anyone imagine it a visible and physical kingdom. He [6] is, He says, like an angel or messenger, as if to say, "One still has an angelic home," that is, everything merely lies hidden in the Word. It is still a kingdom of faith. All things are still in shadow, as Paul says, until the day comes when all things will be revealed to us face to face (cf. 1 Cor. 13:12). Therefore with this statement He summons us to the church which is still doing battle. You see, everything is still covered up. We merely believe. Before God, however, all things are always clear and evident. This revelation we, too, await.

9. *And on that day, I will seek to destroy all the nations.* This is a comforting statement, with which He declares that He is speaking about a kingdom of faith, a spiritual realm. Earlier, at the beginning of this chapter, He said the same things about the wicked enemies of the Word and of the followers of the Word: how they are all flexing

[5] Nathan. Both the Weimar and the Erlangen editions misunderstood the word "prophet" as applying to Zechariah and consequently displayed the words that follow as a part of the Zechariah text to be commented on.

[6] Apparently the Christian is meant.

their muscles to ruin and destroy completely Christ's church. Here, too, just as He did earlier, He comforts the faithful against all those ills, as if to say: "Wicked persecutors oppress My church. They want to destroy it by every means. But I shall avenge it. I shall protect it, and I shall protect it in such a way that I shall save My Christians and destroy My foes. I shall watch over it; I shall give it help. I shall look for a way to destroy the heathen. You faithful people of Mine, enjoy My riches in security, as you return to Me My church avenged. I shall save you, even though the gates of hell and all the world's might cry out in protest." This clearly happened even then. For He destroyed the authority of the Romans and also the kingdom of the Jews, and all who have ever set themselves against the church of Christ have perished.

10. *And I will pour out the Spirit of grace and supplications.* All of this is a description of the kingdom of the church. The meaning is this: "I shall not allow My Christians to defend themselves with arms and violence and the tumult of war, for they will beat their swords into plowshares and their spears into scythes. This will be a kingdom of peace. However, I shall give them other weapons with which to battle against their enemies – the Spirit of grace and of supplications. (This is the name He gives the Holy Spirit.) Therefore He calls the Holy Spirit the Spirit of grace, because the Spirit causes God to be kindly disposed toward us and us, in turn, to love God, united as we are in a tightly knit band of minds. This is a very broad statement, if you go into it more deeply, for it is sense and consciousness of the fullest favor of God in the faithful. Here rule gentleness, sweetness, tolerance, kindness, and all of the finest affections with which to oppose the favor of wrath, impatience, gloom, wickedness, as well as every sort of bitter attitude. These are not in the church of Christ, in which there is only favor, for they are well-disposed to God and neighbor, yes, even to enemies. This is what the apostle Paul says: The Holy Spirit is poured into our hearts (cf. Rom. 5:5).

Of supplications. The apostle Paul has explained this: "The Lord is at hand, and in all things . . . let your requests be made known to God" (Phil. 4:5-6). He says, as it were: "Don't worry. You have the Lord as your Protector. The Lord stands by you. He Himself will take up and sustain your case. Put aside all your fear, anger, and bitterness. If you intend to do any fighting, fight with prayers. After all, there is no other way by which we can more sharply assail Satan and cause him to totter than with our prayers or, to translate this more accurately, with our supplications. You see, supplication is something broader than prayer, as if to say that supplication is praying with a sacred formula, as when we add "through our Lord Jesus Christ" to our prayers.

And they will look on Me whom they have pierced. The evangelist John has quoted this passage in chapter 19:37. Here we have a wonderful natural succession. What now follows to the end of the chapter is about mourning and the sort of mourning which occurs over Christ. This, too, we read in the Gospel: "All the tribes of the earth will mourn over Him" (Matt. 24:30). However, we shall not apply this to the day of judgment, for we are involved here in a description of the church. Consequently, I take the meaning to be as follows: A Christian leads a double life – the life of the Spirit, and the mortification of the flesh. You see, when we have been justified and taken into the kingdom of God's grace, we must still also mourn over our flesh; we must not merely mourn and lament our suffering Christ but also imitate Him; we must die along with Him and crucify our own flesh. Here, then, He is speaking about that mortification of the flesh and not about the grief of the Final Judgment, when every eye will see Christ judging the guilty and punishing the ungodly for crucifying Him. After all, the hands of the Jews which crucified Christ are the hands of all the wicked. But while Christians are alive on this earth, they mourn as they mortify their own flesh. This they do because of Christ. Indeed, as the apostle says in Romans 6, our old Adam was crucified, he died and was buried along with Christ. Consequently, to mourn for Christ's sake is to imitate the crucifixion, death, and burial of Christ so that we mortify our flesh and the affections thereof either by ourselves or by others – that is, when Satan, the world, and our foes attack us. In this way all these ideas hold together beautifully, as if He were saying: "They will see how I was crucified for them. In fact, they will see how they themselves crucified Me." After all, as Isaiah says, "He Himself bore our sins" (cf. Is. 53:11). Therefore, they immediately say with the apostle Paul: "Those who belong to Christ have crucified the flesh with its . . . lusts" (Gal. 5:24). They gladly endure poverty, hunger, illness, and every adverse condition, even when they must put life itself on the line. All of these things are certainly serious and deserve to be called "the cross." This is a grief like the grief over the firstborn. It is a bitter, heartrending sorrow.

11. *On that day the mourning in Jerusalem will be great.* This is the extension of that grief. "In Jerusalem" means in Christ's church.

As great as the mourning for Hadad-rimmon in the plain of Megiddo. He looks back into sacred history to the account of the death of the very righteous king Josiah. As he was about to begin battle against Neco, the king of Egypt, he was pierced by arrows and died. This death brought very bitter grief to all Israel, as we see in 2 Chron. 35. Even the prophet Jeremiah composed a lamentation, or dirge of mourning, for him. So great was the grief that was felt when this godly and at the same time prosperous king died. A very great grief of this sort will come also to the church because of Christ's death. The righteous will imitate His death to conform to their Lord.

12. *And the land shall mourn, each family by itself.* That is, each family will mourn separately. Hebrew generally joins two words in this way whenever it speaks distributively. We have this, for instance, in Moses: "They cast down rod and rod" (cf. Num. 17:2, 6). That is, they threw down their individual rods separately. The meaning is: In the synagog the people were separated in a certain order. This the Jews still observe today, as the men occupy their place, and the women theirs. He here reminds the people of this ritual that they may grasp the idea more easily. He says, as it were: "Families will mourn everywhere in the church throughout the world." Moreover, there is great emphasis on the word "separately," as if to say: "I do not prescribe some general rule for mortifying the flesh. Instead, individuals, as suits their convenience and bound by no definite laws, will restrain their own flesh." This is something which ought to have been remembered by the stupid pope and the bishops who impose fasting on nearly everyone without making any allowance for age or physical condition. The monks, too, are guilty of this. Somewhere St. Augustine has made the very pious statement when he prescribes their rituals and ceremonies, "Not the same for all people, because you are not all equally strong." However, monastic jealousy has held that idea in contempt, lest one yield even a fingernail's thickness to the other. This has caused many people to die. Also, many have slipped into insanity and have never recovered their original healthy minds. This is what Satan caused because of stupid ceremonial laws of this kind. Christians mourn separately, that is, as is convenient for them, individuals weaken themselves and afflict their flesh in order to repress their lusts. After all, this is the function of such weakening. You see, individuals have

their own crosses, just as Christ appropriately says: "Let him take up his own cross and follow Me" (Matt. 16:24). He does not say, "He will take up My cross." In this way, then, the prophet neatly carries across into the spiritual ritual of the synagog the fact that each Christian mourns as much as he can endure in order to mortify the lusts of the flesh. Yet we each do this in such a way that we respect our own bodies, lest they die. After all, God Almighty has not given us our bodies for that. The Lord will give the measure of grief, and the Spirit will teach each person to what extent he should weaken himself. The Lord will give temptations which we shall be able to endure. And with the temptation, as the apostle says, He will give a very fruitful and happy outcome (cf. 1 Cor. 10:13). The apostle everywhere condemns "the worship of the angels" (θρησκείαν τῶν ἀγγέλων) which revolves around food, clothing, and other nonsense of this sort (cf. Col. 2:18). Indeed, physical constitutions are not equal. Not all can endure the same thing. Therefore, I shall not allow anyone to foist upon me the examples of the saints – even of Jerome and Bernard, who so tortured himself with fasting that he was unable to distinguish between oil and water even after tasting them. Although Jerome afflicted himself in strange ways (he slept naked on the ground and did all sorts of other things), yet all this could not check the heat and lusts of his affections. This is what we must go toward: we must check all lusts and affections which oppose the Spirit – anger, pride, envy, laziness, greed, passion, etc. The monks are so far from repressing these with their fasting, that all of those sins run rampant almost only on their monastery grounds. This is the way the church appears according to the inner and outer man.

CHAPTER THIRTEEN

THE prophets who considered the function of the Law and of the rituals in the Law often had at the same time an understanding of the future as the Spirit inspired them. Therefore they often turn legal matters into proverbs and metaphors. Zechariah also does the same thing here. After he has described the condition of the church as regards the justification of the spirit and the mortification of the flesh, he now confirms what has come before as if alluding to it with some allegory. He does this either for his own pleasure or from an abundance of the Spirit. Paul also does the same thing in the Epistle to the Galatians (Gal. 4:21-31) when he speaks of the son of Abraham born according to the flesh and about the true seed according to the promise. There he makes an elegant distinction between carnal sons and the true spiritual seed, which comes from the faith of Abraham. The meaning, then, of this section is this: In our legal rituals we have many different ablutions. The many righteousnesses of the flesh cause us concern, as the Epistle to the Hebrews explains beautifully (Heb. 9:10-11): "with food and drink and various ablutions, regulations for the body imposed until the time of reformation. But when Christ appeared, etc." Furthermore, when that kingdom comes in which everything rests on justifying the spirit and mortifying the flesh, as we have said, then the true washing will occur. This will be very different from those many external ablutions which have been commanded in the Law.

1. *On that day.* That day will be the day of the new covenant under the rule of Christ.

There shall be a fountain. He emphasizes the word "fountain," as if to say: "There will be a living vein of water which is the Word of the Spirit." Christ says in John 7:38: "Out of his heart shall flow rivers of living water." This He said about the Spirit. No one will be able to empty or dry up that fountain in his ablutions. It will never become stagnant. It will always flow fresh and abounding, just as John also says: "welling up to eternal life" (John 4:14).

Opened, or "open," that is, the fountain will pour out publicly. The whole world will see it openly. As I have said, the prophet always looks back to the Law and the rituals thereof. The Law established many ablutions, but they were set up for a specified situation. It scheduled and limited everything to definite places, times, and persons. To this binding character of the Law he contrasts grace, which the Gospel reveals throughout the world among all nations. He adds:

For the house of David. That is, this will happen not merely for Levi, as it is in the Law, but also for the house of David. In fact, it will be for all the inhabitants of Jerusalem; that is, for all the faithful throughout the world. I have mentioned earlier that the prophet makes this kind of spiritual use of the words "house of David," "inhabitants of Jerusalem," "Israel," "Judah," etc.

For the cleansing of sin. In the Hebrew the word "cleansing" is not present, but this is not a bad addition. The Hebrew reads thus: "in sin and separation." He says in substance: "That fountain will be prepared for taking away sin as well as for uncleanness." There are two types of uncleanness – voluntary and natural. The external washing of the Law would cleanse the voluntary, but we could do nothing about the natural. Therefore there was also established a dual cleansing: one for purging voluntary sins, as happened if someone had touched a dead person, a leper, a menstruating woman, etc.; the other, for washing away natural sin, as was the uncleanness of women after bearing children, etc. All this one can see in Leviticus.

So the prophet is alluding to those legal matters, as if to say, "All sorts of uncleanness trouble us who are under the Law. The Law makes many things unclean, and we torment ourselves in washing away all that uncleanness. But this is all ridiculous and not at all serious. The responsibility of washing away sin and genuine uncleanness will belong to the Holy Spirit. He Himself will at last wash away both present and past sins." Consequently, here I properly call sin original sin along with all its results. All this the Holy Spirit takes away. However, there still remains an uncleanness in the flesh – the uncleanness of a menstruating or unclean woman. But the Holy Spirit strengthens the heart and comforts it with the grace of forgiven sin so that it has no further fear of damnation or judgment because of sin. Then, with their hearts thus justified, Christians daily crucify their flesh more and more that the remnants of the old man may be washed away. In this way, too, the flesh finally becomes clean until it completely passes away. This is what the prophet has said in great detail in the previous chapter regarding justification through the Spirit and about grief by families (cf. ch. 12:10 f.).

2. *I will cut off the names of idols from the land.* He again is comparing the old and new covenants, as if to say: "Under the old covenant the major task was to get rid of idols. Many godly kings tried this. They demolished the statues of idols and the sacred groves. But they could not remove the names of the idols. So whatever they did, they did only in the letter. On the other hand, the new covenant functions effectively. Not only does it remove the idols but even the names of the idols." You see, once the truth is known, once the Holy Spirit has been sent, the idols topple by themselves. The Spirit – not mortal hands – breaks them; for those who have the Spirit of God are completely free of idolatry. In the fashion of the Hebrew, he says "the names of the idols." The prophet has used the same practice also in Ps. 9:6: "The very memory of them has perished," along with their noise – the praise and esteem of them. This means to remember someone, as Christ also says: "Do this in remembrance of Me" (Luke 22:19), that is, "Celebrate, declare, praise, and honor, that My esteem may be increased." The memory of the Jews has perished, that is, they no longer have either priesthood or kingdom. Their entire situation has been maligned as ignoble. This is what Scripture calls God forgetting us, as we read in the psalm: "I shall not take their names upon My lips, etc." (Ps. 16:4).

And the false prophets and the unclean spirit. That is, "When I have sent My Holy Spirit, I shall remove not only the worship of idols but also the teachers of that worship." He distinguishes the Holy Spirit from the unclean spirit, because only the Holy Spirit is always that open, flowing fountain. All the other spirits are contaminated spirits. So today, now that the Gospel has been revealed, the contaminated teachers along with their monastic religion are being destroyed in their monasteries, because they cannot bear the Word of God.

3. *And it will come to pass when someone has prophesied.* He uses an elegant comparison but still compares the old covenant with the reign of Christ. He says: "All wickedness will be driven away – wicked laws, wicked teaching, wicked teachers, as well as those who say that they see strange visions." Christians, you see, carefully distinguish between Christ's voice and the voice of strangers, as Christ says: "My sheep hear My voice and flee from strangers, etc." (cf. John 10:4-5). The meaning of this, then, is in substance: "Under the old

covenant, teachers and judges were established who were to pass judgment on visions and prophesies. But this practice clearly will cease under the new covenant, for all people – from least to greatest – will know Me. No man will further teach his neighbor. Son and daughters both will prophesy. I shall put My law into their hearts. Therefore all men will be equal, because they will all have the same Spirit." To summarize, He indicates that the authority for passing judgment on the false prophets will rest upon all Christians.

His father and mother who bore him. This refers to those who have taught them earlier.

They shall pierce him through. They will do this with the Word of the Spirit. We see the same thing happening in our day too. Our children, too, wish to offer new visions, new dogma. However, because they prophesy falsely in the name of the Lord, we pierce them through.

4. *Every prophet will be ashamed of his vision.* From what follows, it is clear about what killing or shame He speaks, namely, the friendly reproach of the godly, who want to call the wicked back from their error. You see, the false prophet himself will say below, when he is asked about his bruises, "I was beaten in the house of those who loved me." Therefore he is speaking about being pierced through spiritually. But about the piercing of the false prophets the apostle Paul says: "Their folly will be plain to all" (2 Tim. 3:9), for when their error has been revealed at last, they will be embarrassed, and they cannot stand in the judgment, as Ps. 1:5 records. All of this He says to comfort the church that the false teachers will not prevail but will be embarrassed.

They will not put on the hairy mantle in order to deceive. It appears, then, that the prophets wore a special garment by which people could tell them apart from others. Thus Isaiah [1] is told: "Loose [2] the sackcloth from your loins" (Is. 20:2). Sackcloth is very cheap material which the prophets used because they were always scolding and accusing the people. In this way, their clothes and teaching were in harmony. The harsh, rough raiment of John the Baptist was like this too. Therefore this passage means: Every external ritual which produces hypocrites will also be taken away. The false prophets will no longer be able to deceive Christians with the appearance of right and godli-

[1] The Weimar text has "Jeremiah."

[2] We have read *solve* for *salve*.

ness. Because the Holy Spirit has taught Christians, they will pass judgment on all false doctrine, no matter how much the false teachers simulate true doctrine and godliness. No sham will deceive the church. The godly will immediately compare the doctrine of the false teachers with the Word of faith to test whether it is analagous to faith.

5. *I am no prophet; I am a tiller of the soil.* This means that the false prophets will be so overcome, when embarrassed and humiliated, that they no longer want to be prophets. They will no longer feel any pride or greatness in themselves. They will easily yield to anyone who admonishes them. This is what the apostle wants: that Christians be one in feeling; that one listens to the other; that one intentionally gives way to the other; that they do not bite at each other or argue about matters of insignificance; but that each honors the other.[3] To summarize this, then, he is saying: "I no longer wish to pursue those heresies. Instead, I submit myself to the unity of your faith. I have no haughty bearing. I no longer preach myself as insolently or greatly as I did before. You see, I am a tiller of the soil. I am a simple man. I am inferior to the person I was when I kept trying to sell myself under the name of prophet." The prophet also alludes to the method of preparing food among the Jews, who lacked trade goods and would feed themselves from fruits and flocks after the example of the patriarchs. Before God that is the most just and best way to prepare food, because all profit motive has been taken away.

Because man has had me from my youth. These are words of confession and humility, with which he subjects himself to the judgment of others who have a more correct sense of godliness. He voluntarily gives way as he indicates that he is no different from the common man. To say, "Man has had me" is a Hebraism. It appears in Gen. 4:1: "I have gotten a man through *(per)* God," that is, "I have acquired." It also appears in the passage (Prov. 8:22): "The Lord created me at the beginning of His ways." We properly translate it with the words "has had," which the Hebrew lacks. The meaning then is this: "From my youth I have been among the country people in their meadows and on their farms. I am far from having learned some new mysteries or revelations about divine majesty. All the false prophets boast that they know such things, but I no longer wish to follow them."

6. *What are these wounds on your hands?* The Word and Spirit have confused, embarrassed, and humiliated him. He bears wounds –

[3] Cf. Rom. 12:9 ff.

the marks of confusion. When asked, he answers that these wounds are good, loving, and pleasant – actually, paternal wounds. It is as if he were saying: "Those who bore me in Christ gave me these friendly wounds. They are friendly because the church strikes with its voice. It does not rage with violence or arms but acts to call back hearts from error and to gain many souls for Christ.

7. *Awake, O sword, against my shepherd.* There appears to be no natural succession from what has come before to the second part of this chapter. Up to this point the prophet has been discussing the reign of Christ: how the faithful are going to be justified in the Spirit; how the Law and its ceremonies have been annulled; and how the faithful are going to be mortified according to the flesh. He immediately brings in the striking of the shepherd and the scattering of the flock. However, up to this point, one thing was missing in this prophet. He did not interpret his earlier vision regarding inscribing the stone about which he wrote in chapter 3. Therefore with these clear words and revelations he interprets that vision. As a result, I connect this section with the preceding sections in this way: The prophet has described what sort of a kingdom Christ's was going to be. He now goes on to describe who is going to be the Head or Prince in that kingdom, what kind of Person that Head must be, and how that kingdom must be established. The prophet, therefore, in sum is signifying two things. First, that kingdom must be prepared according to a far different plan from what the world can understand or believe – through a stricken and humiliated Shepherd, just as Is. 53 depicts Him. That is, the kingdom of Christ is a kingdom of offense, for many people will be offended and will fall away because of the stricken Shepherd. Scarcely a bare remnant will be saved. Against the carnal idea of the Jews he says these things: Not all are to be admitted to this kingdom; many are going to fall away because the humility and wounds of the King will have offended them. His second point is this: a godly man should know that God the Father has ordained and willed that all this should happen, because the Shepherd has been stricken. Even Christ Himself says this in John 14:31: "I do as the Father has commanded Me." Therefore it is pleasing to God that this King first suffer and be humiliated and then be crowned with glory and honor.

But we need not trouble ourselves because the evangelist Matthew has quoted this passage in another person. After all, it makes no difference to what person it is spoken, since the meaning is the same.

This, too, I have spoken of in great detail earlier. We are certain that in Matthew this is said in the Person of God the Father, but here the meaning is absolutely the same, even though God tells a sword to strike. These points are too insignificant for us to dwell on them any longer. Yet, Jerome makes very much of them.

Against the man who stands next to Me, that is, the man who is with or next to Me, as John (1:18) says: "The only Son, who is in the bosom of the Father, He has made Him known." The meaning then is this: "My beloved Son, who is in My bosom, whom I have established as King, My Only-begotten – Him I shall strike in such a way that the whole world will be offended because of Him." You see, it is through the cross and death that He will prepare for Himself that eternal and all-glorious kingdom. And this is what we read in Ps. 8:5-6: "Thou hast made Him a little lower than the angels, and dost crown Him with glory and honor. Thou hast given Him dominion over Thy works, etc." The sword, after all, does signify persecution and crucifixion.

And the sheep will be scattered, that is, very many will be offended. Even the apostles themselves were scattered. Yet generally the statement seems to me to have been spoken not only about that particular moment of time when the apostles fled but universally for the whole time of Christ's kingdom. You see, Christ began to be struck at that time, and He is being struck now and to the end of the world. This happens as often as the wicked persecute and oppress Christians, and whenever heresies arise. This is what Christ means when He says, "Saul, Saul, why do you persecute Me?" (Acts 9:4). Therefore this is the sense: Christ is here set for the fall of many people. He is always being oppressed, always being struck. As a consequence, many are always offended and crushed. In this way, at the time of the Arian controversy, Christ was wretchedly struck and afflicted almost throughout the entire world. With remarkable consent, all the finest and most learned people were denying the divinity of Christ. Therefore we must be certain that even today that sword is being raised against Christ. This is the way that the wicked teachers and persecutors of the church even to this day spit upon Him, crown Him with thorns, crucify, and blaspheme Him, just as the Jews used to spit upon Him. If we were not most sure about the Word of God, all of this could give us opportunity to despair and to desert the Word when we see the great bitterness and frenzy of the numerous and powerful enemies of the Word, all of whom want to destroy and oppress God's Word by every means.

Therefore the scattering of the flock also necessarily follows the striking of the sword. This we have experienced more than enough today, when many who appeared to stand by the Gospel before the striking now flee from the Gospel. The entire crowd with great applause at first would receive the Gospel. But now they shrink away from it and are offended, so that scarcely a handful remain steadfast. Thus for our sakes Christ is the reproach of man and the scorn of the people. Even though we shall have been destroyed, finally He will be declared to be that King of ours – the King of glory.

He says all this for our consolation, lest we be offended by that appearance of a stricken Christ. Otherwise, that appearance is such that we would all become like Sodom and Gomorrah, were it not that He has left seed behind for us.[4] It is the function of divine courage that we not desert our stricken King. You see, this courage is something far too great for the world or for human reason to be able to show. The strength here of free will is nil.

And I will turn My hand against the little ones. That is, "In that offense and fall of many people, I shall still save My remnant – My little ones – for Myself. Otherwise all the greatest and best things in the world will strike out against Christ, as Paul says in 1 Cor. 1:26-27: "Not many of you were powerful, not many were of noble birth; but God chose what is foolish in the world, etc." Christ appears to have looked back often to this section, since He makes mention of His little ones so many times in the Gospel account.

8. *And it will come to pass,* that is, it will occur in this way, it will happen in this way, in all the earth, not merely in Judea.

Two thirds of it shall be scattered. He Himself explains the offense and what He wanted to say with the scattering of the flock, the stricken Shepherd, and the wonderful Preparer of that glorious kingdom. He says, as it were: "The Gospel will be a source of amazement. No one will believe it easily." This is what Christ means when He quotes from Ps. 118:22-23: "The stone which the builders rejected has become the chief cornerstone. This is the Lord's doing; it is marvelous in our eyes." That is, He has offended us greatly. Unless we were divinely kept, we could not persevere. He proposes the same idea to us here, when the two parts are scattered and cease to be, only one is saved. Therefore the greater part always perishes, and the lesser part is saved. At first, when the Gospel is revealed to the world, the world listens with

[4] Cf. Is. 1:9.

great applause. There is hardly a handful that does not wonder at it. But when the sword has been raised and has struck the Shepherd, then the two parts withdraw. Because their own reason and the wisdom of the flesh have influenced them, they are unable to bear that offense of the cross. And, who would endure it, except one who has been divinely encouraged by the Holy Spirit? After all, to believe in life in the midst of death, to believe in glory in the midst of sin, to believe in the peace and favor of God in the midst of persecution – this is something beyond every capability of reason. It is truly a miracle in our eyes.

9. *And I will lead the third part through the fire.* We are forced to bear the reproach of Christ's cross, the apostle says. The weakness of our King is exposed to us. In the meantime, He Himself closes His eyes to the blasphemies of the wicked and keeps silence. Beside this, we are also compelled to endure our private and personal sufferings. Each of us has his own divinely imposed cross to bear so that we complete that which is lacking in Christ's afflictions, as we have it in Col. 1:24. This he here calls being led through the fire. But these, he says, take the place of a test for you so that you are proved by the cross, as silver is proved by the fire. Today there are many who deal with the Gospel to our great disgrace. These are amateurs whom the cross has never trained. They play the part of the sword against us. Yet they meanwhile sit secure beneath our peace and under our fig tree and rage against us. Should any danger threaten them, should evils and the cross oppress them; they then would learn to cling solely to the goodness of God, they would despair of their own counsel and imagination, which otherwise are the wellspring of many heresies. You see, while they are not preoccupied with very serious business, their minds meanwhile are free for leisurely thinking, and they cannot help but dream up new dogmas.

They will call on My name. We have earlier explained a similar passage in Hosea.[5] To summarize, the text says this: The kingdom of Christ, which is harassed in Christ, its very King, as well as in our own bodies, is ruled solely in faith and in the invocation of the name of the Lord. The apostle Paul also teaches this in Rom. 10:13-14: "Everyone who calls upon the name of the Lord will be saved. But how are men to call upon Him in whom they have not believed? etc." Thus it is not

[5] No such passage is found in Hosea. Luther probably had Joel (2:32) in mind.

guards and weapons or our own strength which preserves this kingdom, but the invocation of our Defender and Protector, who does not desert us as we call upon Him. Consequently, Christians cannot help but be secure against the violence and tyranny of the enemies and princes who join together in a single union against the Lord. They know that God cares for them, provided they cry out to Him. He who listens to those who cry out is near. This is the same thing which Paul says: "Have no anxiety about anything, but in everything . . . let your requests be made known to God" (Phil. 4:6). Indeed, we must cry out in the name of Christ; that is, in our unique faith in Christ, which relies on no righteousness or holiness of our own.

You are My people, and they will say: Lord! This is the preaching of the Gospel, for those who believe are the sheep – the flock – of Christ. In short, they are the sons of God, coheirs with Christ. This is the message the faithful hear in the presence of the angels and of the Father. Then, too, the Christians confess the same thing both in their hearts before God and with their mouths in the presence of the world. In these two ideas rests the sum of our justification. But the cross cannot help but accompany that confession. The world and the gates of hell immediately set themselves against it, for the world cannot bear the fact that its powers, its righteousness, and its wisdom are being condemned. So it turns against those who condemn it, persecutes them bitterly, and finally kills them.[6]

[6] The Altenburg manuscript ends here without indication of a reason for the abrupt end.

LECTURES ON ZECHARIAH

The German Text

1527

Translated by
WALTHER M. MILLER

THE PROPHET ZECHARIAH EXPOUNDED

Preface

God the Father Almighty has in our time given us many splendid and learned men who have done very intensive research on the Holy Scriptures, both of the New Testament and the Old. May He help us and grant us grace that we may recognize their work and be thankful for it. Amen. Besides these men, however, there are also to be found daily, in ever increasing numbers, frivolous spirits, who never know where they ought to stop, although, as St. Paul says (1 Cor. 8:2), they "do not yet know as they ought to know." These spirits go about with a lofty air and soar upward and nowhere, just as if they had long worn threadbare the common teachings of faith and love and the cross; they affect figures of speech, mysterious interpretations and allegories, and delight in beautiful thoughts. With these they skip and leap about, as also Origen and Jerome did in times past when they, too, filled the world with allegories, though they contributed little to common, useful teaching. The consequence was that the blasphemer Porphyry [1] was given every occasion to mock the Christians, as though the teaching of these Christians consisted of nothing but this kind of fanciful interpretation. Today, too, everyone claims to be a master interpreter. One studies Daniel, another the Apocalypse, and so on, whichever is most difficult or offers the most allegories; and in this way they hope to show their cleverness. They do not consider, however, whether they are teaching the poor common man anything but only consider how cleverly and brilliantly they may be able to teach. All of them, praise God! are highly learned men who have no need of us. But though they may interpret at great length, they do not offer anything solid to build on.

Now one might be able to put up with the splendid work of these spirits if they did it only among themselves or among scholars and, at the same time, gave the unlearned people their due – that is, the

[1] One of the most distinguished Neoplatonists, Porphyry (A. D. 232—305) wrote prolifically in defense of philosophy and against Christianity. Cf. Eusebius, *Ecclesiastical History,* VI, 19.

simple teaching of faith in Christ. For I can see every day that there are very few preachers at this time who properly understand the Our Father, the Creed, and the Ten Commandments and are able to teach these to the poor people. But because these spirits rise to great heights in Daniel, Hosea, the Apocalypse, and similar difficult books, the poor people flock to these fine actors, listen to them, and gape at them in great amazement. When the year is ended, however, these people know neither the Our Father nor the Creed nor the Ten Commandments – and these, after all, are the principal things and the genuine old Christian catechism or common instruction for the Christians. I just wonder how much more useful these idle prattlers are to the poor people than the men who formerly preached on Aristotle and canon law.

Of the same stripe are also certain enthusiasts of our day who boast of their great learning and their understanding of the old stories of the Bible. The tabernacle of Moses, the garments of the priests must be presented; for underlying these, they say, are *imago et veritas*[2] and I do not know what other great and splendid things. In this way they merely cause the curious crowd to open their mouths wide, and they make it appear as if that which has been revealed to us were something insignificant: that through Christ we are redeemed and saved from sin and death; that we know that God's law is to be kept and that cross and affliction must be borne, etc. No, these things are nothing. They know this very well – just as a goose knows the Psalter. I myself, I am telling you in all honesty, have had about 10 of these exalted prophets before me; and they have always wanted to teach me lofty things and the most spiritual spirit. And when I refused to accept their teachings but instead wanted to remain true to the simple, crucified Christ, they became angry, left me, and started a sect.

With all Christian faithfulness I therefore ask and admonish everyone, teachers as well as students, first, not to despise those who can expound the Scriptures and ably interpret and teach the difficult books. For St. Paul tells us (1 Thess. 5:19 f.) not to despise prophesying or quench the spirit. But this expounding should be done at places and in the presence of persons where "it is good for edifying," as Paul teaches the Colossians.[3] One should not, however, regard those interpreters as great who devote all of their cleverness to allegories and,

2 Cf. p. 347, n. 7.

3 Luther quotes the words of Eph. 4:29, but Col. 4:6 has a similar message.

I fear, seek not great good but rather great glory. For one can very well be a Christian and be saved without this cleverness, because these interpreters either interpret nothing at all or very rarely anything that is sure. One ought, however, to regard those teachers as the best and the paragons of their profession who present the catechism well – that is, who teach properly the Our Father, the Ten Commandments, and the Creed. But such teachers are rare birds. For there is neither great glory nor outward show in their kind of teaching; but there is in it great good and also the best of sermons, because in this teaching there is comprehended, in brief, all Scripture. There is no Gospel, either, from which a man could not teach these things if he only were willing and took an interest in teaching the poor common man. One must, of course, constantly prompt the people in these brief things – that is, in the Our Father, the Ten Commandments, and the Creed – and then insist on them and urge them upon the people in all Gospels and sermons. Even then, unfortunately, the people will learn little enough of these things and, as St. Paul says (2 Tim.4:4), "will turn away from listening to the truth and wander into myths."

For this reason I, too, lectured on this prophet Zechariah and am now having my lectures published, not indeed for the common crowd but for those who like to read the Scriptures at home and wish to be strengthened in their faith. I have done this primarily, however, because of the frivolous spirits who give way to allegories and then very masterfully fail in their efforts. For since this prophet has many visions and requires much expounding, I have wished to anticipate these spirits and show, as far as I can, that to present allegories and interpretations is not so great a feat as they boast and glory, but that one should rather, at all times and in all prophets, seek the truly important thing – faith. Unfortunately, however, very few do that; instead they seek to skip it, as if it were something unnecessary.

May Christ our Lord, however, grant us His Spirit and gifts, not for our glory but for the good and welfare of Christendom, for which alone the Spirit is given, as St. Paul says, 1 Cor. 12:11: He "apportions to each one individually as He wills." In other words: To us be shame and disgrace for our evil and sin; but to the Lord be praise and honor, love and thanks in all eternity for His inexpressible grace and gifts. Amen.

CHAPTER ONE

FROM the prophet Habakkuk we have learned that the office and the preaching of the old prophets were twofold. First, they were to educate the people and prepare them for the coming kingdom of the Messiah, as St. Paul says to the Galatians (Gal. 3:24), "The Law was our custodian until Christ came." The position of the people was like that of a young son. For though he is the heir and master of all his father's possessions, he is not intrusted with these possessions until he is of age and properly trained; and he must submit to a custodian until he becomes the new master of the house. Second, the prophets were to prophesy concerning this kingdom of God and glorify it, and in this way they were to admonish the people to submit to the custodian patiently for a season. They were also to comfort the people, so that these people might not despair of this kingdom, even though it might appear to them that the kingdom would never come, because they were so greatly tormented, oppressed, taken captive, and led away by the Gentiles. In this way one might admonish a young heir to be good, study diligently, and obey the custodian, because it would not be long before he would be rich and a great master. One might also admonish him to endure it gladly if his father used the rod and at times flogged him and not to think that his father would therefore abandon him or put him out of his home, but rather, as a good child, to submit to such sternness, anger, and bitter looks until he has reached maturity.

While the prophets perform these two offices through their preaching, they at times perform miracles or offer comforting visions of God in order to confirm their teaching among the people. A father does not always use the rod or employ a taskmaster, but at times he buys his son and heir a pair of red shoes or a purse or a gift from the fair, or he sends or brings them to him, so that the son will not hate the rod excessively or even hate his father but will submit patiently to this harsh rod and always, despite rod and taskmaster, keep a place in his heart for the love of his father. In brief: just as a good, wise father brings up his child, so God dealt with these people and also deals with us today. He has us suffer much according to the flesh and holds a harsh rod and stern taskmaster over us, but at the same time He comforts us with the promise of future great joy and bliss in heaven.

Now in these offices, and especially in the second, the prophet Zechariah is a model, and in my opinion the outstanding one. For he, too, lived in an age when it was most necessary to comfort the people by means of the coming of the kingdom of Christ and to keep them in order, since neither before nor after have the people, as long as they have been called God's people, been so scattered, dispersed, and dispelled as at the time of the Babylonian captivity. For at that time the people of Israel were like a flock of sheep when the wolf has come among them in the absence of the shepherd: the greater part are slaughtered, while those that get away and escape are so confused and timid that one can hardly direct them again and lead them back to the fold. Or, when a marten steals his way among the chickens at night, then, too, there is such a slaying, scattering, and lamenting that the other chickens also become so fearful and timid that they do not know what to do; and one must again act very carefully if one is to gather them together once more. And that is how the Jewish people also felt when they had just been troubled by the Babylonians, so that, regardless of what they were planning or undertaking, they always had the feeling that the land was full of Babylonians. Therefore it took much coaxing and many a good, pleasant word on the part of the prophet before he could again gather and strengthen them. We, who have not been in the same difficulties, are not moved by the prophet's words but consider them vain and of no significance for our times. But they show us a very fine example of faith, which we should never have had, even if we had lived among the Jews in the days of the prophets, as we shall see later.

1-2. *In the eighth month, in the second year of Darius, the Word of the Lord came to Zechariah the son of Berechiah, son of Iddo, the prophet, saying: The Lord was very angry with your fathers.*

In order to understand this text, we must consult a bit of ancient history. In the first chapter of Ezra (Ezra 1:2 ff.) we read that Cyrus, the first king of Persia, in the first year of his reign, permitted the Jews to be free and go to Jerusalem to rebuild the temple, as had been foretold by the prophet Jeremiah (Jer. 29:10 ff.). In this first year, then, the foundation was laid and building begun. But when Cyrus went to Scythia to do battle against Queen Tomyris, he left behind

Darius Hystaspis, who was king with him and had helped him to gain Babylon and the Chaldean empire. Darius, however, died in the second year, and Cyrus carried on the war for about 20 years, until the queen slew him and cast his head into a vat of human blood and said, "Now drink the blood you have always thirsted for." [1] Because Darius now was dead and Cyrus was at war away from home, the local officials in Judea took it upon themselves to hinder the Jews so much that they had to suspend operations and were unable to do any building during the 20 years of Cyrus (Ezra 4:4 ff.). And they fared as poor wretched people usually fare at the hands of tyrants, and as Zechariah later confesses (Zech. 8:10), "Neither was there any safety," etc.; and no one was able to do anything. So badly did the work fare that God had begun through King Cyrus!

After the death of Cyrus came Artakhshasta. Read about him in Ezra (4:7 ff.). Elsewhere he is called Artaxerxes or Cambyses and Ahasuerus Priscus; his captain, Holofernes, was slain by the Jews at Bethulia through Judith (Judith 13:9), provided the story is true. Therefore Artaxerxes became angry, for the Jews had also been accused before him at other times by the governors, as we see in Ezra 4:7 ff.; and for that reason he forbade them to build the temple. This period also lasted 20 years – as long as he reigned. Think of it, for so long a time the Jews were delayed and hindered. Ought they not quite properly to have despaired and grown weary in their faith, since in 42 years they had had no success but only hindrances? Therefore the prophets had to offer many signs and wonders at this time to comfort the people and to preserve their faith in their many misfortunes.

Next came the third king, Darius Longimanus, of whom Zechariah and Haggai speak and in whose second year and at whose command the temple was built, Ezra 6. Then there was progress, and at that time the prophets arose and urged the people on. For that reason the Jews say, John 2:20, that it had taken 46 years to build the temple and that Christ would raise it up in three days. That is, for 46 years, through many hindrances, men were active before it was completed – as Daniel had also foretold (Dan. 9:25), "in troubled times," that is, it would be built with difficulties and grief. From all this we know when this

1 The Weimar editor cites as Luther's probable source for this story Antoninus Florentinus, *Summa historialis,* I, tit. IV, cap. 1, par 4. The likelihood that this is Luther's source is strengthened by the fact that the report on Artaxerxes in the next paragraph agrees almost verbatim with par. 5 of this source. Cf. *Luther's Works,* 17, p. 122, n. 1.

prophet Zechariah lived, namely, in the 45th year after the children of Israel had been released from Babylon; and he began to preach two months after Haggai. For Haggai began in the sixth month of the second year of Darius. And that is what he says here: he began in the second year of Darius, in the eighth month. The Hebrew language calls this king *Daryavesh*, and King Cyrus *Koresh*.

Zechariah begins his first sermon with the words, "The Lord was very angry with your fathers"; that is, he reminds his people of the Lord's wrath and punishment because of the past sins of their fathers. And the whole first sermon sticks to this theme in order to induce them, in view of their present punishment for earlier disobdience, to be so much the better and more obedient from now on. This is the way one shows a child the rod with which he has been whipped before to try to induce him to be better in the future. It is as if the prophet were commissioned to say: "You see how angry the Lord was with your fathers and how severely He punished them for their disobedience. Be careful therefore and take heed that you do not follow their example. For we are now coming to you with God's Word and command that you be good and build the temple. But if you, too, will be disobedient, then the rod and the punishment will not be long in coming," as one sees from the text that follows, where the prophet further emphasizes his sermon.

3. *Therefore say to them: Thus says the Lord of hosts: Return to Me, says the Lord of hosts, and I will return to you, says the Lord of hosts.*

Before the prophet tells the people of their fathers' disobedience and lets them see the punishment and wrath of God, he first cries out and preaches to them that they should be obedient, and he says: "Return to Me," that is, "Prepare to be My people, to serve Me alone, and to obey My commandments. Then I will return to you and again be your God and do all good things for you and defend you against all the world, as I did before I turned away from you, when your fathers still were good and had not turned away from Me either. One turn brings the next: as your fathers turned away from Me, so I turned away from them. And thus, if you now turn back to Me, I will turn back to you, too." I say this because the pedants and sophists [2]

[2] E. g., Erasmus, *De libero arbitrio* διατριβή, trans. E. Gordon Rupp, in *Luther and Erasmus: Free Will and Salvation*, Vol. XVII in *The Library of Christian Classics* (Philadelphia: The Westminster Press, 1969), p. 56.

use these words to refer to the free will, as though a man could convert himself because the Lord here says, "Return to Me," though obviously the text here is not saying anything about what a man is able to do but what he is supposed to do. For when it says, "Return to Me," it indicates that men should make a turn, that is, keep all the commandments and be good. But Scripture does not say here whether a man can do this of himself, but it does speak clearly enough elsewhere. These two things are far apart: being able to do a thing and being required to do it. Therefore one must not use or understand Scripture as referring to a man's being able to do a thing when it speaks only of his being required to do it. I have written more fully about this in my booklet *Servum arbitrium.*[3]

Now let us see why the prophet, who is to comfort the poor frightened flock, first of all frightens them even more by beginning with threats and showing them the rod. These are, however, the ways and means of the Holy Spirit; He first begins harshly and sternly and later becomes friendly and sweet. The devil, on the other hand, enters softly and begins sweetly; but later he leaves his stench behind him and departs sour. So a father at first rears his child severely and sternly; later, however, it is his dear child, who is shown nothing but sweet love. And so it is here. Because the prophet wants to offer much comfort, he begins harshly and sternly. And not only is this the Spirit's ways and means; but because we are as we are, necessity demands this procedure. For as was said before, for more than 40 years the poor people had suffered much opposition from their neighbors and the emperor of Persia himself; they also fared badly, as Haggai tells us (Hag. 1:5 ff.), so that the great manifestations of evil, which at all times arise to oppose God's Word and work, might well have made the people weary enough to turn away from God, as their fathers had done. And some indeed did turn away and join the Gentiles, like the high priest's son who took the daughter of the Gentile Tobiah, as Nehemiah writes (Neh. 13:38; 2:10). Therefore it was necessary first to show them the rod and frighten them, so that they might not let those evils turn them aside and cause them to become like their fathers in sin and wickedness.

For man is in the habit of excusing himself thus: "What am I to do? If I do not follow the crowd, I must give up wife, child, possessions,

[3] *De servo arbitrio,* trans. Philip S. Watson, *Luther's Works,* 33.

honor, and life.[4] How am I to support myself? Where am I to live?" Men talk as if they must give up God's Word for such reasons, or as if God could not prevent all these evils or recompense His people for the things they had to lose for His sake. In this way the people in the Gospel, too, excused themselves, the one saying that he had bought fields, the other oxen, the third that he had married a wife (Luke 14:18 ff.). In this way also Ahas, the king of Judah, wanted to have the favor of the gods of Syria and thus lost the favor of his God (1 Kings 16:3 ff.). Oh, it is a great and powerful and nobel sermon that Zechariah here preaches, even though his words may sound simple; but when one considers how things stood at that time, then it was surely a splendid and necessary sermon – necessary to keep the people from turning aside from God and falling away from His Word. In the same way one must continue to shout and cry out among us Christians when persecution, rebellion, or heresy breaks forth and rages, if one is to keep the people from turning about and away from God. And so it was then with the Jews, the poor scattered little flock.

And therefore the prophet is so vehement and in these brief words employs the name of God, the Lord of hosts, three times, when otherwise one time would have been enough. For it means something to him and is very important that the people remain true to the Lord of hosts and not fall away because of their blows and temptations. Nor is it to be ignored that the Spirit in this way subtly wished it to be known that there are three Persons in the one Godhead, each of whom is called Lord of hosts. And while the Jews neither believe this nor regard it as significant for themselves, we Christians still believe that it has pleased God thus to reveal Himself to His people.

4. *Be not like your fathers, to whom the former prophets cried out: Thus says the Lord of hosts, Return from your evil ways and from your evil deeds. But they did not hear or heed Me, says the Lord.*

Here the prophet holds up as an example for his people the disobedience of their fathers, as if to say: "Your fathers also had reason and tribulations enough from their neighbors, even as you are suffering them now, to fall away from Me. But I sent prophets and had these preach to your fathers that they should cling to Me. It did not do any good, however; they fell away and turned from Me. Take care that you do not follow their example. For what did your fathers gain?

[4] Cf. *Nehmen sie den Leib, Gut, Ehr, Kind und Weib* in stanza 4 of *Ein feste Burg.*

They wanted to escape the rain and fell into the river." They wanted to avoid tribulation and thereby perished, as follows:

5. *Your fathers, where are they? And the prophets, do they live forever?*

Here the prophet lets the people see the punishment of their fathers and says: "They were not willing to listen to Me through My prophets, but they did listen to their own prophets. For the latter promised them peace, happiness, and good fortune if they would only turn to the Gentiles and pray to their gods and forsake Me; because then, of course, they would not suffer anything from the Gentiles because of Me. But how wonderfully well did they fare? Your fathers, who obeyed those prophets and forsook Me, where are they now? They are dead, as you can see, and their hopes have deceived them. And the prophets that offered them comfort, are they still living? But because you see and feel that these men were deceived and gained nothing but ruin by falling away from Me, take care and do not let any evil or tribulation be so great as to turn you aside. Cling to Me; I will watch over you."

You can see here that this sermon has to do primarly with faith and unbelief; because Zechariah presents the prophets and teachers in such a way as to make one understand that the greatest sin of their fathers was that they did not put their faith or trust in God in their tribulations but rather sought help among men and thus became disloyal and idolatrous. He also wants the word "return to Me" to penetrate deeply and probe the heart. For one "turns to God" when one depends and relies on Him in all things and needs and supplications. Contrariwise one "turns away from God" when one does not put one's trust in Him; and in that case neither the sacrifices nor the good works which their fathers together with their prophets practiced so diligently avail at all. In the case before us, too, in the building of the temple, when there was much affliction, there was need of turning to the Lord of hosts, of clinging to Him and depending on Him, though the emperor in Persia or their neighbors might rage. God says that He will and desires to and can help so that they might not once more fall to the Gentiles. We need this admonition and similar ones at all times against the mobs and tyrants, however, if we are not to fall away because of them. For we can see very well what happened to the Romans and all other tyrants. Where are they now? And the Arians and all other heretics, where are they now? And the princes and mobs who are raging now will shortly be like the others too. Therefore let every one turn to Christ and cling to Him and not fall away; and let no one be intimidated or misled. God speaks. And God will keep His Word.

6. *But My words and My statutes, which I commanded My servants the prophets, did they not overtake your fathers? So they repented and said, As the Lord of hosts purposed to deal with us for our ways and deeds, so has He dealt with us.*

This means: "My prophets and I must have been wrong at that time: what they said did not mean anything at all. And the false prophets must have been right; your fathers followed them. But how did it all end? My Word prevailed; and what I had said, that happened, and not what the false prophets had said. Very well, let that be a warning to you, and learn from the experience that you have had that all their teachings and hopes are vain, which they themselves ultimately, in the midst of their punishment, had to confess – that is, that things were not working out as their prophets had told them, but rather as I had told them. At the time, however, nothing did any good; now that it has happened, they believe and can feel it. But you take heed, too! Oh, if only someone could get the tyrants and mobs of our time to believe God's words! But that will not happen. They want to experience it themselves and must experience it if they, too, are finally to hear this preaching and confess that it was true and at the same time to say that they had not believed that things would take this course." In sum: one does not believe God until one learns from experience. But then one has waited too long.

This, then, is a brief outline of this first sermon of Zechariah: he first wishes to make the people pious and God-fearing by means of threats and promises; and in order to frighten them, he offers them the example of their fathers. For while they are to build the temple and the city of Jerusalem and do good deeds like these, he first wants them to be pious, so that they might not think that God would be satisfied with their work of building the temple and the city, as their fathers had thought that it was enough if they sacrificed. No, my good man, rather than all good works He wants faith and a heart converted to Him. That is all He is interested in. This must come first and be preached first: "Return to Me, and after that build Me a temple," and not, "First build Me a temple, and after that return to

Me." Good works inflate us and make us proud, but faith and conversion humble us and make us despair of ourselves. For this very reason the people had to be kept for more than 40 years from building the temple; since obviously there was not a hindrance in this but rather a strong exhortation to believe and to be pious, patient, and holy; that is, there were so many afflictions and persecutions that they ought to have learned from their experience that being pious and having faith were worth far more than building temples and houses and offering sacrifices to God; as Hosea 6:6 also says: "I desire steadfast love and not sacrifice, etc." So God always teaches faith and true piety first, and only then outward deeds. Men, however, who have got far beyond faith and piety, teach first and foremost mere outward deeds, as though these were the important things. But God tells us here that He will not look at the temple unless the people are first converted and pious, though the temple be of pure gold, rubies, emeralds, and diamonds.

7. *On the twenty-fourth day of the eleventh month, which is the month of Shebat, in the second year of Darius, the Word of the Lord came to Zechariah, the son of Berechiah, son of Iddo, the prophet; and Zechariah said.*

The Jews do not count the months according to the calendar, as we do, but according to the course of the moon in the heavens; nor do they begin the year as we do. For with them the first month and the beginning of the year is April; that is, when April becomes new, when spring comes and everything is new. To be sure, according to the course of the moon it frequently is April in the heavens when it is still March on the calendar. And so it is with all the other months. Among the Jews the 11th month is February;[5] it may well be, however, that it is still January according to the calendar and for us, when among the Jews February has already begun. So Zechariah began this first sermon, in which he told the people to be pious, in the eighth month, that is, in the winter month, at the very time of the vintage – according to the calendar, then, in the wine month. And he prepared his second sermon, in which he encouraged the people to build, about the day of Our Lady's Candlemas,[6] when spring is bursting forth and it is almost time to work and build.

[5] Luther uses the Germanic name for February, *Der Hornung*, which means about as much as "the stepchild," the one deprived of its full complement of days.

[6] February 2 is the day for three church festivals: The Presentation of Our Lord, the Purification of Mary, and Candlemas. At the latter observance the

After the first sermon, the second now follows, in which the prophet begins to encourage the people to build. For during the three months he had undoubtedly preached the first sermon more than once and also emphasized and explained his words by means of illustrations, as one commonly does in preaching. In the second sermon he now shows the people a comforting vision: a man on a red horse is standing among the myrtle trees with many others who have come to report to him that all the lands are at peace. For the prophet had received his visions that he might preach them to the people as an encouragement and admonition. And this is the sum and meaning of this vision: The people are not to be afraid, neither of the emperor in Persia nor of their neighbors, but are to feel sure and confident that from now on no one would prevent them from building, as they had been prevented until now. For there was neither war nor discord anywhere, but all the lands were quiet, everywhere there was peace, and the time was good for building. But it was difficult for the people to believe this, because during the preceding 40 years they had experienced altogether different things, and therefore the prophet had to strengthen their hearts with both word and vision and assure them that God had ceased being angry and was gracious.

All the details of the vision, moreover, in both action and words, show that there was peace and quiet. The first detail is that the angels appear and speak with men. For where there is wrath, the angels leave us and conceal themselves, so that they are neither seen nor heard. The second detail is that the angels do not stand with horses in columns or battle array, nor do they carry shield or sword. Instead, they stand in a happy meadow or orchard, where one is not in the habit of quarreling but of singing, dancing, and being happy, as when there is peace in the land. The third detail is that the angel stands among the myrtle trees. Myrtle trees are not to be found in German lands, nor have I seen them elsewhere. It is a matter of record,[7] however, that it is not a wild tree but a domesticated one, like pear or apple trees. But it is green in winter and in summer, like the fir, the pine, and the boxwood; and it has berries, of which one makes must and oil and which taste like grapes, and it has many narrow leaves. But it is not

candles to be used in worship were ceremoniously blessed and carried in procession in memory of the Gospel's words: "A light for revelation to the Gentiles and for glory to Thy people Israel" (Luke 2:32). The German name of the feast is *Lichtmess.*

[7] Cf. Pliny, *Historia naturalis,* XV, ch. 35.

able to protect itself. One also makes short spear shafts of it, as one makes pig spits of hornbeams among us, for it is not a tall tree. The Romans used it for wreaths when they celebrated a triumph and also in reconciliations. The fact, however, that the angel is standing among the domesticated trees is a sign that there is peace, just as it would be a sign of peace if we saw horsemen standing among the lindens. For under the lindens we are in the habit of drinking, dancing, and being gay and not of quarreling and being serious; for among us the linden is a tree of peace and happiness.

The fourth detail is that the angels become articulate in words and also freely confess that there is peace everywhere. "We have," they say, "gone through all the lands, and behold, all the lands are quiet." That means: "You do not have to be afraid of anyone; there is no strife or hostility toward you anywhere." Shortsighted reason, however, will not yet believe this but will always fear the opposite. Because it has once been struck on the mouth, it fears that there must be more blows coming. The Jews, too, who indeed had gone through the mill before and been beaten severely, felt that way and therefore always feared that more evil was coming. For this reason, too, this vision has an outward appearance that conforms to their inmost thinking; for though all is comforting and peaceful, reason cannot see it thus or accept it. Therefore the prophet himself begins by saying with fear, "What are these, my Lord?" as if he would say, "Alas, there are horses and horsemen present. What does it mean? What do they intend to do? Is there no peace yet but still war and hostility?"

When God begins to comfort, he always makes things seem terrible. Thus the Virgin Mary was frightened when the Angel Gabriel brought her that most happy annunciation (Luke 1:29). And the shepherds in the fields were at first frightened by the brightness of the angels (Luke 2:9). And so were the disciples when they saw Christ walking on the sea (Mark 6:49). Here too, then, Zechariah feared for his own person and for his people when he saw horses and horsemen. For horses are beasts of war, as Solomon says in his proverbs (Prov. 21:31) and Job in chapter 39:21.[8] The fact, however, that the prophet sees the horses and horsemen in the meadow and the glen, as in a clever, dangerous ambush, moreover at night, when everything is more dangerous and frightening anyway than in the day, indicates how fearful and timid their hearts had been. For visions and revela-

8 The Weimar editor corrects the text's "Job 31."

tions accommodate themselves to the state of the heart. Therefore the angel, or the man who is standing among the myrtle trees – for Zechariah mentions both – comforts him, as though he were saying: "It is true: you see horses, and they are red, sorrel, and white; that is, kings and princes are still living and reigning. But do not be afraid. We are mounted on them and are keeping them at peace in a beautiful meadow among the myrtle trees; and you do not see us in armor. They will not harm you or your people but rather serve and help you."

Here we must say something about horses and angels. The first horses are red; the next are sorrel, which Vergil [9] calls *spadices*, chestnut-brown ones, strong horses of a good breed; the third are white. By horses are meant all the dominions which prevailed at that time, especially round about the Jews. Some to be sure regard the Babylonians as the red horses, the Assyrians as the sorrel, the Persians as the white. But as I have said, because the angels say that all the lands through which they have passed are at peace, we must content ourselves with this, that they are referring to all the kingdoms and dominions round about them and especially to the empire which was in power at that time and of which they were afraid. The fact, however, that the first color is black, the next sorrel, the last white, indicates, I think, what I have already said: that revelation is given in accordance with the thinking of the people to whom it is given. Now the people always remembered the murdering and capturing that they had experienced before and that they always feared, and therefore the first color is red and blood-colored. But because comfort was at hand, the second color, next to the red, was sorrel, as a sign that the fear was soon to be modified and that the fear would soon be changed to a feeling of security. And this security is indicated by the last color, the white, which is a cheerful color, like light.

This text in Zechariah, however, is one of those words from which one learns how God rules the world by means of the angels, though of course He does everything by Himself. For God has instituted a fourfold rule: one, in which He works by Himself alone, without the cooperation of His creatures and in which things run their course solely and alone through His might. He acts in this way when He creates and multiplies His creatures, preserves them, and gives them various powers and skills. In this rule no one assists Him. In the second He puts such created and preserved creatures into the care of His angels

[9] Vergil, *Georgics*, III, 82. Cf. p. 16, n. 11.

so that these might lead, guide, preserve, guard, and help these creatures, and especially us men, from without. For from within the One God alone preserves and helps. But while the angels, to be sure, do not help from within, as God does, they nevertheless do their part from without by inspiring men with good, useful, or necessary thoughts and by keeping or removing evil, harmful thoughts from them. In this way they help to preserve and improve men and creatures outwardly, which God alone does inwardly.

Thus it happens to many a man that he will escape fire, water, murder, and other misfortunes because of some insignificant thing that has moved him. Such a thought, or whatever it may be, comes to him so that he does, all at once, the thing that saves him, a thing which he could never have foreseen or thought beforehand but of which he must say, "Indeed, if I had done this or that, I surely should have drowned, been burned to death or murdered, or died or suffered harm in some other way"; or, as someone else might say, "You had your guardian angel with you there." The Gentiles therefore ascribed such happenings to good fortune and made an idol of fortune. For they saw and learned that such things happened but did not know that the true God had done them through His holy angels. So it happened that St. Augustine, when the heretics were lying in wait to kill him, took a different road without any further thought [10] but undoubtedly because of his angel's doing. And when Emperor Julius leaped from the ship and escaped his enemies by swimming, he surely was of good courage and confidence;[11] yet his counsel and courage had been inspired in him by his guardian angel from without and by God from within. Thus it is with all men when they escape misfortune or have good fortune: it is all the work of God and the angels.

And so we see here that the angel cares and pleads for the Jews and also instructs and comforts Zechariah from without. And in Daniel (Dan. 8:15 ff.; 9:21 ff.) Gabriel has much teaching, comforting, and instructing to do and shows there how Michael, the angel of the Jews, contends for them and how the angel of the empire of Persia opposes him. Such an incident and similar revelations of the angels show that they concern themselves with us without ceasing, invisible and unobserved, that it is their office to help and counsel men, to further and advance them, and also to plead and care for us. And so every em-

10 Augustine, *Enchiridion,* ch. 17, *Patrologia, Series Latina,* XL, 239.

11 Antoninus Florentinus, *Summa historialis,* I, tit. IV, ch. 5, No. 34.

peror, king, prince, master, indeed, every man has his angel, whether the emperor or his empire be Christian or not. For it is an outward office which they exercise for both the good and the evil, because both, good and evil, are God's creatures, created by Him. And for that reason He also feeds, preserves, cares for, and guards and multiplies them as God and Master of His work. Where else should the Romans so often have got such fine agreements, counsels, and ideas? How else should Hannibal have been so apt and ready and courageous? How else should Alexander the Great have been so alert and active, so bold and happy? Whatever they may have or do that is useful or fortunate is all the work of God and the angels.

The third rule is that which God carries on through men, such as apostles and preachers. For although God could teach men the Gospel without preaching and also does that inwardly (even as He preserves and governs all creatures inwardly and without the angels), He nevertheless does not wish to act in this way but uses the preachers outwardly by means of the Word and lets them contribute to the teaching and the Spirit, which He Himself grants inwardly. Thus St. Paul glories in 1 Cor. 3:9 that preachers are assistants and fellow workers of God in saving the Corinthians. And in 2 Cor. 6:1 he says, "Working together with Him, then, we entreat you, etc." Thus also through the angels, as fellow workers and His assistants, He helps and saves all men and does not desire to teach without the preachers or help without the angels. Therefore God wants the office of the ministry and all government to be honored; for they are His work and that of His angels and messengers.

The fourth rule is the secular government, which comprehends the rule of the home and the authority of parents over their children. For although God would be able to rear children without parents, as He proved in the case of Adam and Eve and still proves daily in the case of orphans, He does not wish to do it this way but has ordained that He will do it through the parents and with the parents. He could also rule the house without householders, and He often does that. Yet He does not wish to do it this way but wishes to do it with the householders and through the householders, as Ps. 127:1 says, "Unless the Lord builds the house, those who build it labor in vain." And so He could also maintain peace, punish the evil, protect the good without sword and princes. Yet He does not wish to do it this way but has ordained that the princes should help Him; that is, He wishes to work with them and through them. Therefore all rules are His and are true, divine rules; nor does He need angels or men to prove His wonderful might, wisdom, and goodness.

He has, then, three outward rules and in addition three outward ways or means for His own divine rule. In the secular rule it is the sword and the fist, in the spiritual it is the Word and the mouth, in the angelic it is reason and sense. These are the three means: sword, Word, reason. By the sword, however, I understand all that pertains to the secular rule, all secular rights and laws, customs and habits, actions, stations, various offices, persons, clothes, etc. By the Word I understand all that pertains to the spiritual rule, such as spiritual gifts, 1 Cor. 12:5, Eph. 4:11, Rom. 12:6 f., and the sacraments and the like. By reason I understand everything that the dear angels use to move us and keep us from evil and to further our welfare. For they do not rule by the sword or the Word, though they might. The spiritual rulers, on the other hand, cannot rule by reason, like the angels, nor do they rule with the sword, though they could do that too, but by the Word. The secular rulers cannot rule by reason, like the angels, nor by the Word, like the spiritual rulers, but govern by the sword. Thus each has its designated work and limit: the lowest cannot perform the office of the highest, but the highest can indeed perform that of the lowest. The secular rule, however, is the lowest and least of the rules of God; for it makes no one pious but only punishes the evil and resists the rebellious. But more of that elsewhere.

And none of these rules is against the other, and none crushes or destroys the other; but the one serves the other. The lowest, the rule of the sword, serves the Gospel by maintaining peace among the people; and without that one could not preach. The Gospel, in turn, serves the sword by teaching, holding people to the obedience of the sword and bearing witness to the fact that the sword is the ordinance and rule of God (Rom. 13:1 ff.) and is therefore to be feared and respected. Without this fear and respect, however, the sword would have a very wretched rule. And the angels serve both the Gospel and the sword by helping to promote them and moving the people toward them through reason. The sword and the Word, in turn, serve the angels; for they create opportunities and through peace and prosperity prepare the people so that the angels may all the better approach them and promote their rule. For in the midst of strife and error the angels find it difficult to rule through their reason.

Against this rule of God, however, Satan rages; for his sole purpose is to crush and destroy everything that God creates and does through this rule. First he opposes the rule of God and, as far as God permits him, throttles and destroys and spoils everything that God creates, preserves, and improves. For he is the prince of this world (John 16:11; 2 Cor. 4:4), yes, even a god; in opposition to the rule of the angels he has his own angels, who inspire, counsel, and incite the princes, lords, and all men to nothing but evil and promote all hindrances to good and all furtherance to evil, incite the people against one another, set things aflame wherever they can, and fill the world with grief and heartache. Opposed to the spiritual rule he has the heretics, false teachers, hypocrites, false brethren; and he does not rest until he has destroyed this rule. Opposed to the secular rule he has the rebellious, lawless scoundrels, evil, venomous counselors at the courts of the princes, flatterers, traitors, spies, tyrants, madmen, and everything that promotes war, discord, and destruction of lands and people. But enough of that for the present. From this everyone can go on to think how wonderfully God rules the world, and how easily He can punish us when we sin: by merely withdrawing His hand and letting the devil have his way. Then things go horribly enough in all the world.

12. *Then the angel of the Lord said: O Lord of hosts, how long wilt Thou have no mercy on Jerusalem and the cities of Judah, against which Thou hast had indignation these seventy years?*

The angel must speak this prayer also that the prophet might listen to it, report it to the people, and comfort them. It is, moreover, an excellent prayer: first, because it is spoken by the Jews' very own angel, namely St. Michael, Dan. 12:1, who takes a most sincere interest in his people; and then, because Michael is considered so great and mighty by the others that they come to him and answer him and report that all the lands are resting quietly, so that the timid people might surely be comforted when they hear that this mighty angel cares and pleads for them so sincerely.

Secondly, he makes the prayer fervent and emphatic by adducing two facts: that all the countries are at rest while the very land of God alone must have fear and unrest, and that God had promised that after 70 years He would end this imprisonment, as Jer. 25:11 ff. and 29:10 had announced. It is as though he were commissioned to say: "Lord of hosts, do have mercy, for all other godless kings and countries remain at rest, while Your own people alone must have unrest, when it surely would be more proper if the former had unrest and Your own people had peace. Besides, You have promised that after 70 years You would turn Your indignation away. But because You are just in Your works and truthful in Your words, You surely will regard Yourself and think of Your justice and truthfulness, even if You do not wish to regard the people." Notice how carefully and concisely the angel speaks to God. And those are the right prayers, those that move and impel Him because of His justice and truthfulness and not merely because of our needs and requests. Where will He go? What will He do? His own justice and truthfulness beg, impel, urge Him. He must proceed and hear. Blessed are they who can attain to such a prayer, for they cannot fail; their prayer will surely be answered. See, that is indeed a true and rich comfort. Yet that is not all: for there follows:

13. *And the Lord answered gracious and comforting words to the angel who talked with me.*

Even though the Lord is not speaking with the prophet, the prophet also had to hear how the Lord hears and answers the prayer of the angel; and therefore the prophet can comfort the people all the better, because he is hearing not only the mighty angel but is also hearing the Lord Himself as He speaks with the angel and promises that He will hear him. But what friendly, charming, sweet, and comforting words these were, the angel goes on to tell the prophet, as follows:

14-15. *So the angel who talked with me said to me: Cry out:*[12] *Thus says the Lord of hosts: I am exceedingly jealous for Jerusalem and for Zion. And I am very angry with the nations that are at ease;*[13] *for while I was angry but a little they furthered the disaster.*

Look at all of these words and see in how fatherly and sincere a way they are spoken. They surely do not sound different from the words of a dear father, who after using the rod invites his child to him again and speaks the most kindly words to him, and begins by throw-

[12] Luther translates *clama, dicens* with *predige und sprich* ("preach and say").

[13] Luther translates *gentes opulentas* with *die stolzen Heiden* ("the proud Gentiles").

ing away the rod. Indeed, he is angry at the rod, scolds and kicks it as though the rod had acted and not he. Then he interprets his flogging in the most favorable way: that he had meant well, and that it had not been anger but only love. And he also offers him a farthing or an apple as a token so that the timid child might forget the rod and again act toward him like a child. Just so God is here dealing with the Jews. He begins by scolding the rod as though not He had acted, but the Gentiles, and says: "I am exceedingly jealous for Jerusalem, etc."; that is: "I have not really been angry, so that I might have desired to reject or forsake My people; but as a father punishes his child or a husband his wife and is angry with her, so I have acted too."

For jealousy is not the evil anger which enemies have toward one another; but it is an anger of love, a friendly, fatherly anger, like that of men who are angry with one another, though they love one another. For such anger serves to make the love that follows all the more fervent and quite new; and if this kind of anger did not at times come between love, love would grow lax, and rust would devour it like iron. But jealousy sweeps it clean and constantly renews it, as also the heathen Terence says, "Love is renewed, whenever they who love each other are angry with each other." [14] Therefore I am in the habit of calling zeal or jealousy "angry love"; for when love is angry, it does no harm. But when hatred or envy is angry, it destroys and ruins as long as it can. For our loving anger seeks and desires to remove the bad, which it hates, from the good, which it loves, so that the good and what it loves may be preserved; just as a father desires to preserve his dear child, though he desires to put away the sin. And a husband also wants to preserve his dear wife but desires that her shame and vice be undone. The angry hatred, on the other hand, rushes in and wishes to destroy and annihilate both good and evil.

Thus God says also here that He has been angry with Jerusalem not out of hatred and enmity but has been zealous as a father and angry out of love, so that He might sweep out their vice and preserve them as His children. He Himself explains His anger in this way and says: "I was angry but a little"; as if to say: "My wrath is a brief, little anger. It does not last long and hence does not cut to the quick but flogs a little, that it might remove the evil." Thus He excuses His anger and lovingly invites the hearts of the people back to Him. And indeed, when one sees who it is that is speaking, namely God Himself,

[14] Terence, *Andria,* III, 3, 23: *Amantium irae amoris integratiost.*

then these are truly sweet words, yes, words of life, joy, and every bliss. For even though a man were amidst death and hell and heard these words of God, he would have to become alive and happy because of these words. We, however, ignore them, regard them as though some human being had spoken them, and do not believe that God Himself is speaking. And therefore we do not taste, either, how sweet they are.

Next He upbraids the Gentiles, who have been His rod. He does not say that He is indignant with them but that He is very angry with them; and He calls them proud and accuses them of having furthered disaster; that is, they did not seek ways of punishing Jerusalem – and for that God was using them – but their sole intent was to destroy. I cannot adequately give in German the little word "proud," in Hebrew שַׁאֲנַנִּים. For it means "secure," "certain," "free," "without care and fear"; as when great rulers depend so completely on their possessions and might that they are ready to defy anyone and are situated so securely that they think they cannot fail. So Wisdom speaks in Proverbs of Solomon, ch. 1:33: "He who listens to me will dwell secure and will be at ease without dread of evil." So He also wishes to say here: "My little nation is so timid and frightened that no one will ever be able to comfort it again. But the Gentiles feel so secure and free that no one can frighten them; they do not imagine that distress or anger is facing them for having troubled my people until now." Not so, however, says the Lord: "But I am angry with them; nor are they faring so well as they imagine. On the other hand, I am gracious toward My people; nor are they faring so badly as they imagine."

Here you can see God's judgment and work. He is angry with the secure, free, impudent, proud spirits, and He is gracious toward the timid, humble, contrite spirits. It truly is not a good sign but a terrible one when a man feels so secure and at ease that he lives without fear and danger on the basis of his temporal power and possessions; for in such a case this verse applies forcefully, "I am very angry with the nations that are at ease." On the other hand it is not a bad sign but sheer comfort when one sees fear, danger, hesitation, care, and anxiety; for in this case the verse of Is. 66:2 applies: "This is the man to whom I will look, he that is humble and contrite in spirit, and trembles at My word." All these things have been preached to the Jews for their comfort, so that they might not fear anyone on earth anymore.

For they have two good promises: the one, that God was indignant with them and yet loves them as His children; the other, that He is hostile toward their enemies and angry with them. Who, then, shall do anything against them, when God is with them? Whom shall they fear, when God is angry with their enemies and fights against them? He has been swift to protect His people and also swift to smite His enemies. Who can stand against God? There follows:

16. *Therefore, thus says the Lord: I have returned to Jerusalem with compassion; My house shall be built in it, says the Lord of hosts, and the measuring line shall be stretched out over Jerusalem.*

This is the souvenir, the trinket, or the gift that He adds to the comforting words that were mentioned: He promises that the temple and the city of Jerusalem will be rebuilt and that not even the Gentiles will be able to prevent this, as has happened up to the present, but that the work will go forward and succeed. This is what He here calls "returning to Jerusalem with compassion": they are to experience not only in words but also in deeds and actions that He is gracious and compassionate and that His anger is over.

He presents two kinds of structures: the first, His house, the temple, in which it is of the greatest concern that the souls of the people be first furnished with a spiritual rule through God's Word and worship. For God dwells where His Word and honor are. Therefore it is indeed a great act of compassion, as He calls it here, not just to build the house of wood and stone but that God intends to dwell in it with His Word, His worship, and His office and to be with His people and to teach and sanctify and help them. That is what "God's house" means. For where His Word is not to be found, there He does not dwell; nor is He interested in such a house. For when the Word no longer dwelt there, He had the temple, together with the city, destroyed by the Romans.

The other structure is the city of Jerusalem, by which the external, secular rule is understood, and which is another act of compassion. For one must have the two powers: the spiritual for the soul, the secular for the body. But when he says, "The measuring rod shall be stretched out over Jerusalem," he briefly says the following, as it were: "In Jerusalem one will see many carpenters and builders who will be building here and there in the city, here a house, there a house, so that the measuring rod will not rest or lie idle but will be used and stretched everywhere." And by "measuring rod" he means not only the measuring rod of the carpenters but also that of the stone masons and all other builders, who survey and align their structures with line, lead, iron, and rod.

17. *Cry again: Thus says the Lord of hosts: My cities shall again overflow with prosperity, and the Lord will again comfort Zion and again choose Jerusalem.*

Not only are the temple and Jerusalem to be built, but the cities in the land of Judah are also to be blessed. But Jerusalem is to be chosen above all others; for the Lord will dwell there, and she is to be the capital city. And He will comfort her, that is, He will give her His Word and worship, also wives, children, houses and homes, possessions and honor, and whatever else is a part of a holy city and the habitation of God; even as she had earlier been grieved, devastated, and destroyed by the Chaldeans. All of the latter shall be restored again, so that both land and cities shall again come to their proper rule and standing. This was all a great prophecy and, since matters stood so badly, one that was very hard to believe at the time.

Where we should say, "My cities shall prosper again," the Hebrew would say, "The cities shall be scattered because of great possessions," that is, God will do so much good to His people and treat them in such a way that cities will be built here and there in the land and that the land will be full of cities, as though they had been scattered and sown like seed, as they actually do lie scattered about. With such words He indicates how easy it is for Him to restore a land and fill it with cities, as though He could scatter and sow cities as a farmer scatters and sows seed in his field. He wishes to do so much good for the land! For He values temporal possessions lightly, as something that He scatters about in rich measure and throws away wantonly. Yes, but who believes this? Should a man believe that God could scatter cities about like seeds of grain, indeed, fling out kingdoms wantonly, when we cannot believe that He will and can feed our bellies with a piece of bread for one day? Shame on our unbelief, that such fine, rich, mighty promises of God should be presented to it in vain!

18. *And I lifted my eyes and saw, and behold, four horns! etc.*

This, however, is another sermon and offers us another vision. And the vision shows us two things: first, four horns; next, four smiths who are to cast down these horns. And this vision appears in the same manner as the former vision: it is a terrible thing to see, even though it is comforting. And the prophet is afraid of it too and says, "What are these?" as though he would say, "Horns thrust, smiths cast down! There is nothing here yet but slaying and killing!" For as their hearts were, so the visions appeared to them; and they also receive the visions as they feel in their hearts. That is, there is fear in their hearts and therefore everything they see and hear seems terrible to them. For this is the way of the frightened conscience: it always thinks the sky is falling down and that God is standing behind them with a bludgeon.

The angel himself, however, explains what the horns are. They are the Gentiles, that is, all the kingdoms and rules round about that have scattered not only Judah and Jerusalem but Israel as well. For the four horns do not appear, as some think, in order to refer to the four empires of Assyria, Babylon, Persia, and Rome. (For the Romans had not yet done the Jews any harm or scattered them, as the angel says here of the horns, because the Romans at that time were not yet so powerful. The Persians, moreover, had done the Jews much good and had not yet scattered them.) But the horns refer to the fact that Scripture divides the world into four parts: East, West, South, and North, and from these it also has the winds blow, Matt. 24:31. The four horns, then, as the angel himself indicates, are nothing but the Gentiles, who had scattered the Jews about. For the Jews' neighbors round about, in all four directions, were hostile toward them and helped to destroy them. And it has long been known that in Scripture "horns" means kingdoms and dominions, and that fact is proved especially in Daniel (Dan. 8:3 ff.) and in the Revelation of St. John (Rev. 13:1 ff.).

The four smiths, however, are to frighten and turn the four horns away from the land of Judah. That means: "Do not be afraid of the horns any longer. They have scattered you, it is true; and you think of that too much. But they shall never do it again. For here are four smiths, and they shall surely prevent them. Who are these smiths? They are the angels, into whose care these kingdoms and dominions are committed, as was said above;[15] they shall frighten them away, that is, hold them off and turn them away, so that no harm may come to you from them to prevent the building of the temple."

In Hebrew the word "smiths" refers not only to smiths but to all kinds of workmen that have to do with building, such as smiths, carpenters, masons, stone cutters, cabinetmakers, goldsmiths, and who-

[15] Cf. pp. 169—171 above.

ever works with wood, stone, iron, and bronze. Some might think, therefore, that these four workmen represent all kinds of people who were to help in any way in the building of the temple. But I hold to the opinion that they are the angels, who appear to the people in the form of workmen in order to comfort the people, so that these might feel sure that the work of building will go on without any hindrance. For even as the first vision shows the angels standing among the myrtle trees and all the earth remaining at rest, so this vision shows that in this rest the building is to be furthered without any hindrance. Therefore the dear angels must, for the sake of the weak, come and appear in the guise of workmen: the one carries an adze and a measuring line, the second a stone hammer and a chisel, the third a hatchet and a plane, the fourth a hammer and tongs, as though they would say: "Four horns have scattered Judah, but four workmen shall rebuild her. That is, do not be afraid: you now have as many to help you to build as there were those that crushed you. Besides, the former are better able to build than the latter were to destroy; and the former will chase the latter away and hold them off so that the building must prosper and satisfy their appearance. They have appeared as builders, therefore there must be building." See how very lovingly God comforts the poor, timid, scattered consciences! He surely is a dear, gracious, sweet God. Blessed is he that believes it!

CHAPTER TWO

1. *And I lifted my eyes and saw, and behold, a man with a measuring line in his hand! Then I said: Where are you going? etc.*

THIS is another new sermon and a new vision. Three angels are present. The first appears with a string, or measuring line; the second, who usually speaks with the prophet and who is Michael, comes forward, that is, he comes forward into the vision. For in Hebrew "coming forward" means as much as "stepping forward," "appearing on the scene." This angel is to interpret the vision, as he had done before. The third angel also comes forward and commands the angel Michael what he is to tell the prophet. And, as I understand it, because the two angels come forward and meet, the meaning is to be this: the angel Michael is about to come forward and interpret the vision to the prophet as referring to the physical Jerusalem and to the way it is to be built. Before he does that, however, the third angel comes forward and commands him to speak about the spiritual Jerusalem. For this whole chapter speaks about the spiritual Jerusalem, that is, about the kingdom of Christ, which has been foreshadowed by Jerusalem. And for this reason, too, in the preceding chapter, I held back the allegories and mysterious interpretations for this place, because at this place the prophet produces and offers them himself.

In the preceding, first chapter the prophet had sufficiently offered the people comfort and promises by means of two visions and many words and had shown them that Jerusalem was to be rebuilt physically and temporally. Before saying anything more about the physical Jerusalem, however, he now goes on to tell them how Jerusalem is to fare once it stands fully equipped in its temporal structure, and he says, "That shall not be the end, but Jerusalem shall become so great that it cannot be measured. It shall, however, be without walls as far as the earth extends, because God Himself will be a wall of fire about it." Therefore the angel appears with the measuring line, in keeping with the hearts of the prophet and the people. For these do not yet know of any other Jerusalem than the one being measured and having space with regard to physical length and breadth. For by now we have heard often that visions appear in keeping with the thinking of people's hearts. Therefore, because Zechariah is in his heart measuring the physical city of Jerusalem, he must also see the measuring line. But the line is interpreted to him in a quite different manner, namely, that after the physical area there should arise an unmeasured city, etc.

For the man or the angel with the measuring line must of course know the length and breadth of this Jerusalem or realize that he did not have to know, since the people surely knew and could see before their very eyes how large it must be. Therefore the measuring line has to do with a different kind of measuring, namely, that of the spiritual Jerusalem. The man with the measuring line, however, is Christ, our Lord, the one Master Builder of the New Jerusalem. The fact that He has the measuring line in His hand means, however, that He distributes the Holy Spirit with His gifts, to each his share and proper part, as St. Paul teaches (Rom. 12:3 ff.; Eph. 4:7 ff.; 1 Cor. 12:4 ff.). For Christianity goes no farther nor is it more confined than the Spirit of Christ goes and is offered, and that is this spiritual measuring. The Spirit, however, goes as far as the world goes, as He says through the prophet Joel (Joel 2:28), "I will pour out My Spirit on all flesh," that is, upon all the people in all the world. Not that all men receive the Holy Spirit, for the greater part persecute Him. But He does not say, either, that He will pour out or give His Spirit into everyone's heart but that He will pour it out upon all flesh. And that simply means this: the Holy Spirit is sent out upon all men in all the world through the Word of the Gospel and is offered to all of them. Poured out in this way, it hovers over all men in the world wherever the Gospel is preached.

It is as when Christ says, while casting out the demons by the Spirit, that the kingdom of God has come upon the Jews (Luke 11:20), and when He commands the apostles, Matt. 10:7 and Luke 10:9, to tell the unbelievers: "The kingdom of God has come near to you," and then to leave them. All of which means this: "The Gospel has come near to you. In it and with it there has hovered over you and has been present and has been offered to you the kingdom of Christ, that is, the Father, the Son, and the Holy Spirit with all their grace. But you would not have it, etc." This measuring, then, and the fact that the Holy Spirit is poured out upon all flesh mean this: through the Word the Holy Spirit has been offered to all men throughout the world; He hovers over them all and is present and ready to help them; the heavens are open as far as the world reaches; no place is excluded. And all of this began in Jerusalem and from there has come in the same manner to all the world. Thus the physical Jerusalem has become a spiritual one.

See, it is a mighty comfort that is promised the Jews: they are not only to rebuild the transitory temple and the transitory city of Jerusalem and the transitory land Judah but also and at once an eternal Jerusalem. For in their prophecies the prophets, as I said above [1] and in Habakkuk,[2] combine and connect the two Jerusalems and the two kingdoms: the spiritual Jerusalem to the physical and the throne of David to the throne of Christ, in order to show that Christ should and must come while the physical Jerusalem and the Jewish rule were still in existence. For He was to begin with this physical Jerusalem and make a spiritual and eternal one of it. Therefore in Zechariah, in the midst of the prophecy and within the prophecy concerning the building of the physical Jerusalem, there must also be intermingled and affixed the prophecy concerning the spiritual Jerusalem. And because Jerusalem has been now destroyed and the rule of the Jews has long ceased, the kingdom of Christ must surely have come and the prophecies must have been fulfilled.

And since we have arrived at interpretations, we also want to apply the visions of the first chapter to the kingdom of Christ beyond that which they literally and obviously say about the fate of the physical Jerusalem. First, the angel who stands among the myrtle trees and pleads and announces the sweet, living, comforting Word is Christ Himself, who pleads for us and intercedes for us with His Father through His blood – for us, who with our sins and death had been lying in the real prison of Babylon, that is, under the devil, the "ruler of this world" (John 16:11), for 70 years, that is, all our lives. For 70 years is about the span of a human life, as Ps. 90:10 says. He also proclaims to us in the name of God the sweet comforting Gospel, in which there is forgiveness from sin and redemption from death, and through which the true Jerusalem is built and inhabited by God.

The fact that He rides a red horse refers to His wonderful way of waging war and winning the victory. For the steed is an animal of war, as we have said.[3] So He Himself says later on, chapter 10:3,

[1] Cf. p. 158 above.

[2] Cf. W, XIX, 350 ff.

[3] Cf. p. 168 above.

that He will make Judah like a proud steed in battle. This horse is the human nature of Christ, in which He fought for us against the devil, death, and sin – but only by standing still and suffering. For the angel is standing still among the myrtle trees and is not flaying about himself. The horse must, however, be red to indicate His blood, which He has shed for us. He has done these things among the myrtle trees, that is, among the Jews. For the myrtles are domesticated and cultivated trees. Similarly the Jews were not a wild, brutish, forsaken people, like the Gentiles, whom also Ps. 96:12 calls wild trees, when it says: "Then shall all the trees of the wood sing for joy." For the Jews had the fathers, the prophets, the laws of God, the worship of God, and the promises, through which they were reared to the time of Christ for that which was best. "In the meadow," or "in the glen," and not "in the mountain," refers to the synagog and the Jewish people, who at the time of Christ were lowly and were despised by the Gentile dominions, which Ps. 76:4 [4] calls "mountains of prey." For Jewry lay under the Romans and was altogether subjugated; that is, Christ came at the end of the Jewish rule to make of the glen the highest of mountains, raised above the hills, Is. 2:2.

The other angels, who were standing behind Him with red, sorrel, and white horses and were sent into all lands, are the dear apostles and their successors, who at the command of Christ preach peace and a good conscience in all lands. The fact that some are red refers to those who, like Christ the Lord, shed their blood too, such as Sts. Peter, James, Paul. The sorrel ones, who are not altogether red but not white either, refer to those who did not shed their blood nor were put to death but still suffered much in their lives, such as Sts. John, Luke, Athanasius, Hilary, and the like. The white ones refer to those who have suffered no harm in their bodies but also have stood in honor and have led pure, innocent lives, such as Sts. Ambrose, Augustine, and others like them. All of these answer the man among the myrtle trees, that is, they submissively and obediently do what Christ commands them and lays upon them.

The second vision, that of the four builders, also belongs here. For these are the apostles and teachers sent to the four corners of the world, not only to build the Christian church with the Word but also, with the same Word, to put down and subdue the hostile, such as the

[4] The Weimar corrects the text's "Ps. 51."

wise and understanding, like the Gentiles and the heretics, as St. Paul says to the Corinthians (2 Cor. 10:4 f.): "The weapons of our warfare are not worldly but have divine power to destroy . . . arguments and every proud obstacle to the knowledge of God, etc.," and as he also instructs Titus to appoint bishops who are "able to give instruction in sound doctrine" (Titus 1:9). For we, too, can see very well that in the end the Gospel has triumphed and destroyed tyrants and heretics. The fact, however, that these visions seem strange and horrible to the prophet refers to the fact that flesh and blood shun and flee the works of God and the cross of Christ and His people. For flesh and blood cannot comprehend these things; they seem too insignificant to accomplish such great things, just as the builders seem too insignificant to frighten and cast down the horns of the Gentiles. Warriors ought to have appeared with armor and weapons, with steeds and chariots. How should builders be able to wage war? It does not, then, seem at all possible that the Christians should gain the victory when tyrants and heretics rage. They are horns, that is, kings, that are opposing the builders and that have the upper hand.

Thus all the words and works of our God seem foolish in the eyes of men. He sets and incites builders against the warlike kingdoms; He wages war by building. Who has ever heard anything like that? And above, where He announces peace and quiet rest, He causes steeds to be seen, which are used for waging war, and now desires to build and have peace by waging war. But that is the way things go in the Spirit: when one preaches the Gospel, everything happens: one works and keeps peace and wages war as well; one builds and destroys as well. The warring and destroying are directed against the unbelievers and heretics; peace and building prevail among the believers. He does not, to be sure, say here that He will destroy the horns through the builders but that He will frighten and turn them away. For the Gospel does not lash about or depose the kings, but it comforts one so powerfully in the midst of their raging that these kings cannot do anything to the Christians but ultimately must yield to the cross and leave the Christians alone. Let that be enough of interpretations. Let us look at the text in part.

Enough has been said about the man with the measuring line and about the three angels. Let us hear the words of the third angel, which he speaks to the second angel as he says (v. 4): *Run, say to that young man: Jerusalem shall be inhabited as villages without walls, because of the multitude of men and cattle in it.* These words cannot be understood as referring to the physical Jerusalem, for that will be built with walls as a city should be built, as we read in Ezra and Nehemiah (Ezra 4:12; Neh. 6:15). And so it did not happen, either, that Jerusalem was built without walls, except where it was uninhabited. But he says here that it is not to be uninhabited, but inhabited, and so crowded that because of the multitude of men no wall could be about it. For he adds this to the reasons why it should be without walls, that there would be too great a multitude of men and cattle in it. Now one must indeed admit that a city is not forced to be without walls just because there are so many people in it; for one can, after all, add suburbs and wall these up too. In brief, there never will be so many people living together that one could not build a wall about them or that a city must stand open because of the multitudes, especially since it is the common custom to erect walls first at the place where the most people are living together – so that perhaps the opposite ought to have been promised.

But as has been said,[5] the prophet wants to indicate through his words that Jerusalem is to become a village as large as the world extends; and about such a village no one can build a wall because of the multitude of men. For who would complete such a wall that would inclose all the world, when the number of men is constantly increasing? It is as we have said: the kingdom of Christ shall come to all the world, and the blessing promised to Abraham shall be spread among all the heathen. Thus Lyra [6] presents a Jewish master or rabbi concerning this prophet, and he says that at the time of the Messiah Jerusalem will be so large that its walls will mark the end of the earth. He saw something, but the Jews still do not believe. The remarks can of course not refer to the physical Jerusalem.

He also speaks of the cattle that are to be in the city in such great numbers. But what are cattle to do in the kingdom of Christ, when they were not allowed in the physical Jerusalem but were always kept in the suburbs? Since he is saying about Jerusalem, however, that it is to become a large village or town without walls, he also mentions what usually is to be found in villages and towns. For in cities one has walls, towers, steeds, armor, weapons, and whatever has to do with battle; likewise courts of justice, scholars, rulers, and whatever else

[5] Cf. p. 178 above.

[6] Not in connection with this passage but in his comment on Zech. 14:17.

has to do with secular government. But in villages there are peasants and cattle and whatever has to do with one's daily bread. In this way we are shown once more that this is to be a spiritual Jerusalem, in which one is not to wear physical armor or wage war but seek food for the soul in certain peace. The men and the cattle, then, are two kinds of Christians, the strong and the weak. For the strong are men who can outwardly instruct and bear the cattle, that is, the weak, as St. Paul teaches in Rom. 14:1 and 15:1.

Third, God says: *I will be to her a wall of fire round about* (v. 5). Here we again see that this is to be a spiritual Jerusalem. It is to be without walls and still have a wall. Where God Himself, however, is the wall, and where there is to be no physical wall, at that place there surely must be a spiritual city. For God cannot be a physical wall. But are these not extremely comforting, kindly words? Where are the Christians, however, who will believe them? Show me one who really regards this word as true and believes that God is round about him like a wall of fire and that, wherever he goes or is, he does not have to fear anyone. There have been some kings who have had two or three hundred thousand men about them; and in times past Attila, the king of the Huns, had five hundred thousand men about him,[7] so that he frightened not only the Roman Empire but the rest of the world as well. The Turk also had many soldiers about him; indeed, the king of Persia, Xerxes, had about eleven hundred thousand men with him.[8] Now put all of these into one group, and what are they in comparison with him who has God about him like a wall of fire? They are beggars and poor defenseless people. And despite their great outlay and heavy armor, which cost much and require much, they cannot so much as make themselves feel sure of their lives for a moment. Did not Attila, in his gayest night, have to choke on his own blood, which usually issued from his nose? And did not the king of Persia have to escape in a boat on the sea? But the Christian does not need to pay wages for his soldiers, nor does he need armor or food, but can walk about freely, because he has a wall of fire about him that will keep his life safe in all eternity.

Thus Ps. 125:1-2 sings most beautifully too: "Those who trust in the Lord are like Mount Zion, which cannot be moved, but abides forever. As the mountains are round about Jerusalem, so the Lord is

[7] Antoninus Florentinus, *Summa historialis,* II, tit. XI, ch. 8, No. 3, 5 resp.
[8] Ibid., I, tit. IV, ch. 1, No. 13.

round about His people, from this time forth and forevermore." Mountains are round about Jerusalem, and the Lord Himself is round about His people. Mountains surely are better than walls; indeed, who would wish to wage war against a city on the other side of a mountain? But here it is even stronger and safer, because the Lord Himself will be a wall of fire. Who wants to fight through fire or who is able to? In this way God comforts us: by telling us that He will not only be a wall to protect us but will also be a terror to our enemies and will devour them like a fire. And He had, morever, proved this earlier in the case of the Children of Israel, Ex. 14:19 ff., when the angel of God with his cloud of fire placed himself between the Egyptians and Israel, so that they could not come near each other all night; but in the morning God plunged the Egyptians into the sea and killed them. Read also in the Fourth Book of Kings, in the sixth chapter (2 Kings 6:16 f.), how the prophet Elisha showed his servant fiery mountains and horses round about the city and said, "Those who are with us are more than those who are with them." But here faith is needed, because God keeps His walls of fire concealed in such a way that not only can a man not see them, but He even lets His own be pursued and killed, as though He had not drawn even a blade of straw or a spider's web, let alone a wall of fire, about them. Therefore the flesh is too weak to comprehend or believe these sayings or comforting promises. The Holy Spirit must grant grace and teach.

Finally, He also wants to *be the glory within her.* That is: with His Spirit He wants to be in the Christians and dwell with them, to teach and lead them in such a manner that because of it they may be honored; that is, through His deeds he wants to add this factor, that they may not only glory in themselves and be defiant in God with a good, happy conscience, as men who are sure that God belongs to them and they belong to God, but He also wants them to be praised in all the world because of His deeds – above all the nations with their idols, who cannot do for their people what this God can do for His people. For thus also St. Paul says, Rom. 5:11: "Not only so, but we also rejoice in God," that is, "with a happy conscience we are defiant and boast and are sure that God is ours, that He cares for us, and that fire and walls, mountains and armor, are round about us." On the other hand, He says of the ungodly, Rom. 3:23, "They fall short of the glory of God." This is the honor or the glory that He wants here when He says that He will be the glory within Jerusalem; just as they had earlier been scattered in all disgrace and had not been able to boast that God dwelt with them and was their own, and therefore had to let themselves be decried in all the world as men who had been forsaken by their God and now were without a God. There follows therefore:

6. *Ho! Ho! Flee from the land of the north, says the Lord; for I have spread you abroad as the four winds of the heavens, says the Lord.*

After He has promised that the spiritual Jerusalem would come soon after the earthly Jerusalem has been rebuilt and restored, He now admonishes and invites the Jews to gather together. They are to come from all lands and help to restore the earthly Jerusalem for the sake of the coming spiritual Jerusalem, which they are to await in the earthly one. For here it is to begin and from here be spread throughout all the world. He desires to say this: "Because it is true that I wish to make this small earthly Jerusalem a great splended spiritual one and wish to be the wall Myself and to dwell in it with great honor, so that you shall no longer live among the Gentiles in dishonor as men that are without their God and forsaken by Me; therefore come, flee, flee from the land of the north, that is, from Babylon and Assyria, where you have been led as captives by the kings of Assyria and Babylon. And not only you, who are to come from the north, but also all others who had fled round about at the time of the destruction, all, all of you round about and everywhere, come back again and restore Jerusalem again, so that you may share in the coming honor." Especially, however, does He call the Jews, and above all the citizens of Jerusalem, saying:

7. *Ho! Escape to Zion, you who dwell with the daughter of Babylon.*

These same citizens of Zion are to be the first to take an interest in it, because Christ was to come from the tribe of Judah. And He very aptly calls them Zion, even though they are still in Babylon. For they do not belong to Babylon but to Zion. He also says specifically, "You who dwell in Babylon," and does not say, "You who are a stranger in Babylon," though Scripture elsewhere says of their fathers Abraham, Isaac, and Jacob that they had been sojourners in the land (Gen. 21:34, etc.). In this way the prophet indicates that many of the Jews had completely become Babylonian and settled there to stay forever, since they had taken wives and children, houses and possessions there among the Gentiles and had abandoned their fatherland Zion and despised it. For not all the Jews went up to rebuild Jerusalem; in fact, as Ezra well shows (Ezra 2:2 ff.), only the smaller part of them, even as it always happens that God's Word draws the smaller number of students. Therefore the prophet stirs them up and gives them a prod, as if to say: "Ah, my dear Jews, you are citizens of Zion; how can you forget your fatherland and despise the promises concerning the coming Christ and settle in Babylon? You are no longer willing to be guests and captives there but want to be citizens and stay and live there; you let wives, children, houses, possessions, and friends hinder and prevent you from coming and helping to build. Shame on you that you want to be of Babylon when you are of Zion! Who has ever despised his fatherland? It surely is but natural to love one's fatherland, as all Gentiles say and as experience teaches."

Thus this sermon was written to be sent to Babylon, to admonish the unbelievers and those slow to believe and heedless, or even the hardened Jews. For without a doubt there were many Jews who had their sport with the Word of God, as though it would be impossible to rebuild the Jerusalem that had been so shamefully destroyed, and even more impossible that it should become so glorious. For it is always typical of God's Word to present absolutely foolish and impossible things, at which reason with its cleverness must take offense, while faith can scarcely maintain itself. Therefore at that time many no doubt scoffed and said, "Go on, go and build, you will build something fine, you are the right people for it, just as the donkey is for singing," and the like; even as the citizens of Succoth and Penuel mocked Gideon, Judg. 8:6 ff. For God's Word must be a mockery to reason, and few must believe in it. And so He Himself will later confess [9] that some have considered it impossible, others ridiculous, when He says: "If it is marvelous in the sight of the remnant of this people in these days, should it also be marvelous in My sight?" And also in ch. 4:10: ". . . whoever has despised the day of small things."

Therefore He also touches upon such thoughts of theirs when He says above: "Ho! ho! Flee from the land of the north; for I have spread you abroad as the four winds of the heavens," as if to say: "Flee, flee and escape, let nothing detain you in Babylon or elsewhere. Whoever does not wish to join you, let him stay, be it wife, friend, possessions, or honor. Do not think that building Jerusalem is impossible or a jest; for I, who have spread you abroad in all the world and brought you

[9] Zech. 8:6.

dishonor, can and will gather you again and bring you to honor. The Gentiles did not spread you abroad thus, but I did; otherwise they would have had to stop; and I can also help you again. What are you seeking in the land that faces the north and darkness and that means utter misfortune? Return to your fatherland, which faces the south and light and which means sheer happiness and salvation." It is so very hard to forsake the world and cling to the Word that the prophet has to use these words, "Flee and escape!" that is, "Do violence to yourselves and renounce boldly; otherwise you will not succeed." For the old Adam is too troublesome and opposes one too strenuously; or as St. Paul says, Rom. 7:18, and Gal. 5:17, "The flesh and the Spirit are opposed to each other." Therefore one must give oneself a jolt and tear oneself free and force one's way through. That is what he expresses here in this way, "O Zion, escape," that is, "Tear yourself away and do not be too fond of Babylon."

Here, however, you see that it is the custom of the Scriptures to mean the whole world when they speak of the four winds of the heavens or of the four directions: West, East, South, North. Thus Christ says, Matt. 24:31: "He will send out His angels with a loud trumpet call, and they will gather His elect from the four winds, etc." The inhabitants of all the cities and adjoining places, morever, are called "daughters." Thus "the daughter of Babylon" here means the people of Babylon; and later (ch. 2:10 and 9:9) we read, "Rejoice, O daughter of Zion." Likewise when Jacob announces the blessing of God upon Ephraim, he says, Gen. 49:22, that the daughters [10] shall rule, that is, the cities shall have a principality and rule. For to have a rule of the land is a great gift and a gracious blessing of God. And in the Book of Joshua (ch. 15:45 ff.) we find that the "towns with their daughters",[11] that is, with the adjoining places and little cities and villages, are scattered about. This is altogether a Hebrew way of speaking. In German we do not speak in that way.

8. *For thus says the Lord of hosts: He sent Me to the Gentiles who have plundered you. The glory is gone. He who touches you touches the apple of My eye.*[12]

Here the prophet explains and further emphasizes the promise concerning the spiritual Jerusalem. In the Hebrew, however, the text

[10] RSV has "branches" for "daughters" in this passage.

[11] RSV has "villages" for "daughters" in this passage.

[12] Compare the RSV.

reads thus, "For thus says the Lord of hosts, 'After the glory He sent Me to the Gentiles,' etc." The word "after the glory" is a bit obscure, either because we do not know the ways of the Hebrew language well enough or because the Holy Spirit, for good and sufficient reasons, wanted to speak obscurely here concerning Christ. So much we know for certain: this message is to come "after the glory"; that is what the words say: "after the glory," that is, subsequent to it, when the glory is past. The text does not tell, however, what kind of glory it means. Therefore it causes much thinking and many kinds of interpretations. The first one may be this: Christ is to come after the glory, namely, after that of the kings of Babylon and Persia, that is, when they have perished and their kingdoms are gone, so that the Jews would not think that Christ was coming very soon – while the empire of Persia was still standing. Therefore he wishes to tell them: "The glory of the empire must first be gone; He will not come during the time of the empire." In this way Paul also speaks to the Thessalonians (2 Thess. 2:3) concerning the Antichrist: he would come, but not before the Roman empire had fallen. In keeping with this interpretation and in order that we might understand the text all the more clearly, we have translated and arranged it in this way: "He sent Me to the Gentiles; the glory is gone."

The second interpretation is approximately this: Christ is to come after the glory of the Jewish nation, and the Holy Spirit is indicating in this way that with Christ's coming the earthly Jerusalem and the physical kingdom should end. For it did indeed happen thus. When Christ came, the tribe of David had lost the rule, and the tribe of Maccabees of the family of priests was ruling, and after them the Romans and Herod ruled, so that the glory of the Jewish kingdom was completely gone, and various men of foreign blood were kings. For Jacob, too, had prophesied, Gen. 49:10, that the tribe of Judah should have princes and teachers until Shiloh, the Messiah, would come. For later, when Christ had come to the Gentiles and been preached to them, then Jerusalem, beyond the fact that its glory was already gone, also was destroyed. The text then must have this meaning: "After the glory He sent Me," or this one, "He sent Me when the glory was past"; in this way it would set the time and give a sign when the new Jerusalem should begin, that is, when the people would see that it was all over with their splendid kingdom and they had strangers as their kings, then they were to look for Him and wait for Him. I like this interpretation best, and it seems to me it is the correct one. For it agrees with the words of Jacob in Gen. 49. And since he is speaking with the Jews, it is to be believed that he is speaking of their glory, which they valued most and desired so greatly.

The third interpretation, which is not far removed from the second one, is this: Not only is the time fixed in this way concerning the coming kingdom of Christ but also the way, the manner, and the form which Christ and His kingdom will have outwardly, and it runs in this manner: "You Jews desire to understand us prophets in a carnal way, as though we were preaching about a physical, earthly kingdom of Christ that will be glorious and splendid in the eyes of the world, which was true earlier and has been until now. No, that will then all be over and ended. Forget that and believe that all that ever was to be has already been. But this kingdom that is to come in the future will outwardly, in men's eyes, be without honor and shameful and miserable. For it will be under the cross. Hence, after the glorious earthly kingdom, there will come, according to outward appearance, a poor, miserable kingdom, so that in the future you will no longer be able to gape at the glory of a secular kingdom, or hope for it.

It is easy to prove that these words speak of Christ and His kingdom. First of all, this has just never happened, that this prophet Zechariah was sent to the Gentiles who had robbed his people. For he would have had to go and preach to the Assyrians, Medes, Babylonians, Chaldeans, and, as he said before, to the four winds, that is, to all the Gentiles round about. For all of these Gentiles had done the Jews harm and plundered them. Second, this has not happened either, nor will it ever happen, that the Gentiles, to whom the Jews had to be subject, in turn became the prey of the Jews, as our text says here in plain words. The Assyrians had indeed become the prey of the Chaldeans, the Chaldeans of the Persians, the Persians of the Greeks, the Greeks of the Romans, and so forth – but never of the Jews. Christ, however, has fulfilled this text. Through the Gospel He has come to all the Gentiles and has spiritually subjected to Himself all who formerly had physically subdued the Jews, His people. The words also say that, when He speaks:

"Thus says the Lord of hosts, 'After the glory He sent Me to the Gentiles.'" Who is this "Me"? Is it Zechariah? No. For these words precede: "Thus says the Lord of hosts, He sent Me." With all its power this text persuades one that the Lord of hosts Himself is here speaking in His own person and saying, "He sent Me." Now the very one who is speaking here is also being sent: the Lord of hosts is sending the Lord of hosts. Now obviously one cannot send oneself. But through this sending He testifies to the fact that there is one who is sending and another who is being sent. Now all Jews confess, and it is true, that this name of "Lord of hosts" is ascribed to no one but the true, natural God, who is but one. Thus it is revealed here that in this same one Godhead the two Persons must both be the true, natural, one God, both the sender and the one that is sent. And this verse confirms that our Lord Jesus Christ, sent by God the Father, as the Gospels teach, is the true, natural God together with the Father. For if the Person who is here being sent should not be God Himself, our text would have to read thus, as Scripture commonly does otherwise, "The Lord says, 'Go, do this, talk to him,'" in other words, that He would turn to another and give a command. But here He does not turn to anyone else, nor does He give anyone else a command; but the Person who speaks in God's place remains and tells what has been commanded Him. So the Lord says, "He sent Me." Here it surely is stated in sufficiently plain German that the Lord says and confesses that He has been sent, just as when he writes above (ch. 1:16), "Thus says the Lord, 'I have returned to Jerusalem,'" and the like. There one hears of course that God is speaking of Himself and that He that is returning to Jerusalem is no one but the same God who is saying this of Himself. And so there is no one here either who is being sent but the Lord, who is saying these things of Himself.

And what is more, look at what follows in the text, and you will find that the same Person who says, "The Lord sent Me to the Gentiles," at the same time and in the same tone and words says, "He who touches you touches the apple of My eye." And God is surely saying this Himself, for this is a divine promise. Now it is obviously the very same Person who had said earlier in the same speech, "He sent Me to the Gentiles," and now goes on to say, "He who touches you touches the apple of My eye." But if this were said about the person of Zechariah, how would it read? And what sense would it make if he had said, "He sent me to the Gentiles who have plundered you; he who touches you touches the apple of my eye"? The stiffnecked Jews and the contentious wiseacres may twist and invent things here and maintain that in any one speech of the prophets various persons may be introduced. But they cannot twist this fact around that God here says of Himself that He has been sent by God; the text is too clear. For where an "I" follows the words, "Thus says the Lord," the "I" certainly is the Lord Himself, as the writings of all the prophets prove and as the ways of all languages persuade one with all their might. How would it sound if I should introduce the word of a prince and say, "So says the prince, 'I have ordered that the poor be provided for, etc.,'" and then interpreted the "I" as referring not to the person of the prince but to mine? Neither reason nor the ways of languages suffer any other interpretation than this that the "I" refers to the person that is presented as speaking.

This, then, is the sum of this text: "Until now you Jews have endured shame and disgrace from the Gentiles, like men that have no God. Very well, now things shall be different; from now on I will be your God, and I will be that God by being sent Myself and by coming into the flesh Myself as a prophet and teacher. Formerly I sent prophets. Now, however, I desire that I Myself be sent and come, so that I, too, may be a prophet and teacher. But I will come and be sent as a prophet in this way, that my preaching may not only reach you but may come to all the Gentiles in all the world. For I desire to be sent to all; and when that happens, then I have indeed come sufficiently close to you, because I Myself am taking care of you. Therefore he who touches you touches the apple of My eye. For I shall indeed be present everywhere among the Gentiles, because I am being sent to all; and for that reason you will never be without Me or I without you; wherever you may be in all the world, men must touch Me when they touch you."

There would be much to say about these words if there were time and occasion. For in the word "sent to the Gentiles" there is comprehended the whole man Christ together with His office. He is God, as we have heard; if He now is to be sent, He must also be man. For "to be sent" means in the Scriptures to receive the office of preaching among men. Because God now is sent, He must become a preacher; and He cannot preach without being a man like the other prophets. For angels cannot dwell among us. If, however, He is man and God, He must be conceived and born without sin. For God cannot be a sinner; and therefore He must become man by the Holy Ghost of a woman without a husband, that is, of a virgin. If He is to be a prophet for all nations, then He must have such an essence that He can be and teach everywhere; and that cannot be this mortal life, for that would find the task impossible. He must, then, be mortal, as one born of a woman; and yet He must be immortal, that is, He must arise from death and spiritually be the Master Himself everywhere through the Word. But we do not have occasion to speak at greater length about that now. It is enough if it is referred to briefly, and it is emphasized sufficiently elsewhere.

Let us permit the words "He who touches you touches the apple of My eye" to count for something. They are to be our protection and comfort in the kingdom of Christ; and these are indeed something inexpressible. For He does not stop with being a wall of fire round about us but says here that we are as dear to Him as the apple of His eye. And that truly is much. How disgraceful our unbelief still stands there whenever such comforting promises are held out to us and we do not honor and cherish them more. These matters, however, are too far removed from our way of thinking; for according to outward appearance things are happening quite differently when He permits us to be persecuted so cruelly. John the Baptist was beheaded because of a harlot (Matt. 14:8 ff.). Is that an example of "He who touches you touches the apple of My eye"? And so it has been with all other martyrs and saints. The pope and his followers, however, have surely known how to use this verse to their advantage: whoever did not give tithes or deprived the clergy of worldly goods had touched the apple of the Lord's eye. Thus the Scriptures had to be helped along – God help us, whether we are Christians or not. But let us forget the devil and his followers.

But wherever there is a Christian who believes that these things are true, what shall he think when he regards him who does him harm? He must of course not think of great rage or vengeance. He must be not only patient but also merciful and compassionate toward his enemy and say, "O you poor man, what are you doing? You are not harming me but are rather putting your finger into the eye of Him who unfortunately is too powerful for you and whose name is God, etc." In this way the Christian will be moved not only to suffer patiently but also to plead, yes, even to die for his enemies, if only he might save them from the wrath of Him into whose eyes they are putting their fingers. Now there is nothing that is harder to bear than to have one's eyes touched with a heavy hand; and thus God, as a comfort to us and a terror to His enemies, shows Himself as being most sensitive and tender about allowing us to be touched; and therefore it is not necessary for us to get angry or avenge ourselves. He does indeed not deny that we have to be touched; for He says, "He who touches you"; but he who ventures that will not succeed. So He wants to say: "Dear Jews, until now you have been tormented by the Gentiles round about you. Very well, henceforth we shall have things in this way: not only these Gentiles, but all the Gentiles that touch you shall have touched Me. They shall be brought down again and be made subject to you who are Christians and hear Me," as follows:

9. *Behold, I will shake My hand over them, and they shall become plunder for those who served them. Then you will know that the Lord of hosts sent Me.*

He who confesses that He has been sent by God is still speaking, and He again presents Himself here as a God who has power over all the world and who will make the Gentiles the plunder of the Jews. And this He mentions as a great miracle, and He boasts that one should learn from it that He has been sent by God. And He boasts once more that He has been sent by God; and yet He says that as a God He would make the Gentiles a plunder. He claims that He is God and yet that He has been sent by God. Above [13] we have said enough concerning the fact that this passage proves mightily that Christ must be true God and man. And to confirm the statement that through the Word He would "bring about obedience to the faith among all the nations," Rom. 1:5, He now explains the work for which He has been sent and with which He will effect this faith and says, "I will shake My hand over them, etc.," as if to say: "I am being sent among the Gentiles who have plundered you not only to defend you in a pleasant and friendly way so that he who touches you will be touching the apple of My eye; but I will carry things further, so that they shall in turn become the plunder of you, who had formerly been their subjects." For the passage where He says above, "He sent Me to the Gentiles; he who touches you, etc.," is broken off abruptly and simply speaks of a sending, but it says nothing at all about how He would carry out this sending or what His command might be. The Jews could therefore fill in the gaps of this passage with their carnal reason and think: "Since He is being sent to the Gentiles to do such great things that no one will touch us, He will carry out His plans with steeds and chariots and mighty warriors and defend us with His power."

[13] Cf. pp. 31 f. above.

But to prevent such a thought, He not only prefixed the statement that He would be sent only "after the glory" and that His command would be carried out without worldly splendor and glory, but He also indicates here the very way in which everything will be done: "I will shake My hand over them." "Not your sword, not your bow, but My hand shall do these things, and it shall do them in this way, that I will shake it over them." We see, then, that things will not be done with the blows of a sword but that God's hand will do them. For the word "shake" does not refer here to the raising of the hand, as He is in the habit of using it elsewhere and as we find it here and there in the Psalter: "He raised His hand . . . that He would make them fall" (Ps. 106:26), and, "Arise, O Lord; O God, lift up Thy hand" (Ps. 10:12), etc. But it means a hovering over and a waving, as the priests waved their offerings before the altar to the four corners of the world, for which reason the offerings were called "wave offerings" or "waving" (Lev. 7:30). And thus here, too, He wants to let His hand wave [14] or hover over the Gentiles to the four corners of the world, that is, in all the world – but not to overthrow them or cast them to the ground. For that is what is meant by raising or lifting His hand over them. Instead, He desires to move, and hover over, the Gentiles in all the world through His Word and Spirit; and in this way they are to be converted to Him and to offer themselves both to God and to the apostles gladly and willingly as plunder and for submissive service, as Paul writes that the Macedonians had done, 2 Cor. 9:2. For this shaking of the hand is a friendly and gracious shaking, as He also says in Ps. 68:9: "Rain in abundance, O God, Thou didst shake out," [15] and that is the very word that we find here.[16]

And this deed, He says, shall be a sign from which people shall know that God has sent Him; that is, people will then believe that Christ is true God, sent by God. For it is an unheard of and inexpressible work that Christ came into the world, as St. Paul also glories, 1 Tim. 3:16: "Great indeed, we confess, is the mystery of our religion: He was manifested in the flesh, vindicated in the Spirit, seen by angels, preached among the nations, believed on in the world, taken up in glory." For when one considers how foolish it is to reason that one should preach that a Jewish man is the Son of God and Lord over all when, after all, He was crucified by His own people and died;

14 Or, "shake."

15 RSV: "shed abroad."

16 The Hebrew words are תָּנִיף for Ps. 68:9 and מֵנִיף for Zech. 2:9.

when all who were high in the world opposed Him with all their might; and when the very apostles were active in His work without any weapons and resistance but indeed with much suffering and dying: then one must admit that this is not the work of men; for if it were, it would have fallen a thousand times because of so much opposition. In fact, because it makes such foolish and impossible claims, it ought soon to have fallen of itself. But now all the kingdoms and all the worlds that have opposed it are falling, while His kingdom remains above all and before all. Therefore there must be a divine power behind it which preserves it against all devils, all kings, all wise men, all of this world's saints; and for that reason the Jews ought properly from now on to grasp and, as He says here, know that this Christ has been sent by God. Yet they do not do it.

Saint Paul now calls this a "great mystery of our religion . . . believed on in the world" (1 Tim. 3:16), however much the world may at first have persecuted it. And it has been preached to the Gentiles, however much the devil and his great ones may have opposed it. It has also appeared to the angels; that is, in heaven He is revealed to the angels and is not hidden in the Word and faith, as in the world. It has also been revealed to the world in the flesh through Christ's own person and that of the apostles. Though these had flesh and blood like other men, yet it was revealed to them and was justified in the Spirit. For although it is damnable folly to reason, it is received and approved as God's Word and work wherever one finds the Spirit and faith. In sum: It fills heaven and earth, it must be and desires to be everywhere: with God in the presence of the angels, in the saints, among men, in the world, on earth, etc. But it is called a mystery, and it remains one. Therefore it is hidden from men in the Word and in faith, but to God and the angels it is evident and revealed. Whoever, then, refuses to know from this that Christ is sent by God will indeed have no excuse and deserves to be blinded and hardened. God has proved and let it be known sufficiently well that He has so shaken His hand over the Gentiles that not only they who had formerly plundered them but also they who are still plundering them today shall submit to His people; and that, in brief, Christ has no friends except those whom He has made of His enemies. For if He should destroy His enemies, He would not create any more Christians either, and thus "the wheat would be rooted up with the weeds" (Matt. 13:29). Where would St. Paul be, if he had been destroyed when he was an enemy?

Thus Ps. 110:2 sings of the kingdom of Christ that He shall "rule in the midst of His foes," and Ps. 45:5 that His "arrows are sharp in the heart of the king's enemies; the people fall under" Him. And here in Zechariah He says that He is to be sent not to the Jews or to friends but to His enemies, to the Gentiles, who are the plunderers of Him and of His people. His kingdom therefore is entirely different from worldly kingdoms, and all His efforts aim at making friends of enemies by offering them only that which is good, though He suffers every evil from them. A worldly kingdom, however, prefers to make enemies of friends by taking and demanding what is good and by being neither willing nor able to suffer evil. For how would a worldly king maintain himself if he did not demand or take anything from his subjects and friends but instead tolerated every evil, punished nothing, and let everyone ridicule him and make a fool of him? It will not do and is not good, either, in a secular kingdom. When the Jews also, therefore, wanted to have secular kings, 1 Sam. 8:4 ff., He let it be shown to them what burdens and loads they would have to bear which they had not had to bear before under the judges and prophets, when through these God Himself ruled. There follows:

10. *Sing and rejoice, O daughter of Zion; for lo, I come and I will dwell in the midst of you, says the Lord.*

This is an admonition to those that are despised and are under the cross, as the Jews were at that time, to confirm to them the near promise of Christ's coming; as if to say: "Since all these things are now at hand, and since because of these great things Jerusalem is to be restored, you should quite properly not be indolent, lazy, or unhappy in view of them, like the unbelievers, but you should be awake, alert, and happy to build and to act in view of the splendid great hopes of future blessings under Christ's kingdom. 'For I come and I will dwell in the midst of you'; that is, I Myself will rule, and there shall no longer be a worldly kingdom; but I Myself will dwell in the midst of you spiritually through the Gospel and through faith, all of which is effected by the Holy Spirit; as St. Paul teaches, Eph. 3:17, 'that Christ may dwell in your hearts through faith'; as Is. 66:1 says, that God does not dwell in earthly houses; and as also St. Stephen indicates, Acts 7:8." But these are all spiritual and exalted words, which require faith, that I, a poor man, am to believe that God dwells with me when outwardly, after all, I am subject to the devil and all the world and besides am a sinful man, who falls often and is weak. This matter of being God's dwelling place here, then, is a most incredible thing.

11-12. *And many nations shall join themselves to the Lord in that day, and shall be My people; and I will dwell in the midst of you, and you shall know that the Lord of hosts has sent Me to you.*

Here He repeats once more that He will dwell in the midst of the Jews, because not only the Jews but also the Gentiles are to be added to Him and because Jews and Gentiles are to become one nation as though they were all Jews. But He extends the same promised dwelling farther – also to the Gentiles – so that the Jews might not think that He desired to dwell only among them as Jews, as was said above.[17] He accordingly desires to dwell among the Jews not as Jews alone but as Jews mingled with Gentiles, so that Gentiles and Jews will be regarded as one and the same. And this is a miracle, undoubtedly as great as none other; and He Himself says that we are to know from this that He has been sent by God. For when one considers how hostile the Gentiles and the Jews had been toward one another, it is impossible to believe that the two should ever become one people of God, and one must confess that this is a great and miraculous work of God – one that the apostles and the disciples themselves could not believe at first, Acts 8:14; 10:45; 11:2, and accepted only with difficulty, so that God had to give St. Peter a special sign from heaven, Acts 10:10 ff., while the apostles held a great council about it, Acts 15:1 ff.

In this way He also lets us know that, because the Gentiles are to become His people, the law of Moses will cease. For Moses was not given to the Gentiles; and they surely were to be joined to the Lord Himself and not to Moses, and to become the Lord's people and not Moses' people, so that He might dwell with them together with the Jews. For this matter of dwelling, which He repeats twice and in which He includes the Gentiles, cannot be the physical dwelling in the temple but, as has been said, must be a spiritual one, especially since He had dwelt in the midst of the Jews even before and without these promises. This new promise, then, refers to another, a new dwelling.

[17] Cf. p. 200 above.

And the Lord will inherit Judah as His portion in the holy land and will again choose Jerusalem.

This is spoken in a parable and is to be carried over from the physical to the spiritual in this way: When all of these things happen and God has made one people of Jews and Gentiles and is dwelling in their midst, then this state will truly begin that the Lord will inherit Judah as His portion. This had often been discussed and often wished for and yet could not succeed in a physical way. But Jerusalem is to be chosen properly, so that no one henceforth shall prevent it. Therefore Christ says, John 15:1, "I am the true vine," where the physical vine refers to the spiritual; and in the next chapter Zechariah will also say (ch. 3:10): "In that day everyone of you will invite his neighbor under his fig tree," that is, in the time of Christendom all that one now does physically when one invites another to be one's guest will be done more than ever. For here He adds to His words and says that these things shall happen in the holy land. For in the earthly land there dwell and remain many non-Christians, who will not let the land be a holy land and who will not be God's heirs for their portion either.

13. *Be silent, all flesh, before the Lord; for He has roused Himself from His holy dwelling.*

This is an admonition to all the world; and with it He indicates that what He has said here regarding Judah and Jerusalem applies to all the world. For if He were referring to the earthly land of Judah alone, what need would there be for Him to cry out to all the world that it should be silent before the Lord? The Jews alone would have to be silent, because they alone were before Him. But now He says, "Be silent, all flesh, before the Lord," as though the Lord were coming or were already present before all flesh. The meaning, then, is this: God desires to do these things in all the world and to dwell everywhere in the midst of the Jews and the Gentiles. Let everyone therefore be silent, that is, make way, permit God to rule and act; let no one oppose and resist, and let no one consider himself too intelligent, pious, and mighty, or depend on men; but let everyone permit Him to rule while confessing himself to be a sinner and a poor, lost man before Him, so that he might be helped. For therefore the Lord has roused Himself from His holy dwelling, that is, He has gone forth, has let men preach of Him and announce to all the world that He desires to be Lord alone and to do all, and that He alone is able to do all, as Christ says, Matt. 28:18, "All authority in heaven and on earth has been given to Me."

The term "be silent" specifically means as much as "to keep quiet," as one tells those to keep quiet who are talking and making a noise by talking, and as Caleb silenced the people of Israel when they were murmuring, Num. 13:30. This shows that Christ rules through the Word alone and that He alone should speak and be heard and believed; while false teachers, heretics, and those that claim to be clever should keep their mouths shut before Him in His kingdom – an important admonition indeed, which one, however, heeds but little. For wherever Christ speaks at some place through one mouth, there the devil, too, wants to be and babble and prattle with ten mouths. His kingdom is based on speaking; therefore He must suffer every kind of interruption and much of it, so that there is an eternal quarreling in words and in preaching.

CHAPTER THREE

1. *Then he showed me Joshua the high priest standing before the angel of the Lord, and Satan standing at his right hand to accuse him.*

AFTER the prophet has comforted and strengthened the people in general and has interpreted the visions and consolations and has applied them to the coming of Christ's kingdom, he now begins to comfort the heads and leaders, both spiritual and secular, in particular. In connection with his interpretation and its application to Christ he first comforts the spiritual head in this chapter and then the secular head in the following chapter. For if the heads despair and are unwilling to take on their work, what are the people to do? It is said that everything depends on a good leader, and that a good leader is worthy of all honor.[1] The people have now been admonished and aroused so that they might say, "Very well, we should like to get to work. But who is to take the lead? Whom are we to follow? We must have a headman for our work." He therefore now gives them leaders and heads: Joshua, the high priest, and Zerubbabel, the prince of Judah; and he treats both of them in a wonderfully friendly way and thus indeed makes them bold and anxious to begin.

In a masterful way, however, he touches upon the thoughts of each of the men that make them fainthearted and unhappy. For when the high priest, the spiritual leader, sees so many obstacles before him, he thinks that his sin and that of his people are to blame for the fact that God is not yet truly gracious toward them. The prince, Zerubbabel, thinks that his secular power is altogether too insignificant to undertake anything against so many Gentiles. Thus they both stand there depressed: the high priest because of a bad conscience, the prince because of the timidity of his impotence. He therefore frees both of them from their timid thoughts and shows that before God the high priest is worthy and acceptable, and He also shows where Prince Zerubbabel is to gain the strength and power that will make him feel secure. Let us first consider the high priest.

[1] Cf. p. 34, n. 1.

"Then he showed me Joshua the high priest," he says; that is: "In a vision I saw the high priest Joshua and what was wrong with him so that I might preach to him and the people that he should not dwell on his shortcomings but be bold and joyful as one who is sure that he has a gracious God." His shortcoming, however, was this, that a twofold thought weighed on him and gave him a bad conscience. The first was that Satan was standing at his right hand and was assailing him; and that means nothing else than this, that the devil is standing there rigidly and is magnifying his sin and giving him a timid, despairing conscience. For that is the way of the devil: he greatly inflates one's sin and magnifies it and makes God's judgments horrible, even as Rev. 12:10 tells us that the old dragon accuses the saints day and night before our God, while the Holy Spirit, on the other hand, is a Comforter[2] and Advocate (John 16:7), who excuses our sins before God and makes them small and pardonable. The other thoughts follow from the first: that he thinks his priestly office and work are unacceptable to God; and this he indicates by saying that his garments, that is, his priestly garments, are filthy and inglorious. For the prophet did not regard Joshua as an ordinary man but as a high priest in a high priest's garments; and these were to be beautiful and glorious, even as God had commanded Moses, Ex. 28:2, to adorn Aaron and make him garments for the glory of the priestly office. Among the papists for that reason the garments for the Mass or the church vestments are even now called *Ornat,* that is, "adornments." Joshua, then, was wearing the garments of a priest, but they were unclean. Not that they were filthy or befouled but that they were not beautiful or adorned as they were supposed to be, but instead they were old and threadbare and worn or were of ordinary material like other, everyday clothes – all of which is called filthy or unsanctified, because it is not in keeping with the Word of God, who had commanded that the garments be beautiful.

The fact, however, that his clothes were not the proper ones indicates that also his conscience stood in a similar relationship to God so that, though he considered himself a priest of God as one born of a priestly family – which he could not deny – his conscience nevertheless was not happy or beautiful, that is, it did not consider itself sufficiently right, beautiful, or worthy before God to do acceptable service. For that reason he has to be seen in threadbare, bad garments, like a poor

[2] RSV: "Counselor."

village priest in a threadbare and shabby chasuble. The sum and meaning, then, is this: The high priest Joshua had such thoughts, and his conscience put words like these into his mouth: "Very well, I am born a high priest according to God's decree. But, dear Lord, we have sinned, and therefore God has allowed the priestly office to be destroyed by the Babylonians, so that there is little hope for it. And it is truly a wretched priesthood, one that has grown quite musty and that the moths have devoured. Perhaps it will rise again and become glorious. But at present it still looks bad and will need much sunshine; for it is a shabby thing and mere trash." Conscience acts thus by nature when it is bad and is tormented by sin. It cannot adorn itself at all; that is, it cannot be happy or have good courage in God but always fears that its works are worth nothing. Or it is held by doubt, so that it cannot say joyfully, "I know that my work is pleasing to God, etc." I have David as a witness that this interpretation is correct; for he himself interprets beautiful clothes as referring to a righteous, joyful conscience when he says, Ps. 132:9: "Let Thy priests be clothed with righteousness, and let Thy saints shout for joy"; and Solomon says, Eccl. 9:8, 7: "Let your garments be always white; let not oil be lacking on your head, for God has already approved what you do"; and Christ says, Matt. 6:17: "When you fast, anoint your head, etc." Adornment, therefore, refers to a joyful, good conscience before God, one that is sure that its works are pleasing to God. But rags and shabby garments refer to a bad, despairing conscience.

In order to offer consolation in these two things, the angel of the Lord now also appears with two things. The first is that he rebukes Satan and says, "The Lord rebuke you, O Satan! etc.," as if he would say: "O Joshua, I see indeed that you, as a poor sinner, are timid and have a bad conscience. But look, I am coming with a consoling sermon. For I have seen an angel who rebuked Satan in the name of God and who has only good things to say of you. Therefore be of good cheer and know that it is not your sins that are making you so timid; but it is the devil that is assailing you and is giving you such a bad conscience and wishes to hinder this work of building. Therefore be of good cheer; do not be afraid. God is gracious to you. Begin to build, so that the people may follow your example." And here let us learn what it means that "Satan is standing at your right hand." "Satan" in Hebrew means "a hostile one," as the prophet himself is interpreting it here and speaks of "Satan standing at his right hand to accuse him."

For it is the devil's way to oppose God and all His people, even as John calls him the "Antichrist" (1 John 4:3), that is, the enemy of Christ, while Paul, 2 Thess. 2:4, calls him the one "who opposes," and thus gives the Hebrew word "Satan" in Greek as ἀντικείμενος, which commonly refers to all that oppose. But here it surely refers to the devil himself.

He is standing, the prophet says: he is neither lying nor sitting. For the devil is in earnest[3] and gets on his feet armed and stands rigid; he does not rest and is not slow to spoil and harm, as also Peter says, 1 Peter 5:8:[4] "Your adversary the devil prowls around like a roaring lion." And when he begins to oppress one and magnify one's sins, then one can feel very well in one's conscience how desperate and timid a man can get, especially in the presence of God, also how tightly and firmly the devil holds those whom he has caught in error and heresy, so that they will neither yield nor be persuaded. But especially does he like to stand at the right hand, that is, in matters that are best and spiritual; and that means: most of all he prevents true faith and a good conscience from arising; instead, he wants vain unbelief or doubt and despair to remain, just as Ps. 109:6 says of the Jews: "Let an accuser stand at his right hand." For there is no angel present there to rebuke Satan, and therefore it is impossible for them to give up their unbelief. Satan stands too rigidly and firmly, as he also does in all sects and heretics. But here, in the case of Joshua, he also wanted to stand at the right hand and hinder the faith. But there is a stronger one at hand, who tells him to be gone and to make way for faith. Blessed is he who is worthy of this!

The second thing is that he adds a deed or a sign and tells Joshua to take off his rags and put on glorious garments; as if Zechariah were saying: "Dear Joshua, you think the priestly office does not mean anything, and you are timid. But I have seen that you are well pleasing to God and that your priestly office is acceptable to Him." These surely are splendid words and visions. How great a man must Joshua have been before God if for his sake such a glorious sermon and such glorious visions were ordered by God. Ought it not to give him joy

[3] *Der Teufel meinet es mit Ernst* echoes the lines *Der alt böse Feind, mit Ernst er's jetzt meint* in st. 1 of *Ein feste Burg.* This passage and other similar echoes of Luther's hymn in the lectures on the minor prophets have been used in attempts to determine a plausible date of composition for the hymn. Cf. W, XXXV, 188 ff.

[4] The Weimar editor corrects the text's "2 Peter 3."

and courage when he hears how God is acting for him, is letting him see His angel fighting for him against the devil, and is announcing to him that his sins are forgiven and that he has a gracious God? Yes, what good would it have done him if he had not believed it? And how could he have committed a greater sin than by doing God the dishonor of doubting? If one looked at Zechariah only as he was preaching these things, it would seem as though he were flattering the high priest hypocritically. But oh, what very necessary flattery it would have been, since good Joshua was feeling so very insignificant and timid in his own mind. It would have been an entirely different flattery from that of calling the pope a God on earth and a person compounded of God and man.[5] Here Joshua is wretched and a nonentity; and therefore God, who looks upon the lowly and wretched, makes him so glorious, in accordance with the words of Mary (Luke 1:52), "He has put down the mighty from their thrones, and exalted those of low degree." So Joshua is now strengthened, both by word and sign, as Scripture is in the habit of doing. The word is that Satan is rebuked; the sign, that his rags were taken from him and glorious garments put on him. Let us now look at the text.

Once again he here shows that there is more than one Person in the Godhead. For Zechariah first tells how Joshua had stood before the angel of the Lord, and immediately thereafter he says that the Lord had rebuked Satan, as if he were pointing out the fact that the angel had been the Lord Himself. For he says nothing of the Lord's having been present, but rather of an angel's; and yet he says that the Lord was speaking, even as Abraham, Gen. 18:2 f., adored the Lord in the person of an angel and spoke with Him. For give attention to the words, how they follow one another. He speaks thus: "Joshua was standing before the angel of the Lord. And the Lord said to Satan, 'The Lord rebuke you, etc.'" If the angel were not the Lord Himself, the text would have read better thus: "Joshua stood before the angel of the Lord. And *the angel* said to Satan, 'The Lord rebuke you, etc.'" And one Lord is speaking of another Lord as one God of another God (for "Lord" at both places here is the one true name of the true, real God). It is as if I spoke thus: "God said to Satan, 'God rebuke you, etc.'" Here it would of course be understood that one God was speaking of another God, as in Ps. 45:7: "Therefore God, Your God, has anointed You," from which psalm, as we know, the Epistle to the

[5] Cf. Karl Hefele, *Conciliengeschichte*, VIII, 531.

Hebrews proves that Christ is God.[6] And the remarks of the prophet are obviously the same as these: "God says to Satan, 'God rebuke you.'" Besides, the whole speech says that too. For Joshua is standing before the angel with Satan as before God, so that all these things are happening and are as valid in his conscience as before God, as was said before. And the angel also gives commands like a God to the others who are standing before him, that is, to the angels: that they should clothe Joshua. And so in every way Christ is here shown as being God and an angel coming into the world.

This rebuking on the part of the Lord is also spoken in the manner of the Scriptures, which testify that God does and creates all things through His Word, and as Ps. 33:9 says, "He spoke, and it came to be." When God therefore is speaking, it is as much as saying, "He is doing and creating something." When He blesses, that is, when He speaks in a good and kindly way, then He is doing good and helping and enlarging, and in the Old Testament goods and temporal possessions are called God's blessing. Again, when He curses, He is destroying and annihilating, so that the destroying of possessions is called cursing. Malachi therefore says, ch. 2:2, "I will curse your blessings," that is, "I will make small your possessions, which you have through My blessing." For this reason we must grow accustomed to this divine way of speaking, that God's rebuking means as much as preventing and deterring the devil so that he must abandon his intentions because of God's might, as Ps. 9:5 says, "Thou hast rebuked the nations, Thou hast destroyed the wicked." St. Paul, Rom. 16:20, also speaks thus of this rebuking of God in different words: "God will soon crush Satan under your feet." This "crushing" is as much as the "rebuking," though St. Paul in using the word "crush" is also considering other portions of Scripture that say the same thing (Gen. 3:15).

But he adds, "The Lord who has chosen Jerusalem rebuke you!" in order to comfort Joshua and the people all the more when they will hear that the devil is being rebuked for the very thing they are interested in, that is, for Jerusalem, which they are to build. And they are now to feel sure that from this time on they are not to be hindered by the devil and any other opponents. For God has chosen Jerusalem to be His dwelling place and wants to build it and is no longer willing to allow the devil any hindrances. Such varied great consolations, however, show that without any doubt the people and their headmen

[6] Heb. 1:8.

have been very, very timid, frightened, and confused, and have suffered great opposition and affliction. For where God comforts mightily, there indeed must be mighty persecution. He does not grant His Word and comfort lightly or without necessity; He holds Himself and His Word dear, as it is right and proper too. Therefore there has been great misery and need here, as the following shows:

2. *Is not this a brand plucked from the fire?*

This is as much as saying: "Has it not been enough that God has allowed the whole Jewish nation to be destroyed, as if a whole city were burned down? And you, Satan, do you not want to let anything survive, not even a brand or spark? Not so! Rather shall you yield and give over to this Joshua a remnant, through which the whole Jewish kingdom is to be restored again." And here we see how wretchedly the Jews were faring at this time; nothing seemed to indicate that anything would ever become of their building. For the prophet compares the high priest to an ember that remains and is barely preserved and plucked out when a house or a city burns down. And what is such an ember compared with a house or a city? Who can hope that a house is to be built of an ember? It just is not possible or humanly thinkable. Just so the Jews and especially Joshua felt and therefore thought like this: "What shall we do? Shall we build? We are surely to be compared with the former city as an ember is compared with a beautiful house that has burned down; and we are nothing at all compared with the former inhabitants of this city, and they of course were all destroyed and brought to ruin together with the city. We, however, have survived – like coals and embers."

Consider, then, if it was not needful in this distress to comfort richly and to flatter well. But the Scriptures have their own way of speaking of God: He makes everything out of that which is nothing or insignificant (cf. Rom. 4:17), and when He destroys something, He still leaves a remnant and keeps a seed through which He will restore it again. Thus He had the world, together with its men and animals, destroyed through the Flood and restored it again (Gen. 7:21 ff.) through eight people and a pair of animals of each kind, which were the seed. And so He says Is. 1:9: "If the Lord of hosts had not left us a few survivors, we should have been like Sodom, and become like Gomorrah"; and again, Is. 10:22: "Though your people Israel be as the sand of the sea, only a remnant of them will return"; likewise Lam.

3:22:[7] "It is the Lord's mercies that we are not cut off"; and in Is. 49:5 f. He says that Christ is to restore the dregs, or the sediment, of Israel; while in Is. 65:8 He says that He will remake Israel out of a grapestone. Now He who can make an anker[8] of wine out of dregs, vineyards out of a grapestone, acres of seed out of a grain of corn, and whatever else of that nature He presents in Scripture, He can also easily rebuild a holy city out of an ember that remains over. For has He not proved it before and made all men on earth out of one Adam, the whole people of Israel out of one Jacob, and so many trees every day out of one cherry stone or nut kernel that from year to year one kernel would yield enough cherry trees and cherries for all the world, if one wished to grow them? And so in all other things He makes abundance out of dregs, riches out of poverty, honor out of dishonor,[9] life out of death, everything out of nothing.

This, then, is said for the comfort of Joshua, so that he may hear that he is an ember plucked from the fire and preserved, so that out of him a great and glorious city may be built – not through his own might but through that of Him who in one year can make of one grain a hundred, the next year can make of these hundred ten thousand, the third year a hundred times ten thousand, and so on till the world is filled. He does this every day. Therefore this word is intended not for Satan alone, but rather for Joshua, so that he may not consider himself a miserable remaining ember from the fire but one that has been preserved by God to be a seed, a kernel, a root, to rebuild an entire city more glorious than before. And though the devil might not like it, he shall not prevent it. Therefore, dear Joshua, do not consider the fact that in your own eyes you are a small piece, a short stub, and a wretched ember; it is God who will and can very easily make of this ember beams, pillars, rafters, yes, houses, cities, forests, and everything. And you have been ordained to that by God, who through you and out of you desires to build that glorious Jerusalem, no matter how insignificant you may be.

From this example we learn, first, how difficult a matter it is to produce a good, trusting conscience and how hard it is to accept what God commands and whom He calls to do His work. Indeed, in Joshua there is neither pride nor ambition nor boldness but only fear, hesita-

[7] The Weimar editor corrects the text's "Jer. 10."

[8] A wine cask of about 10-gallon capacity. The German word is *Fuder.*

[9] The Weimar text has *aus ehren schande,* an obvious inversion.

tion, and humility. But the flighty spirits and Enthusiasts strut along; if only one thought occurs to them to teach or do something, then it must be the Holy Spirit. God can scarcely instill the Spirit into Joshua to the extent of an individual little drop; while these men drink Him in by pailfuls. But God's work at all times proceeds in a sickly and weak manner; yet it does progress confidently. But as swiftly as the spirits, on the other hand, run and hasten, so they succumb and stop just as swiftly. Second, the doctrine of grace is here confirmed as against that of works. For Joshua is here undressed and dressed again before the office and the command are given him as to what he is to do. The person must first be clean and beautiful through faith; thereafter his works are pleasing, as is shown in the case of Abel and Cain (Gen. 4:5). There follows:

6. *And the angel of the Lord enjoined*[10] *Joshua: Thus says the Lord of hosts: If you will walk in My ways and keep My charge, then you shall rule My house and have charge of My courts, and I will give you the right of access among those who are standing here.*

In keeping with the way of the Law, He here commands Joshua what he is to do and does not offer the promise freely on the basis of God's goodness but on the basis of Joshua's obedience. For this is the difference between the Old Testament and the New: the promises of the Old Testament do not extend beyond the people's goodness and obedience. Therefore all these promises run thus: "If you will do this, then that will happen"; "if you will be obedient, then I will do good to you" – all with a duty, distinction, and condition attached. But the promises of the New Testament are given altogether freely, out of pure kindness, and all read like this, without the addition of one's own duty: "This will I do, says the Lord"; "that shall be done, says the Lord." At times He adds: "Not for your sake, but for My sake and My name's sake, will I do it." Of that St. Paul wrote enough to the Romans and the Galatians. Therefore, because Joshua is still to carry on the old priesthood here, He bases His promise on Joshua's obedience. In this way, on the other hand, He again keeps Joshua from becoming too proud because of the earlier visions, consolations, and promises: Joshua must remain humble and walk in the fear of God.

For that is the way we poor people here on earth are: When God punishes us and permits evils to prevail, we become altogether too

[10] Luther uses the German word *bezeugete* ("testified," "bore witness") to translate the Vulgate's *contestabatur.*

timid and fainthearted, so that He has enough to do to comfort us and restore us. Again, when He consoles and blesses us, we become altogether too proud and secure, so that He has enough to do to threaten and frighten us. Our flesh is much too weak and fragile to be able to bear God's deeds – both evil and good; whatever He does with us, He gets work to do. Evil we cannot suffer; good we cannot bear. Therefore, after His great promises, He must once more humble Joshua and hold him in check, so that he may not grow too conceited because of those glorious promises. Saul and many kings of Israel were deceived by the fact that they had the promises of God, and they became proud so that they perished. And this did indeed put the Jews, one and all, into the Babylonian captivity, that they depended on God and yet were not willing to be good but wanted to live secure and without fear. Again, many were deceived by the wretched captivity, so that they stayed abroad and did not return from Babylon. Oh, if we could only see what poor people we are before God!

The word "bear witness to" [11] in Scripture means as much as "to proclaim the word of God." Ps. 122:4: "The tribes go up . . . to bear witness [12] for Israel," that is: God's people are ascending to the temple, where God's Word is proclaimed to Israel; and Ps. 81:8: "Hear, O My people, while I bear witness to you." God's Word, then, is called a "witness" because God speaks to the people through men, who are His witnesses; Acts 1:8: "You shall be My witnesses." But what one bears witness to, that men do not see but only hear; and it must be believed. Therefore "bearing witness" is nothing but God's Word spoken by angels or men, and it calls for faith. Also the words "If you will walk in My ways," ought to be quite intelligible to us; that is, that "God's ways" means God's commandments and works; and "walking in them" means practicing God's commandments and works and being obedient within their framework. And this He commands Joshua in particular: he is to keep His charge, as Moses also spoke in Exodus and Leviticus.[13] The "charge" is what we call performing the office of the church and of the worship of God; for in that one has to do not with men, but one waits on and attends to the Lord and gives

[11] Cf. n. 10 above.

[12] Luther's German translation of this passage uses *zeugen* in the meaning *predigen*.

[13] The Weimar editor suggests Lev. 8:35, "performing what the Lord has charged," and Num. 1:53, "the Levites shall keep the charge of the tabernacle of the testimony," as the passages Luther may have had in mind.

attention to Him alone and to what He says and desires. This attention and care is here called the "charge of the Lord" or a "waiting on the Lord," which befitted Joshua the high priest especially and above others.

Thus upon the fulfillment of this duty comes the first promise: that Joshua shall rule the house of God in peace and have charge of His courts; that is, he is to be confirmed in his office not by men but by God Himself, so that he may know that God has given him these commands and be assured that he is well pleasing to God in his office, because he has received it not of his own choosing or presumption but by God's command. In addition God will give him peace and occasion to conduct this office; that is, the city is again to come into existence and be protected by God; for if this did not happen, how could he carry on his office within it? Ruling God's house, however, is this: being judge and ruler over the office in which God's Word and worship are to be found, that is, in the priesthood of Levi and in the spiritual office. And it is indeed a high and glorious command for him to be told that he is to rule over the Word of God, the worship of God, and the souls, and to be appointed pope in Jewry. He includes the courts, however, in the house of God, because the Word of God and the worship of God are cultivated not only in the temple but also in the courts.

The second promise is that God will also give him obedient subjects. For where there is a rule without obedience, there also is sheer disorder and nothing worthwhile. And that promise is certainly needed by Joshua. For the Jewish people were a haughty, stiffnecked people, so that Joshua might well worry and say: "You entrust to me the spiritual rule in this wretched time. What if this happened to me, that the others would not believe and each one would boast that the work had been entrusted to him? After all, Moses and Aaron were not able to maintain themselves; for Korah and the leaders of the tribe of Levi rose up against them (Num. 16). Should not that happen to me all the more, who am so much more insignificant than Moses and Aaron?" Therefore the promise runs thus and says: "Be not afraid. I, who entrust this office to you, will also give you subjects who shall follow you and not resist you or rebel. For I will have my angels present, and they shall see to it that they keep you in the rule and your followers in obedience." That is what He says here: "And I will give you people who will do the walking (that is, who will be obedient) among or in the midst of those who are standing here (that is, among the angels), who are standing here for the purpose of attending to this matter and keeping the people on your side against every devil and his rebellious angels. Of that you shall be sure."

From this word we know that it is altogether God's grace and gift when there are obedient subjects, and that God creates and preserves these blessings through His angels in the world against the rebellion and the disobedience which are found in the hearts of all men and are incited by the devil. Hence there is no doubt that, wherever one finds disobedience and rebellion, there the devil has slacked the reins, and the angels have ceased watching, so that God might punish those that deserve it. So the latest rebellion [14] in the German lands without a doubt was a punishment for us who have despised His Gospel and refused to obey His Word, though we have become all the worse because of the punishment, as is common among the godless, and as Is. 9:13 says: "The people did not turn to Him who smote them." Again, it is sheer grace and goodness when He institutes and gives men a government, especially when this government is a Joshua, that is, pious and useful, as the text here teaches and as also Solomon says in Prov. 20:12: "The hearing ear and the seeing eye, the Lord has made them both." The seeing eye is pious government, the hearing ear is pious subjects: neither of them is within the power of men; God must give both.

8-9. *Hear now, O Joshua the high priest, you and your friends who sit before you, for they are men of good omen:*[15] *behold, I will bring My Servant Zemah.*[16] *For behold, upon the stone which I have set before Joshua, upon a single stone with seven facets.*

This text speaks of the coming of Christ. For the prophet connects the Levitical priesthood with the priesthood of the coming Christ, to which it also points and in which it is to find its end, as we have heard above. Thus the prophet himself teaches what Joshua's priesthood means, so that no one should seek another allegory or interpretation here. For by now he has said enough about the priesthood of Joshua: how he stood with God, what he was to do, what God in turn would do for him; so that there was no need of teaching anything more

[14] The Peasants' War of 1525.

[15] Luther translates: *sie sind eitel wunder* ("they are sheer wonders").

[16] Luther transliterates the Hebrew צֶמַח ("the Branch," or "the Bud").

about it. He therefore now announces what is to follow all this and how long the priesthood should stand and his office should run, and says: "Hear now, O Joshua, with your friends, I will announce to you even more and greater things." He also includes the friends of Joshua, however, who are also to hear these things, and in that way he lets us know that the promise of the coming kingdom of Christ will benefit the pious and faithful only, those who are like Joshua and one with him in spirit. For very many of the Jewish people have despised, and despise to the present day, both this promise and its fulfillment, so that these are left for Joshua and his friends alone.

And he says that they are sheer wonders. For all who are to accept Jesus are strange beings and wonders to the world. For the kingdom of Christ on earth is so offensive, foolish, and wretched a thing that all who believe in Him are considered mere fools and wretched people, as also Paul says (1 Cor. 4:9), "We have become a spectacle to the world,[17] to angels, and to men." And Is. 8:18 speaks in the same vein: "Behold, I and the children whom the Lord has given me are signs and portents" and are set for the fall and offense of both houses of Israel, etc. "Christ is a stumbling block to the Jews and folly to the Gentiles," 1 Cor. 1:23. Whoever therefore preaches and confesses Christ must also be an offense and a fall to the highly intellectual, wise, and saintly. And so the angel remarks also here that this promise of Christ is so offensive that his friends, who are to hear it with him, must permit the other Jews and the whole world to consider them fools and nothing but strange, peculiar people. It is therefore necessary for the angel to admonish them to hear, as though he would say: "Listen, listen, dear Joshua and your friends, you must listen and simply give attention to the Word and cling to it. If you do not hold to the Word, you will not be able to stand against the offense which the kingdom of Christ brings with it."

From all of this Joshua must now learn that he is indeed to build the temporal temple and conduct his office. He is not to become so attached to his office, however, as though there were nothing else; but he is to know that it is to last for a short time only and that then another one will come. And it is also strange that he is told so very seriously to build when, after all, he is to be nothing in comparison with the coming Servant. Joshua, however, knows very well that he is

17 Luther actually quotes "to God, to angels, and to men." Cf. the same quotation p. 39 above.

the high priest; yet he must believe here that this "Zemah" will be greater and more glorious than he and all his descendants, and therefore he understands well that another High Priest will come who will set aside his own Levitical priesthood.

He says, "My Servant Zemah," as if He did not have any other servant or the others were not His servants. But Christ is called the Servant of God in particular and above all others, as Isaiah more than the other prophets is in the habit of calling Him, for example, Is. 52:13: "Behold, My Servant shall prosper"; and 42:1: "Behold, My Servant," which the evangelists translate *puer meus,* for example, Matt. 12:18 and Acts 4:27: "[They] were gathered together against Thy holy Child Jesus, whom Thou didst anoint, etc." For this Servant was to do the actual work of which all the other servants had prophesied, even as He Himself in the Gospel of John often praises the work that the Father has commanded Him, namely, that of redeeming the world through His suffering, etc. (John 4:34; 5:36). Thus He is the real, one Servant of God, the pattern for all other servants. He calls Him "Zemah," which in German means a plant – like a branch, a sprig, or a rod; as also Is. 4:2 says: "In that day the Branch of the Lord shall be glorious"; and Jer. 33:15: "At that time I will cause a righteous Branch to spring forth for David, etc." He is called a Branch, however, because without ceasing Christ is being preached in the Gospel and is growing and increasing in the world. For until Judgment Day Christ's kingdom will be growing and increasing and will always gain new and more Christians out of this world.

But this is a strange growing, one that looks to the world like something that is withering and perishing. For we find the cross of Christ in it and all kinds of persecution. But we also find pure growth in it; for in the midst of death there is life, in poverty riches, in disgrace honor, and so forth – amidst all evil there is sheer goodness. Is. 53:2 therefore says very aptly: "He grew up before Him like a young plant, and like a root out of dry ground," that is, before God and in the spirit there is nothing but growth, even though it does come forth out of the dry ground where there is neither water nor moisture. In other words: in the eyes of the world it is growing up out of utter misery, distress, and grief. Even here, therefore, Christ is not simply called "Zemah" or "Branch" but "a Branch of the Lord." Because in this growing He is the Servant of the Lord and not something that is growing in the eyes of the world, where there is fertile and moist land, that is, possessions, honor, and pleasures.

For behold, upon the Stone which I have set before Joshua, upon a single Stone with seven facets.

Here the prophet himself gives the allegory or interpretation of the physical temple. He speaks of the spiritual building of a living temple, in which a foundation Stone is to be laid that is altogether different from that of the former temple. It is to be a single Stone, while in the physical temple many stones were laid; and it is the Stone of which Is. 28:16 and 1 Peter 2:6 speak: "Behold, I am laying in Zion for a foundation a Stone, a tested Stone, a precious Cornerstone, . . . He who believes in Him will not be put to shame." The Stone is Christ, as He Himself explains, Matt. 21:42: "The very Stone which the builders rejected has become the head of the corner." And God is laying this Stone Himself – not Joshua or Zerubbabel. For God Himself is building this temple, as He says here: "The Stone which I have set before Joshua." God was already beginning to build the spiritual temple while He was having the physical temple built for the sake of the spiritual one. And furthermore: this spiritual building is set before Joshua, that is, before the priesthood of Joshua. For Christ's temple and kingdom began while the tribe and priesthood of Joshua were still in existence, which indicates that Christ should come before Joshua and his tribe and priesthood had ceased. This Stone, then, was set among Joshua's descendants, into their presence, though they neither saw nor understood it, yes, even rejected it.

Seven eyes [18] are to be found on this stone. A strange building! There stones are being placed upon other stones; here eyes are being built upon that one Stone. Who can tell how that can happen and be? And why not just as well have seven ears or seven mouths? It is like this: The kingdom of Christ stands in the faith and knowledge of Christ, as Isaiah, Peter, and Paul teach. For whoever knows Christ is enlightened and has spiritual eyes. Now not all that hear Him also know Him, but only those who believe. Therefore not ears but only eyes must be built on this Stone. The seven eyes, then, are the various kinds of true Christians, who have been enlightened by the Holy Spirit, and especially those Christians who teach, instruct, and guide others. But it is sufficiently well known that in Scripture the number seven is as much as a common number or means "all kinds of" and that the seven eyes therefore refer to all Christians. In addition, reference is

18 "Eyes" literally translates the Hebrew עֵינַיִם and the Vulgate's *oculi*. RSV has "facets," as applied to a stone.

here made to the fact that in Jewry there should be no eye but only blindness – indeed, everywhere all that is not in Christ must be blindness. For all the eyes are to be found on this Stone, and nowhere else. And they are quite properly called "eyes," for a Christian knows and sees and understands all things, as St. Paul says, 1 Cor. 2:10: "For the Spirit searches everything, even the depths of God"; and (v. 15): "The spiritual man judges all things." For the Christian knows what is meant by God, Christ, Spirit, life, righteousness, sin, death, hell, devil, world, flesh, future, and present. In him everything is eye and knowledge.

Behold, I will engrave its inscription, says the Lord of hosts.

Not the stone masons but God Himself will polish this Stone. He says: "I, I will prepare this Stone properly, and polish and engrave it, so that it will be a beautiful, suitable Stone." Some interpret this "polishing" to mean that in His mother's womb Christ was furnished by the Holy Spirit with many kinds of beautiful gifts. I let that stand. I think, however, that he is speaking here about the suffering of Christ, through which Christ was prepared and made ready to be a Cornerstone for all who believe in Him and were to be built on Him. For thus He says, Luke 24:26: "Was it not necessary that Christ should suffer these things and enter into His glory?" And the Epistle to the Hebrews says (cf. ch. 2:9 f.) that He "should be made perfect through suffering, to be a pioneer of our salvation and be crowned with glory and honor because of suffering, etc." The Jews and Pilate, however, were our God's chisels, picks, and stone mallets, which He used to polish this Stone so that He might lay the foundation of His new temple. For as we know, the seven eyes and all the Christians have been born of His suffering and His blood and are also built up on His suffering. All that the following text proves.

And I will remove the guilt of this land in a single day.

The stone is to be polished so that in this way sin may be removed. Now sin, as we well know, is removed by nothing but the suffering of Christ. For that is the power and the fruit of His suffering, the forgiveness of sins, as Is. 52 and Peter and Paul teach in many places. This polishing, then, must be His suffering and not His birth or conception. By promising to remove the sins of the whole world, however, He shows that no sin can be forgiven through the old priesthood. Yes, everything that is not, and cannot be called, the suffering of Christ cannot remove sin; and before God all good works are worthless and sinful. The polished Cornerstone must do the deed, and nothing else can do it.

He lets us know, however, how strong and mighty this forgiveness is by saying that He will effect it "in a single day." That is as much as saying: In a single day, and once, He will effect this great reconciliation and forgiveness, which will make satisfaction for all sins from the beginning of the world to eternity. No new forgiveness for new sins will have to be effected every day and every year, as was true under the old priesthood, where forgiveness of sins was sought every day and every year through sacrifice and the worship of God. No, the one polishing on the day of Christ's suffering is to effect a complete and sufficient forgiveness; and so the Epistle to the Hebrews (ch. 9) also teaches very beautifully that Christ has made the saints perfect by one offering.

When he speaks "of this land," however, he means that He will remove the sin of the Jewish land. For the promise of Christ was given to the Jews. Moreover, they had the Law and the priesthood, which had to do with the atonement for sins. It is as though He were to say: "Every day and every year there is much ado in this land and among these people about the blotting out of sins, but to no avail. Therefore I will take one day for Myself and do away with sin, so that all this hubbub and ado no longer will be necessary." And with this word, then, the Old Testament and its priesthood are rebuked and abolished as incapable of removing sin and to be kept in force only until the day when sin really will be removed.

Now ask yourself whether Joshua's friends do not all have to be "sheer wonders" to tolerate this offense: first, that there is to be another temple and that this physical one will not be adequate; then, that the other temple is to be so unusual as to contain only one single Stone with nothing but eyes built on it; also, that their own priesthood is to be ineffective and that whatever they do, it will all be sin, as though no sin had ever been forgiven with and under their priesthood. All these things are to take place, however, when the new temple is built and their own priesthood and temple have been abolished. It is nothing but offense, nothing but offense!

10. *In that day, says the Lord of hosts, every one of you will invite his neighbor under his vine and under his fig tree.*

This means: When sin has been removed and God in this way has been reconciled through Christ, then at this one time the true and eternal peace will come; as Paul teaches Rom. 5:1. For where there is sin, there can be no peace in one's heart before God; as Isaiah says (Is. 48:22): "There is no peace for the wicked," and Ps. 14: "They do not know the way of peace." [19] For these words, "every one will invite the other under his vine," are spoken in the way of a proverb, to indicate that there is peace in the land. For where conditions in the land are so that men can live secure and invite one another as guests, be merry, and can eat and drink, there one finds peace. Scripture therefore also tells of the great peace under King Solomon (1 Kings 4:24 f.), when every man lived "under his fig tree and under his vine." But when there is war, one must go out and lie on the field of battle, and no one is sure of himself or his property. For that reason the prophet now wishes to say: "Heretofore, when sin still prevailed, everyone was looking for peace. But sin would not have it. Peace was more desired than found. But now that sin has been removed, really perfect peace shall prevail for once. For the first time it shall really happen that everyone can sit under his vine and invite his neighbor to be his guest.

Not that Christ gives physical peace – like the world – so that His followers might now invite one another under vines and fig trees. The prophet is rather using the same language to praise spiritual peace that the Jews were using to praise physical peace. It is as if someone were talking about the cleansing of the law of Moses and said: "The cleansing will come when Christ comes," and, "One will eat the true Paschal lamb some day – when Christ comes," and the like. For the forgiveness of sins which is mentioned here and the resulting peace cannot be understood as referring to the Old Testament, as has been said, because the Old Testament has to do with the forgiving of sins every day and every year. Here, however, it is all to take place on one day.

[19] This passage is in the Vulgate only.

CHAPTER FOUR

1-3. *And the angel who talked with me came again, and waked me, like a man that is wakened out of his sleep. And he said to me: What do you see? I said: I see, and behold, a lampstand all of gold, and a bowl on top of it, and seven lamps on it, with seven lips on each of the lamps which are on top of it. And there are two olive trees by it, one on the right of the bowl and the other on its left.*

THE prophet here wishes to comfort the other head, Prince Zerubbabel, who was also tempted by two thoughts to become inactive and timid about building, as was said above.[1] The first thought came when he considered his weakness and his powers, which amounted to nothing at all when compared with the might of the Persians and all his other enemies; the second came when he considered that heretofore his enemies had succeeded in preventing the building and simply had not been willing anywhere to abandon what they had determined to do. In these two temptations the prophet here comforts him and admonishes him not to consider his own weakness but rather the power of God. For what is impossible with men is possible with God (Luke 18:27). And he should also consider that the great kingdom of the Persians amounted to nothing at all when compared with God, who wanted to do this thing. For even though something might be a great mountain in the eyes of the world, it is no mountain at all in God's eyes but only a plain like any other flat fields. For in His eyes nothing is great, high, broad, mighty, wise, pious, blessed, or anything else, but everything is nothing.

The prophet is preaching in this way: he has seen a vision of a lampstand of gold standing between two olive trees. And he interprets the vision himself and adds this word and says that it is the Spirit of God, who desires to be among them and to strengthen and help both Zerubbabel and Joshua. For as I have often said, the signs and visions that God gives in addition to the Word are needed to

[1] Cf. p. 204 above.

strengthen all the more the faith of weak or saddened souls who cannot cling to the mere Word as well as to a picture or sign. For it is a great thing to believe that God is gracious and favorable to us but a difficult thing for human hearts to achieve. The frivolous fanatics, however, come rushing and roaring along and at once can praise the Spirit so confidently that they tolerate neither picture nor sign but in one moment are able to believe everything without a sign – even the bare Word. But though Joshua and Zerubbabel are great men in the eyes of God and indeed have a strong faith, conditions are still so bad that God must use visions and interpretations to nurse them along in the faith as though they were young children. Faith and the Spirit are not so easy a matter, however glibly the noisy spirits may be able to chatter about them.

As a portent of these things the prophet says that the angel has wakened him as one is wakened out of one's sleep. For there is to be another sermon, again addressed to Prince Zerubbabel. And this sermon is to point out that Zerubbabel is timid and inactive in his heart and lax through his unbelief, and that he cannot see the light of the Spirit, who is ready to help him. For the fact that the prophet is to be wakened indicates that Prince Zerubbabel is to be wakened out of his sleep. It is as though the prophet were to say: "Zerubbabel, you are fixing the eyes of your heart on your weakness. Therefore you can see neither light nor help but are asleep in the darkness and night of your unbelief. But wake up and see that it is day! God's mercy is shining upon you and desires to be with you. Open your eyes and forget your weakness! Someone else is here who desires to accomplish the task, etc."

The vision of this lampstand of gold, however, is a little different from that of the lampstand of Moses, Ex. 25:31 ff. The lampstand of Moses has branches issuing from its sides or stems. But this one stands up straight with its stem and on its top has a round, large, broad plate or bowl, which I have translated as a "ring" *(reiff)*. And round about on this plate, in a circle, there are seven lamps that are all burning and lighted. And to keep the light from being extinguished because of a lack of oil, there are seven ladles or pipes [RSV: "lips"] on the stand that are filled with oil, one to follow the other. We cannot know, however, what form these ladles had, and whether they were like little pots or cans or pipes. But oil was poured into the lamps by means of them – and that is enough for us, may they have been cans or jars or what –

and all were of pure gold. And the Hebrew text also says that there were more of these ladles than only one times seven, for it reads *Septem et septem*[2] *infusoria pro lucernis,* that is, "each seven and seven ladles for the lamps." That almost sounds as though there were seven ladles for each lamp, to indicate that the lamps were very plentifully supplied with oil and that no one had to worry that the lamps might go out.

4-7. *And I said to the angel who talked with me: What are these, my lord? Then the angel who talked with me answered me: Do you not know what these are? I said: No, my lord. Then he said to me: This is the Word of the Lord to Zerubbabel: Not by might, nor by power, but by My Spirit, says the Lord of hosts. What are you, O great mountain? Before Zerubbabel you shall become a plain; and he shall bring forward the top stone amid shouts of Grace, grace to it!*

This is the interpretation of the lampstand and of the whole vision. As the lampstand with its burning lamps is standing between the two olive trees, so God with His Spirit desires to be among and in the midst of His people, especially between and in the midst of the two heads, Joshua and Zerubbabel. And at the same time He touches upon the very thoughts of Zerubbabel and tells him that everything shall take place "not by might, nor by power, but by My Spirit," as if to say: "You cast your eyes about and look where the power might be that will hold off the king of Persia and all your other foes and will help you and strengthen you. For you can think of no other way in which all this shall and may happen. But I will show you a different way, so that this way of yours will not be needed. My Spirit shall perform it. He shall strengthen you and your people, shall give the king of Persia a gracious mind to let you build in peace, and in addition shall help you with all his captains – and all this because My lampstand, My Spirit, is standing among you, and because I am gracious to you and wish you well." For when God wishes a man well, no one shows him any enmity. And Solomon says (Prov. 16:7): "When a man's ways please the Lord, He makes even his enemies to be at peace with him."

The meaning, then, is this: "Dear Zerubbabel, you have My Word, which is shining upon the lampstand; and through Zechariah and Haggai that tells you to build. Therefore look up and let that satisfy

2 This Latin translation of the Hebrew is Luther's. The Vulgate has only a single *septem.*

you. For where My Word is, there My Spirit is, there I am Myself. But if I am with you, who will be against you? I will give you peace for the building that I am demanding of you. Just do what My Word says and let Me see to it that you have peace before the king of Persia and all your other enemies. I am mighty enough and can also change their hearts as I like, so that the very men that you fear most shall help you the most." This surely is another defiant, mighty promise: Zerubbabel is to feel secure before such great enemies, and that very easily, without trouble, war, or the stroke of a sword. Thus God once again, as a comfort to all of us, demonstrates His omnipotence and shows us how firmly He has our hearts and the hearts of all our enemies in His hands: men cannot do anything to us unless He wills it but must even help us when He wills it. Moreover, in the New Testament our enemies help us most when they harm us most, so that even death, the greatest enemy of all, must help us to life at the very time when it destroys us.

The interpretation, however, is this: The lampstand refers to the position or office of the preacher. The lampstand is single; that is, the preachers and teachers among the people of God are of one heart and of one mind and teach one and the same thing, as Zechariah and Haggai and their companions do here. And it is of gold; that is, it is pure divine wisdom and not of clay or earth, which means that they do not have men's words. The seven lamps on it mean this: Though they teach one and the same thing, and though there is one Spirit in them, they still have varieties of gifts, as St. Paul testifies Rom. 12:6; 1 Cor. 12:4; Eph. 4:7. The light is the Word that they preach physically, each one in accordance with the capacity of his lamps and his gifts. In this way they let their light shine before men and are the light of the world, Matt. 5:14; 1 Thess. 5:5. The oil is the grace of the Holy Spirit, which preserves this light among the people of God and at all times is in and with the Word, so that this Word may always have power and success and may never stop or cease. The ladles and pipes are the prophets, from whom the other teachers and preachers take and receive what they are teaching. For those men are prophets who have been enlightened not by men but by God, and other men learn from them. And for this reason there are many times seven ladles because he wants to indicate that God has always given – and been willing to give – prophets to these people, so that they would truly be richly furnished with prophets and with the Word and Spirit of God.

The angel of course also has this interpretation in mind when he answers the question of the prophet and says, "Do you not know what these are?" as if to say, "You really ought to know this, because you, too, are a part of the lampstand." For otherwise this answer of the angel sounds unnecessary and superfluous, as though he did not know that the prophet did not understand the vision. But as it is, it is a very friendly conversation, as when a father is talking to a child: "Don't you know, dear Zechariah, what these are? Why, you yourself are one of them, etc." But what the two olive trees and the two snuffers are, will follow later in the text.

7. *What are you, O great mountain? Before Zerubbabel you shall become a plain.*

To give further comfort, he comes back to the mountain, that is, to the kingdom of the Persians, of which Zerubbabel is afraid and by which he is being tried in his faith, as we have heard. For just as he had rebuked Satan above [3] in the presence of Joshua, so he here rebukes the empire of Persia in the presence of Zerubbabel and calls it a great mountain – for it was a mighty empire – in the manner of Scripture, which calls all kingdoms and principalities mountains. But these words are sweet and fatherly, as when a father has punished his child and now wants to calm it again and draw it back to him. He rebukes the rod before the child and says, "O you bad rod, did you strike my little son? Just wait, you will never do that again. My little son is good, etc." So it also is here; when God had chastised the Jewish people severely by means of the Babylonians, so that even Zerubbabel was still afraid of the rod and timid about believing in God, He rebuked the empire in his hearing and said: "Before Zerubbabel it shall no longer be a great mountain which he has to fear, but it shall be as a beautiful merry plain"; that is, through God's Spirit it shall be merry, friendly, and helpful to the Jews.

And he shall bring forward the top stone amid shouts of 'Grace, grace to it!'

Here, then, he is encouraging the pacified child and promising that from now on things will be good and go forward. He will, he says, bring forward the first stone; that is, he will erect and raise the building from its foundation, which had been laid earlier – the building that had been delayed for a season. And he will do this so quickly and

[3] Cf. p. 209 above.

joyfully that everyone will feel favorable and well-disposed toward it – yes, even joyful. These again are beautiful words and promises of God intended to awaken and preserve the faith of Zerubbabel. We can see, however, how difficult it is to revive a frightened conscience. For God must offer Zerubbabel comforting words in two directions: here to rebuke the enemy and make him humble, and there to comfort and lift up Zerubbabel's heart. For a conscience is a tender, soft thing.

These Latin words, *Exaequabit gratiam gratiae eius* ("he will match grace with its grace"), which read thus in Hebrew, *Cum clamoribus gratia gratia ei* ("with shouts of 'grace,' 'grace for it' "), I have translated in this way: "So that people will cry out, 'Grace, grace upon it!' "[4] The words reveal the joy that one has when one is happy about a building that is making progress; everyone offers congratulations and expresses the wish that it were finished. The fact that *gratia vel favor,* that is, "grace!" is given twice means about this in Hebrew usage: There will be one here, one there, and many others besides who will be happy about the building and will wish it well. This is what the logicians call "speaking *distributive.*" It is as though one were building and here one came, there another, who would praise the work and say, "Ah, how beautifully that is rising," and it pleases everyone. This praise and rejoicing over the building on the part of so many is here expressed as *gratia, gratia ei, i. e., habet gratiam, est egregium certe;* which one might translate: "Ah, how fine that is. It is indeed a splendid structure! etc." In this way he wants to assure Zerubbabel that he is not only to build but also to build well and beautifully, so that everyone will like the building, regard it with favor, praise it, and wish it well.

8-10. *Moreover the Word of the Lord came to me, saying: The hands of Zerubbabel have laid the foundation of this house; his hands shall also complete it. Then you will know that the Lord of hosts has sent me to you. For whoever has despised the day of small things, etc.*

Here the prophet comes with another sermon to strengthen Zerubbabel further in a new tribulation which his people were causing him. For some of them considered the work small and impossible, so that Haggai rebuked them and said (Hag. 1:2): "This people say the time has not yet come to rebuild the house of the Lord." And in Ezra 3:12 f.

[4] Luther's German translation is: *das man ruffen wird glück zu, glück zu.*

we read that many of the old men who had seen the first temple wept when they saw the foundation of this temple. And later Zechariah himself will say (Zech. 8:6): "If it is marvelous in the sight of the remnant of the people in these days, should it also be marvelous in My sight, says the Lord of hosts?" From all this we can see that many of the people were unsure in their faith. Some perhaps even scoffed at the work, especially those that were on good terms with Tobiah, their enemy. Nehemiah writes about that (Neh. 2:19). Thus Zerubbabel had to hear these words and others like them: "Oh, why are we building anyway? Nothing will come of it anyway. We are too poor and insignificant." The others, however, said, "Yes, yes, go on and build. You will do it. You are the right people for it, etc." Zerubbabel thus had to contend with his own people to keep them from despairing, backsliding, getting tired of building, and hindering him because of idle mouths. For what God orders and desires to have, that has to be attacked on all sides and tempted by Satan within and without.

Then it follows that Zechariah again repeats his first sermon: that Zerubbabel is to complete the building. And then he adds this bit, "Whoever has despised the day of small things?" In this way he rebukes the idle mouths, just as he had above rebuked Satan and the great mountain in order to comfort Zerubbabel.[5] The meaning is this: "You judge according to outward appearance and not according to My Word. According to outward appearance the work is insignificant; and yet My Words are glorious. But if you believed My Words, the insignificant beginning would not offend you. Therefore keep your mouths shut and do not cause Zerubbabel and the others to become confused or discouraged, as men did in the desert in earlier times and deterred the people from entering the land of Canaan. For who are you despisers that you are more impressed by the insignificant appearance of the building at this time than by My Word, and that you confuse those who are more impressed by My Word than by the insignificant appearance?" For He calls it a time of small things because at that time the building was insignificant, even as Paul calls the days evil in which evil is done (Eph. 5:16), while he calls those days good in which good is done. And in Hebrew we read this: *Quis contemnit ad diem parvorum,* which I cannot translate better than in this way: "Who despises at the time of the insignificant," that is: "Who is it, I pray, that despises My Word because at this time everything is still

[5] Cf. pp. 206 and 226 above.

insignificant and not in keeping with My Word?" as if to say: "I will surely make it sufficiently proper and great enough." Therefore I am not able to give a better translation than this, "Who despises these insignificant days? etc."

He shall rejoice and shall see the plummet in the hand of Zerubbabel. These seven are the eyes of the Lord, which range through the whole earth.

In Hebrew a weight or measure is called a stone. Therefore the "stone of tin" is here translated as the "plummet." It is what our masons call a plumb rule, in which the plumb hangs, or whatever other kind of rule the Jews and the people of the East used in building. But what kind of great joy will be involved in seeing the plumb rule or plummet in the hand of Zerubbabel? I think the prophet is referring not to simple seeing but rather to the fact that through Zerubbabel the building will be so far advanced that people will have to admit that God's eyes and Spirit have accomplished these things and have guided the plumb rule in Zerubbabel's hand and that therefore the mouths of all will be stopped who have despised the day of small things and despaired of the building. For the seven who are to be with Zerubbabel, he says, are the eyes of the Lord; that is, His Spirit with His manifold gifts shall be present and with His favor shall strengthen and help the people of both the Jewish nation and the kingdom of Persia, that is, of all lands. Hence, as he said above, progress will come not through the sword or the might of armies but through the Spirit of God. And we also heard above [6] that the seven eyes signify the Spirit of God with His gifts.

11-14. *Then I said to him: What are these two olive trees on the right and the left of the lampstand? And a second time I said to him: What are these two branches of the olive trees, which are beside the two golden pipes from which the oil is poured out? He said to me: Do you not know what these are? I said: No, my lord. And he said: These are the two anointed who stand by the Lord of the whole earth.*

Here the prophet himself explains what it means that the lampstand is standing between the two olive trees and the two oil buds or olive branches and says, "The two olive trees and the two olive

[6] Cf. p. 218 above.

branches are the two anointed," that is, Joshua, the high priest, and Zerubbabel, the prince of Judah. These men are to be comforted and assured by the vision that God's Word and Spirit will graciously be and remain with them in their work. In Hebrew fashion the prophet calls them "sons of oil," [7] not only because of the olive trees and olive branches, which refer to them, but also because of the power and meaning of the oil. In German we should have to speak thus: "There are two who are fat and well filled, that is, who have enough and have a gracious God," as Is. 5:1 also says: "My beloved had a vineyard on a very fertile hill," that is, he is well situated and is pleasing to God. And the fact that he has a twofold vision, as of two olive trees and two olive branches, or olive buds, has only a single meaning, as Pharaoh's dream (Gen. 41) about the seven cows and seven ears had a single meaning. It is common with God to point to a single thing with a twofold sign. If one likes, however, one may interpret the two olive trees as the priestly and the princely offices of the Jewish people, from which the two branches, Joshua and Zerubbabel, have sprouted forth above others as the outstanding and distinguished ones that stand at the very head and serve the Lord of the whole world or the whole land.

What the two gold pipes are, however, and how they were fashioned, I really do not know and shall let anyone advise who can. It is beyond my knowledge, nor do I find anyone who can offer us anything definite. But I have translated in this way: "two snuffers which one breaks off." But in order not to have to leave a gap in the text, I used the lampstand of Moses, Ex. 25:38, as an example. That also had snuffers, and I felt that this translation would be good in view of the interpretation. For among the teachers there must also be those that polish and clean the light so that it will not go out because of foulness, as is indicated by the lampstand of Moses. For the first teachers, as mentioned above,[8] lay the foundation and do the planting. But if others do not follow who will do the necessary teaching and watering and maintaining, flesh and blood get lazy and indolent and allow the light to get a snuff and core, so that it grows dim and at last goes out altogether. This, then, is the office of the teachers who admonish and exhort men with the teaching that these men have already received. St. Paul speaks of this, Rom. 12:8: "He who exhorts, (let him use the

[7] Cf. *Luther's Works,* 16, p. 58.

[8] Cf. p. 225 above.

grace given to him) in his exhortation." They do not kindle a new light but cleanse and maintain the light already kindled; for they do not teach anything new but constantly rouse, urge on, and exhort men against their lazy Adam with the same old teaching.

Now this interpretation is not wrong, but, as I have said, I cannot base my stand on the text. St. Jerome gave this Latin translation: *Quid sunt duae spicae olivarum, quae sunt juxta duo rostra aurea, in quibus sunt suffusoria ex auro?* that is, "What are the two olive branches beside the two golden lips or pipes, in which are the pitchers of gold?" From this one can see that St. Jerome meant to say: "Two lips or pipes were attached there, as a tap or spigot, through which the wine flows, is attached to a keg." And beside these pipes there were pitchers or some other golden vessels, into which the oil was poured through the pipes and later into the lamps. But in his commentary on Zechariah he says this: *Quid sunt duo rami olivarum, qui in manibus duarum narium aurearum sunt, et quae infundunt et retrahunt suffusoria aurea?* that is: "What are the two olive branches that stand between the two golden noses, or lips, and fill and empty the golden pitchers?" [9] From this I take it that St. Jerome did not understand the text altogether either. What shall I make of it then? The Hebrew word צַנְתְּרוֹת they translate as "noses" or "snouts," through which something flows, as the mucus flows from the head through the nose. If this is the correct translation, it would apparently mean that these noses, or snouts, in keeping with the above interpretation, had been beside the lampstand for the purpose of cleaning the light. The Hebrew reads thus: *Quid sunt duae spicae olivae in manu duarum narium aurearum, evacuantium supernae aurum?* that is, "What are the two olive buds between the two golden snouts which empty the gold from above?" From that I get so much: the two gold snouts, or spouts, or whatever they were, were suspended above the lamps and overflowed, perhaps into golden vessels, which he here calls "gold." Or he uses the term "gold" for the whole lampstand together with its lamps and everything else, *ut evacuantium a superioribus auri scilicet candelabri feces supernas in lampadibus* ("as emptying from the tops of the gold, that is, the lightstand, the impurities above in the lamps"). Now I do not know whether that which flowed out was oil or the residuum of the oil. But why should I grope for a long time in darkness? I will not hit it anyway. I tell you

[9] Jerome, *Commentaria in Zachariam prophetam*, on Zech. 4:11 f., *Patrologia, Series Latina*, XXV, 1445.

that I do not know and therefore shall abandon the little passage like other obscure passages. Nor does it matter so much, since we have the sum of it: that Zerubbabel is to be comforted through the help and assistance of God's Spirit, etc.

CHAPTER FIVE

1-2. *Again I lifted my eyes and saw, and behold, a flying scroll! And he said to me: What do you see? I answered: I see a flying scroll; its length is twenty cubits, and its breadth ten cubits.*

THIS is the way the holy apostles work. When they have preached faith and the Christian doctrine, they announce the seducers and false teachers who are to come, as Christ also does when He says (Matt. 24:5): "Many will come in My name, saying, 'I am the Christ,' and they will lead many astray." In this way the apostles warn us to be on our guard and to cling to the pure doctrine. And so Zechariah does here. After he has preached that the temple and the worship of God are to be reestablished, he now announces how things will be among those who are to come: they no longer will have the Spirit among them, the lampstand will be lost, and they will stray into men's teachings and their own works, as the Pharisees and Sadducees did, as Christ tells us in the Gospel. And the prophet has the golden lampstand before him, because at his time all was well: the Spirit of God was with the people. But when he turns about and looks behind him, he notices something else, namely, a large book that was to come after him. For to look behind one is to see what is coming, even as Abraham saw the ram behind him in a thicket (Gen. 22:13). To have something before one's eyes, however, is to see the present.

But note: this vision is a masterful painting or picture that teaches us in the very best way what men's teachings are, both before God and the world. First of all, there is a book, and therefore one cannot doubt that it represents the knowledge and wisdom of scholars. For books are the marks of scholars – and Moses and the prophets have also written books. But it is a flying book; that is, it is a teaching that is spread through the office of preaching. For "flying" refers to speaking or preaching, as the cherubim with their wings also do (Ex. 25:20). For the spoken word flies through the air like a bird; and for that reason the poets have put wings on the feet of their god Mercury. The tender fruit, the teaching of men, accordingly does not want to be a book that will lie under a bench or in a chest but wants to get out among the people and be preached and heard – more so even than God's Word. And for that reason it could not be better named than "a flying book" – "a book," because it offers splendid and great wisdom, knowledge, and understanding and wants to help and advise the world, as St. Paul says, "These have the appearance of wisdom," Col. 2:23; "flying," because it has many preachers and scholars to promote it; and if they did not talk and chatter about it, their bellies would burst because of their great knowledge and understanding, so greedy and anxious are they to teach, just like the good-for-nothing chatterer Elihu, Job 32:18 f. Thus the book flies back and forth; and thus the laws of the Pharisees had so powerful an influence among the people that by means of them they even suppressed God's commandments, Matt. 15:3. And St. Paul says (Titus 1:11) that they are upsetting and misleading whole families, and that they are increasing and "their talk will eat its way like a gangrene" (2 Tim. 2:17). In short: false doctrine does not walk or ride, but it flies, and the people join it and cling to it as if they were mad. We can also see this very well at present from our factious spirits.

Some say that the prophet had seen this book flying out of the temple, to indicate that false doctrine pretends to be holy and spiritual and boasts of having the Spirit of God. But because this is not in the text, I shall not go beyond the fact that the prophet has simply seen it flying and not coming from any particular place. For the teaching of men does not have any particular origin either but flies and swarms along like a swarm of bees, or as a dream comes to one, so that these men do not know themselves where they got this teaching, except that the devil inspires it. It is not stated either whether the book was open or closed. I think, however, that it was open, because Zechariah can see at once how large it is – perhaps as large as the tables of Moses: a large scroll, which one can roll up and close. For thus the Hebrew word מְגִלָּה presents it, *a volvendo*.[1] For this is the way one formerly made books: one rolled them up, as painters roll up their canvases. Now this great learning wants to stand open and be seen – that is the first thing. For we do not read that there was idolatry among the Jews in later times. But in place of the former idolatry there come this book, knowledge, wisdom, and doctrine, which effect the real idolatry of the

1 That is, "from the verb 'to roll,'" Hebrew גָּלַל.

heart, that is, self-conceit and men's laws in the things of God. And therefore the prophet does not see an idol, but a book.

The second thing is that it is a large book and has the same length and breadth as Solomon's vestibule in the front of the temple had (1 Kings 6:3), to indicate, as was said above,[2] that in the eyes of the world everywhere the teaching of men is something great, that it has great outward show and appearance, many adherents and followers, and that it commands great power and obedience – much more than God's Word. Moreover, it is something big and hard to bear, for it has many, yes, countless laws, as Christ says, Matt. 23:4: "They bind heavy burdens, hard to bear, etc." God's commandments, on the other hand, are easy and light, 1 John 5:3,[3] and they are small in number and are all summed up in one commandment, Rom. 13:9. And yet one abandons the easy commandments and subjects oneself to the hard and unbearable laws of men, though all of these teach merely external things and go outside the Scriptures, just as Solomon's vestibule stood outside the temple (1 Kings 6:3).

But whoever will, may also interpret the flying in this way: the teaching of men is of such a nature that it will never give rest or quiet to the conscience, as St. Paul says, Eph. 4:14, that men's teaching moves and tosses us about as the wind tosses a reed, so that we must be uncertain and unsure. And therefore this book must move and soar about and not rest or lie quietly anywhere. The book of Moses, however, lies and rests in the golden ark (Ex. 40:20), for God's Word and doctrine are quiet and peaceful and give one a calm, secure, and peaceful conscience, wherever they are accepted in faith. St. Paul therefore also rebukes the teachers, 1 Tim. 1:7,[4] who do not understand "either what they are saying or the things about which they make assertions"; that is, they teach nothing that is constant or certain but only cause men's consciences to become confused and restless. We can see, then, what men's teaching means to the people: a splendid thing that has great knowledge, wisdom, outward show, might, and many adherents; and yet it is hard and very complicated, besides being uncertain, inconstant, insecure, and vacillating, with nothing in it. It is an altogether vain, deceptive splendor and specter. But what it means before God, now follows:

[2] Cf. p. 233 above.

[3] The Weimar editor corrects the text's "1 John 2."

[4] The Weimar editor corrects the text's "Eph. 1."

3. *Then he said to me: This is the curse that goes out over the whole land.*

Before God this book is a curse and an execrable thing, for through it a whole land is accursed and robbed of a blessing. For God's Word is a blessing and brings a blessing and grace with it, because it preaches not our works and righteousness but the blood of Christ and the righteousness of God. For that is what the Pharisees did among the Jewish people when through their teachings of men they annulled the commandments of God, Matt. 15:3, as we shall hear. For it is the nature and manner of men's teaching to lead men away from the truth, Titus 1:14, and then indeed curse and wrath must follow. And the prophet himself here clearly interprets what the flying of this book means when he says, "This curse goes out over the face of the whole land," as if to say: "You have seen correctly that it is flying; it indeed is flying and going out over the face of the whole land." For the teachings of the Pharisees had subjected the whole land to themselves, even as men's commandments and ordinances do in Christendom.

And we ought to be quite properly frightened away from all the teachings of men by the horrible fact that before God they are regarded as a curse and damnation. For who, I ask, would want to stand accursed before God and earn that curse with so much toil and trouble as they do who torture themselves with men's commandments? Where there is a curse, the blessing of Christ cannot be found. Nor does the curse go out through only a few houses but over the face of the whole land. But this curse now goes out in full over the Jewish people, because they have despised the Gospel which had brought the blessing promised them in Abraham; and now they are tortured with their Talmud and rabbinical writings, which make them accursed before God. It is as Ps. 109:17 says concerning them: "He did not like blessing; may it be far from him! But he loved to curse; let curses come on him!" To such an age, however, this vision of the prophet applies most of all. For at the time of Christ the curse had begun through the Pharisees; later, however, it was really spread when the Jews were disturbed and took up the Talmud. And that is the real curse and the really great flying book.

For everyone who steals shall be judged innocent according to it, and everyone who swears falsely shall be judged innocent according to it.

Here the prophet touches upon and indicates the teaching which is written in this book, which is taught from it, and by which men are condemned. And although the statement is not clear, I still think that the angel is combining the teaching of men given in these two parts and that he wishes to say this: "All their teaching is this: they teach and glorify thievery and godless living." For all Scripture ascribes to false teachers and to the commandments of men these two parts: they teach hypocrisy and serve their own appetites (Rom. 16:18). Through hypocrisy and the fine glitter of works they lead men away from the faith and God's Word and into a godless life, as St. Paul says, Titus 1:14,[5] that they who give heed to commands of men reject the truth; while in Rom. 16:17 he says that they create dissensions and difficulties in opposition to the right doctrine. In sum: At all times they contend against the saving Word of God and the pure faith. Through thievery and greed they devour widows' houses, Matt. 23:14. For their entire teaching aims at gaining money and possessions, honor and glory, as St. Paul says, Rom. 16:18: "Such persons do not serve our Lord Jesus Christ, but their own appetite"; and Phil. 3:19: "Their god is their belly"; and Ps. 5:9: "Their throat is an open sepulcher"; and Ps. 14:4: "They eat up My people as they eat bread." And so they are rebuked by all the prophets as greedy men and belly-servers.

False teachers, then, are first of all thieves and greedy men. For with a show of holy living and teaching they deceive the people, so that these may bring them gifts in great abundance. For that is thievery, when one furtively takes a man's possessions from him. Yes, they are thieves in a twofold way: first, because they steal from the people through hypocrisy and deceit; second, because they steal from the mouths of the true preachers. For true preachers ought to have what these men steal, but they always come short. How the Pharisees carried on the Gospels teach us well. Thus in Matt. 15:5 Jesus rebukes them for making void the commandment of God and teaching that sacrificing was better than honoring father and mother. According to Matt. 23:16 ff., they taught that the gold on the altar and in the temple was better than the altar itself and the temple. And in addition, they had money changers and hucksters in the temple (Matt. 21:12). These were all thievish tricks, intended for their own profit. Yet all these things were not punished but praised; and their teaching declared

[5] The Weimar editor corrects the text's "Titus, at the end."

those to be good who taught and did such things. There is no need, however, of telling how these things are being done also in the papacy by the greedy, insatiable servants of the Mass and the paunches of the monasteries; for it is quite evident that they have acquired the goods of this world as thieves and rogues. And yet, according to their books and teachings, they are called good and holy people; and besides they persecute those who do not agree with them. The deeds of the Pharisees were child's play, etc.

Second, they are perjurers; that is, they are liars and blasphemers of God. For at that time it was the custom of false prophets to present their teaching in the name of God and to swear by the name of God. Is. 48:1 therefore laments: "Hear this, O house of Jacob, who are called by the name of Israel . . . who swear by the name of the Lord and confess the God of Israel, but not in truth or right"; and again (Jer. 5:2): "Though they say, 'As the Lord lives,' yet they swear falsely, etc." But since men's teaching is nothing but lies and yet is taught in the name of God as the true Word of God, and since the false teachers also base their stand on it, swear and give oaths, ban and curse, as St. Peter did when he denied Christ (Matt. 26:70 ff.), they are properly called false swearers, or perjurers. These, however, are two qualities that are hateful and hostile even to the world and are commonly mentioned together in speaking: "He steals and lies very much." Much more frequently are they found together in spiritual offices. For men must preach lies, otherwise one will not give much to them. He who will preach the truth cannot remain anywhere. If, then, they are to get rich, they must talk the riches out of the people and steal it from them through the preaching of lies – as was said in times past, "The world wants to be cheated." [6] But all these lies remain unpunished too; yes, they must all be called saving teaching, and men that teach these lies must be adjudged and praised as true preachers, while they who rebuke the lies must be persecuted and damned. These are the dear, fine thieves and liars that devour all the world and to boot mislead it and spoil it in body and soul.

6 This proverb appeared in Sebastian Brandt, *Narrenschiff* ("Ship of Fools"), in 1494 in the form *Die weltt die will betrogen syn.* Its Latin form is variously quoted, but perhaps the most characteristic version is the one Büchmann's *Geflügelte Worte* assigns to Carlo Caraffa (1517—1561): *Quandoquidem populus iste vult decipi, decipiatur.* The American showman P. T. Barnum is sometimes quoted as defending his enterprises with an adaptation of this proverb: *Populus vult decipi, ergo decipio.*

4. *I will send it forth, says the Lord of hosts, and it shall enter the house of the thief, and the house of him who swears falsely by My name; and it shall abide in his house and consume it, both timber and stones.*

Here the prophet announces the punishment of these false teachers. For as long as false teachers will prevail, there will be this swearing of oaths and boasting and bragging that with them there is nothing but the truth, nothing but the Holy Spirit, nothing but God, so that anyone opposing them may well despair simply because of their great boasting and swearing. Therefore God must comfort the latter and announce that this boasting and swearing will not last. Oh, how I have suffered in these short years from prophets who with their swearing and boasting tried everything to persuade me that the Spirit was with them! How confidently and defiantly did Müntzer proceed, and everything that opposed him was nothing! How defiant are our blasphemers now, how proudly they proceed, how everything stinks that is said against them, as though they had gained the victory for all times. But here stands the text and brings them to fall and comforts us.

"I will send it forth," he says. What is this "send forth"? Nothing else than to bring it to the light of day: "I will reveal the book to all the world and show that it is a book of thieves and liars. It now shines in the darkness as a truthful and useful book; but I will remove its gloss and take away its paint, so that everyone can see the thieving and lying and also see that because of these the false prophets will be disgraced and brought to nought. I think, indeed, that Christ has brought the teaching of the Pharisees to light through the Gospel, so that all the world can see what a thoroughly godless and greedy thing it was. So all heretics have fared, and so our factious spirits will also fare, and neither boasting nor outward show will help them. He says, "I will send it forth," as He also says in the Gospel (Matt. 15:13): "Every plant which My heavenly Father has not planted will be rooted up." And St. Paul says, 2 Tim. 3:9: [7] "They will not get very far, for their folly will be plain to all." In short: God will send it forth. This is the first punishment of the false teachers: they are brought to shame.

Then comes the second punishment: "It shall enter the house of the thief, and the house of him who swears falsely by My name . . .

[7] So the Weimar editor corrects the text's "1 Tim. 4."

and shall consume it"; that is, it will condemn them and destroy them. For it will leave its resting place and, once it has been revealed, never again mislead anyone. But the false teachers themselves will cling to it and not forsake it but will try to defend and preserve it. Therefore they will be wrecked and destroyed so that they will scarcely leave a token or memento, like a house that burns down so that neither wood nor stones remain but only the deserted place and scene of the fire. For the seducers must suffer this torment, that, though their lies are exposed and brought to shame, they will not yield or leave but will refuse to let their stubborn heads be persuaded. Instead, they will retain the lies for themselves and meanwhile flee the true saints until they have been completely destroyed. Thus the Jews have retained their lies, nor have they ever been willing to desist from them, so that they have been completely destroyed like a house that has burned down. So the Arians have acted and all other heretics; no one was able to talk them out of their thoughts. But what are they now? Nothing but a memory. Our present-day sects and all the seducers under the pope refuse to listen to us, even though their lies have been revealed most clearly. They want to cling to their lies and remain with them until they, too, perish and neither stick nor stone remains. This is what I have often said: factious spirits cannot return to that which is right. For they sin against the Holy Spirit, and for that there is no forgiveness in all eternity. That is what is expressed here in this way: "the book shall enter the house of the thief, and the house of him who swears falsely, and it shall consume them."

5-6. *Then the angel who talked with me came forward and said to me: Lift your eyes, and see what this is that goes forth. And I said: What is it? He said: This is the ephah that goes forth. And he said: This is their form*[8] *in all the land.*

Also this vision of the prophet, like the second last one, is directed against the false teachers. For, as we have seen above,[9] this prophet likes to use two visions for one event, even as Pharoah had two dreams about one event (Gen. 41:26), to indicate how very surely false teaching would in the future be found among the Jewish people after the pure teaching, even as it is true at all times that wherever the Word

[8] Luther translates the Vulgate's *oculus eorum* with *ihre Gestalt,* which is also the meaning of the original Hebrew word עֵינָם, literally, "their eye."

[9] Cf. p. 230 above.

of God appears, there also false teaching appears beside it. For the devil cannot endure it to have the Word of God remain pure and clean.

What the ephah means the angel himself indicates when he says, "This is their eye, or form, in all the land." That "eye" means "form" in Scripture Moses himself indicates, Ex. 10:5, where he says that locusts shall cover the "eye" of the whole land, that is, the appearance, or form, of the earth. And Ps. 6:7 says: "My eye wastes away because of grief," that is, "my form, etc." Here too, then, we take "eye" to mean "form" or "outward appearance." But why is it that their outward form so greatly resembles an ephah? The many uses of an ephah may here yield a manifold similarity. First, even as the ephah is a special measure and has its own size, so the life of the hypocrites and their outward behavior are also contained in various customs and rules and are joined to special works, places, foods, and clothes. And it is something completely regulated by men's teachings and commandments, and in these there is neither spirit nor freedom. Second, even as the ephah is empty without either corn or grain in it, so it is the nature of hypocrites to offer only an empty show and form of a good life without any real substance. It is as St. Paul says (2 Tim. 3:5): "Holding the form of religion but denying the power of it."

But I shall now continue to show that this vision agrees with the former one. Thus I regard the ephah as the spiritually greedy life of the false teachers, which he above [10] has called a thieving life. For by means of their fine appearance and teaching they deceive all the world and devour all its goods; and for that reason it is properly compared to an ephah, with which corn and foods are measured into a sack. For they are solely interested in their bellies, in eating and drinking. There is a constant weighing-out into the sack, which cannot be filled, and there is the ephah, which cannot be satisfied. Thus their form is that of an ephah – pretty and beautifully formed, of fine proportions and appearance, but greedy and thievish, so that one cannot fill them, though they are always letting themselves be filled and are always being emptied into the sack. This interpretation pleases me not only because it agrees with the former but also because of the use of the ephah, since the ephah is used primarily to measure grain in and out. Now that interpretation is always the surest and best with which one explains the use of a thing instead of explaining its appearance or form.

[10] Cf. p. 237.

7-8. *And behold, the leaden weight was lifted, and there was a woman sitting in the ephah! And he said: This is Wickedness.*

This agrees with the second last vision, that the false teachers are not only greedy but also wicked and that they mislead the people. Therefore the woman is here sitting in the ephah and has the name *Impietas,* that is, godless teaching. For the sitting refers to the office of teaching, Ps. 1:1; Matt. 23:2: "The scribes and the Pharisees sit on Moses' seat." But she is sitting in the ephah, that is, she is ruling among the greedy hypocrites; they are listening to her and clinging to her wicked teaching. Moreover she travels far, for in the whole land, he says, that is her appearance. Hypocrisy and lies at all times have a large following. And it is a woman. Why not a man? Because her teaching teaches what is neither human nor godly – for "man is the image of God," says St. Paul (1 Cor. 11:7) – but teaches according to fine tender reason: how that thinks and judges, so the teaching must be; let God's Word stay where it will! Now reason is indeed fine to look at, even as a woman is when compared with a man; but it is not good for teaching or having authority, even as a woman is forbidden to teach or have authority, 1 Tim. 2:12. Yet it teaches and has authority here in a hypocrite's life. For the woman is sitting in the ephah and is a fine doll to look at when compared with pure teaching, which offers the serious face of a man – one that is shaggy about its mouth and has a bristling beard; for it is not hypocritical but serious. Women, however, have smooth mouths, and the hypocritical preachers do, too.

8. *And he thrust her back into the ephah, and thrust down the leaden weight upon its mouth.*

Here, then, we again have the punishment that follows such hypocrisy and godless teaching. The angel thrusts the woman into the ephah, so that she may no longer sit so high and look out from above but must squat and bend down into the ephah. This means: through the Gospel hypocrisy is dethroned and brought to shame – for the angel represents Christ and all the teachers of the Gospel – even as above [11] the book was sent forth and brought to shame. But no improvement follows; the false teachers only become all the more hardened and fall all the more deeply and want to defend and preserve their teaching against the truth. And it is for this reason that the woman is not lifted out of the ephah but is thrust back in and to the bottom, even as the

[11] Cf. pp. 239 and 240 above.

book remains in the house of the thieves and perjurers and consumes them. For they hold fast to their teaching and do not regard the fact that it is recognized by others as error and unchristian teaching, but gather themselves together and remain set in their minds. The leaden weight on the ephah, however, is the divine judgment on those who are hardened in their error and neither can nor may get out to preach to others. For they are no longer heard or believed, because the truth has come to light. But they must bear within themselves the great, heavy burden and load of their unchristian teaching and nature. For all false teaching is called אָוֶן in Scripture, that is, "burden and great weight." And one can see, too, how much more difficult and bitter life is for false saints than for true saints; and this is shown very well here by the picture of a heavy leaden weight that is lying on the mouth of the ephah. For it is the nature of the Christians to be cheerful, because they have a happy and good conscience, which no hypocrite can have. The fact, however, that the leaden weight was moving or floating about before it was thrust down upon the ephah means that this punishment of God is at first merely threatened to the wicked so that they might be frightened and improve. But they despise both threats and promises, etc.

9. *Then I lifted my eyes and saw, and behold, two women coming forward! The wind was in their wings; they had wings like the wings of a heron, and they lifted up the ephah between earth and heaven.*

The wicked are indeed separated from the people of God, so that their ephah and their woman, that is, their teaching and life, no longer are tolerated among the godly, as Ps. 1:5 says: "The wicked will not stand in the judgment, nor sinners in the congregation of the righteous." Nevertheless, they do not stop their teaching but at all times find teachers and students to further and carry on their error and deceit. We see that especially in the Jews, who do not cease from their error concerning Christ and to whom this vision refers especially too. The two women represent the office of preaching, or office of teaching, or all teachers and preachers, even as the two cherubim on the ark of Moses represent that also (Ex. 25:18). The fact, however, that there are two cherubim and two women, means that in all preaching or teaching, be it right or wrong, these two parts are regularly to be found, *mine et promissio,* "threat and promise," which we call Law and Gospel. For even the wicked could not maintain their teaching if they did not present a false law, that is, if they did not compel and incite the consciences with false terror and threats; and again, if they did not present a false gospel, that is, did not attract and occupy the hearts with false comfort and promises. For every teaching must be so constituted that it frightens and comforts the consciences by pretending that God commands and demands this or that and that He promises His grace and reward as a comfort to those who act in accordance with this teaching.

Now in the true office of teaching and over the ark there are two cherubim in the image of men; but here in the false office of teaching there are images of two women on the ephah. For as I have said above,[12] reason is a beautiful woman, but she is not to teach; she may indeed make a fine appearance, but she is not fit to preach. Man's image, however, is God's image and teaches properly, that is, God's Word is to do the teaching. There is, then, in the false office of teaching nothing but reason and whatever is in keeping with reason: it is the master and doctor and applies God's Word in accordance with its own conceit and pleasure. The two women, however, are they who teach nothing but reason or a law and a gospel of the flesh and not the law of the Spirit or of God and the true Gospel. But the fact that they have the wind in their wings, or outspread wings, means that the wicked are forever chattering and babbling, or, as St. Paul says (Titus 1:10), they are *vaniloquos,* "empty talkers"; they can chatter more about a single flower than a godly teacher can about a whole meadow. In sum: They know how to conduct their activities and are not slothful, they never drop their wings or let spiderwebs grow in front of their mouths but spread their activities far and wide. They are more diligent and alert to spread their error than the children of light are to spread their truth (Luke 16:8). The mouths of the seducers never are at rest.

Their wings are herons' [13] wings. Some say they are storks' wings, some hawks'. We have given the bird everywhere as "heron." Be it what it may, it is an unclean bird not to be eaten, according to the law of Moses, Lev. 11:19. The wings surely are not wings of a dove. That means as much as this: What they offer is nothing but unclean, unspiritual, and unholy preaching, and in that there is sheer reason

[12] Cf. p. 242 above.

[13] Cf. p. 59 and n. 7 above.

and no Spirit or anything pure. But they nevertheless soar to great heights and move the ephah between heaven and earth. For their activities wish to hover above and to soar on high before the world and reason. They lift the ephah, however, between heaven and earth; that is, their nature in their teaching is neither of heaven nor of the earth. For they have neither Joshua nor Zerubbabel, neither priesthood nor kingdom, neither spiritual nor worldly rule, but they hover between both and reach neither one. Heaven does not want them, nor does the earth want them, as we can tell from the Jews. Or this hovering between heaven and earth may also be this, that their teaching does not give the consciences any rest – with neither temporal nor eternal possessions. For they are without God's Word.

10-11. *Then I said to the angel who talked with me: Where are they taking the ephah? He said to me: To the land of Shinar, to build a house for it; and when this is prepared, they will set the ephah down there on its base.*

The land of Shinar is Babylon, as Moses writes in Gen. 11:2. The people of Israel had recently been redeemed out of Babylon and brought back to Jerusalem. So this ephah is being brought back from Jerusalem to Babylon, and not simply to Babylon but to the land of Shinar, that is, to old Babylon, where the tower was built because of which the tongues were confused and divided (Gen. 11:6 ff.). By that, I think, we are to understand that because of this wicked teaching the Jewish people were to be exiled out of the true Jerusalem of the communion of God and be brought to Babylon, that is, scattered among all the Gentiles and languages – as we see it fulfilled. And Christ Himself says, Luke 21:24, that the Jews were to be scattered and led captive among all the Gentiles. For why should the prophet otherwise have mentioned the land of Shinar, where the languages were first confused and scattered into all the world? For we of course do not read that all the Jews had gone to Babylon, though many had gone there and many before them had also remained there because they did not want to return to Jerusalem. They therefore also had two translators there, Jonathan and Onkelos,[14] who were very famous among them. And they also had the Babylonian Targum, in which are found the Jewish law and teaching.

[14] Jonathan ben Uzziel, Pseudo-Jonathan, and Onkelos were authors and editors associated with early Targums (Aramaic interpretative translations) of the Old Testament.

But what kind of house is it that was built for the ephah? I feel that the hardening of the Jewish people in their unbelief is indicated by it. For a house is a place where one stays and lives. And they live scattered in all the world and yet cling firmly to their thinking and error. This is indicated, too, by the fact that this house is set down there on its base. For it is not built on the rock Christ; but they stand fast on their own righteousness of works, as St. Paul writes of them (Rom. 10:3). The Christians, however, are not set on their own base, but Christ is their foundation stone, laid not in Babylon but in Zion; and all who believe in Him will never be put to shame (Rom. 9:33).

From all this one can know that this vision of the ephah is completely formed and fashioned after the vision of Moses which he saw on Mount Sinai, when he was to fashion the ark after this vision (Ex. 25:9), even as godless hypocrisy at all times tries to imitate pure teaching and truth and be like them. There we find the golden ark, here an ephah; on that we find a mercy seat, on this a leaden weight; there God is sitting on the ark and mercy seat, here a woman is sitting in the ephah, and she is wicked; there we find two angels with wings, here we find two women with wings; there the ark is standing at Jerusalem, here the ephah is moving to Babel. Everything is imitated and yet is different in the extreme. For the wicked wish to appear holy and also do have that appearance. But it is only an accursed and condemned thing; for they have no ark with the bread from heaven and the tables of Moses; in their consciences they have neither the true Law nor the true Gospel but only their own inventions – for the sake of their bellies. Again, not Christ is sitting there with His mercy, but the wicked woman; nor is the true office of preaching there, the golden cherubim, but rather a self-chosen office and way of teaching. And so it goes on, without being like pure teaching and truth in any part, though it desires to be like these in every part.

CHAPTER SIX

1-3. *And again I lifted my eyes and saw, and behold, four chariots came out from between two mountains; and the mountains were mountains of bronze. The first chariot had red horses, the second black horses, the third white horses, and the fourth chariot dappled-gray*[1] *horses.*

THIS is an obscure vision and has been interpreted by others in various ways, and thus it has become even more obscure. I will not begrudge anyone his honor and will thank him for his zeal. What I understand I will also present, until someone does better. In the preceding chapter the prophet showed by means of two visions that false teachers would appear among the Jewish people. And that prophecy was fulfilled by the Pharisees to the time of Christ, who rebuked them on that account; and when they would not mend their ways, He forsook them until they were scattered in all the world, as we have heard. And now the prophet shows in this chapter how the pure teaching of the Gospel is to go out into all the world after Jewry with its teaching has perished. And so it happened, too, that after the teaching of the Pharisees the Gospel soon came and was preached in all the world.

Above, in the first chapter, we heard that the number four meant the four corners of the world, that is, the whole circuit of the earth round about Jerusalem.[2] If we therefore see four chariots here, they also signify that in all the world round about Jerusalem and in the four directions of the heavens the Gospel is to be preached. For not only horses are seen here, as above,[3] but also chariots. Nor do these horses come together at this place from other lands, as they did above, but they go out from one another into all the lands, so that we have an altogether different vision from the first. The first brought news from all the lands that there was quiet and peace everywhere; these, how-

[1] Luther translates *bundte starke* ("mottled, strong").

[2] Cf. pp. 179 and 191 above.

[3] Cf. p. 168 above.

ever, in turn carry the Spirit of God outward, even to the land of the north. What the horses are, however, we shall see later on in the text. But the two mountains of bronze, I think, are the two testimonies of the Gospel given in the Old Testament, namely the Law and the Prophets, as St. Paul says, Rom. 3:21, that the Law and the Prophets bear witness to the righteousness of God, even as Moses and Elijah bore witness on Mount Tabor by their appearance there (Matt. 17:3). For the apostles draw the Gospel out of the Law and the Prophets and prove it from them. Therefore it is a good thing that these chariots come out from between these two mountains. But the mountains are of bronze, that is, they are fixed and constant. For rust does not devour bronze, as it devours iron. Thus the Law and the Prophets are great, strong, constant witnesses of the Gospel; thus Christ also opened the minds of His disciples that they might understand the Scriptures (Luke 24:27); and thus it is also needful for our faith that it have a good and firm foundation, so that it might be sure of its grounds.

4-5. *Then I said to the angel who talked with me: What are these, my lord? And the angel answered me: These are going forth to the four winds of heaven, after presenting themselves before the Lord of all the earth.*

In the Hebrew language "spirit" and "wind" are the same words. Therefore, where "wind" is written here, one may read "spirit"; and even if one does read "wind," it still means "spirit." Now according to the angel's own interpretation these four chariots are the four winds of heaven, that is, they are the Spirit in the apostles, sent out from Jerusalem into all the world. And then the angel says that they are presenting themselves or standing before the Lord of all the world; that is, they are the servants of Christ, who is a lord set over all the world, as Ps. 8:6 tells us. In His service these spirits stand and walk. For as the angels that stand and serve in the presence of God are called winds or spirits in Ps. 104:4: "He makes His angels spirits or winds and His servants fire and flame," so the apostles are here also called spirits or winds, who serve in the presence of Christ and are sent forth by Him to the four corners of the world, that is, to all parts of the earth. And the fact that he calls them four winds of heaven also signifies that the apostles were to go forth with their preaching into all the world, under all heavens, or from one end of the heaven to the other, as Christ says in Matt. 24:31.

And at this point notice what a splendid testimonial the apostles here receive for their teaching. They are not being presented as preaching their own thoughts or as having their own forms or eyes, as the ephah had them above.[4] But they are serving the Ruler, Christ, and not themselves; they teach what He wants and what pleases Him; and they do not come of themselves but are sent by Him. Therefore they do not bring men's teaching but God's Word. And not only horses are there with them but also chariots; for they do not come with empty words but bring with them all kinds of precious wares and treasures, yes, even armor and weapons; and thus they are equipped for war. That means: Through the Gospel the apostles bring with them all kinds of gifts and favors from the Holy Spirit; and with these the Christians in all the world are adorned and strengthened to fight against sin, death, and the devil, and also against the world. For since horses and chariots are present, war and struggle are indicated, as we have also heard above.[5] In sum: God's Word does not come into the world in vain and void. It does much good among the faithful and fights powerfully against the faithless. Therefore there must be chariots here together with the horses. Yet no rider is seen here on the horses nor a man in the chariots. For Christ sits and rides on these horses and chariots alone, but invisibly, in the Spirit and in faith. Nor does He let men sit on them or direct and drive them. For He does not like men's teaching, nor does He tolerate it. He alone is the one Master and Teacher of us all, Matt. 23:8. And as the angel here says: They do not serve just any leader, rider, or merchant, but rather the ruler of all the world, who here directs, rides, sits, leads, and drives alone. And that ruler is Christ, our Lord. For above, in the first vision, angels rode on the horses, to signify the kingdoms that are governed by men.[6]

6. *The chariot with the black horses goes toward the north country, the white ones go toward the west country, and the dappled ones go toward the south country.*

This passage with its horses, colors, and countries to which these chariots go is the most obscure. Very well, we have made apostles and preachers of the horses. The first, the red ones, are not seen here as going away. These of course are the apostles and Christians who remained in Jerusalem and among the Jews, such as St. James the younger, also Sts. Peter and John for a while, as well as other disciples,

[4] Cf. p. 241 above.

[5] Cf. p. 183 above.

[6] Cf. p. 169 above.

such as St. Stephen and others like him. And these horses are red, that is, they remained among the murderous, bloodthirsty Jews, who killed St. James and St. Stephen as well as many others, also the Lord Jesus Himself, and earlier and at all times the prophets. For I think that the color of the horses signifies the nature of the country or the people to whom the preachers are sent. So the first horses are red and are sent to the Jews, and they remain among them.

But the black horses of the second chariot and the white ones of the third are both sent toward the north country. These are the apostles and disciples that were sent to Assyria, Persia, India, and Syria, such as Simon, Jude, Thomas, and others like them. For in the Acts of the Apostles we read, and especially of Antioch, that Christianity increased there greatly, also that there "the disciples were for the first time called Christians" (Acts 11:26) and that a very vigorous school of Christians was to be found there. There were also many disciples of Christ at Damascus, where St. Paul was converted (Acts 9:19). Now both Antioch and Damascus lie north of Jerusalem, as has been said – not to mention those who went to Assyria and Persia.

But what is the significance of the colors here, that the black ones go first and the white ones come after them? I am of the opinion that they signify the ways of these countries toward the Jews. For black is the color of night and signifies persecution, misfortune, and death; while white is the color of day and of light and signifies mercy and happiness. Now the Jewish people had suffered much from all those lands of the north and had indeed experienced the black color, as the stories of the Books of Kings show and the Jews still had to experience from the kings of Antioch and as the Books of the Maccabees show. Countries like Assyria, Syria, and Media, then, were quite black, dark, and cruel toward the Jews. Still, at this time the kings of Persia were merciful and gracious toward the Jews, as we heard above,[7] and permitted them to rebuild the city of Jerusalem. And for this reason the black horses here go first, while the white ones follow. For at first, under the kings of Babylon and Assyria, everything was black and altogether night, but under the king of Persia everything was altogether white and day.

But the two chariots with their horses go to one and the same place also because Zerubbabel and Joshua and their people are to be comforted even more; because one sends the most chariots to the place

[7] Cf. pp. 159 f. above.

that one fears most. But there is also this reason, that the enemies of the Jews, such as Syria, Babylon, and Assyria, face Jerusalem in such a way that they take in two directions of the earth: the east and the north. And therefore two kinds of horses go to that place, as if the two directions were to be regarded as one direction – though there really were two directions, and not one. And so the eastern direction is not mentioned in view of the fact that both directions lead to the same kingdom. The northern direction alone is named because the land of the Jews had to suffer its greatest evil from that source.

The dappled horses are the apostles, such as Matthew and his companions, who went to Arabia, Edom, and Egypt and Ethiopia; for these lands lie south of Jerusalem and are of many colors, that is, black, red, and white. For at times they were hostile toward the Jewish people, at times friendly; and they often shed Jewish blood, as the histories especially of the Edomites, Ishmaelites, and others like them prove. But thus the Jews again are comforted and told not to be afraid of these lands but to build the temple, as men that are sure that in due time also these lands were to receive God's Word and Spirit and obey the Ruler of all lands.

7. *When the steeds came out, they were impatient to get off and patrol the earth. And he said: Go, patrol the earth. So they patrolled the earth.*

The fourth chariot is here divided into two chariots. For above he says that there were dappled, strong horses in the fourth chariot, and yet he here separates the strong horses from the dappled. It seems therefore that two chariots, that is, the black and the white, had gone into the empire of the Persians and Medes, who occupied the land east and north of Jerusalem; while two other chariots, that is, the dappled and the strong, had gone into the Roman empire, which occupied the land south and west of Jerusalem. And so in place of the red horses of the first chariot, which remained in Jerusalem, the strong horses come to this place. Thus there are still four chariots remaining in the four corners of the world, that is, that are sent into all the world. These, however, are the strong horses: Sts. Peter and Paul and John, the foremost and strongest apostles, who were sent into the Roman empire, where a great persecution of the Gospel took place. And for that reason strong apostles were sent to this place; and St. Paul, the apostle of the Gentiles, was especially singled out for that purpose. Therefore these men were given a special command to that end and were told, "Patrol the earth," that is, "the whole world." For at first the apostles themselves did not know that they were to proclaim the Gospel to the Gentiles, until they were admonished from heaven to do it.

8. *Then he cried to me: Behold, those who go toward the north country have set my Spirit at rest in the north country.*

Here the prophet cites this vision of coming things for the good and benefit of the Jews of the very time when they were to build the temple, so that he might comfort and strengthen them. It is as if he were saying: "Why are you so afraid and worried about the Persians and the enemies of the north? Look! they shall not only let you live in peace now and, as you have already heard, be friendly toward you; but in the future, when the Gospel and Christ with His Spirit will come, they shall be even more friendly. And He will make them your brothers and friends, so that, instead of subjecting you to harm or hindrance, they will have the same Spirit of the Lord as you." That also is the reason why only the horses going toward the north are here mentioned, above all others, as having set the Spirit of the Lord at rest in the north country. For in this way he touches and moves the hearts of those who at the time were most afraid of the lands of the north, as Jeremiah had foretold (Jer. 1:14) and as they were soon to know through their own experience. For no man will believe how much effort is needed if one is again to comfort and console a conscience that is despairing and intimidated, and again, what effort is needed to terrify a hardened conscience and bring it to fear. To our view both tasks are impossible. God must perform them Himself. Therefore, as we can see, he uses so many words and visions here and yet cites them all for the comfort and strengthening of the poor, timid little flock of his people. For when God once gets angry and punishes, the human heart cannot forget it; it will flee from Him forever and think that God will always be angry, and it will tremble even at the rustling of a leaf and worry that the sky will fall down upon it. Again, when He blesses and is gracious, the human heart becomes so secure and hardened that it thinks this will go on forever; and even though constant crashes of thunder should threaten, it does not think that these are directed against its wickedness. Therefore He gives us a sign of His mercy here to show that the kingdom of Christ will surely come and bring us assurance and says:

9-10. *And the Word of the Lord came to me: Take from the exiles Heldai, Tobijah, and Jedaiah, who have arrived from Babylon; and go the same day to the house of Josiah, the son of Zephaniah.*

Now that the visions are over and ended, the prophet offers a sign in addition to the Word of promise regarding the coming Gospel, even as it is a custom of all the prophets to add and attach to their Word a sign that is like the Word. Thus Isaiah did in Is. 20:2 ff. when he walked naked as a sign that the king of Assyria would pillage the land of Egypt; and Jeremiah wore thongs and yoke bars on his neck (Jer. 27:2 ff.) when he proclaimed the tyranny of the king of Babylon to all the Gentiles. Thus, too, the rainbow was given to Noah as a sign (Gen. 9:12 ff.) and circumcision to Abraham (Gen. 17:10), etc. But to us Christians Baptism and the Sacrament were given, etc. And thus a sign of two crowns is here being given to the Jews to confirm the prophecies of the Gospel, which is indicated by the vision of the chariots, so that these Jews might be sure that hereafter the Persians and their other enemies no longer would torment them but that very soon the kingdom and priesthood of Christ should come and that through these they would be made completely and forever free and safe from all their enemies.

11. *Take from them silver and gold, and make two crowns, and set them upon the head of Joshua, the son of Jehozadak, the high priest.*

This, then, is the sign, two crowns, to be set not upon the head of Zerubbabel, the secular prince, but upon the head of Joshua, the priest. Also they are not given to Joshua as his own or committed to him that he should wear or use them; but this act of setting them upon his head is merely to be a sign, and afterwards the crowns are to be hung up in the temple as a reminder, so that their faith might be strengthened in the coming Christ, the true King and Priest. Whether the two crowns were of gold mingled with silver, or one was of gold alone and the other of silver, I do not know. The text is there and says that he was to take silver and gold for his purpose, and I shall let the matter rest there. It is enough that by means of the two crowns the two rules of Christ are indicated: that He is to be Priest and King, not in a worldly way but in a spiritual way through faith. And this is indicated by the fact that he does not place the crowns on the head of the prince, Zerubbabel, but on that of the high priest Joshua, the spiritual person. This also is indicated, then, that the priestly office is to be superior to the princely office. For through His priestly office Christ sacrifices Himself for us and acts as our Advocate before God and reconciles us to Him. But through His kingdom or His princely office He protects us with might against the devil, death, sin, and all evil, and rules us as His heirs and kingdom in spirit and in faith.

And this is a special comfort that is offered to the prophet, that he is to take gold and silver only from the Jews, moreover from such Jews as had been captives in Babylon. The prophet thereby indicates that Christ was to come from the blood of the same Jews who had been captives, so that they might not be afraid anymore but be sure of everything that this prophecy and this sign indicate. The names of these men, however, are not to be found in the Book of Ezra except those of these two: Jedaiah and Tobiah (Ezra 10:18; 2:60), though no one knows if these are the same ones. I think, however, that one half of the men were of the tribe of Judah, the other half of the priestly tribe. And the fact that this sign and this setting on of the crown did not take place in the house of the high priest Joshua but in that of another, Josiah, the son of Zephaniah, I take to mean that the priesthood and kingdom of Christ were to be something different from the Levitical priesthood and were also to come to the Gentiles and not be confined to the Jews alone.

12-13. *And say to him: Thus saith the Lord of hosts: Behold, the man whose name is the Branch, for He shall grow up in His place, and He shall build the temple of the Lord. It is He who shall build the temple of the Lord and shall bear royal honor and shall sit and rule upon His throne. And there shall be a priest by His throne, and peaceful understanding shall be between them both.*

Here the prophet himself interprets the sign of the two crowns. For this text cannot be understood as referring to Joshua, because the two crowns, that is, the worldly rule and the priesthood, are here assigned to one person, who shall occupy both chairs, or thrones, at the same time and be both king and priest. And that is something that happened to no one in the ancient priesthood but solely to the one Man, our Lord Jesus Christ. For although at the time of the Maccabees the worldly rule had by chance fallen to the priests, it never developed into a kingdom or permanent rule. But here he also calls Christ צֶמַח

("Zemah"), as above in the third chapter,[8] and he does this, he says, because under Him there is to be a growing, that is, whatever He does shall go on and prosper, though all the world, together with the gates of hell, should oppose it. For "Zemah" means a plant or a twig which grows to be a large tree. For Christ at first was a small shrub, or plant, in the Jewish land, but then He grew until He has become a tree which fills all the world with its branches, its top reaching to heaven and its roots reaching to the abyss of hell. For He has everything in His hands: Ps. 8:6; Eph. 1:22.

Note, however, that the prophet does not designate any special place for this "Zemah." For he does not say that He shall be at Jerusalem and there build the Lord's temple but says that under Him, that is, wherever He will be, wherever His place may be, there growth will be found. However, He is not at one place, but through the Gospel He is in all the world. And therefore this growth is spiritual and cannot be understood as referring to the priesthood at Jerusalem. But under Him the growth is spiritual. For physically it looks much different, because under Christ's cross, persecution, and death alone are mighty. Still there is growth, and that is by no means hindered under Him, but rather it is greatly furthered. And when the prophet says that the temple of the Lord is to be built through Him, he reveals publicly that it is to be a much different temple from that which the two men, Joshua and Zerubbabel, are now building – namely, it is to be a spiritual one. For this spiritual temple is to be built by the one Person who at one and the same time will be King and Priest.

And He shall bear royal honor. For the priestly garments are called "glory and beauty," Ex. 28:2 ff., because they are becoming to those who are clothed in them and cause them to be laudable, honorable, and adorned. But even as the temple here is to be spiritual, so the adornment of this priest and king must also be spiritual, as Ps. 104:1 says of God: "Thou art clothed with honor and majesty," and Ps. 8:5 says of Christ: "Thou dost crown – or surround – Him with glory and honor," though this bodily adornment of the Jews has been retained under the pope. But this spiritual adornment is interpreted in Ps. 132:9, where the writer says: "Let Thy priests be clothed with righteousness, and let Thy servants shout for joy." This adornment of the priest, then, is righteousness, that is, all the virtues, such as love, loyalty, joy, peace.

[8] Cf. p. 217 above.

And in sum, as St. Paul says, Titus 1:7 ff. and 2 Tim. 3:2 ff., a priest is to be adorned and apt, so that he may be blameless, that is, righteous in every way.

And this priest is to be a Lord and Prince upon His throne and also a Priest upon His throne. Thus we have sufficiently strong evidence, as was said before,[9] that this word cannot be understood as referring to Joshua but solely to Christ, because one single person is to have both offices. And it is very well stated that He shall rule upon His throne and be a Priest upon His throne, as one having His own throne. He is, therefore, not a priest on the throne of Aaron or Moses; nor is He to rule on the throne of Zerubbabel, but on His own throne, so that in every way there is to be a different priesthood, a different rule, from that of Joshua and Zerubbabel. And he says that there shall be a peaceful understanding, or counsel, between the two – not between Zerubbabel and Joshua, but between the two, that is, between the offices of priest and prince; for these offices indeed at times had been opposed and hostile to each other when they were held by two persons and families and when, for example, the kings would persecute the priests. Thus we read in the Books of Kings that the one would tend in one direction, the other in another; that the one would give this counsel, the other a different one, so that there was no peaceful harmonious opinion or understanding. But now that both offices are combined in one Person, everything henceforth will be peaceful and harmonious, and no rebellious counsel or discordant conceit will interfere. But as He intercedes for us before God, so He will also rule us on earth. At the times of the kings, however, the priests often interceded for the people before God in a very godly manner, while the kings again and again ruled the people in a very godless manner.

14. *And the crown shall be in the temple of the Lord as a reminder to Helem, Tobijah, Jedaiah, and Hen the son of Zephaniah.*

The man who was called Heldai above [10] is here called Helem; and he who was called Josiah above is called Hen. For it is common in Scripture for one person to have two or three names, even as among us St. Peter is also called Simon and Bar-Jona and Cephas (Matt. 16:17; John 1:42). What such names mean, however, does not bother me

[9] Cf. p. 254 above.

[10] Cf. p. 253 above.

greatly. It is enough that according to the text the two crowns are to be hung up in the temple as a sign for the coming promises and as a reminder to these four men, so that it might be said among their descendants: "Behold! these four men had these two crowns made at the time of the prophet Zechariah as a sign and confirmation of the prophecies concerning the coming kingdom of Christ, which was to begin while this new temple was still standing and the crowns were still in it." Following the example of these crowns, many other precious treasures were presented to the temple at Jerusalem and hung up in it, as the apostles bear witness, Matt. 24:1, when they showed the Lord Jesus the buildings and treasures of the temple, and as we can also see them in the temples which have been established under the pope. But for the latter there is no command from God, nor do they serve as a sign, but they are there only for show and pride, serving neither love nor faith. But these two crowns served to strengthen the faith of the Jewish people in the coming Christ and His kingdom.

15. *And those who are far off shall come and help to build the temple of the Lord.*

This is being said, in my opinion, of the temple of Christ and not of the physical temple at Jerusalem. For although many treasures had been given to the temple at Jerusalem by many Gentiles, it was nevertheless built by the Jews alone through Zerubbabel and Joshua, as he says above (Zech. 4:9): "The hands of Zerubbabel have laid the foundation; his hands shall also complete it, etc." The temple of Christ, however, that is, holy Christendom, was built and is still being built by all the bishops and teachers among the Gentiles and by all who are preaching and keeping the Gospel properly. For these really have come from afar, because they are not of the Jewish race and yet are the closest and the very own friends of Jesus.

And you shall know that the Lord of hosts has sent me to you.

This means: At that time you and your descendants will know by deed and experience that I have been a true prophet and that my prophecy concerning these horses and chariots has been truthful; for at that time the prophecy will be there and pass before your eyes in fulfillment, which you now find very difficult to believe, because you have your thoughts fixed on the physical temple and are looking for an external rule.

And this shall come to pass, if you will diligently obey the voice of the Lord your God.

Here is the commentary for the whole chapter. "It is essential," the prophet says, "that you believe the coming Gospel which your God will cause to be preached to you. If, then, you believe, you will understand me in this prophecy and will know that it was God that had me prophesy these things to you. But if you will not believe, then you will understand none of these things – in fact, nothing at all; you will not understand anything about the Branch ("Zemah") or His rule and priesthood but instead, hardened and blinded, you will cling to this physical temple and priesthood and abandon the other, yes, even persecute it." And here the prophet touches on the fact, and has us understand, that the Jews would not accept the Gospel and Christ, for in no other chapter does he offer this same admonition that we obey the voice of God as he does in this one, where he prophesies of Christ and His kingdom.

CHAPTER SEVEN

1. *In the fourth year of King Darius, the Word of the Lord came to Zechariah in the fourth day of the ninth month, which is Chislev.*

UNTIL now the prophet has been preaching for about two years and has brought the people back to the true faith. He has also comforted them so that they might feel safe in the presence of their enemies from the north, because two chariots were to go there; and these were to bring the Spirit of God there, as well as to all the world. And now, in the midst of this, there appears a case or question concerning self-chosen good works, so that one might see that nothing else beside the Word of God is to be tolerated. And this question has to come while the prophet is still living and teaching, so that it may be condemned publicly and emphatically and be an example for us that all of the works that we may choose, however good they may seem to be, are useless, and that we should adhere solely to the pure Word of God. For this plague clings to all human teaching that it destroys or weakens God's commandment and makes itself high and mighty, as we shall see from this example. The Jews begin the year in March, at their Easter. If we reckon from there, their ninth month is the one we call the winter month and they, in Hebrew, Chislev.

2-3. *Now the people of Bethel had sent Sharezer and Regem-melech and their men to entreat the favor of the Lord and to ask the priests of the house of the Lord of hosts and the prophets: Should I mourn and fast in the fifth month, as I have done for so many years?*

In this chapter four fastings are mentioned, namely those of the fourth, fifth, seventh, and tenth months; and the Jews had accepted these fastings and chosen them for themselves and imposed them upon themselves because of four misfortunes, they say, that had happened to them. For in the fourth month the city of Jerusalem was taken and starved out by the Babylonians and was abandoned by the warriors of the city, Jer. 52:6 ff.; but in the fifth month the temple, the king's house, and the whole city were burned down, 2 Kings 25:8 ff.; and in the seventh month the captain Gedaliah was killed and the people were taken to Egypt, 2 Kings 25:25 f.; but in the tenth month this news and this mourning were brought to Babylon and reported to the captive Jews who were there, Ezek. 33:21. These people, then, are asking if, while the temple is being built, they should continue to fast during the fifth month or cease. For they had vowed this fasting and accepted it as a commandment. And therefore we must once more discuss vows and laws here.

The people point out two things, however: first, that they have fasted; second, that they have disciplined themselves, that is, that they have abstained from good morsels and delicate food and drink, especially from wine and strong drink, as is written Num. 6:3 ff. concerning discipline. And in keeping with this law and example, they had accepted this discipline and avoiding of wine, even as they had accepted fasting in keeping with the example of the seventh month, of which Moses speaks in connection with the Day of Atonement, Lev. 16:29 ff. Now look! fasting and discipline are indeed good works and not bad ones; moreover, they were accepted for good reasons; besides, they had been vowed and commanded among the Jews. But listen how God rejects and condemns them as He says:

4-6. *Then the Word of the Lord of hosts came to me: Say to all the people of the land and the priests: When you fasted and mourned in the fifth month and in the seventh for these seventy years, was it for Me that you fasted? And when you eat and when you drink, do you not eat for yourselves and drink for yourselves?*

Is it not inappropriate for God to reject this fasting and discipline so strongly and say that it does not mean anything to Him and has not been done in His service or honor? Yes, He considers both their eating and fasting as the same and says that they have indeed fasted and eaten, but in their own service and not in His, as though He would say: "Why do you tempt Me with your fasting? Who has commanded it? Why should I be interested in your fasting and eating? How do your fasting and feasting help or serve Me? If you do not want to eat, stop it; if you want to fast, do it – as long as you know that I am not interested in it. The reason? It is not My fasting. I have not commanded or ordered it, and therefore I neither want nor heed it. Whoever has commanded it or demanded it of you, for him you may do it, and to him you may offer it. But you have chosen it yourselves without My commandment; therefore you have not done it for anyone but yourselves; and so you may also accept the reward for it from yourselves. Whomever you have served with it, let him reward you. You have not served Me with it, therefore I pay no attention to it."

And in this text one must give special attention to the word "ME" and to the word "YOU," for with these two words He separates the commandments of men from the commandments of God. "For ME, for ME you have done none of that. Why? Because I have not commanded it. But for YOURSELVES, for YOURSELVES you have done it. Why? Because you have invented and chosen it of your own selves and therefore have been pleased with it." In this very way they lament in Is. 58:3: "Why have we fasted, and Thou seest it not? Why have we humbled ourselves, and Thou takest no knowledge of it?" And in Jer. 7:21-22 He speaks to them: "Add your burnt offerings to your sacrifices, and eat the flesh. For in the days that I brought them out of the land of Egypt, I did not speak to your fathers or command them concerning burnt offerings and sacrifices, etc." There we hear again that God does not want all these things that He has not commanded Himself. And there are many more passages like these in both the Old Testament and the New.

But why all this? Because, as has been said, all of our own self-chosen works and commandments, which have torment and grief in them, please us better than what God has commanded. We also heed them more and apply much more diligence to them than to God's commandments. And that properly vexes God to the highest degree, so that He in turn despises and rejects our own works and commandments, even as we have despised His commandments and works. For see from these men, who are sending their message from Babylon and are inquiring of their priests, what a perverse, blasphemous sanctity they are revealing. They are not inquiring about God's commandments and about what they are to do and leave undone in order to keep God's laws – oh, they at Babylon know that much better themselves than all the priests and prophets in Jerusalem! They do not send so much as a dog out about that, they do not give a messenger a penny as a tip to cross the street and ask about it; all of that has been done, and nothing more has to be added! There is no conscience there, no shortcoming, but only pure sanctity and full perfection. They have gone perhaps a hundred thousand and more miles over and beyond what God has commanded by fasting and disciplining themselves. But when it is a matter of having someone plead for them at Bethel and inquire if their self-chosen fastings could have any further meaning, then there is care, conscience, fear, and time for asking, then they find money and messengers to have someone plead for them; then no work is too great, no road too long, no care too burdensome. But is not this a vexing, shameful thing?

But consider also our own way. Faith in Christ and love for our neighbor are commanded us, and on that we are to stake all that we can do and have. But everybody knows that and has long worn it threadbare; nobody regards it, so why should one invest anything to learn and do, even a penny or a step across the threshold? But to build churches, to endow a Mass, to vow fasts, pilgrimages, a monastic life to the saints – oh, that is something that glitters; for that one has money in abundance; for that one can fast, wear coarse clothes, eat bad food, watch, work; for that one must study and ask questions, toil and mortify oneself, so that one may become pious and holy, etc. But Christ will speak on Judgment Day and say: "Ah, when you endowed churches, did you endow them for ME? Who told you to do it? When did I command it? And when you were living in the monastery obedient, chaste, and pure and were keeping the rule, were you keeping the rule for ME? Where did I command these things? Very well, then go and let him reward you for whom you were living and keeping the rule." What will all the priests, monks, nuns, and people of holy orders say to that? They will have to be silent and in addition hear that they had not only chosen and kept all these things to serve and please themselves but also that they had meanwhile neglected and despised God's commandments.

And therefore Is. 58:2 ff., as has been said, preaches against these perverse fasters and saints, who also had neglected the commandments of God and desired to fulfill everything by means of fastings and gloomy faces, and speaks thus: "They dare to ask of me righteous judgments and delight to draw near to God and say, 'Why do we fast, and Thou seest it not? Why do we mortify our souls, and Thou takest no knowledge of it?' Behold, on the day of your fast you pursue your own business, and you oppress all your debtors. Behold, you fast only to quarrel and fight and hit wickedly with your fists. Do not fast as you are doing this day, lest your voice be heard on high. Should such be the fast that I choose: that a man this day mortifies his soul and binds his head like a bundle of rushes and makes his couch in straw and ashes? Is that to be called a day of fasting and a day acceptable to the Lord? This, rather, is a fast that I choose: Loose the bonds of wickedness, undo the heavy burdens, let the oppressed go free, and tear down every yoke. Share your bread with the hungry, bring the poor beggars into your house. When you see a man naked, cover him; and do not hide yourself from your flesh, etc."

See, these great saints left the unchristian bonds and burdens on their neighbors; that is, they oppressed the poor and treated them in accordance with the severity of the law and without any mercy at all. At the same time they did not do good to their neighbors but went on and fasted and bound up their heads and lay on hard couches, made gloomy faces and hurt their bodies with all kinds of severe living. And because of these things God should take knowledge of them; they boast of them and trust in them, and they quarrel with God and ask why He is so unjust as not to see their sanctity, and they presume to teach Him what is right and holy. And now He, in turn, answers that this is true fasting: when we forgive our enemies, when we remit that with which we have burdened them in an unchristian way, and when in addition we do good to them and help them. Whoever does this, fasts well, though he continue to eat and drink. But whoever does not do this, does not fast, though he live off the wind. To fast and lead a severe life is easy; but to help and serve one's neighbor, to forgive him and cancel his debts, that no one wants to do. Why? Oh, the former is our own doing, our own choosing, our own pleasure. But the latter is God's commandment; therefore it does not mean anything. For this reason, too, Isaiah calls these things *colligantias impias et fasciculos jugi* – bonds or knots of wickedness.[1] For what we impose on our neighbor is firmly tied and knotted together. We do not like to yield but prefer to make the burden and load greater and to fetter our neighbor all the more firmly, so that he must go on without freeing himself, but must pay and do what he owes if he is not to remain entangled and enmeshed and burdened – and the longer the more. And what is harshly laid and bound on him the prophet here calls the bonds and burdens of wickedness, etc.

We see, then, that one's own works with their fine outward appearance completely nullify the commandments of God and at the same time effect a presumption in the heart that wants to contend and

[1] Is. 58:6 in the Vulgate reads in part: *Dissolve colligationes impietatis, solve fasciculos deprimentes.*

quarrel with God, as though God must take knowledge of these works or else be unjust, so that Paul well says, Titus 1:14, that they "reject the truth," and tells the Thessalonians (2 Thess. 2:4) that the Antichrist "exalts himself against every so-called god or object of worship" – surely by means of his self-invented holiness. Christ bears witness, Matt. 15:3,[2] that the Jews transgress the commandments of God so that they might keep the traditions of men. We can also see this in the hostile monastery life and holy orders. There we find fasting, holiday-making, lying in hard beds, watching, keeping silent, wearing coarse clothes, being tonsured and locked in a cell, living unmarried – and God has commanded none of these things. But meanwhile they devour land and people with their rents and possessions, they wear the people down to their bones; and in that there is neither love nor mercy. They do not work but nevertheless consume the blood and sweat of the poor, who have no bread in their houses but still must fill the bellies of these men with all abundance, work day and night, etc. Could this also be called *impiae colligantiae et fasciculi jugi?*[3] Yet they boast of this and expect God to crown them as special saints. If He does not, then He must be wrong and must hear them complain: "Why have we fasted, and Thou seest it not? We live severely and spiritually, and Thou takest no knowledge of it, etc." But it is our choice and therefore will come to nought and not be otherwise. God wants His commandments to be kept, and we have enough to do to keep them.

Moreover, these men also have this vice in them that they send to Bethel to pray, while they send to Jerusalem to get counsel. Thus they divide their holy life into two parts: they worship God in Bethel, in the place where previously worship had always been forbidden them by the former prophets and where in his time the king of Babylon had settled Samaritans and all kinds of other people, each of whom prayed to his own god. The Book of Chronicles describes this in the last chapters, so that Bethel at one and the same time had to be the house of the Lord and the house of idols, ordained by the choice of men.[4]

[2] The Weimar editor corrects the text's "Matt. 12."

[3] Cf. n. 1 above.

[4] Luther is apparently referring to the report of 2 Kings 17, according to which the king of Assyria, not of Babylon, had carried the inhabitants of Samaria off into captivity and resettled their lands with people from other territories. The result was that Samaria was host to a variety of religions beside the worship of God, and 2 Kings 17:33 sums up the situation Luther here has in mind: "So they feared the Lord but also served their own gods, after the manner of the nations from among whom they had been carried away."

But the teaching of men always acts in this way. It follows the conceits of men, or at least it intermingles them so that surely the whole lump may not remain unleavened. The prophet, to be sure, is not occupying himself here primarily with this vice but rather with the people's self-chosen fasting, for which they neglected and despised God's commandment.

7. *When Jerusalem was inhabited and in prosperity, with her cities round about her, and the South and the lowland were inhabited, were not these the words which the Lord proclaimed by the former prophets?*

It is as though He wanted to say: "I forbade these self-chosen works and this worship of God all the while Jerusalem was still standing. And it was destroyed because the people would not obey Me. And you, though you are still in the midst of the same punishment, nevertheless will not desist, but you cling to your opinion and will not better yourselves. What would you do, I wonder, if Jerusalem were still standing and you were living in it in peace, as your fathers were, since this great punishment has not yet been able to subdue you or bring you to your senses?" And that is another one of the virtues that men's teachings have: they do not let anyone tell them anything and, as St. Paul says of them, Titus 1:16, they are "disobedient, unfit for any good deed." For they "obey not" – that is a lost art; only what they themselves think and resolve is right and good.

8-10. *And the Word of the Lord came to Zechariah, saying: Thus says the Lord of hosts: Render true judgments, show kindness and mercy each to his brother, do not oppress the widow, the fatherless, the sojourner, or the poor; and let none of you devise evil against his brother in your heart.*

"This," He says, "was the sermon that I had the former prophets preach. In it you will find no fasting, no mortifying of the flesh, or other obscure works that they chose themselves, but only the good works of love toward the neighbor. But they ignored and disregarded all these works and meanwhile began to fast and lead a hard, severe life, as it pleased them. I was to see these works and abandon and despise My commandments, as they did. I commanded the kings, princes, and priests to render true judgment and to attend to their offices to which they had been ordained, so that there might be true peace and protection in the land. This they neglected and judged unjustly and abused their offices in violence. In this way there arose complaints, discord, and lamentation in the land. But then they came with their fastings, sacrifices, gloomy, severe lives, and claimed to be holy because of these and wanted to adorn and cover all their faults with them; they acted as though I were a child or fool, who could be beguiled into taking copper coins in place of gold, who therefore would accept their lazy works of straw and forget My golden works and commandments and become a scoundrel like them and take pleasure in their roguish tricks.

"I also commanded them all to do good to one another and to be merciful, to give, lend, advise, and help anyone in need of these things. But that was no good; that was something insignificant. Instead, everyone looked out for himself and left his neighbor in need; no one took an interest in the other. But meanwhile they sacrificed or fasted or did something else, so that they would not have to obey My commandments; and I was expected to laugh about that and be gracious. I had also commanded that one should not hurt or harm the widows, the orphans, the strangers, and the wretched. Oh yes! Not only did they not do these people any good but rather committed all evil and injustice against them — solely that they themselves might be rich and filled. And then they came along with their fasting and praying and their grey and black clothes and looked gloomy. These prattlings and hypocrisies of theirs were supposed to deceive Me and make Me regard them as saints and not insist on My commandments. Again, I had commanded that they should be peaceful and patient with one another; if one should suffer harm from another, he should forgive and not take vengeance or repay evil with evil, not return a curse for a curse, not slander or defame anyone. But all these things had to be considered worth nothing: a fool must have issued such commandments, and they would be fools to keep them. So it came that everybody was his neighbor's enemy, that he bore an eternal hatred and envy against him; and whenever he could do him harm and avenge himself or show him malice otherwise, hinder his welfare or at least not prevent his harm — all of this was right and just could not be sin. Why? Because they offered Me sacrifices of dill and anise and burned offerings of incense or slept on hard beds once a week or ate no meat on Wednesdays or committed similar hocus-pocus."

Here consider if it was not all a most vexing thing that men despised

God's commandments so shamefully and glorified their own works. But things have gone on like this also among us until now and are still going on, both in the spiritual and the secular realms. One found no justice there but only tyranny: the pope, the bishops waged war and shed blood; for that, however, they endowed perhaps a Mass or seven *horae*. The world was full of usury and fraud; for that, however, they lighted a wax candle or two for St. Anne and fasted for St. Barbara or St. Catherine. The chapters, priests, monks, and nuns were filled with hatred and envy and devoured the world's goods with joy; but for that they wore hoods and howled in chorus day and night. It is always like that: what God commands, that is nothing; what we do, that is everything. God should recognize it and be satisfied with it. Now if God were not so inexpressibly gracious but would let His wrath prevail over us as we deserved, would it be surprising if pestilence, war, famine, the French, sudden death, and every other kind of misfortune plagued us every day? Ought not the earth by rights swallow us up when we try to make a fool of God by doing everything and anything that vexes Him and at the same time doing other things that please us? And still we refuse to listen or permit men to tell us these things, as we can see from what follows:

11-12. *But they refused to hearken and turned a stubborn shoulder and stopped their ears that they might not hear. They made their hearts like adamant, lest they should hear the Law and the Word which the Lord of hosts had sent by His Spirit through the former prophets.*

How fittingly he depicts them with their virtues, and how horrible does he show the teaching of men to be when they make a human heart that they have gained so blind, so stopped up, and so hardened against God's commandments! First, he says they turn their backs to God's Word when it is preached to them; that is, the more one tells them about it, the more they turn from it and go their own way, as is written here in the Hebrew: *Et dederunt dorsum declinationis.*[5] Second, they stop their ears because they do not want to hear it. Not only are they unwilling to act according to it; they do not even want

[5] The Vulgate text has *et averterunt scapulam recedentem* ("and they turned away a withdrawing shoulder"). To show the force of the Hebrew background, Luther translates the Hebrew וַיִּתְּנוּ כָתֵף סֹרֶרֶת more literally "and they presented an unwilling back." The picture is that of oxen trying to prevent the imposition of the yoke.

to hear it. Third, they set their hearts against it like adamant, because they not only do not think about it but resist it and persecute it most horribly. There is nothing harder or firmer than adamant, for one can neither force nor subdue it with iron or stone. And now in our own day look at the clergy in the papacy with their followers and see how they insist on their Masses and human works. I think you will also have to say that their hearts are pure adamant, their ears stopped, and their backs turned. And though they hear God's Word against them clear, loud, and powerful, it does not do any good: it is as though a goose were hissing at them. But they cannot deny that their lives are nothing but greed, haughtiness, pride, laziness, idleness, fornication, and mercilessness over against the poor. But the tonsures and surplices, the chasubles and Masses no doubt will make all these things right with God and gain them heaven – close to Lucifer in the abyss of hell.

12-14. *Therefore great wrath came from the Lord of hosts. As I called, and they would not hear, so they called, and I would not hear, says the Lord of hosts, and I scattered them with a whirlwind among all the nations which they had not known. Thus the land they left was desolate, so that no one went to and fro, and the pleasant land was made desolate.*

Hard against hard is not good; two hard stones do not grind well; God's commandment is hard, yes, it must remain forever. Whoever resists it and wants to be hard against hard, surely will not fare well; but, if he will not yield, he will be broken to pieces and crushed to mere fragments, yes, to mere dust. And thus He says here that the hard Jews, like adamant, were broken to pieces because of their hardness and were scattered among all the lands, and it did not help them that they called and prayed for grace and mercy. For they did not give up their hardness of heart but continued to cling to their own works and despise God's Word. For the fact that God here says He would not hear when they called is not to be understood as meaning that He refuses to hear when one calls Him, since, after all, He tells us to call in time of need, as He says in Ps. 50:15: "Call upon Me in the day of trouble; I will deliver you, and you shall glorify Me, etc." But it is to be understood in this way: If we do not listen to His commandments, He will not hear our prayer either; and if we resist His commandments and become hardened and oppose them, He will also resist our prayer and oppose it, so that it must be sin, as Ps. 109:7 says, "Let his prayer be counted as sin." But whoever accepts God's commandments or at least confesses his sin, his prayer is surely heard. But those people insist on being right and do not allow their sin to be sin; they also pray and cry to Him in their trouble, but in vain, as Ps. 18:41 says: "They cried for help, but there was none to save; they cried to the Lord, but He did not answer them."

CHAPTER EIGHT

1-3. *And the Word of the Lord of hosts came to me saying: Thus says the Lord of hosts: I am jealous for Zion with great jealousy, and I am jealous for her with great wrath. Thus says the Lord: I will return to Zion and will dwell in the midst of Jerusalem, and Jerusalem shall be called the faithful city and the mountain of the Lord of hosts, the holy mountain.*

THIS is the last prophecy of the prophet to the Jewish people concerning their building of the temple. For now that he has rebuked the false saints and given the people an object lesson that they should no longer act as they had acted, he takes steps to keep them from thinking that more wrath is to follow and from becoming timid and frightened. He therefore consoles them further and gives them the very rich promise that they would not only have peace from their outside enemies round about them but also that the whole land would prosper, that Jerusalem would be a mighty and famous city, filled with people and possessions, etc., and that it would enjoy full safety and peace until the coming of Christ. Therefore this whole chapter is full of sweet, friendly words, and with these he describes how this peace is to be fashioned. First, there is to be forgiveness of sins, and the wrath of God is to be ended, for He says: "I am jealous for Zion with great jealousy." For where there still is wrath, there no peace can be found in the heart, and the conscience is timid and despondent and cannot do anything. For its sins still oppress it, because it cannot feel forgiveness. Second, this forgiveness and this mercy are to be proved by deeds, for He says: "I will return to Zion." From now on there will be nothing but peace and laughter, joy and happiness in the heart, while the conscience will feel secure and will trust in God's mercy. And therefore it can also build with joy and do what it has been commanded.

Third, this grace is not to cease but is to remain and endure forever in Jerusalem, for He says: "I will dwell in the midst of Jerusalem." For "if God is for us, who is against us?" (Rom. 8:31). And what harm can sin, death, the world, and the devil do where God dwells? Must not all the angels be present there too and serve and help to administer this peace and bliss? Fourth, there are to appear there the fruit and the good of this dwelling and grace; that is, spiritually everything is to be splendid, for He says: "Jerusalem shall be called a faithful city and the mountain of the Lord of hosts, the holy mountain." That is, there shall be no idolatry or hypocrisy or unholy living in Jerusalem as formerly, but truth and faithfulness shall be there, so that the teaching shall be pure and godly and the worship of God on Mount Moriah, that is, in the temple, shall also be righteous, pure, and holy. For the people will be believing and pious, they will avoid men's teaching and idolatry, they will cling to God's Word alone, and through that they will become holy and faithful, that is, righteous and pious without any hypocrisy at all. For wherever God dwells, there God's Word and Spirit are, as we have said often; and where God's Word and Spirit are, there it produces holy and righteous people, both through teaching and living, and as a result these blessings burst forth also among many others, and the city becomes famous as an example for many others. And so He says here that Jerusalem shall be called a faithful city or a city of truth; and that is, translated: "It shall become famous as a city where right and honesty prevail and not hypocrisy or deceit, which prevail where men's teaching rules without God's Word or beside God's Word."

4-5. *Thus says the Lord of hosts: Old men and old women shall again sit in the streets of Jerusalem, each with staff in hand for very age. And the streets of the city shall be full of boys and girls playing in its streets.*

Fifth, temporal good is to follow also; that is, also in a temporal and physical way life is to be splendid there; for He says: "Old men and old women shall again sit in the streets of Jerusalem." But this cannot be where there is war and discord, where young men are slain and where there is little playing or dancing in the streets. All must be well in a land where the children of the city leap, dance, and play in the streets and the old people dwell and walk secure. And here let us note what a great gift it is to have temporal peace in the land, because God Himself praises this gift of His, though we unfortunately do not give thanks for it or acknowledge it. And note too that the children's activities, such as the playing and dancing of the young world in the streets, are not an evil thing but are well-pleasing to God. For He praises also these things here as His gifts, though to us they may seem to be something wasted and useless. The foundations and monasteries ought to be willing to give half their possessions and sanctity to have half as much support in Scripture for their existence and work. How will they stand the test, however, when Christ will say that the singing and dancing of the children in the streets are dearer to Him than all their howling and mumbling in their churches, and that the little girls' wreaths and dolls, the boys' hobby-horses and red shoes please Him much more than all their hoods, tonsures, surplices, chasubles, and adornments? For though their activities also are nothing but child's play, still, because they are without God's Word, they are not to be compared to real child's play but rather to buffoonery and fool's play.

6. *Thus says the Lord of hosts: If it is impossible in the sight of the remnant of this people in these days, should it also be impossible in My sight, says the Lord of hosts?*

Here He anticipates a weak faith, which considers everything impossible when it hears these great and splendid promises and then looks at the present; nothing at all tallies with these promises and everything seems altogether at odds with them. He therefore here wishes to strengthen this weak faith and does it in this way: He tells the people to close their eyes and not look at the present but solely to consider the Word of Him who surely is greater than all things present. It is as if He were to say: "You must not consider your thoughts or conceits but rather Me and My Word. Your conceit fixes its eyes on the present; and because this conceit sees the city so desolate and finds neither young people nor old in it who are playing or rejoicing; and because it rather finds nothing but weeping and lamenting and the city still lying in ashes and the enemies still raging and storming round about it, so that there can be neither peace nor commerce, therefore this conceit thinks everything is in vain and lost and quite impossible. But if you look to Me alone, you must surely confess that with Me nothing is impossible." See how much it takes to strengthen and console a timid, frightened heart so that it may be strong in the faith; and how tender, fragile, and noble a thing a conscience is, how easy it is to corrupt it and how hard to heal it.

7-8. *Thus says the Lord of hosts: Behold, I will save My people from the east country and from the west country; and I will bring them to dwell in the midst of Jerusalem; and they shall be My people and I will be their God, in faithfulness and in righteousness.*

This is a confirmation of the preceding promise and is meant to say this: "What I am promising you now seems impossible to you, because there are so few of you and things are proceeding so haltingly. But My Word shall be true, for I will and can indeed make your numbers great, namely, in this way: I will bring My people here from the east country and from the west country, where they are captives and are scattered about, so that they may live in Jerusalem. And there they shall be My people, and I shall be their God, in faithfulness and righteousness; that is, they shall serve Me in true faith and life, and I in turn will show Myself as their true God with mercy and help, and I will no longer be their judge in wrath and punishment as I had been before, when they did not want to be My people in faithfulness and righteousness either."

And note here very carefully the two words "in faithfulness and in righteousness." For God does not like hypocrites nor does He desire to be the God of the wicked. These indeed would like it if He were a God in riches and honor, that is, if He would make them rich and glorious in the eyes of the world – let piety and righteousness remain where they will. No, He is not a mammon, or a god of the belly. He desires to be a God in faithfulness and righteousness and also to have a people that loves faithfulness and righteousness. Temporal goods, however, shall indeed come, as will follow. "In faithfulness" means that the people are righteous toward God and not hypocritical, and that they serve God in true faith and sincerity; "in righteousness" here means the love and mercy with which they do right toward their neighbor. On these two commandments depends the whole life of a holy people.

9. *Thus says the Lord of hosts: Let your hands be strong, you who in these days have been hearing these words from the mouth of the prophets, since the day that the foundation of the house of the Lord of hosts was laid, that the temple might be built.*

This is an admonition and a consolation. It is as though the Lord should say: "Because you hear these faithful promises through the prophets, be of good cheer and begin your task cheerfully and happily and in complete faith." Thus the prophet not only teaches the people by means of promises regarding what is to happen, but he also incites and arouses them to believe these promises and not to think again in this way: "Yes, it may all be true what the prophets proclaim; and Jerusalem may become the kind of city they say. But who knows when that will happen, or if it is to be delayed even longer, as by now it has been delayed for about 40 years? And who knows if we are the ones who are to share in the work, or if our descendants will do it alone? Thus they say in Haggai (Hag. 1:2): 'The time has not yet come to rebuild the house of the Lord, etc.'" Such a delusion and doubting slackness He dismisses here and says: "You, you, who now and at this time are hearing these words of the prophets – and I am not speaking of your descendants, but you who are present now – to you these promises apply, and you are to begin the work."

10. *For before those days there was no wage for man or any wage for beast, neither was there any safety from the foe for him who went out or came in; for I set every man against his fellow.*

Haggai also says (Hag. 1:6) that conditions in the land were bad. When they sowed much, little grew; and whoever gathered much put his grain into bags with holes. And besides, there was unrest everywhere because of the enemies and neighbors, as Ezra and Nehemiah well show and also Zechariah shows here. Therefore the people were discouraged and complained that the time to build the temple must not yet have come. To this complaint the prophet here puts an end, so that they might surely not plead any excuse or hindrance. He says that the things of which they were complaining had happened, but he also says that they would not happen again, as we see from the following:

11-12. *But now I will not deal with the remnant of this people as in the former days, says the Lord of hosts. For there shall be a sowing of peace and prosperity; the vine shall yield its fruit, and the ground shall give its increase, and the heavens shall give their dew; and I will cause the remnant of this people to possess all these things.*

The prophet is again interpreting these promises of a happy time as applying specifically to his contemporaries who were hearing these things, so that they might indeed be certain and sure that they had been chosen for the work at hand and might firmly believe that henceforth everything would be better and prosper. Everything is designed to strengthen their faith, which had been very faint because in the past the people had indeed been plagued and tormented by all kinds of hindrances and misfortunes. And although the words that the prophet here speaks concerning temporal things, such as growth and rain, may to us seem easy to accept, they were most difficult for the Jews, because they demand faith in the presence of so manifold an affliction. And they who did believe them were surely very pious children; we at the present time fail to believe much more insignificant things in much more insignificant afflictions. I am saying this so that no one may think that it is a jest or joke when certain promises are preached in Scripture. Though these promises may have to do with insignificant temporal things, they require a great, strong faith, and they are great, strong words, even as the words here following are great:

13. *And as you have been a byword of cursing among the nations, O house of Judah and house of Israel, so will I save you, and you shall be a blessing. Fear not, but let your hands be strong.*

Here there is another great, fine promise: The Jews are to fare so well that all the Gentiles, when they desire to wish a man something good, will wish and say: "God grant that you fare as well as the Jews!" Thus a good and blessed saying is to proceed from them, even as earlier, when they were destroyed, they had been a bad example and a byword so that, when a man desired to wish another something evil, he might say: "May you fare like the Jews!" Now note what a great thing it is and what a faith is needed by the Jews to believe that they are to be nothing but a blessing when, after all, their misfortune and grief are so apparent that all the Gentiles use them as a horrible example, yes, as a curse and byword. That indeed is making life of death, heaven of hell, and everything of nothing. Of this curse and blessing Moses wrote at length in his fifth book (Deut. 28) and threatened that the Jews would become a curse, example, and byword among all the Gentiles if they prayed to strange gods. He also mentions the house of Israel, however, and not only the house of Judah — not that the kingdom of Israel, which had been completely rejected and abandoned, was to be restored, but that many from the house of Israel would join the house of Judah and cling to Jerusalem and the temple.

14-15. *For thus says the Lord of hosts: As I purposed to do evil to you, when your fathers provoked me to wrath, and I did not relent, says the Lord of hosts, so again have I purposed in these days to do good to Jerusalem and to the house of Judah; fear not.*

This again is a promise of temporal blessings. For in order to console the timid hearts, He promises the same thing many times and often repeats the same thing. For what has been said is true: It is exceedingly hard to quiet a crushed heart so that it will look to God for grace and mercy. Therefore God must act here as a father acts toward his child when it weeps and is afraid; he must use many kind words and say again and again: "Be still, be still, my darling child, etc." On the other hand, however, to keep the bad children from being spoiled and emboldened to do mischief, there follow, further on in the text, suggestions on how they may be good.

16-17. *These are the things that you shall do: Speak the truth to one another, render in your gates judgments that are true and make for peace, do not devise evil in your hearts against one another, and love no false oath, for all these things I hate, says the Lord.*

God wants to keep the Jews from accepting His promises of temporal blessings under the false impression that He wants to have servants of the belly and hypocrites, that He is a mammon and a god of the belly, and that He would be pleased with everything they might do (as the presumptuous and wicked always do; they accept the good promises and at the same time ignore God's commandments; while the godly, in turn, give careful attention to the commandments and find it difficult to accept the promises). At this point therefore God must again oppose men in two directions: with comforting promises He must keep the godly from despairing; but with severe commandments He must keep the wicked from becoming bold. For He wants to bless us and satisfy us; He does not, however, want to bring up scoundrels. No, He wants us to be good; and then He will be gracious.

But note once more that He is giving no orders here about fasting or eating, about clothes or holidays, about sacrifices or the burning of incense. For if He liked these things, he surely would not keep silent about them while He is saying: "These are the things that you shall do, etc." For with these words He is of course taking it upon Himself to teach them everything that is needed for their salvation.

But in this teaching there is nothing but the two parts, faith and love, as we have also heard above [1] on the same matters.

First, they are to "speak the truth to one another." That has to do with their teaching. And though it applies to everyone, it of course applies primarily to clergymen or priests, from whom the others are to learn to speak the truth too. They do speak and teach the truth, however, when they ignore men's commandments, their own works, and the falsely glittering worship of God but teach men to serve God in true faith and confidence and without any presumption of righteousness of their own.

The second part has to do with the secular rulers. These are to "render judgments that are true and make for peace" in their courts or offices. That simply means this: They are to administer their offices well, so that no tumult or unrest may arise in the land against them. The third applies to all of them: they are not to "devise evil in their hearts against one another," that is, as was also said above,[2] they are to show patience and love toward one another, gladly forgive if the one has offended the other, not seek revenge or reprisals, but do their best to help and counsel wherever there is need. Finally, they are to "love no false oaths." It may be that this is to be understood as referring to the false oaths which are taken in the name of strange gods. I think, however, it means that no one is to defraud his neighbor in his business. For in business men are in the habit of using seal and document, witnesses and oaths and similar bonds in order to confirm good faith with one another, as Ps. 15:4 says, "Who swears to his own hurt and does not change"; that is, men are not to lie or deceive one another but to keep faith. For it is one of the worst complaints in the world that there is no faith among people. They swear and make vows so faithfully, and yet there is nothing but frivolity and knavery in them. God therefore well says here that He hates all these things and is opposed to them. And this is indeed a hateful thing; through it many a good man is deceived and utterly ruined.

18-19. *And the Word of the Lord of hosts came to me, saying, Thus says the Lord of hosts: The fast of the fourth month, and the fast of the fifth, and the fast of the seventh, and the fast*

[1] Cf. p. 273 above.
[2] Cf. p. 265 above.

of the tenth shall be to the house of Judah seasons of joy and gladness, and cheerful feasts; therefore love truth and peace.

Here He answers the question which was presented at the beginning of the chapter[3] concerning fasting and discipline and says: "Keep only what I command you, and let fasting be fasting. Yes, if you keep My commandments, then these fastings shall not only be over and ended but, because I will do so much good at Jerusalem, all the sufferings for which you have chosen and observed these fastings shall be forgotten. And in the future it will be a joy for you to think of your fastings and the heartaches which had occasioned your fastings at that time – namely, in this way: when the fourth or the fifth month comes, you will say: "See, today is the season when I fasted and mourned because of the destruction of the temple and the burning of the city. But God be praised! There the temple is standing in all its glory, and the city in its most splendid state! Give me the jug of wine, the wreath, and the fine cloak; let us be merry and praise God instead of fasting and mourning as we were in the habit of doing at this season of the year." See, that is turning discipline into joy, mourning into delight, and fasting into a cheerful feast.

At the same time, however, we read that the people are to love truth and peace, so that the presumptuous wicked may not think that it is enough if they are glad on these days while, at the same time, they are scoundrels. "No," He says, "be joyful and forget your fastings and sorrows and turn your discipline into cheerful feasts, yet in such a way that you do not forget My commandments. Instead love truth, that is, first, toward God: pure teaching, the pure commandments of God, unfeigned faith, and righteous worship, so that you may not grow superstitious or become hypocrites and dissemblers. Likewise, toward your neighbor, love peace, so that there may be no hatred, envy, and strife among you, but rather love and friendship, peace and goodwill, patience and mercy. If these two loves prevail, all is well; then give up fasting and have cheerful feasts and be glad. Do you see, then, how God overturns the vanities of men and insists on His commandments alone?

But what do you think of our teachers who at this point have applied these words about the four months to the four ember weeks, or Quatember fasts?[4] Do the words not agree beautifully with this ap-

[3] Cf. p. 259 above.

[4] The use of this passage from Zechariah can already be found in the letters

plication? God says that these four fastings shall be over and that there are to be only cheerful feasts; yet they interpret these words in this way: There are to be four sad fastings a year. How beautifully God's Word and men's teaching agree! Yes, how beautifully men look at God's Words, and how diligently they read them! At the very place where God commands that the four fastings are to be nothing but that instead there are to be cheerful feasts, they teach that there are to be four fasts. Here one can see that in this text they looked only at the word "fast" and then at the "four months" and that from these words they invented the Quatember fasts, regardless of whether the months or the fasts of this text agreed or disagreed with their interpretation. It was enough that they found "four months" there and the word "fast." And that is the way they act elsewhere, too, so that where God teaches no, they teach yes, where God teaches faith and mercy, they invent works and merit. Yet they grow angry and will not listen when one says that till now the Scriptures have been lying under the bench [5] among them and that their wild dreams alone have had to rule in place of these Scriptures. For here you can surely see and must comprehend that they have interpreted this text, which says no to fasting, as saying yes, that they have straightway and just as senselessly applied God's Word to their hocus-pocus, and that they have, nevertheless, by means of the latter – as though it were by means of God's Word – confused the world and confirmed their claims.

20-21. *Thus says the Lord of hosts: Peoples shall yet come, even the inhabitants of many cities; the inhabitants of one city shall go to another, saying: Let us go at once to entreat the favor of the Lord, and to seek the Lord of hosts; I am going.*

I understand this passage and promise to mean that not only the Jews are to meet again in Jerusalem from all lands, as was said above, but that Jerusalem is to become so splendid and famous that also many Gentiles shall gather there to adore the Lord. And all of that was

regarding the Quatember fasts that were ascribed to Pope Calixtus I (3d century) by Pseudo-Isidore. Cf. p. 74, n. 3, above, concerning the name Quatember.

[5] The anger which was felt about this assertion of Luther was expressed, e. g., in the title of a writing by Petrus Sylvius (c. 1470—c. 1536): *Von den vier Evangelion, szo eyn lange tzeit untter der banck seyn gelegen. Das ist von den irrigen Artickeln, der vier unchristlichen ketzereyen. Nemlich der Pickarden, der Muscouitern, des Wigkleffs, und des Husss. Auss welchen allen Lutther seyn funfft Euangelium, wie mans hie vor awgen wirt sehn, tzusamen gelesen und tzuhauffen gesetzt, etc.*

fulfilled, and so Josephus writes that many kings and princes and also others bestowed great honors on the temple at Jerusalem.[6] And Luke also writes (Acts 8:27) that the minister of Queen Candace went to Jerusalem from Egypt. And without a doubt many others like him came from other cities and countries, as the following also indicates:

22. *Many peoples and strong nations shall come to seek the Lord of hosts in Jerusalem, and to entreat the favor of the Lord.*

This is the sum total of it all: Jerusalem is to become very splendid and, as Haggai also says (Hag. 2:9), the latter splendor of this house is to be greater than the former and first one. For one does not read that so many Gentiles and kings went to that former temple, which Solomon had built, and entreated His favor as went to this latter temple, which drew almost the whole world to itself, as history proves. Therefore this is a very great promise that the temple at Jerusalem was to be so very splendid and much more splendid than the first one, though everything looked so wretched when it was about to be built. What is meant, however, by "seeking the Lord" and "entreating His favor" has been told adequately elsewhere.

23. *Thus says the Lord of hosts: In those days ten men from the nations of every tongue shall take hold of the robe of a Jew, saying: Let us go with you, for we have heard that God is with you.*

Some[7] have applied this passage to the time of Christ, when many Gentiles of all tongues attached themselves to an apostle and came to Christ. That is a good interpretation, but at this point it does not strike me as being the correct one. The prophet here wishes to show how it will come about that many cities and people will go to Jerusalem to entreat the favor of the Lord in the temple, as he has said. And it will come about in this way: While the Jews are scattered among all the Gentiles, they will attach many Gentiles to themselves and bring them to their faith. And when the Jews would then go to Jerusalem for their festivals, these same Gentiles would go with them, because they wished to serve God together with the Jews. And when he says, "In those days," he means: at the time when many Gentiles will go to Jerusalem, as he said above; this "going" will take place in this way: the Gentiles

[6] Josephus, *Antiquities of the Jews,* XI, ch. 8; XII, ch. 2.

[7] E. g., Jerome, *Commentaria in Zachariam prophetam, Patrologia, Series Latina,* XXV, 1477.

will attach themselves to the Jews because they have heard from the Jews that God dwells in Jerusalem. That seems to me the simplest and surest interpretation, for by means of it God declares how splendid Jerusalem and the temple are to be, even though at that time they were still lying in ashes and in disgrace. All these sayings must of course point to the coming kingdom of Christ, as has often been said.

But when he says, "ten men from the nations of every tongue shall take hold of the robe of a Jew," this is not intended to mean that exactly ten Gentiles, no more or less, shall do that, nor that every individual Jew will bring exactly so many with him. But this is spoken in a general way and in this way: Here a Jew and there a Jew will bring many Gentiles with him from the midst of all kinds of Gentiles and countries; and so St. Luke also writes, Acts 2:5,[8] that on the day of Pentecost there were dwelling in Jerusalem men from every nation under heaven, etc.

[8] The Weimar editor corrects the text's "Acts 1."

CHAPTER NINE

1. *The burden of the Word of the Lord against the land of Hadrach and Damascus, on which it depends.*

UNTIL now we have heard that the prophet has consoled and strengthened the timid and frightened Jews and encouraged them to build the temple as a preliminary to the coming of the kingdom of Christ. But although temporal and physical blessings are promised in these prophecies, the prophecies are nevertheless not to be despised; because they are God's Word and because great examples of faith are presented in them. Some, however, who profess great spiritual insights, despise these physical blessings and fail to see how great a faith lies in these promises; they look for spiritual promises, when they have never believed for even an hour that God would feed them with bread and drink. I am repeating this so that no one might disregard the examples of faith and the divine promises found in the ancient stories, as Origen and Jerome are in the habit of doing, as though these were dead, useless stories, and as though one ought to look for something greater in them. If one looks at the things that are promised, they are indeed nothing but temporal, physical blessings. But if one looks at the promise, it is the living, eternal Word of God, which justified and saved those who in their day had faith in it. And such a faith is a great and powerful example for the strengthening of our faith.

From now on, then, the prophet wishes to prophesy how things will proceed from this time on and how Christ is to come, to whom all these things have been pointing that till now have had to do with the temple. And though many explanations have been offered on this point, I still think that the meaning and sum of it all is this: The countries and neighbors surrounding the Jews, such as Syria and Palestine with their cities: Damascus, Tyre, Sidon, Antioch, Accaron,[1] etc., are to be devastated and humbled in this way, that even as until now they have been hostile and opposed to Jerusalem, so in the future they will also become friendly and will accept Christ at His coming. That is

1 The Philistine city Ekron.

what he means when he says: "This is the burden, of which the Lord speaks concerning Hadrach." Among the prophets, however, "burden" means a punishment, as we have heard in Habbakuk,[2] and as it is especially common in Jeremiah [3] (ch. 23:33 ff.). This burden and punishment, however, as we shall see in what follows, is that they are to be destroyed, burned down, and taken captive.

"Hadrach" is an unfamiliar word and is to be found nowhere else in Scripture except at this place. But since it is certain that the prophet has the land of Syria in mind, of which Damascus is the royal capital, I think the prophet is giving this land a new name compounded of two words – "had" and "rach." "Had" means to be happy, and "rach" means tender or delicate, as we Germans might say of a woman: "She is so delicate and coy that she would not put her hand into cold water unless she really desired it." This, then, would be the prophet's meaning: "This is the burden over the land of Hadrach" (that is, over this tender, coy land, which till now has been accustomed to nothing but pleasures, happy days, and honors, and which would never put its hand into cold water either or suffer anything bad or unpleasant); "some day also misfortune will come upon you, and you will get a foreign ruler." He also calls Damascus "the rest of that land." For in Hebrew it reads "and upon Damascus, which is its rest," and this we have translated "on which it depends." And that is the real meaning of the words too, even as in Is. 7:2 "Syria rests upon Ephraim" means "Syria depends on Ephraim." Thus the land of Syria depended and rested on Damascus as on a strong, mighty city, through which it might feel quite secure and protected and have happy days.

For the Lord looks upon men and upon all the tribes of Israel.

I shall let the masters of Hebrew determine whether I have translated this text correctly. I am not sure myself that I am right. The Hebrew text reads thus: *Quoniam domini est oculus hominis et omnium tribuum Israel,* which may yield various meanings that cannot be tabulated here. I will hold to this interpretation: The prophet wants to say that the surrounding lands are before the Lord just as much as the tribes of Israel and that no one can conceal himself from Him or escape Him. And therefore, even as He has punished the tribes of Israel, so He will not let these lands go unpunished either.

[2] Cf. W, XIX, 350.

[3] Isaiah may be meant. Cf. Is. 13:1; 15:1; 17:1; 19:1; etc.

2. *Hamath also, which borders thereon.*

Hamath is the city which later was called Antioch, where the disciples were for the first time called Christians, Acts 11:26.[4] This city borders on the land of Syria and the city of Damascus; indeed, it belongs to the land of Syria. If, then, the burden rests upon Damascus, it will also rest upon Antioch, because the two are so close to each other.

Tyre and Sidon, though they are very wise.

Tyre and Sidon, both on the sea, are also in Syria and border on the Jewish land and on Damascus. They also were strong, rich, and mighty cities in that day and subject to no one. And the prophet says that they are wise, or intelligent – not, however, in spiritual wisdom but in worldly wisdom. For they had a splendid government and were rich and mighty, for all of which, no doubt, wise and sensible people are needed. Therefore also Ezek. 28:3[5] says that the prince of Tyre "was wiser than Daniel." For where fools and clods rule, there you will not find rich cities or lands.

3. *Tyre has built stoutly and heaps up silver like dust, and gold like the dirt of the streets.*

Here you can see what kind of wisdom the prophet ascribes to the people of Tyre. They are wise and intelligent enough to build their cities strong as a protection against their enemies and to heap up much money and many goods for their future needs and thus to provide for their temporal rule in the very best way. For it surely is to be called governing wisely when one guards one's land and cities well and provides for them. But against God neither buildings nor provisions avail anything, and therefore we read the following:

4. *But lo, the Lord will strip her of her possessions and hurl her wealth into the sea, and she shall be devoured by fire.*

This is the burden of which the prophet spoke above and which was to come upon these lands and cities. For if Tyre was to fare thus – and she surely was the mightiest and strongest of them all – how much more would also the others fare thus. This destruction and devastation was of course brought about by Alexander the Great; for it

[4] The Weimar editor corrects the text's "Acts 15."

[5] The Weimar editor corrects the text's "Ezek. 35."

was he who put this burden into execution, especially at Tyre, which he besieged and against which he waged war a long time. And thereafter these countries had much war at all times, and they almost never enjoyed peace under the kings that ruled Syria and Egypt after Alexander, until the Romans conquered the land. Now, where war is waged often and for long periods of time, the only result can be that lands and cities are destroyed by it. All vanity, then, was driven from this tender and coy land, for all these mighty cities had lost their rule and had at last become subject to Rome and humbled in such a way that in future days they were well able to tolerate and receive Christ.

5. *Ashkelon shall see it and be afraid; Gaza, too, shall writhe in anguish; and Ekron will be saddened when she sees it.*

Here the prophet also adds the land of the Philistines, who had also opposed the Jews at all times and had always had their own rulers until now. But now that Alexander and his successors have become rulers and have conquered such mighty cities as Tyre and Sidon, which no one was able to conquer before, the Philistines also have to become frightened, because they see these things and note that their rule will soon be over. And that really happened, as we see from the following:

5-6. *The king shall perish from Gaza; Ashkelon shall be uninhabited; a mongrel people shall dwell in Ashdod; and I will make an end of the pride of Philistia.*

Heretofore, as has been said, the land of the Philistines had always had its own kings and rulers and had always been a well-populated, mighty land. But later, as has also been said, it was horribly devastated and destroyed by wars when it was overpowered by the successors of Alexander. And since that time these cities have not regained kings or rulers of their own and even today are quite desolate, so that Luke in Acts 8:26 [6] calls Gaza a desert. But when he says that "a mongrel people shall dwell in Ashdod," he is saying, in Hebrew fashion, as much as this: "Ashdod will be so completely under strange hands that the natives shall no longer rule or dwell there, but only strangers." Now strangers in a city are not true children of that city but are like mongrels in a house; they were not born in it and do not belong to it. Thus, he says, the splendor, conceit, rule, and might of the Philistines shall come to an end. And all of this took place, too, during the time

[6] The Weimar editor corrects the text's "Acts 4."

which elapsed between the coming of Christ and the building of the temple; and whoever has read history knows that very well. And Zechariah here has foretold all this and has really hit the mark.

7. *I will take away its blood from its mouth and its abomination from between its teeth; it, too, shall be a remnant for our God.*

Although the Philistines were the most stiffnecked of all the enemies, "yet," He says, "once they have been destroyed and humbled so that they no longer are anything, they will be friendly toward Me; and I will then receive them, and they shall be kept for Me for the time of My coming and shall become good Christians and the best friends of My people." But when He says that He "will take away its blood from its mouth and its abomination from between its teeth," I understand Him to mean that He is going to make them friends of His people. For until now, as has been said, they had been a people fierce toward the Jews and murderous in its intentions to destroy them. And that is why He says that their mouths are bloodthirsty and their teeth full of abomination, because they were devouring the Jews with war and wrath; that is, they were always shedding the blood of the Jews and killing them and were as anxious and fierce as bears and lions to kill and to shed blood. All this is now to stop: they shall no longer thus devour or shed blood; "I will have them humbled so greatly that they will be happy to become the friends of My people and henceforth keep their mouths and their teeth clean of the blood and flesh of My people."

It shall be like a prince in Judah, and Ekron shall be like the Jebusites.

This means: I will choose bishops and preachers from their midst as well as from Judah. "Prince," however, is here given as אַלֻּף , which means the kind of prince who has charge of the doctrine, as teachers, preachers, and bishops are supposed to do. "And Ekron shall be like the Jebusites," that is, the citizens of Ekron are to be Christians the same as the citizens of Jerusalem, whom he here calls Jebusites after the old Gentile name. For Jerusalem was called Jebus in ancient times, as we read in Joshua (Joshua 15:8; Judg. 19:10). And perhaps he is using the old name to obscure the prophecy or to indicate that at the time of Christ Jerusalem would properly be called Jebus because of its unbelief, while Ekron would properly be called teachers and bishops, that is, called the real Jerusalem because of its faith. All this was said so that the Philistines might be prepared for the coming of Christ in such a manner that, when He did come, they would receive Him.

8. *Then I will man my house with warriors who shall march to and fro; no oppressor shall again overrun them, for now I see with My own eyes.*

This text cannot be understood as referring to the temple at Jerusalem. For, as the text presents it, it refers to the time after the Philistines were to have become Christians; and at that time the temple was already destroyed or very near its destruction. Therefore it must be another house, Christianity, in which there were also to be Philistines; and that happened, too, at the time of the apostles. It was at that time that Christ "manned his house with warriors," that is, with apostles and consecrated teachers, who went to and fro in that house, that is, guarded it with their preaching and admonitions like genuine, well-equipped warriors, sent with the weapons of God and with the "sword of the Spirit" (Eph. 6:17) against the devil, error, sin, and death. "No oppressor shall again overrun them" and be able to rule over them, that is, no deceiver with the Law and the works of men. For the oppressors are none other than the teachers who desire to make men good through works, without faith. But Jesus will not let such teachers continue to rule over His Christians; instead, He will send warriors to oppose those oppressors and fight against them valiantly, as we can see in the case of Sts. Paul and Peter. And all this will be done, "for now," He says, "I see with My own eyes," that is, "I Myself am now looking on and Myself am the Bishop, and no longer am I giving commandments to Moses and the prophets, as I did at the time when I was looking on with the eyes of a stranger. Now, however, I am looking on Myself and Myself am ruling in My house, so that the oppressors do not rule over it."

9. *Rejoice greatly, O daughter of Zion! Shout aloud, O daughter of Jerusalem! Lo, your King comes to you; just and a Helper is He, poor and riding on an ass, on a colt, the foal of an ass.*

This happy and beautiful verse I have explained in my postil, within the limits of my ability, for the first Sunday in Advent.[7] For this reason,

[7] Cf. Luther's *Enarrationes epistolarum et evangeliorum, quas postillas vocant* of 1521, W, VII, 477—479.

and also for the sake of brevity, I do not consider it necessary to repeat the explanation here. But this is strange: He has just promised that He would "man His house with warriors so that no oppressor should again overrun it"; all of His words, moreover, sound so warlike, as though He were about to equip an army with great worldly splendor. (He speaks like a mighty emperor. For in Hebrew צָבָה means *militia* ["warriors"], and חָנִיתִי means *vallabo* ["I will put a rampart"], *castra metabor* ["I will lay out a camp"] which means this: "I will surround my house with the might of an army, etc." And for this reason He Himself is called Lord of Sabaoth, Lord of hosts.) And all at once, after this warlike talk, He presents the King of this army: extremely unpretentious, without military splendor, poor, too, and riding on an ass. Is this the warlike King? Is this to be called surrounding the house with the might of an army? All of this, however, was done that the former words concerning military forces might be understood spiritually and that the Jews might not expect the kingdom of Christ to be physical and earthly with worldly, external splendor but to be in poverty and humility externally, but inwardly and spiritually in great splendor. And therefore He says here that He is coming "as a just Man and a Savior," and yet "poor and riding on an ass."

10. *I will cut off the chariot from Ephraim and the war horse from Jerusalem; and the battle bow shall be cut off.*

Here He Himself goes on to explain that the kingdom of Christ shall not be furnished physically with weapons; for He says that He will have neither chariots nor horses nor bows in His kingdom, as He also says in Is. 2:4: "Neither shall they learn war any more, etc." And He also calls the old kingdom Ephraim, that is, Israel, which was of the tribe of Ephraim; for under Christ the two kingdoms were to be joined, as Hosea says in chapter 1:11.

And he shall teach peace to the Gentiles.

It is for this reason that He will need neither chariot, nor horse, nor bow, nor battle. For He will be a "Prince of Peace," as Is. 9:6 also says; and this peace is to be not only among the Jews, of whom only a few will accept it, but also among the Gentiles. Therefore His rule will consist in the Word or in speech, because He says here that He will speak, or teach, peace to the Gentiles.

His dominion shall be from sea to sea, and from the River to the ends of the earth.

These words are taken from Ps. 72:8, so that one may see that the psalm is not to be understood as referring to Solomon, as the Jews think, but to Christ Himself. For in these words the whole earth is made subject to Christ: "from one sea" – that is, from the Dead Sea in Judea – "to all other seas" round about; and "from the River" – the Jordan – "to the ends of the earth." For His kingdom began in Judea, where the Dead Sea and the Jordan are, and from there spread about into all the world.

11. *You also, because of the blood of Your covenant, set Your captives free from the waterless pit.*

He has just said that the dominion of this King shall not consist in external worldly splendor but in poverty, and that He shall nevertheless bring justice and salvation to His people and shall also establish peace among the Gentiles – not only by reconciling the Gentiles with the Jews and making the two nations one throughout the world, although heretofore they had always been deadly enemies, as St. Paul also says, Eph. 2:14 – but also by establishing peace between God and us, Rom. 5:1. If one should ask how He will accomplish all these things when, after all, no worldly power has ever been able to accomplish them, He gives the answer here and now and says: "Because of the blood of Your covenant, or testament, etc." And He holds up this blood against the blood of the Old Testament, and thereby He also abolishes the latter. It is as though He would say: "Moses led his people out of Egypt through the blood of his testament; but You, the new King, will institute a new testament and abolish the former through the blood of Your own testament; and through it You will not lead the people of Israel out of Egypt but Your own captives out of another Egypt, out of the waterless pit. And that is the power through which You will bring about that righteousness and salvation and peace – not with sword and armor but through Your suffering, blood, and death."

Thus this text tells us, first, that this King shall die and shed His blood in order to gain for His people righteousness, salvation, and peace – that is, forgiveness of sins and eternal life; second, that He shall rise again from death and live eternally; and then there follows that He will expand this testament by means of the Gospel and rule

His people, as we shall hear. This no dead man can do. Therefore we have the statement "that it was necessary that the Christ should suffer and rise and thus enter into His glory," as Luke 24:26 describes it. But that in times past some understood these words to mean that this pit was the outer limbo of hell, in which the ancient fathers were supposed to have been, and that Christ is supposed to have come to these fathers when He descended into hell and to have led them out of it [8] – that I shall leave to their simple conceits and pleasures. One cannot, however, prove this interpretation from Scripture or from this passage, especially since Zechariah is here not considering so small an area as the fathers represent but is considering the whole kingdom of Christ as far as the world goes, the complete salvation of all the saints, and the blood of the whole new covenant together with all its power and fruits. And he speaks most gloriously of all these things. For the text is all one, and everything has to do with the complete salvation of all the saints.

He has given the name "waterless pit" to the prison of sins in the Law, in which we all lay as captives under the devil and which is indicated by the captivity in Egypt; and he has given it this name because there is no water of life in it to refresh and comfort the soul, but only eternal thirst in eternal heat. Ps. 8:8 [9] also has this prison in mind when it says, "Thou didst ascend the high mount, leading captives in thy train, etc." And in the Hebrew he contrasts it very excellently with the Old Testament when he says: "You also, because of the blood, etc.," that is: "Moses indeed led his people out through the blood of a covenant; but You too, You too have blood, the blood of Your own covenant and not that of Moses, and You did not want to lead Your people out without blood either, etc." Likewise he says, "Your captives" – not the captives of Moses. For the people of Moses were captives physically; but "Your captives," that is, "those whom You are leading out through Your blood are a different kind of captive, even as You are a different blood, a different covenant, a different Man from Moses." I am showing all this from the text so that everyone can see for himself that Zechariah is here not prophesying about the dead but, as I understand it, about the full salvation that Christ has gained

8 Lyra, for instance, paraphrases the passage: *Patres in inferni limbo detentos eduxisti.*

9 The Weimar editor corrects the text's "Ps. 63."

through His blood. But if anyone likes something else better, let him go on with it.

12. *Return to your stronghold, O prisoners of hope.*

"Because so great a salvation has been accomplished through My blood, see to it that you do not despise it. Until now you have been lying under the Law in sin, captive and mired down in filth and sand; in fact, you have been everyone's prey and booty; whoever came along would lead, drive, and scatter you about at his pleasure. For you were captives and without protection against your oppressors. Then the taskmaster of the Law came and chased you from one work to the next and still did not do you any good. There was no peace. Here the devil came and drove you from one sin to the next; and there was no security but only the fear of death. But now you have a firm stronghold, in which you can rest secure and in peace from both the Law and the taskmasters of sin – and that stronghold is the blood of My covenant. Cling to it; for nowhere else is there rest or peace from the Law and sin. But he calls them *vinctos spei,* "prisoners of hope." They are the people who were hoping for salvation and, like Simeon, Luke 2:25, were looking for the consolation of Israel. For in the prophets they had the promises of God that they were to be redeemed by Christ. They were looking for this hope with great longing until it came; for they surely felt the burden of Moses, the taskmaster of the Law, and that of the devil, the taskmaster of sin.

The prisoners of hope, then, are all that despair of their works and, humbled by the Law, are captives in the knowledge of their sins. They are also the ones whom he here calls "prisoners of Christ" when he speaks of "Your captives." For the haughty saints who claim to be pious and righteous through the deeds of the Law are not prisoners of hope. For they are not looking for any redemption. Nor does the blood of this covenant mean anything to them; indeed, they feel quite free and are anything but prisoners, not to mention the fact that they are not prisoners of hope. In the same way they who occupy themselves with men's teachings and works are holy and free too and have no need of this stronghold at all; for they feel quite secure and dwell in rest and peace. But we poor sinners, who are compelled by the Law to feel that it demands what we neither have nor can do, who therefore stand before God overburdened with sin and with a timid, despairing, bad conscience, and who then learn that because of our sins we are condemned to death and must lie in this miserable prison – we are the prisoners of hope, for we look for redemption not through our works but through the blood of this testament. It is as St. Paul says, Gal. 5:5, drawing on this verse, "For through the Spirit, by faith, we wait for the hope of righteousness." Thus our text applies solely to those who through the Law and sin and with a wretched conscience are conscious of their prison and who hope for mercy through the blood of Christ, through which they are redeemed and justified and have peace and dwell in a firm, safe stronghold.

Today I declare that I will restore to you double.

Read the Letter to the Hebrews in the third and fourth chapters (Heb. 3:7; 4:7),[10] and you will find what the Holy Spirit wants men to understand by the word "today," namely, that at the present time, when Christ will come – and that is the real today – the Jews should give attention to this preaching and mercy and not gape and look for another time to come. This, then, is the meaning of *hodie annuncians reddam tibi duplicia,* "by what I am preaching today I will restore to you double blessings for your misery," that is, "through the preaching which is to take place at this time, when I am freeing My prisoners through My blood, I will give you double comfort and blessings for all your sorrow (such as the Law and sin), namely, a double redemption, from both the Law and sin, so that the Law and your conscience may not depress or frighten you. Sin shall not frighten you with death or condemn you. For both of these shall be completely abolished through My blood; that is, the Law is to be fulfilled so that you may become righteous, and sin is to be destroyed so that instead of dying you may live. These, then, are the two blessed freedoms of which eternal life consists; and it is of these two freedoms or redemptions that Is. 40:2 speaks: "Jerusalem has received double for all her sins. For her iniquity is pardoned, and so her warfare (that is, her servitude under the Law) is ended."

Once more the little word "also" is to be noted here, as above;[11] for it reads as if He wanted to say: "You have many teachers and taskmasters of the Law who preach much and burden you with sins; you are accustomed to them and know of nothing else. But I also want to preach and not let only the taskmasters do the talking. My preaching,

[10] The Weimar editor corrects the text's "Heb. 2 and 3."

[11] Cf. p. 289 above.

however, is quite different from their preaching. For they torment and humble you with a twofold evil: through the Law they give you a conscience that is heavy with sin, and through sin they give you a heart that is frightened and despairing because of death, which is the 'wages of sin,' Rom. 6:23.[12] But My preaching shall make you free and independent of both, if only you give attention to it today and at this time." Note, however, that this twofold blessing is to be distributed through the Word and preaching and that it must be received and preserved through faith. For he says: *Annuncians reddam duplicia,* "by preaching I will restore to you double." But that is the most offensive thing, and it hampers the Jews to this day. They would like to feel and grasp the blessing as a physical one, so that they would become physically free and independent; but they give no attention to their spiritual redemption. This, however, is the thing that must be preached, heard, and believed. This is a spiritual kingdom, and in it all things, with all their blessings and riches, are done spiritually.

13. *For I have bent Judah as My bow; I have made Ephraim its arrow. I will brandish your sons, O Zion, over your sons, O Greece, and wield you like a giant's sword.*

These words almost sound worldly, as though there were to be a physical battle. But according to what has gone before, all this is spoken about the office of preaching, which was to begin at first at Jerusalem among the Jews, as has just been said, and later was to go farther out, even to the Gentiles, as he says here. The "bent bows of Judah" are the dear apostles from the tribe of Judah, as Ps. 68:27 also speaks of the prince of Judah in Christendom. "Ephraim" is the apostles and disciples from the tribes of Israel whom He fills (Note!) and equips well with arrows. For in Christ the two kingdoms of Judah and Ephraim again had to combine into one kingdom, as we heard above.[13] The "bending of the bow" and "equipping with arrows," then, is nothing but the sending out of well-equipped teachers taught by God. And the "sons of Zion" whom He has "brandished over the sons of Greece" are also the same, that is, the apostles and disciples sent into Greece with the Gospel from Zion, when they had begun their work and on Pentecost Day became spiritual sons of Zion through the Holy Spirit. And their sword is to be "like the sword of a giant," that is, the

[12] The Weimar editor corrects the text's "Rom. 8."

[13] Cf. p. 288 above.

Word of God that they are "to wield" is to be powerful and active and able to penetrate mightily. And we read, too, that the Word of St. Paul and his companions was mighty in Asia (Acts 19:20).

14. *Then the Lord will appear over them, and His arrow go forth like lightning.*

This means: He Himself will be with them; and one will be able to see from the Holy Spirit and from the signs and miracles which they will do that the Lord is upon them and with them. For the words of the apostles are not their own words, but they are the arrows of the Lord; the apostles are His bows and equipment; and therefore they go forth like lightning; and their words are powerful and fruitful and terrify the proud and comfort the humble.

The Lord God will sound the trumpet and march forth in the whirlwinds of the south.

There will be a blowing of horns and trumpets different from that of the Law ordered by Moses. "The Lord will sound the trumpet Himself," that is, He will cause the very same Gospel to be sounded forth by the apostles. And in this "sounding" the announcement will be made that before God the whole world is sinful and guilty. It will, however, be like a great tempest with thunder and lightning, as the tempests from the south commonly are, in that "it reveals the wrath of God against all ungodliness and wickedness of men," Rom. 1:18, so that the haughty might be terrified and humble themselves to seek mercy. But the world will confidently resist and oppose the Gospel and persecute the Word and the apostles. But that will not do them any good, for:

15. *The Lord of hosts will protect them, and they shall devour and tread down with slingstones; and they shall drink and rage as with wine, and be full like a bowl, drenched like the corners of the altar.*

The prophet is intentionally using fine and ornate language here about strife, whirlwinds, battles, etc., to indicate that there is nothing inactive or inept about the Gospel but that it does great things. For it overthrows and casts down everything that is great, learned, sacred, wise, strong, and proud and humbles everyone under Christ, as Paul says, 2 Cor. 10:4: "The weapons of our warfare are not worldly but have divine power." But since the world cannot bear such humiliation and subjection, it opposes and persecutes the apostles and rages against them as though they were poor, forsaken, weak people of this world. But here see what a Protector they have against such attacks: "The Lord of hosts will protect them." That does not mean that they will not suffer anything in their bodies; for they must be persecuted and killed. Their office, word, and preaching, however, cannot be hindered or repressed; but the more these are hampered, the more they press forward and onward. For "the Word of God is not fettered" (2 Tim. 2:9), even though Paul is fettered.

But how is it that "they shall eat and tread down"? How can a thing be subjected that has been devoured? The devouring, then, must be a spiritual one: through their mouths and with the Word the apostles will draw the Gentiles to themselves and embody them into their congregations, and in this way they will subject them to the obedience of the faith in Christ. And this they will do with slingstones, even as David subjected Goliath to himself with physical slingstones (1 Sam. 17:50). Their slingstones, however, will be spiritual: the Word of God, with which they will throw accurately and strike the consciences of men in such a way that they will not be able to defend themselves or conceal themselves but will have to give themselves up as captives and say, "That is the truth."

They will also "be turbulent, or rage, as though they were full of wine." That means the very same thing as the above: through the Word they will cause many Gentiles to become Christians and will boldly press forward, like drunken men. For they are so full of the Holy Spirit, who makes them bold, that they go among the Gentiles confidently and, rather than fearing danger, will be quite brave and turbulent among these Gentiles until they have swallowed them up and made them fellow Christians.

I should prefer, however, to understand this "devouring and drinking" in this way: The apostles are not only to be guarded and protected so that their work may go forward unhampered, but they are also to have enough to eat and to drink – to eat, so that they may maintain themselves and grow strong enough to subject the Gentiles to Christ; to drink, so that they may grow cheerful and bold enough to be confident and turbulent among the Gentiles with the Word and not fear any danger. This eating and drinking, however, is spiritual; for first they themselves are to be satisfied and filled with the Word and the Spirit and are to increase more and more every day so that they may not become tired in their office or because of griefs, just as the body must have its food every day if it is to bear the day's work.

But what does it mean that "they shall be full like a bowl, drenched like the corners of the altar"? The prophet in this way refers to the old priestly office and points to the new priesthood, as though he wanted to say: "When the apostles will be so turbulent among the Gentiles, then the priestly office will be conducted properly and fully; and when through God's Word they will punish and kill the old man with all his works and sacrifice in this way to the glory of God, then a slaughtering and sacrificing will begin just as when the old priests sacrificed unreasoning beasts, etc." Such sacrifices St. Paul urges when he says, Rom. 12:1, "Present your bodies as a living sacrifice, holy and acceptable to God, etc." The prophet mentions the "bowl" and the "corners of the altar." For, as Moses writes in his third book (Lev. 4:5 ff.; Ex 24:6), the bowl was used to catch up the blood of the sacrificed beasts and to carry it into the temple, and from it the priest was to sprinkle the ark with his finger seven times, to paint the horns of the altar with it, and then to pour the rest of it at the base of the altar. By means of all this the prophet here wishes to prophesy that the Gentiles, according to the old man, were to be killed through the Gospel as a sacrifice that would be pleasing to God, and that their blood would also be holy and glorious before Him.

16. *On that day the Lord their God will save them, for they are the flock of His people.*

This means that through the Gospel He will gather into one faith, as into one group or flock, those who have been scattered throughout the world and separated by various ways of teaching. For the Jews also were scattered about in all the world in their fashion and had various ways among themselves of getting pious, as one can see from the Pharisees, Sadducees, and scribes. But that is even more true of the Gentiles, who were separated throughout all the world into countless numbers of idolatrous sects. But when they were punished for that through the Gospel and their wrong beliefs together with all the cunning and wisdom of the old Adam was killed, then they were all brought together into an harmonious faith and teaching.

For like the jewels of dedication they shall be set up over His land.

These jewels also are the apostles and preachers of the Gospel; and they are not only precious stones but consecrated stones. For נֵזֶר

in Hebrew refers to the consecration, or dedication, through which a person or something else is set apart for the service of God – like the Nazarites, Num. 6:22 ff. In the same manner St. Paul says, Rom. 1:1, that he was "set apart (that is, was a Nazarite) to preach the Gospel"; even as Acts 13:2 also says concerning him and Barnabas, "Set apart for me Barnabas and Saul, etc." But the fact that they are to be elevated does not refer to an ordinary elevating, either, but is rather like the raising up of a banner or of battle insignia, to which the whole army looks and by which it is guided, as the Hebrew word מִתְנוֹסְסוֹת indicates. This, then, is the meaning: The fact that the Christians everywhere, as has been said, are to be gathered together into one faith through the Gospel is to be accomplished in this way: they are not to gather at physical places, as has happened until now in Jerusalem, but they are to attach themselves to the apostles and cling to their teaching. For these apostles are to be elevated among the Gentiles as sacred stones and battle insignia or as markers in Christendom; and all Christians will look to them and will be guided by their teaching, so that unity of doctrine and of faith may be maintained and not every one may start his own doctrine and teaching, through which the flock would be scattered and become separatistic in the faith.

17. *Yea, how good and how fair it shall be! Grain shall make the young men flourish, and new wine the maidens.*

Christ will not use armor and weapons to redeem or gather His people but will accomplish everything through meat and drink. That is surely a strange King, however, who does nothing but serve bread and wine and in that way not only gathers His people but also begets strong people, both male and female. The sum of this text, however, is this: Among the people and in the kingdom of Israel this happens: children are begotten, physically, in the natural manner of man and wife. But in this kingdom things happen in a wondrous way. There one finds the very finest and most pleasing bearing and increasing of people. For there no children are begotten that will lie in cradles. What else, then? Only fine, strong young men and full-grown, beautiful maidens are begotten there. All, then, that are born and added to this King are young men and maidens, grown boys and grown girls who from their very birth are ready for marriage. For when a man becomes a Christian, he can immediately teach and act and at once beget other Christians, just as if a mother bore a boy who at once could take a wife and beget children. That would be an unusual child. But so are all the Christians: they are full-grown young men who through the Word can beget other Christians, and full-grown maidens who can carry and bear other Christians.

This bearing and increasing is brought about through grain and new wine, that is, through the Gospel, as Paul says in 1 Cor. 4:15, where he admits being such a young man and father: "I became your father in Christ Jesus through the Gospel." Again, in Galatians (Gal. 4:19), he makes himself one of these maidens and mothers, when he says, "My little children, with whom I am again in travail until Christ be formed in you." Hence the people of Christ are people that are increased through the Gospel and are increased in such a way that they can at once be fathers and mothers and beget others, who in their turn can also be fathers and mothers. That is what the prophet expresses here in this way: "Grain shall make the young men flourish, and new wine the maidens." Of this begetting Is. 66:7 ff. speaks: "Before she was in labor she gave birth; before her pain came upon her she was delivered of a son. Who has heard of such a thing? Who has seen such things?" – that is, who has heard of or seen a land that could beget a nation in one day or a nation that could be born all at once, as Zion bears her children, etc? It is as if the prophet should say: "A woman can give birth to a child but not to a man; but Zion gives birth to men. Also, a woman must be given time before she can bear a child; she must be at least 14 years old. But Zion bears children at once – when she is one day old. And when a nation is to be begotten on earth, many years are needed; but Zion bears a nation quickly and at once – in one day.

CHAPTER TEN

1. *Ask rain from the Lord in the season of the spring rain, from the Lord who makes the storm clouds, who gives men showers of rain, to every one the vegetation in the field.*

THIS is said about a spiritual rain, that is, about the teaching of the Gospel, and with this meaning: Because the promise was made in the preceding chapter that the Gospel would come, therefore prepare for it, and do not merely wait for it but also ask for it. For now it is time to ask for the true spring rain so that you may not be hindered by men's teaching and the works of the Law and be found unprepared for this rain. It will surely come; but it wants to be accepted and not despised; instead, it wants to be desired and received with careful attention. If you act in this way, then enough rain will come for the growing of all the good fruits of the Spirit. Christ Himself speaks very much like this text in Matt. 9:36 ff.: [1] "When He saw the crowds, He had compassion on them, because they were harassed and helpless, like sheep without a shepherd. Then He said to His disciples, 'The harvest is plentiful, but the laborers are few; pray therefore the Lord of the harvest to send out laborers into His harvest.'" These laborers are the preachers, whom the Lord here calls "storm clouds," in Hebrew חֲזִיזִים, which comes from חָזָה, and that means "to look, or see," because these clouds look down and take their places and let one see that they are about to give rain. And so the prophets, too, were ready and prepared to give the true rain. And the rain is called a "spring rain," which comes when the grain has sprouted and is shooting forth, and when the soil is dry from the heat. And so the Gospel also comes when the consciences have become hot and thirsty because of the Law.

2. *For the teraphim utter nonsense, and the diviners see lies; the dreamers tell false dreams, and give empty consolation.*

Here we can see that the prophet was speaking above about a spiritual rain, because he is giving the reason here for his admonitions and

[1] The Weimar editor corrects the text's "Matt. 10."

is contrasting false teaching with the spring rain, which comes from the Lord. It is as if he were saying: "I am admonishing you to request the spring rain of the Lord, so that you may not request it of men and expect it of them. For when the Lord does not give rain and teach, then the things happen that the text mentions: false teachers utter nonsense, lies, and dreams and give nothing but empty consolation; yes, they keep one from desiring and waiting for the spring rain." And therefore he warns people to guard against them and admonishes them to seek the spring rain. He presents three kinds of teachers and three kinds of teachings. The first he calls teraphim, idols. And with that name he indicates the teachers of the Law, who conduct a worship of God of works. For the Hebrew word teraphim means idols or the worship of God, especially a worship that consists in external actions, such as the worship of our clergy is now, as one can see from Hosea 3:4 and Judges 17:5.[2] Hence he wishes to say at this time: "The teraphim, they are the teachers of the Law that teach men that they may become God-pleasing through many sacrifices and similar outward forms of worship; but besides hampering this spring rain of the Gospel, they do nothing more than teach nonsense, that is, demand many works, through which, after all, no good conscience can come." And so their teaching remains sheer nonsense, both outwardly in their many and manifold activities and inwardly in an insecure conscience. For they teach neither faith nor the right understanding of the Law, as we can see in the Gospels, where the Pharisees taught much about sacrifice and nothing about faith.

The second group of those that prophesy are the false prophets who mislead the people with false promises and threats. Such were the prophets among the Jewish people who cried out "Peace, peace!" when there was no peace, as Jeremiah laments (Jer. 6:14). That is: for the sake of their good works, which they had invented and taught, they promised the people all good things from God, even as the Pharisees taught and said that it was better to give as a sacrifice than to feed one's parents (Matt. 15:5), and as in our times the clergy have until now sold their Masses and worship services as the best of works and, on the basis of these, have promised the people God's mercy and eternal life. This the prophet here calls "uttering lies and dreams," and that is what their teachings are in truth. For they invent all these

[2] The Weimar editor corrects the text's "Judg. 19."

things themselves according to their own conceits, without having a Word of God to support them. These things, however, are to be called men's teachings – nothing but lies and dreams.

The third are the "comforters." These are the same as the two mentioned above, or all those who defend and protect these false teachings and dreams against the true teachers, who punish such dreams. For these comforters admonish and urge the poor people by all means to cling to their teaching and, as they now say, to the old faith. They always put off and comfort the poor people with pleasant words and praise their works most highly, as though these were the right and good thing, etc. But all this comforting does not mean anything. See, these are the teachers and idols whom Christ found when He came; and He will always find them, whenever He comes. But what follows?

Therefore the people wander like sheep; they are afflicted for want of a shepherd.

This is what the people get from such teachers: they are driven away and scattered like a flock into various kinds of superstitions and schisms. Moreover, they perish and famish like abandoned sheep which have no shepherd and which no one tends with the divine pure Word. And therefore Is. 53:6 says: "All we like sheep have gone astray; we have turned everyone to his own way, etc." Christ also alludes to this verse in Matt. 9:36 ff., as we heard above.[3] God accordingly is properly vexed when they not only scatter the flock into their schisms but also keep them from desiring the spring rain. Therefore follows:

3. *My anger is hot against the shepherds, and I will punish the he-goats.*

He calls these men "shepherds" because they have the office of shepherds, though in fact they are teachers of idolatry and are dreamers. Such were the Pharisees, and such are all false prophets; and such are also the he-goats, which butt their way among the sheep by force and rule them. Christ also calls them he-goats that He will place on His left hand on Judgment Day, Matt. 25:33. He punished these he-goats, however, when He deposed them from office and destroyed them.

[3] Cf. p. 299 above.

For the Lord of hosts cares for His flock, the houses of Judah, and will make them like His proud steed of battle.

This means that He will redeem His flock from the he-goats and will Himself be their shepherd and visit them with mercy. For in the Hebrew we read that He will visit the goats with punishment and His flock with blessing, so that a twofold visiting is being announced here – one of anger and wrath against the goats, another of mercy and pity for the flock. And not only does He desire to visit His flock and His people graciously, but He will also make of them well-equipped steeds; and on these He will ride and do battle in order to bring others into subjection to Him too, such as the Gentiles. And this He has done through the apostles and disciples, who were chosen from the Jewish people. But in order to keep people once more from thinking that a physical battle is implied, there follows:

4. *Out of them shall come the cornerstone, out of them the tent peg, out of them the battle bow, out of them every ruler.*

This means: things shall not go on there in a physical way. No vanguard shall be there; no arrow or spear or bow shall be there; nor shall there be a commander in chief there who would urge them on to battle. For there will be no need of all that. Instead, things will be done in a spiritual way. Some, however, understand this text in this way: From the land of Judah there shall come spikes, bows, spears, and drivers, or captains, who will wage this spiritual war under Christ, their leader in battle. And this interpretation does not agree badly with what precedes and follows. It is a good interpretation. I will, however, stay with the first explanation, but will undoubtedly find enough people who will want to stay with the others and against me.

5. *Together they shall be like mighty men in battle, trampling the foe in the mud of the streets.*

The warriors, however, shall be like this, the prophet says: They shall all be great heroes and mighty men and not ordinary military rabble, who only make the crowd larger and take a beating. Instead, they shall gain the victory and conquer and always be victorious. For through the Word they are to be so mighty that they not only will never yield to anyone or flee but will trample all their foes in battle as one tramples the mud in the streets, so that these enemies will lie there disgraced, as we see from the following:

They shall fight because the Lord is with them, and they shall confound the riders on horses.

Not by their own might! But Christ is with them; and therefore they will fight in such a way that all the riders on horses and all that oppose them will be confounded and lie like mud in the street. Look at history. Have not the Jews, the philosophers, the heretics, and all who have prepared for war against the Gospel been trampled by now like mud in the street? What are the Arians? Mud trampled in the street. What are the Manichaeans, Pelagians, and so forth? Mud in the street. What are Müntzer and the pope now? Mud in the street. What will our Sacramentarians be? Mud in the street. It is as Ps. 83:10 says: "They became dung for the ground"; and Ps. 18:42, "I cast them out like the mire of the streets." Yes, you say, the Sacramentarians do not think like that but intend to have the victory. Of course they do not think like that. The Jews, Arians, Müntzer, the pope did not think like that either, but it happened like that anyway. And for that reason he says here, "They shall fight." There must be fighting; and it will always seem as though the others had won. But the Lord is with us, so that the riders who think they have won will be confounded, and that at the very time when they think that we have been confounded and they have won. So it has gone at all times and will continue to go.

6. *I will strengthen the house of Judah, and I will save the house of Joseph.*

This means: In this contest I will be with them in such a way that they shall be the strongest, shall win, and shall gain the victory over all that fight against them. And this shall not only happen in the tribe of Judah; but I shall also save the house of Joseph, the kingdom of Israel – that is, as it reads in the Hebrew, Israel as well as Judah shall win and gain the victory. For, as was said above,[4] both Judah and Israel shall again be joined under Christ and have the same grace and spirit.

I will bring them back.

Not into the old kingdom but into the spiritual one; and it is of the latter that He is speaking, as follows:

[4] Cf. p. 293 above.

Because I have compassion on them.

The old kingdom was founded on Israel's obedience; for the promise was made to them that they were to possess the land insofar as they were good. Therefore the kingdom was weak [5] and had to perish. But this kingdom is founded on God's mercy without our own goodness or merit, and therefore it will stand fast to all eternity. And so He says here that He will bring them back – not because they deserve it but because He has compassion on them. Yes, they shall stand – on the basis of His mercy, and not on that of their own righteousness.

And they shall be as though I had not rejected them.

This mercy, which has nothing to do with their righteousness, makes everything good and right, so that they are as though He had never been angry with them and as they were when they were most obedient and when the promises were quite new and fresh. All that they have done till now is forgotten, and only the forgiveness of sins remains.

For I am the Lord their God and I will answer them.

This means that there is to be nothing but grace, because the kingdom is one of mercy. "Formerly, when they called upon Me in their physical kingdom, I did not hear them but let them perish with their righteousness, on which they depended, so that they were destroyed. But now I am near them, and because of My mercy I answer them when they call. This answering, however, shows that they call and pray much; and their frequent calling and praying show that they have much distress and sorrow. Therefore this must be a kingdom of the cross, in which there is a God who answers, as Ps. 50:15 says: "Call upon Me in the day of trouble; I will deliver you, etc." For the devil does not remain passive toward such a kingdom.

7. *Then Ephraim shall become like a mighty warrior, and their hearts shall be glad as with wine. Their children shall see it and rejoice, their hearts shall exult in the Lord.*

Since He has begun to speak about the house of Joseph in connection with the house of Judah, He continues the same remarks about

[5] To express "weakness" Luther uses the picture of a coat which betrays its insufficiency by showing fur trimming only on the sleeves. His expression is *es stund wie auf Pelzärmeln.*

the house of Joseph to the end of the chapter, in order to proclaim that the kingdom of Israel (which was in the house of Joseph and in the tribe of Ephraim) should also be subject to Christ together with the house of Judah. What He prophesies therefore of Judah, He also prophesies of the house of Joseph, as of fellow citizens of the same kingdom of Christ: first, that they too, as was said above about Judah,[6] are to be mighty warriors, that is, victors and heroes, not rabble or a mob gone astray. Then they "are to be glad" in their spirits, like those who are glad "with wine"; and their children are likewise to be glad when they see this victory of mighty warriors on the part of their fathers, because this joy does not come from temporal goods or honors but from the Lord, who makes the victory and the victors, and that not through their own might but through His mercy and His answer to their prayers. In sum: You hear of mighty warriors here, of strife and victory – all of which is out of keeping with a physical kingdom enjoying peace and comfort. But there is always to be strife without peace, and yet nothing but victory shall prevail.

8. *I will signal for them and gather them in, for I have redeemed them, and they shall be as many as of old.*

This is said in the Hebrew manner. "I will signal them," that is, "I will touch them with My Spirit." Is. 7:18 [7] uses a similar expression when he says: "In that day the Lord will whistle for the fly, etc." For in the Hebrew language "spirit" and "wind" are expressed by the same word, רוּחַ . And here we see that He is speaking of the Ephraim that is scattered, because by means of His signaling He wants to gather it – namely, to the same faith as Judah's, so that it may increase as of old, that is, that it may consist of many. This time, however, the increase is to be spiritual, as follows:

9. *Though I scattered them among the nations, yet in far countries they shall remember Me.*

The increase is to take place in this way: They will be scattered among the nations, like a seed which is increased in a field. This must of course be a spiritual increase, because they are not to return home from the nations but are to be sown there among the people and then increased. All of this takes place in this manner, that they will be sent

[6] Cf. p. 302 above.

[7] The Weimar editor corrects the text's "Is. 8."

by God among the nations as preachers and thus draw many people to themselves and through themselves to Christ. "For," He says, "they shall remember Me in far countries, that is, they shall preach and teach of Me, and thus they shall be increased and shall convert many others to Me." It was not proper for the Jews, either, to remember the Lord or to worship Him outside of Jerusalem, as Ps. 137:4 says: "How shall we sing the Lord's song in a foreign land?" Since He says, then, that when they are sown and planted in strange lands, they are to remember the Lord, it is sufficiently clear that He is speaking of spiritual things and that the spiritual Jerusalem is to be as broad as the world. Otherwise, if He had a physical kingdom in mind, He would sow and plant them in Jerusalem and let them increase and remember the Lord there.

And with their children they shall live and return.

According to the preceding text, the children whom they beget through the increase which results from the scattering among the nations must of course be spiritual children, as was said above. As a result, then, both the seed which is sown among the nations and the fruits which have grown out of this seed and have increased, the converted Gentiles, shall live, that is, shall be of good courage and be satisfied. For in Scripture "to live" means to experience and enjoy life, as men do who live without misfortune and danger. But because the life of the apostles and preachers is a struggle as was said above, He means to say that, even in the midst of death and all danger and where no life seems to be, they shall still live, as Paul says in 2 Cor. 6:9: "We are . . . as dying, and behold we live." So, too, shall the return be: Ephraim, scattered throughout the world, shall now truly come back to the home where it shall stay forever, namely to Christendom.

10. *I will bring them home from the land of Egypt and gather them from Assyria; and I will bring them to the land of Gilead and to Lebanon, till not one of them is missing.*

According to what has gone before, all of this must be understood spiritually; otherwise that which has gone before cannot stand. For it does not make sense if by His signaling He should gather the people in such a way as to sow them among the nations and yet bring them physically into the Jewish land, though such an interpretation is pleasing to the Jews. Nor was He to bring them to Gilead and Lebanon, but to Samaria and into the midst of the land where they had dwelt before. Therefore this is the meaning: At that time, and for once, the true returning will take place, namely, when Christ through the Gospel will bring the children of Israel out of Egypt and Assyria and back to the faith, that is, to the true Gilead and Lebanon. For how should the ten tribes of Israel get into Gilead and Lebanon alone when formerly scarcely two tribes, Manasseh and Gad, were in it? Then the former, old kingdom of Israel would have been more glorious than this one, because at that time each tribe occupied its own inheritance, while here all ten of them were to live in the inheritance of two half tribes. Besides, what sense would it make if Ephraim were to live in the inheritance of the tribes of Gad and Manasseh beyond the Jordan, since this surely is all contrary to the decree of Moses and Joshua that the tribes of Israel were not to be mixed? If this, however, is contrary to Moses, then Moses in turn is contrary to Zechariah, and the one must yield to the other.

It is fitting, however, that Moses should yield and permit Zechariah to talk about the spiritual Gilead and Lebanon. The name *Gilead,* however, means "many witnesses," while *Lebanon* means "clear" or "white." The names, then, refer to Holy Scripture or Christianity, in which there is much witnessing, through which Christ is preached, and which in addition is clear and white in pure innocence and holiness. To this host of witnesses and to this whiteness comes Ephraim – that is, he comes to the Word of God and to faith, through which the hearts become clean, white, and pious, Acts 15:9. "Till not one of them is missing." In the Hebrew we read *Et non invenietur eis,* which some understand to mean: So many of them will come that they will not find enough space to live in. This might be correct if only the ten tribes of Israel were to come into Gilead physically. But in Scripture and in Christianity enough space would of course be found or provided. Let each accept the interpretation he likes.

11. *And distress shall come upon the sea, and He will smite the waves of the sea.*

Some translate this text in this way from the Hebrew: "He will pass through a narrow sea"; and I prefer this translation. The text may, however, yield both; and they are of the same meaning. For He is speaking of the spiritual passage which was made through the Red Sea when He led His people out of Egypt. It is as though He wanted to say: "When God will redeem the tribes of Israel in the new way and bring them into the true Gilead and Lebanon, as has been said, then He will also introduce a new passage through the sea — a passage much greater than the one through the Red Sea." For this sea will be the whole world, and through that He will lead His people. The world will resist and oppose these people and not want to let them pass through, and as a result it will become a very narrow sea for the people of God, just as the Red Sea resisted and was narrow at the place through which the Children of Israel passed. Then distress will come, not only upon the people of God but also upon the sea. For the world's resistance and opposition will not help it, it will have to let the people pass through. For He will smite the waves of the sea, that is, with the Gospel He will punish everything that is great and mighty in the world, even as Moses smote the Red Sea with his rod (Ex. 14:16).

And all the depths in the water will dry up.

Even as the Red Sea vanished when Moses had struck it, so the world will pass away when it has been struck by the Gospel: it will become humble, will give way, and will no longer resist the apostles and preachers; that is, all the depths in the water will be dried up by the Spirit of Christ, even as the Red Sea was dried up by the east wind. Thus the Spirit is here playing with the interpretations of the old histories about the future essence and course of the Gospel.

The pride of Assyria shall be laid low, and the scepter of Egypt shall depart.

Here he himself shows what kind of sea he has in mind, namely, the world with its power and splendor. And he specifically calls the two kingdoms Assyria and Egypt, because these two did the tribes of Israel the greatest harm. But when he himself speaks of "all the depths of the waters, etc.," he undoubtedly wants also the power and might of the entire world to be understood. For they have all been humbled by the Gospel and have all had to come to an end. The Gospel, however, has remained. We can here see plainly, therefore, that the prophet is not speaking of the physical redemption of the Jewish people. For this passage and battle in the sea, which dries up Assyria and Egypt and all the depths of water, cannot lead into that Gilead. But the place where the sea is smitten, that is, where the kingdoms are humbled, must be a spiritual Gilead, which is everywhere in the world.

12. *I will make them strong in the Lord and they shall walk in His name, says the Lord.*

This means that they shall gain the victory and shall conquer all the waves of the sea; not, however, by the might of arms or the power of men but by the power of God, in Spirit and in faith. And so they walk not in their own names but in the name of Jesus Christ. For they do not live and build on the foundation of their own works or righteousness, nor is anyone saved except on the basis of His name. For here neither Paul nor Apollos nor Cephas avails them anything, but they must walk in the mercy and righteousness of Christ: Gal. 2:16: "A man is not justified by works of the Law but through faith in Jesus Christ."

CHAPTER ELEVEN

1. *Open your doors, O Lebanon, that the fire may devour your cedars!*

UNTIL now the prophet has been preaching the kingdom of Christ and the power and fruit of the Gospel, namely, faith among the Gentiles. Here, however, he preaches the destruction of the temple of Jerusalem and of the Jewish people. For they wished to keep the old kingdom and not accept the new; and for that reason they perished and lost both. Here he calls the newly built temple Lebanon, because it was built of the cedars of Lebanon – as the grammarians teach that a part is called by the name of the whole, by synecdoche. It is as if I should say, "The men of Wittenberg drink Faulbach and Frischbach," that is: "Wittenberg beer"; "The Thuringian Forest yields many warm rooms," that is: "the wood from the Thuringian Forest, etc."; "The Rhine flows through the whole German land," that is: "the Rhine wine, etc." The prophet uses this way of speaking frequently at this point, without a doubt not only to veil the prophecies but also to spare the Jews who at the time were building the temple, so that they might not be frightened away if they heard that the temple was to be destroyed.

This, then, is the meaning: "Open your doors, O Lebanon!" that is: "O you sacred temple at Jerusalem, you will stand open to the Romans so that no one will be able to keep them out or protect you. But they will walk in freely, as though you were standing there opened by yourself, were abandoned and without any protectors. And they will burn down the structure of cedarwood because of the people, because they did not know the time of their visitation," Luke 19:44.[1] Of this we are told in the next chapter.

2. *Wail, O cypress, for the cedar has fallen, for the glorious trees are ruined!*

He commands the cypresses to wail; that is, the cypresses and cedars will give the Jews cause for wailing during that destruction of

[1] The Weimar editor corrects the text's "Luke 21."

the temple, since both the cypresses and cedars and every glorious edifice will be felled, destroyed, and burned, as also Dan. 9:26 foretells.

Wail, oaks of Bashan, for the strong forest has been felled.

Here, I think, he has the whole city of Jerusalem in mind, which had built its houses of the oaks of the forest of Bashan. Because of the great amount of wood from Bashan, however, the city is also called a forest of Bashan, even as above the temple was called Lebanon. For Bashan is famous in Scripture for its oak trees, even as Lebanon is famous for its cedar and cypress wood. He calls Jerusalem a strong forest, however, because it was also a strong city, as the Romans themselves admitted.

3. *Hark, the wail of the shepherds, for their glory is despoiled.*

These are the high priests and scribes, who were to feed the people as shepherds. These are not spared, either; but their splendid palaces and glorious edifices, which they had furnished as though they would inhabit them forever, also had to share in the destruction.

Hark, the roar of the lions, for the splendor of the Jordan is laid waste.

These are the counselors and the men of wealth of Jerusalem. All of them had to wail, for not one stone was left upon another there. "The splendor of the Jordan" is also a difficult term. I think that by it he means the splendid decorations of the city and the building – the tiles and marble, palms, bronze, silver, gold, and similar treasures, which had been brought from the Jordan to Jerusalem and had been prepared about the Jordan. For Solomon had had all the brazen vessels cast at the Jordan, 1 Kings 7:46.

4-5. *Thus says the Lord my God: Become shepherd of the flock doomed to slaughter. For their masters slay them and do not regard it as sin; they sell them and say: Blessed be the Lord, I have become rich.*

Here he begins to report and enumerate the sin and guilt with which they merit their destruction. Of these there are three. The first is that they teach falsely; the second, that they are greedy and teach falsely because of their greed; the third, that they sell Christ and deny and reject Him. He presents the first guilt when he says, "Become shepherd of the flock doomed to slaughter." This the prophet is saying to Christ in the Person of God and tells Him to tend the sheep, for then He would learn how matters stood among the people. He would find nothing but sheep doomed to slaughter. For Christ found nothing but wolves, thieves, and murderers – that is, false teachers – among the people, as He Himself said John 10:1; and therefore the prophet properly calls the people a "flock doomed to slaughter." For with their false teachings the Pharisees and scribes were slaughtering and killing them like thieves and wolves; moreover, they did this with so great a feeling of security that they did not make it a matter of conscience but thought their deeds were right and proper. But this is the way of all murderous and wolfish teachers: they desire to be praised as men who do everything better than all other and wholesome teachers. But because they not only sin but also with all wantonness defend their sin as right, they thereby also sin against the Holy Spirit, so that their sin cannot be forgiven but must fall into punishment. For if sin is to be forgiven, it must be confessed and repented of.

He presents the second guilt by saying that they "sold" the poor sheep that were doomed to slaughter; that is, as St. Peter says, 2 Peter 2:3: "In their greed they will exploit you with false words." This exploiting Zechariah here calls "selling." For the Pharisees had started a genuine annual fair with their sacrifices, even as our clergymen have sold and exploited us with Mass, indulgence, and other forms of worship. For they take our money and possessions from us and give us to the devil to boot; and he gives us the sacred indulgences, merits, and other good works in return; and on these then we build and so go to hell. And just as they did not let their consciences trouble them because of their false teaching (as has been said), so they do not make their exploitations a matter of conscience either, but think they are doing something good with them, and they thank and praise God for getting rich in that way. "Blessed be the Lord," they say, "we have become rich"; that is, "Now we are in good standing; for the fact that we are getting rich is a sign that these things are pleasing to God." Of course the opposite is being proclaimed here. Much could be said here about how very masterfully the prophet portrays the belly-servers and false teachers and their ways, that they are so blind, so sure of themselves, so greedy, and that they do not praise God for His grace and mercy but for the fact that they have become rich –

that is, for the sake of their bellies and their temporal possessions and desires. Otherwise they indeed do not bother about God and the things of God.

And their own shepherds have no pity on them.

This means: They killed their people with respect to their souls through false teaching and robbed them of their possessions through hypocrisy. And they showed no moderation, no stopping, no sparing; but the longer they carried on, the more they increased their killing and robbing, exactly as has happened to us under the papacy. Shepherds, of course, ought to be of such a kind and kindliness as to spare the herd and deal gently with it. But here they are wolves, and it is the nature of these not to spare. For the wolf has this shameful vice about it that, when it gets into a stable, even though it could eat its fill in peace, it will not devour a sheep unless it has first killed them all, so that not one remains alive. That is how greedy and grasping it is. Nor are the false teachers satisfied to mislead a few people, but they want to have them all and altogether and do not rest as long as they hear the bleating of one pious person that opposes them. Therefore he also says above that "their masters slay them," as if to say, "They have subjugated the people and rule over them as the country squires rule over their ancestral estates, so that no one dares to open his mouth against them." St. Peter, however, teaches, 1 Peter 5:3, that the shepherds are not to domineer over the Christians as over an ancestral estate; and Paul, 2 Cor. 1:24,[2] does not desire to lord it over the faith of the Corinthians.

6. *For I will no longer have pity on the inhabitants of this land, says the Lord.*

How much God is vexed by such guilt He shows here by saying that He will withdraw His hand and let the people go their own way, as Ps. 81:12 also says, "I gave them over to their stubborn hearts." But what could be greater wrath than when He permits us to act according to our own conceits, takes His Word from us, and permits men, yes, even the devil, to be our masters? What else can one have then but sects and disunity in teaching? Later, outward disunity with strife and rebellion follows from this disunity in teaching: and so we

[2] The Weimar editor suggests that this may be the passage meant when the text reads "1 Cor. 3."

read in Josephus[3] that horrible sects and rebellions arose among the Jewish people shortly before the birth of Christ, when they had to fulfill the prophecies that follow.

Lo, I will cause men to fall each into the hand of his shepherd, and each into the hand of his king; and they shall crush the earth, and I will deliver none from their hand.

Thus the Jewish people fared, especially at the times of the Sadducees and Pharisees before the birth of Christ, when there were nothing but factions and sects and also all kinds of kings, as the Book of Maccabees shows. They were not saved by all of these but rather were abandoned, so that they always had different kings until Herod, commissioned by the Romans, came upon them with his descendants. Herod first of all fulfilled the prophecy of the above verse by treating the Jews terribly with his sword. But the factions of the Pharisees treated them even more terribly with their tongues and teachings; and the Jews fared as though they no longer had a God who would regard them. I think, however, that we ought also to see something here concerning the papacy: into how many factions of the clerical office we have been separated within it, and how very violently we have been set against one another; how in addition, and as a consequence, so much war has arisen among pope, emperors, kings, and princes that it is frightening to read and hear about it, as if there no longer were a Christ in the church. He has indeed permitted us until now to shift for ourselves; and as a result there has been nothing but a killing of souls and bodies, and indeed nothing but a devilish rule has prevailed mightily with seductions and killings. The devil is a murderer and liar or seducer (John 8:44), and he has proved this sufficiently among us and is again beginning to prove it by means of the new spirits and factions. Wherever God is not present, there things fare in this way.

7. *So I became the Shepherd of the flock doomed to be slain for the sake of the wretched sheep.*

Here comes the true Shepherd, Christ, and says that He is accepting the office of Shepherd, as His Father had commanded Him above.[4] For with these remarks the prophet is presenting Christ. He had to

3 Josephus, *The Jewish War,* II, esp. chs. 5—7.

4 Cf. pp. 311 f. above.

be the Shepherd of the sheep doomed to be slain, in this way: He preached among the sects of the Sadducees and Pharisees, who were slaying the people with false teachings. He did not do this, however, for the sake of the sheep doomed to be slain, for they despised Him, but did it for the sake of the wretched sheep; that is, as He Himself says, Matt. 11:5, "The poor have the Gospel preached to them."

And I took two staffs: one I named Gentle, the other I named Painful. And I tended the sheep.

And here the third guilt of the Jews begins, namely, the fact that they deny and sell Christ. A shepherd should have a staff; and therefore Christ here presents Himself as a Shepherd and takes two staffs to Himself and begins to teach and tend the sheep. What the two staffs are has been interpreted in various ways. Because Christ, however, here is a Shepherd and tends the sheep, we feel that the staffs cannot be anything else than the teaching that He has carried on. For it is also shown later in our text that the one staff, when it is broken, signifies a covenant and that by means of this breaking He confesses that He no longer wishes to tend the sheep. We must, therefore, consider what kind of preaching and teaching Christ practiced, and then we shall find the two staffs. For also elsewhere in Scripture God's Word is called a staff, as in Ps. 23:4: "Thy rod and Thy staff, they comfort me." And the staff of Moses, with which he struck the sea and the rock, of course means God's Word (Ex. 14:21; 17:6). The Gospel is also called Christ's scepter, Ps. 110:2 and Ps. 45:6: "Your royal scepter is a scepter of equity."

The first staff, then, is the Holy Gospel, which is a delightful, merry sermon of grace. He therefore calls it נֹעַם here, that is, "merry and pleasant." We have translated it as "Gentle," so that it might agree all the better with the second word. For "Gentle" and "Painful" go well together as opposites. The second staff, however, is the Law, which is a hard, bitter, and difficult sermon for the old man. But Christ interprets the Law masterfully indeed in Matt. 5:20 and thereby proves that all the righteousness of the Pharisees amounts to nothing; and in Matt. 23:3 ff. and everywhere else He rebukes them for forsaking God's law and keeping their own ordinances. He always points out what the Law demands and concludes that they are not keeping it, and thus He always makes of them and their righteousness a sin and a shame. This they were not able to bear, and it hurt them. In fact, it pains everyone when the Law makes him out a sinner; then there is anxiety and distress, as St. Paul says, Rom. 4:15, "The Law brings wrath," and 1 Cor. 15:56, "The power of sin is the Law." The Law therefore is a staff whose name is Painful, Distress, and Anxiety, and that is contained in the Hebrew word חֹבְלִים, which means much or many kinds of anxiety, such as a woman has in travail. It is indeed a heavy, thick staff, yes, a club or bludgeon, which the shepherd throws into the midst of the dogs or wolves.

Now it happened to Christ that men could not bear any of His teaching. When He preached the Gospel, He had to be called a sinner who kept neither the Sabbath nor the law of the fathers, a sinner and a companion of the tax collectors, a glutton and a drunkard, etc., who respected neither their fasting nor their praying nor their alms. When He preached the Law, He had to be called a fool, and they mocked Him, yes, became angry with Him because He rebuked them for their greed and hypocrisy. Whether He sang sweet or sour, it did not do any good. When He led them with His staff *Gentle*, they did not follow Him; when He threw the club *Painful* into their midst, they became angry – as He Himself says, Matt. 11:17, "We piped to you, and you did not dance; we wailed, and you did not mourn." When He promises them every good thing through the Gospel, they reject it; when He threatens every evil through the Law, they despise it. What is He to do with these vipers except finally to break both staffs and let them go on in their own conceits forever, without either the Gospel or the Law?

8. *In one month I destroyed the three shepherds.*

These three shepherds are the three kinds of teachers and rulers among the people whom Jer. 18:18 lists thus in accordance with the boast of the wicked: "The Law shall not perish from the priest, nor counsel from the wise, nor the Word from the prophet." At the time of Christ, however, the place of the prophets had been assumed by the scribes, who dealt with Scripture and made laws in accordance with their own conceits, and not as the prophets in accordance with the Spirit of God. Above these three kinds of shepherds were the Pharisees and Sadducees. But these were factions and sects, not ordained by God like the above-mentioned shepherds but devised and invented by men. The three kinds of shepherds, however, were in the midst of the people by the ordinance of God. Yet they had to pass away when Christ came. For when He says, "In one month I have destroyed them," He means that when He began His prophetic office, He abolished all the teachers of the Old Testament, in as short a time as one month. For when Christ began to teach, Moses was through with his teachings, as Christ Himself says, Matt. 11:13, "All the prophets and the Law prophesied until John." From that time on the kingdom of God was preached, etc.

But I became impatient with them, and they also detested Me.

This is a quick separation. I was not able to bear their false teaching and therefore condemned all three of them, so that they would have no further significance. That vexed them, and they would not have it. Therefore we separated in that I let them go their own way.

9. *So I said: I will not be your Shepherd. What is to die, let it die; what is to be destroyed, let it be destroyed; and let those that are left devour the flesh of one another.*

This means: "They will not hear Me, therefore I must let them go their own way, die, be destroyed, devour one another, as must happen wherever God's Word is despised and men's trifles rule. For at such a place the devil dwells with all his angels; and separatistic spirits will have it so. For they will not let anyone tell them anything, and therefore Christ has to say to them: "I will not be your Shepherd." We coarse Germans would express it in this way: "Because you will not hear me, let the devil and his dam[5] tend you."

10-11. *And I took my staff Gentle, and I broke it, annulling the covenant which I had made with all the people. So it was annulled on that day.*

This means: "Since they would not hear Me and My Gospel, I proceeded to take it from them and turned to the Gentiles." For that is what He means when He says that He has annulled the covenant, that is, has taken the Gospel from the Jews and shortened it so that it no longer touches or reaches them – the covenant which He had made, after all, that it should come to all the Gentiles. And yet it is broken and shortened only with respect to the Jews, as St. Paul also teaches concerning the shortened Word on the basis of Is. 10:20 and says that it will not touch or reach them (Rom. 9:27). In Acts 13:46 Paul also confesses that they must turn to the Gentiles because the Jews did

[5] Cf. Luther's comment on Ps. 23:3.

not want the Word. And so it came about that the covenant was annulled by the Jews and the rod or staff shortened. Thus one can see here that this staff is the Gospel, which is the covenant of God among all the Gentiles but is taken from the Jews and shortened for them.

And the wretched sheep, that clung to Me, knew from that that it was the Word of the Lord.

"The big crowd fell away. But the wretched and lowly clung to Me and through the Holy Spirit saw that the staff was the Word of God. And it is in truth a great credit to the wretched that when they saw that the big crowd had taken offense at Me and would not hear Me, they still clung to Me and believed that the staff was God's Word, as Peter said to Christ, John 6:68: 'To whom shall we go? You have the words of eternal life.'" Yes, the poor and wretched act like this; for the poor have the Gospel preached to them, Matt. 11:5; Is. 61:1.

12. *Then I said to them: If it seems right to you, give Me my wages; but if not, keep them.*

This is the prophecy concerning Christ's being sold by the traitor Judas, as St. Matthew shows (Matt. 27:9 ff.). All of this the prophet here sees and hears in a vision. And these are words which are spoken with great seriousness; as if He wanted to say: "Not only do you not care to hear Me or tolerate Me, but you are also so exceedingly hostile toward Me that you will be happy to be rid of Me, even though you will have to sell Me very cheaply, just as your fathers did in the case of Joseph (Gen. 37:28). Very well, then: Go on, fill up the measure of your fathers (Matt. 23:32). And oh, let us see what price you are putting on Me, and for how much you are going to sell Me!"

And they weighed out as My wages thirty shekels of silver.

Christ, who was promised and commended to men so highly and dearly in order that they might receive Him, is in the end considered to be worth 30 shekels of silver and is sold for that amount. All of this is caused by the foul greed and honor of this world, and all of it we find completely fulfilled in the Gospel, especially in Matthew.

13. *Then the Lord said to Me: Cast it to the potter – the lordly price at which I was paid off by them.*

The prophet saw in a vision what Christ has done; and later on it was fulfilled in this way, too. For St. Matthew writes (Matt. 27:7) that for 30 shekels of silver the Jews bought the field of a potter, this potter to whom the 30 shekels of Christ were cast; and the vision indicates that these shekels were to be given for the field — a lordly price, He says, and a precious sum for which I am sold! Are not these sellers most properly accursed?

So I took the thirty shekels of silver and cast them into the house of the Lord for the potter.

This does not mean that the potter was in the house of the Lord, but that He casts the shekels into the temple so that they might reach the potter later on. And thus it is prophesied that Judas would first cast the shekels of silver into the temple and that these would then later reach the potter, as Matthew writes. But if anyone wishes to understand here that the prophet had cast 30 shekels of silver into the temple as a symbol, I shall let that pass. I think, however, that he is speaking of a vision in which he saw how Christ was sold, how the shekels of silver were cast into the temple, and how these were kept to buy the potter's field.

14. *Then I broke my second staff Painful, annulling the brotherhood between Judah and Israel.*

Not only the Gospel is taken away but also the Law. For the Jews no longer have a priestly office now, or a sacrifice, or the right understanding of the Law. And thus "the brotherhood is annulled between Judah and Israel." For through the Law the Jews were joined to one another as brothers and all Gentiles were excluded, as David says, Ps. 147:20, "He has not dealt thus with any other nation." And Paul, Eph. 2:12, also shows that "the Gentiles had been without God and strangers to the covenant, etc." Hence that thing, too, is gone and foreshortened by which the Jews had been most firmly joined to one another.

15. *Then the Lord said to me: Take once more the implements of a foolish shepherd.*

By means of the last prophecy the prophet prophesied that the Gospel and the Law were to be taken from the Jews because of their guilt. Now another vision follows concerning that which they would teach in place of the Gospel and the Law, namely, nothing that was good for the poor souls but rather mere belly-teaching to satisfy their greed. And he says that Zechariah or Christ should in a vision "take the implements of a foolish shepherd" – such as staffs, horns, pouches. For, as has often been said, God is in the habit of adding signs and visions to His Word in order to strengthen men's faith by means of them. Here too, then, two visions must serve as signs: the one being that of a shepherd with two staffs who casts the shekels of silver into the temple; the other that of a foolish shepherd and his implements, in order to signify the Jews' foolish, mad teachers, who would teach their dreams in place of the Gospel. For that reason, too, they are here called foolish teachers. For while they have the name of a shepherd, they do not perform the office of a shepherd.

16. *For lo, I am raising up in the land a shepherd who does not care for the perishing, or seek the crushed, or heal the maimed, or nourish the sound, but devours the flesh of the fat ones, tearing off even their hoofs.*

This verse has been applied to the Antichrist, and I shall let that pass. I think, however, that it is speaking of the troubles of the Jews, who had to deal with the Pharisees and similar extortioners, as Christ speaks of them Matt. 23:4 ff. and as Zechariah also reports here. For he speaks of "the land," that is, the Jewish land, though we have experienced the very same thing from the pope and for the same reason too: because in times past we did not receive God's Word. And also at present there are factious spirits who will toy with us in the same way. God keep us, Amen! But what do such teachers do? First, "they do not care for the perishing," that is, they allow the souls to remain fixed in their bad consciences and do not bring them the food of the Gospel; second, they are not able to comfort those that are grieved and faint-hearted, that is, "they do not seek the crushed"; third, "they do not heal the maimed," that is, when a man falls or is afflicted, they do not help him, do not bear or suffer his burden, but with severity and harshness always drive the poor consciences to works; fourth, "they do not nourish the sound" either so that it might become stronger and increase. You may read more about that in Ezek. 34:2 ff. and in the sermon for the Second Sunday After Easter.[6] But whatever is fat, that they devour and tear off its hoofs; that is, their preaching is intended

[6] The Weimar text has *Sermon Dominice 4. post Pascha.* Luther is apparently referring to his sermon on John 10:12-16 for Misericordias Domini, 1523. In this sermon he discusses Ezek. 34:2 ff. at considerable length. Cf. W, XII, 531—535.

to suppress everything that amounts to anything, especially if it opposes them and does not do their will.

17. *O idol shepherds, who desert the flock.*

Here you can tell that he is not speaking of one shepherd but of many. And he calls them shepherds of idols, that is, men who are not living shepherds that would perform their duties but that would rather sit like idols and let men serve them. He has surely called them idols fittingly and well; for they indeed are idols and specters and nothing else. For they let the flock go its own way, as long as they themselves can devour and tear to pieces, until not even one hoof is left without their tearing it to pieces. Look at the bishops and priests and monks, and you will have in rich measure glosses, examples, and the fulfillment of this text, even if there were no Jewish Pharisees of whom it was to be understood.

May the sword smite their arm and their right eye! Let their arm be wholly withered, their right eye utterly blinded!

The "sword" is God's punishment and judgment, with which they will be tormented to such an extent that they will be "unfit for any good deed," Titus 1:16; and besides, they will neither teach nor understand anything wholesome. This is their right arm and eye. Ps. 109:6 also says this of them: "Let Satan stand at his right hand, etc." But their left arm and their left eye are strong and whole. For they do much and are very clever in their fleshly minds and their own conceits to mislead themselves and others, as is the manner of all false teachers, etc.

This chapter raises the question why Matthew ascribes the text of the 30 shekels of silver to Jeremiah (Matt. 27:9) when, after all, it is found here in Zechariah. This question, to be sure, and others like it do not bother me greatly, because they do not serve any great purpose. Moreover, Matthew does quite enough when he quotes certain Scripture passages even though he may not hit upon the exactly correct name, especially since at other places he quotes passages without using the words exactly as they are in Scripture. If one can bear with this practice of his, and if the sense is not endangered when he does not quote the exact word, what harm is there if he does not put down the exact name, especially since the words are more important than the name? Furthermore, it is the custom of all the apostles to do this: to present the sense of Scripture without such a quarrelsome zeal for the exactness and completeness of the text; and about this custom one might question these apostles much more sharply than one might question Matthew here about the name of Jeremiah. But whoever likes idle strife, let him go on questioning; he will find that he is doing more questioning than answering.

CHAPTER TWELVE

1. *This is the burden of the Word of the Lord concerning Israel: Thus says the Lord, who stretched out the heavens and founded the earth and formed the spirit of man within him.*

I UNDERSTAND this chapter to refer to the burden of the cross which was to come upon the true people of Israel because of the Gospel. For in the last chapter He had separated Himself from the physical Israel when He said, "I will not be your shepherd" (Zech. 11:9). And yet He would keep the poor remnant; for He says: "And the wretched sheep that clung to Me knew that it was the Word of the Lord"(Zech. 11:11). These same wretched sheep, however, are the true Israel; and of these he prophesies here that they are to suffer and yet become much stronger in their suffering, as Paul says 2 Cor. 12:9,[1] "Power is made perfect in weakness." This chapter, then, is a sermon of comfort, to strengthen the apostles and disciples in all the persecutions that they had to suffer in all the world from both Jews and Gentiles. For that reason, too, the prophet here introduces the Lord with a title that he has not used before, namely, that it was He "who had stretched out the heavens, founded the earth, and formed the spirit of man within him," and who rules – as if to say: "Both the persecutors and the persecuted, together with all their powers, are in His hand, so that the persecution, whether it come from tyrants, heretics, sects, the devil, or his mother, can do no harm but must further and help His people to their best interests."

2. *Lo, I am about to make Jerusalem a cup of reeling to all the peoples round about.*

"Jerusalem" is the apostles and first disciples; while the "peoples round about" are the Gentiles and Jews who opposed them and would drain them like a cup, yes, like a spoon. For the dear disciples, compared with their enemies, looked so insignificant that the Jews thought they would not only eat and devour them but devour and kill them as

[1] The Weimar editor corrects the text's "2 Cor. 14."

easily as one drains a cup or a spoon. Against this presumption the Lord says here: "Very well, come on, try your tricks, go on and drink. I will present you with a drink that will serve you well: you will stumble so that you will reel along very violently and will not digest the drink as you had thought." This reeling, however, means that they will fall and act like drunkards and no longer be able to do anything at all. And so the Jews and Gentiles ultimately stumbled and fell over the disciples and were undone: some were converted through grace; the others, however, were destroyed. For they had become sated and had drunk themselves full of guilt because of Jerusalem.

The fact, however, that this drinking refers to the persecution which the Jews and the Gentiles had carried on is shown by the words that also Judah will be involved in the siege against Jerusalem. Here he is of course speaking of a siege as enemies do. Hence "the peoples round about" must all be enemies, who persecuted and desired to swallow up not only Jerusalem (that is, the apostles and the leaders) but also Judah (that is, the whole host of Christians). What is Rome now, which also wanted to devour and swallow up the Christians? It stumbled over them, I think, as the Jews did too. It is not a good thing to lay hands on the Christians. Oh, if only our princes and bishops today knew what they have in their dungeons. They think they will take a refreshing drink and quench their thirst for blood and cool their tempers at the expense of the poor heretics. But how they shall stumble over that! How the pope is already stumbling, and many with him! Oh, what drinking and stumbling! Stop, good men, stop! The drink is too strong for you! You would indeed do better if you drank vinegar or the dregs of wine instead!

3. *On that day I will make Jerusalem a heavy stone for all the peoples.*

Another metaphor, which means the same thing. The apostles are to be a heavy stone or a rock of oppression for all nations; that is, Christianity shall not be crushed; but all who try to crush it shall themselves be crushed, some by grace, others by disfavor, as follows:

All who lift it shall grievously hurt themselves.

Then, however, men lift a stone upon themselves when they undertake to cast out the Christians, as one picks up stones and casts them out of the garden as stones that are useless and hindering. To the world the Christians are people who are equally useless and harmful, and therefore it undertakes to cast them aside. But it tears and crushes itself most shamefully in doing that; for the stone is too large and too heavy, and therefore the throwers are crushed in their undertaking. They cannot let it lie and yet cannot remove it, and therefore a tearing and crushing must begin.

And all the nations of the earth will come together against it.

Here he explains clearly enough that he is talking about the persecutions and the cross of the Christians throughout the world. Here you also hear the comfort of those of us who believe in Christ and preach of Him: that no one shall hate us – except the whole world, as Christ also says: "You will be hated by all for My name's sake." But it does not avail the world, as the following shows:

4. *On that day, says the Lord, I will strike every horse with panic, and its rider with madness.*

The power of the world shall not be victorious but shall ultimately be disgraced because of the Christians. And this is the full interpretation of the cup of reeling and the heavy stone. He calls them horses and riders, however, because they boast of their might and strength, as Ps. 20:7 says: "Some boast of chariots, and some of horses; but we remember the name of our God."

But upon the house of Judah I will open My eyes, when I strike every horse of the peoples with blindness.

This means: "I will have eyes of mercy for the apostles and Christians in all their afflictions and will finally blind their persecutors and make fools of them. And all their plots against the Christians shall be as when one plays blindman's buff or throws at crockery, so that their persecution must fail, must rage in vain, and accomplish only this, that men laugh at their failures, while the more they strive against the Gospel, the more it increases."

5. *Then the princes of Judah shall say to themselves: The inhabitants of Jerusalem have strength through the Lord of hosts, their God.*

This means: In this persecution and cross the apostles and teachers will comfort and strengthen themselves and the Christians in the presence of their persecutors – not by arms or armors but in Christ Jesus. For they will gladly suffer all affliction and be content to be strong and comforted inwardly, in the Spirit, through faith in Christ and in His Word. There they find their comfort and strength.

6. *On that day I will make the princes of Judah like a blazing pot in the midst of wood, like a flaming torch among sheaves; and they shall devour to the right and to the left all the peoples round about.*

Not only shall the persecutors rage in vain, but the Christians shall also, through the Word, harvest much fruit among all the Gentiles and shall convert and save many, and thus they shall devour round about them like a fire that is burning in the midst of dry wood or straw. The fire of the Holy Spirit, then, shall devour the Gentiles according to the flesh and prepare a place everywhere for the Gospel and the kingdom of Christ.

While Jerusalem shall still be inhabited in its place, in Jerusalem.

The same spiritual Jerusalem which has been mentioned so far shall not be devastated or destroyed, even though all the Gentiles oppose it; yes, because of this opposition it shall remain all the more – wherever it is; it shall be well inhabited and be full of people, for the princes of Judah shall devour round about them like fire in straw. And lest one think of the earthly Jerusalem, he says: "Jerusalem shall be inhabited in its place" – that is, wherever it is or wherever its place is. And that place is in all the world. For wherever the princes of Judah are, that place is Jerusalem and is called Jerusalem, and at that place Jerusalem shall also be inhabited.

7. *And the Lord will give victory to the tents of Judah first, that the glory of the house of David and the glory of the inhabitants of Jerusalem may not be exalted over that of Judah.*

He is making a distinction here between Judah and the house of David and Jerusalem, when, after all, they are one people and all of them Christians. He is doing this because he wants to indicate that in Christendom neither difference nor respect of person shall mean anything, but that all shall be equal, as also St. Paul teaches, Gal. 3:28:[2] "There is neither Jew nor Greek, neither male nor female, etc., for you are all one in Christ Jesus, etc." These victories, therefore, he says, shall be gained not as before and until now, when the house of David, as the royal family, was more noble than the inhabitants of Jerusalem

2 The Weimar editor corrects the text's "Gal. 5."

and when the inhabitants of Jerusalem, as men living in the sacred, great, royal capital, were more noble than the common man elsewhere in Judah. Instead, all are to be equal. For this is to be a spiritual victory or liberty, in which no one can exalt or inflate himself over the other, etc., 1 Cor. 3:21.

8. *On that day the Lord will put a shield about the inhabitants of Jerusalem so that he who falls on that day shall be like David, and the house of David shall be like the house of God, like the angel of the Lord among them.*

Even those that fall, that is, the feeble, shall do as much as strong David; for though David was insignificant in person and weak compared with others (1 Sam. 17:50), he nevertheless became a greater hero than Goliath and slew him. Therefore, because the Christians all have the same Christ and His Spirit, everyone of them, when he is most insignificant and weak, can do as much as the very strongest. For they shall, all of them, conquer sin, death, the world. They all gain the same victory, however different they may be. For there is one Spirit and one Christ in all of them, who protects them and helps them. To the world they may therefore appear to be nothing but falling and feeble men who would succumb to anyone; but they shall nevertheless all be heroes and victors in that world. The word "falls" here means that someone is so feeble that he must fall, as when Ps. 105:37 [3] says that among the tribes of Israel there was none that stumbled or was weak when he left Egypt. These "feeble" ones are the Christians when they suffer and have affliction, as St. Paul says, 2 Cor. 12:10,[4] "When I am weak, then I am strong"; or Joel 3:10: "Let the weak say, 'I am a warrior.'"

Again, they who are strong and "the house of David, shall be like the house of God, like the angel of the Lord among them." That is: They who are strong victors like David, who conquer and are victorious in their weakness, will be the true house of God among the Christians and like the angels of the Lord; that is, in them God will live, and they will be able to teach others and to proclaim the Word of God rightly. And that is as much as saying that they will truly be the most prominent Christians and like the angels and messengers of Christ, who proclaim His Word.

[3] The Weimar editor corrects the text's "Ps. 77."

[4] The Weimar editor corrects the text's "1 Cor. 14."

9. *And on that day I will seek to destroy all the nations that come against Jerusalem.*

This means: "I will avenge and repay all that the Gentiles have done to Jerusalem with their persecutions, so that these Gentiles shall perish and My Christians shall survive, though these Gentiles intend to destroy the Christians so that they themselves might survive. But things shall be reversed, so that the Gentiles shall be destroyed." Thus the Roman empire perished and was destroyed; thus the papacy is now perishing too; and thus all must be destroyed that would destroy Christ. He says, however, that He would think or seek, that is, strive, how He might destroy the Gentiles, in order to indicate that He does not intend to destroy them suddenly, but at His leisure, and in order to give them an opportunity to repent. And in this way He presents himself as one seeking ways and means of destroying them.

10. *And I will pour out on the house of David and the inhabitants of Jerusalem a Spirit of compassion and supplication.*

The Christians, however, are to survive. And at the same time they are not to avenge themselves but rather suffer all evil patiently. For He does not want to arm them with weapons but to pour out on them the Spirit of compassion, that is, the Holy Spirit, who creates in them a good conscience and bears witness in their hearts that they have a merciful God and forgiveness of their sins in the peace of faith. Moreover, if they lack anything or suffer evil, they have the Spirit of supplication, who prays for them and intercedes with "sighs too deep for words," Rom. 8:26, so that they need neither weapons nor any defense in their affliction but, as St. Paul says to the Philippians (Phil. 4:5 ff.), "The Lord is at hand. Have no anxiety about anything, but in everything let your requests be made known to God, etc."

For they will look on Me, whom they have pierced.

Here, in brief words, He indicates His suffering and dying, through which He has merited the pouring out of this Spirit. And mark that it is the same Person of God who has been speaking until now and who now is confessing that He has been pierced (that is, crucified) and that He will be mourned as a dead man – that is, that He has died on the cross. Thus we learn from this passage that Christ, true God and man, had to suffer and die. But since He is nevertheless to do as much as He has mentioned previously and to give the Spirit, He must obviously not remain in death but must rise and live again in all eternity. But when He says: "They will look on Me, whom they have pierced," this is not said to mean that only they who had crucified Him would look on Him but is said in this way: "Men will see how I have been pierced and crucified, and this fact will be proclaimed through the Gospel to all the world and will be presented to its view." And this, very briefly, is the meaning: "Men will remember Me through the Gospel and will contemplate in their hearts how I have suffered and died, and in that way the Holy Spirit will be offered to them for the forgiveness of their sins. And not only that, but:

They shall mourn for Him, as one mourns for an only child, and weep bitterly over Him, as one weeps over a first-born.

His friends indeed fulfilled this mourning physically when they saw Him physically pierced and dead. But this mourning must go further and extend also to them who view Him in faith through the Gospel and see Him crucified and dead. To bear this mourning or suffering, however, is nothing more than this, that each one, following His example, bears his own cross and thus fulfills the true compassion. It is as St. Paul says (2 Tim. 2:12), "If we suffer with Him,[5] we shall also reign with Him," and as Christ Himself says (Luke 9:23), "If any man would come after Me, let him deny himself and take up his cross daily and follow Me." This is true compassion and killing of the old Adam: when a Christian is constantly in danger of his body, possessions, honor, and life, etc. For it is not a monk's life, which of its own choosing torments its body with fastings and a hairy shirt; but it is a serious and great sorrow and danger of death at every hour, for it is called a sorrow "as for an only, firstborn child." And that is not a thing that is chosen willingly but a serious and great sorrow.

11. *On that day the mourning in Jerusalem will be as great as the mourning for Hadadrimmon in the plain of Megiddo.*

Here the prophet gives the third simile for the mourning which was carried on for pious King Josiah, so that one might see again that in Christianity there is no fictitious or self-chosen sorrow and cross. This is written in 2 Chron. 35:24 f. You may read about the cities of Megiddo and Hadadrimmon in Joshua 12:21.

[5] Luther gives an interpretative translation of the Vulgate's *si sustinebimus* (RSV: "if we endure"), as if the text read *si consustinebimus* to match the preceding *si commortui sumus*.

12. *The land shall mourn, each family by itself; the family of the house of David by itself and their wives by themselves, etc.*

He mentions four families: two from the royal tribe, David and Nathan; and two from the priestly tribe, Levi and Shimei; and after that he takes all of them together. Each family shall mourn by itself, and the wives by themselves. According to ancient history the people of Israel were divided into 12 tribes, and each tribe was divided by itself. In the assemblies the women also had to stand by themselves, as is still customary among the Jews. But with the word "by themselves" he wishes to say here, as is said at present, that each one will bear his own cross by himself. Christ bore His, which men indeed bear in splendor in the monstrances. But that isn't anything. Christ does not say, "Take *My* cross and follow Me," but, "Take *your* cross, etc." (Luke 9:23). The monasteries also have crosses. But that isn't anything: first, because the crosses are self-chosen; second, because they are imitated by the others without variation.[6] Thus the barefoot monks bear the cross of St. Francis, but none of them wants to bear his own cross by himself. The Benedictines bear St. Benedict's cross. For they torment themselves with the very same works and rules – self-chosen and imitated – with which St. Benedict tormented himself. There is no mourning of their own; their mourning is a matter of monkey-sees-monkey-does. But everyone flees his own cross, and no one wants to bear it. Yes, men choose suffering and the cross so that they will not have to bear their own crosses. They crawl into monasteries and have peace and happy days, leave other people in trouble and toil, and still claim to be holier in doing that than all others. But they will surely learn.

[6] *Das sie von den andern als einerley nach getragen werden.*

CHAPTER THIRTEEN

1. *On that day there shall be a fountain opened for the house of David and the inhabitants of Jerusalem to cleanse them from sin and uncleanness.*

ALL this is said to confirm the earlier remarks about the new Jerusalem and Christianity; and therefore he is also speaking here about the washing and bathing of the priests in the Old Testament and contrasting them with the New Testament, when there will indeed be a different washing and bathing – as if to say: In the Old Testament the priests had a washbasin or laver for themselves alone (Ex. 40:30 f.), from which they washed when they entered the tent of the testimony. But in the New Testament, in the kingdom of Christ, a bath and a washing shall be prepared not only for the priests but for the whole house of David, yes, for all the citizens of Jerusalem, that is, for all kinds of Christians, both great and small. For it is to be a free and open fountain, presented to everyone for bathing and washing and not restricted by the court like the priests' laver in the old law. Furthermore, it is not to be a bath to which one has to carry water in a jar, which wastes away and is temporal, and to which new water must always be carried – which also indicates that this bathing is to cease in time and become different. But here there is to be a fountain which always springs up of itself and is fresh and forever yields enough water that will never stop.

This fountain might well and properly be understood as referring to Baptism, in which the Spirit is given and all sins are washed away. But because of the quarrelsome factions, who despise Baptism and ridicule everything that points to Baptism, we shall drop that too and cling to the fact that Christ, in John 4:14,[1] speaks of a spring of living water – and this the evangelist himself interprets as being the Spirit, whom they are to receive who believe in Him (John 7:38 f.). This spring is now open to all Christians, and it washes away two kinds of filth; sin and uncleanness. We have two kinds of sin in us: the one is

[1] The Weimar editor corrects the text's "John 5."

that which we commit ourselves, the other is original sin, which is native to us, which the prophet here in the Hebrew calls uncleanness, and which is the uncleanness that Moses, Lev. 12:3 ff., imputes to women and children the six weeks after a birth, etc. The text, then, means to say this: The old priests washed their hands and feet externally in their lavers; but now there is to be a washing in which not hands and feet are to be washed but all sin and uncleanness is to be washed away, so that, even if someone should sin and still have many of Adam's and Eve's other evil inclinations in him, everything should still become clean. For it is a daily, public, free washing, that is, an eternal forgiveness of sins, which is at all times open to all sinners and unclean persons; and we say this in the Creed: "I believe in the forgiveness of sins," and in 1 John 2:2: "Christ is the expiation for our sins, and not for ours only but also for the sins of the whole world, etc."

2. *And on that day, says the Lord of hosts, I will cut off the names of the idols from the land, so that they shall be remembered no more.*

Yes indeed, wherever the true doctrine springs up that through this open fountain men's sins are forgiven them without merit, and that through this same forgiveness of sins, by grace, man is justified before God, there not only all idol worship must fall and cease (which has indeed been invented merely to effect piety), but also all other teaching which would bring us, through works, to that place where only this open fountain can lead us. For by now the idols may indeed have been removed from our eyes, but not from our hearts. But what does this amount to? It is a matter of destroying idols outwardly but setting up many idols inwardly, in the heart, as the false teachers do, and as also follows:

And also I will remove from the land the prophets and the unclean spirit.

These are the same factious spirits that are unclean and unholy. For contrary to the Holy Spirit they teach their own dreams and conceits, even though they do not have any idols externally; just as the Pharisees and Sadducees were very holy and did not have any idols externally. Nevertheless they were false and unclean spirits, who preached their own doctrine and set up idols in their hearts.

With these words, in which he names unclean spirits, the prophet points, as is his manner, to the office of the old priesthood and makes it spiritual. For the old priests had much to do with unclean persons, as the books of Moses teach. This uncleanness he interprets here as referring to unclean spirits, that is, to teachers who teach unclean doctrine and praise works without grace. And I know of no other prophet who speaks about unclean prophets besides this one alone.

3. *And if anyone prophesies further, his father and mother who bore him will say to him: You shall not live, for you speak lies in the name of the Lord.*

This means: The Christians will at all times be able to judge in spiritual matters – and not only the priests, as in the Old Testament. And for that reason, too, father and mother will not consider their own child, but will condemn and ban it if it prophesies what it should. For by prophesying the prophet here means prophesying like the false prophets; and the following text shows that the speaker is telling lies. And this is the sum: Among the Christians men will cling to pure teaching, without respect of anyone, may he be ever so closely related. For there must be false teaching and factions to test the others. But they will not gain the victory.

And his father and mother who bore him will pierce him through when he prophesies.

They will not do this with weapons of iron but with the Word of God. For it will be a spiritual, friendly piercing, as is done to a child by a father and a mother, and even as St. Paul pierces the Galatians and Corinthians and rebukes their error with God's Word.

4. *On that day every prophet will be ashamed of his vision when he prophesies.*

This is the spiritual piercing; they are put to shame, and their prophecies are rebuked. For they shall not maintain themselves with their prophecies. The Spirit and the Word shall prevail in Christianity, so that no heresy will gain the upper hand, however much it may bestir itself.

He will not put on a hairy mantle to deceive.

The prophets put on sackcloth, that is, rough, simple clothes; Is. 20:2, "Go, and loose the sackcloth from your loins, etc." The false prophets, however, hypocritically employed the speech and behavior and all the ways of the true prophets in order to mislead the people. This will no longer be true among Christians. For one no longer asks whether a man is wearing grey or red, whether he looks sour or sweet, but whether he is teaching the truth. The Word is the criterion here and not the appearance of the person. Yes, the more holy a man acts in his outward behavior and clothes, the more he becomes suspect. One does not believe the hood or tonsure, but only the Word.

5. *But he will say: I am no prophet, I am a tiller of the soil; for I have served people since my youth.*

This means: If a man wishes to remain in the church, he will accept this piercing and rebuking, let himself be instructed, cease his prophesying, and say: "It is true: why should I want to have anything to do with prophesying and to be wiser than other Christians? For I am a tiller of the soil, that is, a simple man like the rest. And I have served people since my youth." All this is like saying: "Although all Christians can prophesy and teach, 1 Cor. 14:31, they will not exalt themselves above others and act in a disorderly way or start factions and heresies; instead, each will yield humbly to the other and regard himself as the most insignificant and simple. For all rebuking shall be done in a fatherly and friendly way, and all obeying shall be done in a childlike and sincere way – if they indeed want to belong to the community. If they do not, then let them go their way."

6. *And if one asks him: What are these wounds on your hands? He will say: The wounds I received in the house of my friends.*

This means: A Christian will be patient when he is thus punished and not be angry or resist. "Why shouldn't I gladly suffer it?" he will say, "since they surely and sincerely mean well with me. The blows are friendly blows; they are better than the flattery of the enemy." See, among Christians everything is done in this friendly way when someone strays or stumbles and is not stubborn; it is as St. Paul teaches the Galatians, chapter 6:1: "Brethren, if a man is overtaken in a trespass, restore him in a spirit of gentleness, etc."

7. *Awake, O sword, against My Shepherd, against the Man who stands next to Me, says the Lord of hosts. Strike the Shepherd, that the sheep may be scattered; I will turn My hand against the little ones.*

How does this agree, that he speaks here of the King, Christ, and says that He is to suffer? The answer: He has just said that the Christians will be humble among themselves and will gladly let themselves be struck and punished when they stray and sin. And this they do as a service to Christ. For He Himself also submitted to smitings without any guilt of His own, and He did this also so that men might not regard the kingdom of Christ as something worldly. For to the world it is to be a very offensive kingdom, as St. Paul says, 1 Cor. 1:23, "We preach Christ crucified, a stumbling block to Jews and folly to Gentiles." For the disciples themselves were offended because of Him, as Christ Himself told, Matt. 26:31, and said, "You will all fall away because of Me this night; for it is written, 'I will strike the Shepherd, etc.' "

The meaning, then, is this: "Awake, O sword," that is, "the power of darkness," as Christ calls it (Luke 22:53). For Pilate and the Jews had the sword and rule in the land. And yet they could not do anything until God had decreed it, as Christ also declared before Pilate: "You would have no power over Me" (John 19:11). Thus He herewith gives to the sword leave and power over Christ and also offers us the comfort that no harm can come to us except insofar as He allows and permits it. He calls Christ "His Shepherd" and "the Man standing next to Him": *qui apud me, vel iuxta me est.* This I understand to mean that Christ is the one true Shepherd in Christendom and at the same time is with the Father in eternity, as John says (John 1:18): "the Son in the bosom of the Father." But whoever likes, may also take these words to mean that God had always been near and with Him to do great signs and wonders until the hour of His suffering had come.

But just as at that time the disciples took offense and scattered because of the suffering of Christ, so it will be to the end of the world. For Christ must still be smitten and still suffer the sword in His spiritual body, which is Christendom; and many will take offense at this. For His is a kingdom of offense. Yet He turns to the little ones, even as above [2] He tells of the wretched sheep and says that they mark His Word. And so it is here. When all that are great, exalted, learned, holy, mighty, and rich among the Jews take offense, then the insignificant, poor, wretched sinners and disciples cling to Him, and He receives them and turns to them.

8-9. *In the whole land, says the Lord, two thirds shall be cut off and perish, and one third shall be left alive. And I will put this third*

[2] Cf. p. 318 above.

into the fire, and refine them as one refines silver, and test them as gold is tested.

The two thirds are the great multitude of those that take offense. One of these thirds allow themselves to be frightened away by cross and persecution, so that they are cut off; the second third allow themselves to be misled by unclean spirits and false teachers, and thus perish. But the remaining third firmly remain with the pure Word and are refined and tested by both persecution and affliction. These are the righteous, though there are but few of them. For the cross drives away many, but false teaching many more; and therefore they are properly called two thirds. But the third that endure will be saved, as follows:

They will call on My name, and I will answer them. I will say: They are My people; and they will say: The Lord is my God.

For through their faith they will be pure and righteous and without any hypocrisy. They will know how to preach rightly about the name of the Lord, for that is what "calling on the name of the Lord" means in Hebrew. For they do not preach their own names, like the heretics and hypocrites. And for that reason, too, they are His people and have Him as their God, that is, have everything that God is and has. For they are His children and heirs. Thus this text announces the cross and offense that arise in Christ and His people: "He is saved who endures to the end" (Matt. 10:22).

CHAPTER FOURTEEN

1-2. *Behold, a day of the Lord is coming, when the spoil taken from you will be divided in the midst of you. For I will gather all the nations against Jerusalem to battle, and the city shall be taken and the houses plundered and the women ravished.*

HERE, in this chapter, I give up. For I am not sure what the prophet is talking about. Men have understood it to refer to the Antichrist and to Judgment Day. But while this interpretation is to be found everywhere and is presented by many, I shall put it aside at present because it does not satisfy me in all respects. Whoever wants to accept it will find it also in Lyra.[1] I want to add my thought too, even though it is not sufficiently certain either in many places, and ultimately I will yield the mastery to the Holy Spirit.

First, while he has been speaking of Christ and His kingdom and telling how this kingdom was to be refined and increased by offenses, he now goes on to prophesy how the unbelieving Jews are to fare, who took offense at Him and crucified Him. And he says that the city of Jerusalem is to be destroyed by the Romans, who had all kinds of Gentiles subject to them and with these went forth against Jerusalem, as Christ also announces, Luke 19:44,[2] where He weeps over the city. This interpretation makes the text easy. For "the day of the Lord" properly means the day when the Lord's death and torture were avenged on the Jews by the Romans, who as it was were hostile toward the Jews.

Half of the city shall go into exile, but the rest of the people shall not be cut off from the city.

Jerusalem fared very much like this. One part of them, who were not able to escape, perished in the city of hunger, pestilence, and the sword; the other part were led away among all the nations, captives to this day.

[1] Lyra on Zech. 14:2: *Hic consequenter resumitur persecutio antichristi, etc.*

[2] The Weimar editor corrects the text's "Luke 21."

3. *Then the Lord will go forth and fight against those nations as when He fights on a day of battle.*

Here it begins to sound as though it were about Judgment Day. But as I have said, I shall at this time put this interpretation aside and maintain that he wishes to say that, after the destruction of Jerusalem, Christ will go forth and by means of the Gospel fight against those nations – for on Judgment Day there will not be much quarreling, since no one will be able to oppose Him. But, as is His custom, He is fighting through the Gospel, that is, through His Spirit and not with weapons. In this fight, too, He has had His opponents, and these have resisted Him stoutly.

4. *On that day His feet shall stand on the Mount of Olives which lies before Jerusalem on the east.*

On Judgment Day Christ will not stand with His feet on the Mount of Olives, but He will hover in the air in a cloud, as St. Paul writes (1 Thess. 4:17). Therefore I hold that, because Christ ascended to heaven from the Mount of Olives outside of Jerusalem, the prophet wishes to say that the fight of the Gospel is to begin there at the Mount of Olives, where He gave the disciples His last command: that they were to go into all the world and preach: Matt. 28:19, Mark 16:15. This shows, however, that Christ no longer wishes to rule in the physical Jerusalem but quite outside the physical city – in all the world, beginning at the Mount of Olives.

And the Mount of Olives shall be split in two from east to west by a very wide valley; so that one half of the Mount shall withdraw northward, and the other half southward.

If this is to take place on Judgment Day, where will the feet of the Lord stand on this mount? But just as the name of Jerusalem is given to the people and persons living in it – the Jerusalem that is described above [3] as extending as far as the world; that is: Christ, the apostles, and the disciples who were in Jerusalem were to go to the ends of the world – so I hold that also here the name of the Mount of Olives is given to people. The disciples, therefore, who were with Christ on the Mount of Olives at the last, were to be distributed into all the world very far from one another: to the east, the west, the south, the north; so that, even as there is a second Jerusalem, spread into all the world, so there shall also be a second Mount of Olives, split into all the world.

[3] Cf. pp. 182 and 186 above.

5. *And you shall flee from this valley between My mountains, for the valley between the mountains shall reach to Azal.*

How shall they flee, and who shall flee? Hasn't he told us that Jerusalem shall at that time be destroyed and deserted? I think therefore that, because the Mount of Olives will be split into all the world, the deserted, empty valley is nothing but the abandoned deserted synagog, or Jewry; and for that reason all the pious Jews who become Christians will flee and cling to the disciples. "For there is a valley between My mountains," He says, that is, between the split Mount of Olives which He now calls His mountains – those that He created by His splitting. But what the Azal is, I do not know. In German it means "close by," though elsewhere it is the name of a city. I think he wants to say that the deserted valley, where the Jews dwell between the two mountains and are now neither Christians nor Jews, will extend far and near, so that it will contain almost all the Jews. For few have been converted to Christ.

And you shall flee as you fled from the earthquake in the days of Uzziah, king of Judah.

During an earthquake people flee from cities and houses. Much more will men flee during this earthquake, when the Mount of Olives will be split and Jewry abandoned in such a way that men will stay with Christ and in Christ. The prophet Amos also tells about the earthquake in the times of King Uzziah (Amos 1:1).

Then the Lord my God will come, and all the holy ones with Him.

These words apply very well to Judgment Day. But because the other texts do not apply in the same way, I shall at this time stay with the interpretation that Christ, who went out to do battle through the Gospel, will also come, together with His apostles and preachers and all the Christians together, to do battle through His Spirit, and that in an altogether different way from the time when He came out of the wilderness with His holy ones. And Moses sings about that in Deut. 32:10.

6. *At that time there shall be no light, but cold and frost.*

What can this be, that Christ is to come in cold and frost, without light? It is this: Christ's Word and Spirit cause the Christians to be altogether insignificant in the eyes of the world: without light and heat, but instead in the darkness and frost of persecutions. Elsewhere of course Christ is mentioned as coming with fire on Judgment Day: 2 Thess. 1:7-8.

7. *And there shall be continuous day (it is known to the Lord), not day and not night.*

Here He is revealing Himself. There will be no light, he says, and still it will be day, that is, a spiritual day, which no one can see except the Lord alone. For He is the very Sun which creates this day in the believers' hearts. But they must believe this; and therefore there is neither day nor night, to speak in a natural way; rather, no light at all, etc.

For at evening time there shall be light.

Face about. All the days of the world become dark at evening time, when the night approaches. But this day will become light more than ever when its evening comes and its night approaches; and as a result this day will be dark by day but light by night. Therefore it is properly called a day which is neither day nor night, as other days are. The evening, however, is the end of the world, when faith shall cease and the eternal light shall be revealed.

8. *On that day living waters shall flow out from Jerusalem, half of them to the eastern sea and half of them to the western sea.*

What? Isn't Jerusalem destroyed? How then shall living water flow out from it? But this is the spiritual Jerusalem, from which the Holy Spirit flows through the Gospel, as John 4:14 indicates the Holy Spirit by means of the water. Now Jerusalem lies between two seas, the Dead Sea to the east and the Great Sea to the west; and water had to be conducted into Jerusalem. How, then, is it to come about that living waters shall flow from Jerusalem, across so many mountains on either side, and as far as the two seas? It is exactly as has been said. The Spirit flows out to the east and to the west, that is, above Himself to God, in order to appease His wrath, which He exhibited in the Dead Sea upon Sodom; and beneath Himself into the world, in order to comfort and strengthen it in the midst of its persecutions and sufferings.

It shall continue in summer as in winter.

Other waters dry out in summer. But these waters continue to flow; that is, the Spirit continues forever and does not cease appeasing God's wrath and comforting the suffering Christians.

9. *And the Lord will become king over all the earth.*

Not only over Judah and Jerusalem will He become king, as was true until now, but over all the earth, Ps. 2:8. And that will be brought about by the living waters, etc.

On that day the Lord will be one and His name one.

Until now men have been dividing God into many gods and giving Him many names. Thus in times past the Jews called Him Baal Astaroth; the Gentiles called Him Jupiter, Saturn; the Babylonians, Bel and Nebo; and so forth. For since all the world knows something about God, everyone proceeds to invest a form of worship according to his own conceit. And that is supposed to please God and must therefore receive a form and a name from us. In the very same manner we, too, in our own time have divided Christ, so that the one serves Him under the rule and name of St. Francis, the other under that of St. Dominicus, and so forth. Each one has chosen a way and a work, and all that under the one Christ. In sum: starting sects and factions in the faith and following them means dividing God into many gods and giving Him many names, though in Himself He surely remains undivided. If, then, sects and factions are ended and one serves God rightly in one Spirit, faith, word, and essence, then God is called One and His name One; and that is accomplished through the Gospel.

10. *The whole land shall be turned into a plain from Geba to Rimmon south of Jerusalem.*

Geba lies to the north of Jerusalem within the tribe of Benjamin; Rimmon lies to the south within the tribe of Simeon. Does he wish to say: "At that time everything will be level ground, just as if there were a straight road and flat land from Geba to Rimmon across the mountains"? All of that amounts to this: everything shall be the same and even, united and level, and no longer shall there be those factions, sects, and differences, as also Is. 40:4 says: "Every mountain and hill shall be made low and every valley lifted up; the uneven ground shall become level, and the rough places a plain, etc.," so that under Christ all shall be considered the same. God grant it! Let a man go from Geba to Rimmon, or from Rimmon to Geba, he will still get to Jerusalem on level ground. For there shall no longer be the differences of the sects. And though there must be many kinds of offices and gifts, and some must go to Geba, the others to Rimmon, some to one place, the others to another; still they shall all enter Jerusalem in harmony on fine, level, even land, without any offense or vexation, so that each may serve the one Lord with his gifts.

For it shall be lifted up and inhabited upon its site.

This means: It shall be situated high upon a mountain which is called Christ, so that one can easily see and reach it round about on level ground. It shall also be built well, but at this time not in the midst of the tribe of Benjamin, where it formerly was situated and now is destroyed, as was announced above,[4] but on its own site, as far as the world extends.

From the Gate of Benjamin to the place of the former gate, to the Corner Gate, and from the Tower of Hananel to the king's wine presses.

You may read about these gates and towers in Ezra and Nehemiah. Here, however, he is not mentioning all of the gates but only the main ones, those that are located at the four corners and are facing the four corners of the world: the north, the east, the south, and the west; because he wants to indicate that Jerusalem is to be in all the world. For even Lyra cites an old Jewish rabbi as writing that at the time of the Messiah Jerusalem shall be so large that its walls will be the ends of the world.[5] The text of Zechariah indeed compelled him to say that.

11. *And it shall be inhabited, for there shall be no more ban; Jerusalem shall dwell in security.*

The holy new Jerusalem will be filled with people. And yet it will at all times be holy and pure, so that there will not be any ban there and no one will be exiled because of some fault of his. For they are all holy and righteous in Christ, and not only righteous and holy but also secure. For they have a good conscience in Christ and are happy and in perfect peace.

12. *And this shall be the plague with which the Lord will smite all the peoples that wage war against Jerusalem: their flesh shall rot*

[4] Cf. p. 337 above.

[5] Lyra on Zech. 14:17.

while they are still on their feet, their eyes shall rot in their sockets, and their tongues shall rot in their mouths.

Those that persecute the Christians shall not go unpunished. And the punishment shall proceed in this way, that they shall perish in a wondrous way, namely thus: they will rot within themselves, lose their strength and power, even while they think they are still on their feet. Thus the Romans perished without one's knowing how. They had flesh enough, that is, land and people enough, and were also standing well on their feet. Nor did they lack eyes, that is, intelligent, sensible rulers. Nor did they lack tongues, that is, teachers and wise counselors. Yet that did not help them, even as it is written of Troy that it was destroyed at the very time when it had its very finest people. Jerusalem also perished when it was mightiest; likewise Babylon. Why? Because God had ceased being with them, and because the hour had come when they were to be punished and destroyed. It is as he says here: the tongue is to rot in the mouth, and the eyes in their sockets, and the body on its legs: that is, power and strength, good fortune and victory are to be withdrawn from them. When that takes place, then shall follow:

13. *And on that day a great panic from the Lord shall fall on them, so that each will lay hold on the hand of his fellow, and the hand of the one will be raised against the hand of the other.*

This means: When they have become so impotent, they shall, in addition, also fall out with and attack one another, so that they quite naturally will soon perish, even as it happened to the Roman empire. The Lord will cause this panic to fall on them when He withdraws His hand from them and no longer administers peace. And not only will the Gentiles destroy one another in this way, but:

14. *Even Judah will fight against Jerusalem.*

This means: Also in Christendom there will be sects and factions that will destroy one another, even as the heretics, generally and at all times, have quarreled with one another, though they rage against the true Christians as one. I fear that this will also happen some day to the German land, because the tyrants are persecuting the Gospel so horribly. For the factionalists are quite at odds with one another and are speedily destroying one another, though in their opposition to the Gospel they are as one.

And the wealth of all the nations round about shall be collected, gold, silver, and garments in great abundance.

This means: Their wealth, which they have been gathering until now and for the sake of which they have been raging against the Gospel, shall be snatched away from them, even as the Jews have lost their land and people, for the sake of which, after all, they fought against Christ. And that is what will also happen to all belly-servants and clergy who are now persecuting the Gospel because of their great fear for their possessions and treasures. They must perish and lose all these things shamefully.

15. *And a plague like this plague shall fall on the horses, the mules, the camels, the asses, and whatever beasts may be in those camps.*

This means: These, too, will perish and decrease and be robbed; so that all the might and power of the Gentiles, of which they have boasted and with which they defied the poor wretched Christians, will perish.

16. *Then everyone that survives of all the nations that have come up against Jerusalem shall go up year after year to worship the King, the Lord of hosts, and to keep the feast of booths.*

The Gentiles who do not cling to their unbelief with the others will be Christians and serve Christ. And more than others, he says, they will keep the feast of booths year after year. Why not the Easter festival or Pentecost? Above he has said often enough that Jerusalem is to be destroyed. Therefore this must be a new feast of booths in the New Jerusalem. Very well, the new feast of booths is this, that the Christians here on earth shall live as guests and pilgrims and hope to enter the city that is to come, even as they who live in booths intend to stay in them for only a little while, such as eight days, and then to go home again. And that merely means that the Christians live happily here on earth in faith and hope and await the coming bliss. Year after year, that is, every day, they will go up to this feast and exercise themselves in their faith and hope, etc.

17. *And if any of the families of the earth do not go up to Jerusalem to worship the King, the Lord of hosts, there will be no rain upon them.*

The people who refuse to keep this spiritual feast are they who look more to their bellies and themselves than to Christ, and in whose case the Word falls among the thorns and is choked, so that it does not yield fruit (Luke 8:7). Upon them will come the plague that there will be no rain upon them; that is, because of their ingratitude the Word of God will at last be taken from them.

18. *And if the family of Egypt do not go up and present themselves, then there shall be no rain upon them either.*

What does that mean to the Egyptians? They do not need any rain; nor do they ever have any rain, either, as Moses writes (Deut. 11:10). But he includes the Egyptians specially so that men would have to understand the rain spiritually – and this the Egyptians need as much as all the other Gentiles.

18-19. *This will be the plague with which the Lord will afflict the nations that do not go up to keep the feast of booths. This shall be the punishment to Egypt and the punishment to all the nations that do not go up to keep the feast of booths.*

He uses very many words about this plague and this feast of booths to say that this shall simply be counted as a sin that will not go unpunished. But these are not idle words. For in truth, there is no greater mercy on earth than when God's Word is preached, and again, no greater woe than when God's Word is not preached. And Is. 5:6 the same plague is pronounced upon the vineyard. For where God's Word does not rain down, there nothing good can be, neither in thoughts, nor in words, nor in deeds; and all effort and work are lost, even as the work of the Jews, the Gentiles, the monks, and the priests at all times has been lost.

20. *On that day the equipment of the horses shall be holy to the Lord.*

It is a mockery, says St. Jerome,[6] that some say the prophet is at this place speaking about the nail of Christ, of which Queen Helena made a bridle for the horse of Emperor Constantine, because the Latin says: *Quod est super frenum equi sanctum erit domino.* But the prophet does want to say as much as this: In Christendom also the laymen, as for instance, the secular rulers with the office they administer, are just as sacred and God-pleasing as the priests, so that not only

[6] Jerome, *Commentaria in Zachariam prophetam, Patrologia, Series Latina,* XXV, 1540.

the priests, as was true in times past, but also the secular rulers are to be sacred. For they, too, serve God, Rom. 13:4. Besides, they are able to believe and to be Christians as well as the others, as we read of the centurion Cornelius, Acts 10:30 ff.; of the proconsul Paulus Sergius, Acts 13:7; and later on of kings and princes. In sum: All, both great and small, both high and lowly stations, are to be subject to Christ.

And the pots in the house of the Lord shall be as the bowls before the altar.

In the Old Testament only those vessels were sacred which were consecrated and dedicated to the altar and the worship of God. But in the New Testament all the kettles or pots in the entire house of the Lord are to be as sacred as the bowls of the altar had been formerly. That is, in the New Testament all Christians that worship God shall be sacred, consecrated, and fit for the priestly office, so that henceforth there will be no difference between the consecrated and the unconsecrated, because they all have been consecrated with the Spirit of Christ. Yes, what is even more:

21. *And every pot in Jerusalem and Judah shall be sacred to the Lord of hosts.*

This means: They shall be priests and sacred through and through; and even though they are not in the office and service, they are nevertheless consecrated to them. For in the Law not all the pots were sacred.

So that all who sacrifice may come and take of them and boil the flesh of the sacrifice in them.

This means: The old priesthood with its sacredness shall be over and at an end. For the new priesthood makes everyone that believes sacred and consecrated. Therefore whoever wishes to sacrifice, that is, preach and serve God, takes whatever Christian he will; and the latter can teach him and boil him so that he is prepared and sacrificed to God according to the old man, Rom. 12:1. For they are all priests and are "taught by the Lord" (Is. 54:13). And here the prophet himself anticipates matters and interprets the old priesthood with its office, so that the frivolous spirits may not come and with their allegories and interpretations profess great learning, even as now our factionalist spirits are boasting that it would be a precious thing if one knew the meanings of *imago* and *veritas,* because then it would become clear what the old priesthood was.[7] They act as if these things were the principal things or otherwise would never have been discovered. But after all, the prophet himself has interpreted many of the symbols of the Old Testament, as he does here in the case of the priesthood and did above in the case of the ark of Moses, and the like.

And there shall no longer be a Canaanite in the house of the Lord at that time.

In times past some Canaanites remained among the people, as we read in Joshua and Judges (Joshua 16:10; Judg. 1:28), so that there were not only true people of Israel in the land. But in the times of Christ there is to be no unconsecrated person in Christendom. They must all be of one spirit and faith, so that neither heretics nor any other false Christians may remain among them. Yes, such false Christians will drive themselves away, like chaff, Ps. 1:4.

These last parts of our text, then, induce me to understand this chapter to refer not to Judgment Day but to Christendom. For the words that "every pot shall be sacred," that "the equipment of the horses shall also be holy," that it shall be a sin not to keep the feast of booths, and indeed almost all parts of it except the one about the splitting of the Mount of Olives fail to fit in well with Judgment Day, but they do fit in very well with Christendom, which lives in faith and in the Word. Whoever can do better has sufficient opportunity and leave for that. Christ, however, help and protect us in the singleness of His mind. Amen.

[7] Cf. p. 156 above. As is known, the Enthusiasts of the time of the Reformation frequently took their wisdom from the mystical writings of the Middle Ages. So they also seem to have appealed to the authority of the thoughts of Jan van Ruusbroeck in his work, *Dat boec van den gheesteleken Tabernacule.* Cf. *Werken von Jan van Ruusbroec, I. deel* (Gent: Maetschappy der Vlaemsche Bibliophilen), e. g., p. 40: *Moyses geboet desen tabernakel te makene, . . . tote dien tiden dat volbracht worden alle de figuren tote der waerheit, die si bedieden; p. 193: . . . daer die cledinghe der joedscher priesteren one figure ave was.*

Index

By JOHN H. JOHN

INDEX TO SCRIPTURE PASSAGES

APOCRYPHA